CAMBRIDGE STUDIES IN PUBLIC OPINION
AND POLITICAL PSYCHOLOGY

Series Editors

Dennis Chong, *Northwestern University*
James H. Kuklinksi, *University of Illinois, Urbana-Champaign*

Cambridge Studies in Public Opinion and Political Psychology publishes innovative research from a variety of theoretical and methodological perspectives on the mass public foundations of politics and society. Research in the series focuses on the origins and influence of mass opinion, the dynamics of information and deliberation, and the emotional, normative, and instrumental bases of political choice. In addition to examining psychological processes, the series explores the organization of groups, the association between individual and collective preferences, and the impact of institutions on beliefs and behavior.

Cambridge Studies in Public Opinion and Political Psychology is dedicated to furthering theoretical and empirical research on the relationship between the political system and the attitudes and actions of citizens.

Books in the series are listed on the page following the Index.

D0036909

HOW VOTERS DECIDE

Information Processing during Election Campaigns

RICHARD R. LAU

Rutgers University

DAVID P. REDLAWSK

University of Iowa

CAMBRIDGE
UNIVERSITY PRESS

CAMBRIDGE UNIVERSITY PRESS
Cambridge, New York, Melbourne, Madrid, Cape Town, Singapore, São Paulo

Cambridge University Press
40 West 20th Street, New York, NY 10011-4211, USA

www.cambridge.org
Information on this title: www.cambridge.org/9780521848596

First published 2006

Printed in the United States of America

A catalog record for this publication is available from the British Library.

Library of Congress Cataloging in Publication Data

Lau, Richard R.
How voters decide : information processing during election campaigns /
Richard R. Lau, David P. Redlawsk.
    p.   cm. – (Cambridge studies in public opinion and political psychology)
Includes bibliographical references and index.
ISBN 0-521-84859-8 (hardback) – ISBN 0-521-61306-X (pbk.)
1. Voting research – United States.   2. Elections – United States.
I. Redlawsk, David P.   II. Title.   III. Series.
JK1967.L38   2006
324.973–dc22   2005021892

ISBN-13   978-0-521-84859-6 hardback
ISBN-10   0-521-84859-8 hardback

ISBN-13   978-0-521-61306-4 paperback
ISBN-10   0-521-61306-X paperback

To Karen, who has meant so much to me that – even if you only consider what I have come to take for granted, or what she *thinks* I take for granted but do not and in fact appreciate daily, or just the relatively little that I manage to convey that she knows I appreciate – would easily constitute the most important decision of *my* life. I am so glad, in so many different ways, that I met you.

(RRL)

To Aletia, Andrew, and Greg, who put up with a husband and father who often couldn't seem to make up his mind exactly what to do in life, and whose support, encouragement, and sometimes even frustration helped me find the direction I needed. And to my father, who has continued to get smarter as I have gotten older!

(DPR)

In his reflective moments even the most experienced politician senses a nagging curiosity about why people vote as they do. His power and his position depend upon the outcome of the mysterious rites we perform as opposing candidates harangue the multitudes who finally march to the polls to prolong the rule of their champion, to thrust him, ungratefully, back into the void of private life, or to raise to eminence a new tribune of the people. . . .

Scholars, though they have less at stake than do politicians, also have an abiding curiosity about why voters act as they do.

V. O. Key (1966, p. 1)

Contents

Contents

List of Tables and Figures

TABLES

FIGURES

List of Tables and Figures

Acknowledgments

Any project that has gone on for as long as this one will accrue debts (both intellectual and personal) too numerous to mention in the space normally allotted to such a task. With apologies to those we will inevitably overlook, in more or less chronological order, we thank Peter Bentler, Thad Brown, Barry Collins, Bob Jervis, Hal Kelley, John Petrocik, Bernie Weiner, and especially David Sears, as well as all graduate school teachers of the first author, without whose knowledge, training, and subsequent friendship all of this would have been impossible. We also thank Gerry Pomper, whose guidance helped the second author decide to pursue his Ph.D. (for better or for worse) after many years in the "real" world, and Milt Heumann, who, although not exactly in our field, gave great Hanukkah parties we always looked forward to, and whose advice and support were crucial to the second author during those initial disorienting days of graduate school and beyond. Thanks also go to Alan Kornberg, who, as the second author's mentor during his undergraduate years at Duke, helped him develop an excitement and appreciation for the joys of academe and research.

John Herstein graciously shared his stimulus materials with the first author at a very early stage in the development of this research; Herstein's dissertation (or at least the 1981 published version of it) was the first time we had seen a decision board in action. Dana Dunn then used those stimulus materials as the basis for a senior honors project at Carnegie Mellon University, which became the infamous "Rick's study" that none of Lau's future students could ever figure out exactly what to do with. Ralph Erber got further than anyone else and helped point the way to a new way of thinking about this type of data.

The National Science Foundation provided the crucial financial support necessary for the development of the dynamic process-tracing methodology described herein, with awards to both authors (SBR 93-21236 and SBR-9411162). Eric Johnson, one of the original developers of the decision board methodology, provided invaluable advice on using a decision board at an early stage in our development process. The Foundation's reluctance to fund subsequent projects has kept us more or less focused on this one. Rutgers University and later the University of Iowa provided the laboratory facilities and countless other relatively minor resources necessary for any research project, which of course cumulatively far outweigh any formal grant award. The second author in particular thanks the Obermann Center for Advanced Study at the University of Iowa; its Director, Jay Semel; and administrative assistant, Lorna Olsen, for space and resources provided during a particularly intense period of manuscript revision.

Racheal Ankrah, Jennifer Holt, Jill Locke, John Manyo, Grace Ann Mumoli, and Jeff Schnug worked as experimenters at various stages in this project. Licia DeVivo was an experimenter who also coded much of the open-ended data. Gail Shirazi, Elizabeth Williams, and Rachelle Brooks worked diligently coding the data that led to our initial conception of the on-line evaluation counter. Jason Humphrey, Andrew Civettini, and Kimberly Briskey all played key roles as research assistants as portions of the project moved to Iowa. At Rutgers, Paul Babbitt and Liz Felter served in the multiple roles of expert judges, project managers, experimenters, and readers of early papers from this research and thus deserve particular thanks.

One of the most interesting tasks early on was the creation of campaign ads, using technology that seemed quite advanced at the time. We would like to thank all those who lent their voices to us to narrate the ads, but we especially thank George Bruce Morgan, the second author's father-in-law and a retired radio announcer.

Larry Bartels and the Center for the Study of Democratic Politics at Princeton University provided a home away from home for the first author and offered the most valuable resources of all, time to think and write, when the book manuscript was beginning to take shape. Numerous colleagues at Columbia, Duke, Iowa, North Carolina, Ohio State, Princeton, Rutgers, Stony Brook, UCLA, UCSD, and Vanderbilt and at the New York Area Political Psychology meeting, have listened to and provided valuable feedback on various aspects of this research. Bartels, Adam Berinsky, John Geer, Jane Junn, Tali Mendelberg, Steve Nicholson, Gerry Pomper, and David Sears have all read and provided feedback on early drafts of several different chapters of the book, as did graduate students in the second author's Experimental Methods and Political Decision Making seminars. Several anonymous readers and Cambridge editors Dennis Chong and James Kuklinski have each read the whole damn thing twice and have provided trenchant criticisms, valuable suggestions, and unflagging encouragement throughout the publication process.

And finally we want to thank Mo's grandmother, who unbeknownst to her (and as far as we know, her grandson) symbolically at least inspired this entire research project.

HOW VOTERS DECIDE

Information Processing during Election Campaigns

Part I. Theory and Methods

I

Introduction

Democracy succeeds when government, in some broad sense, represents the will of the people. Democratic representation can be assured if informed citizens freely elect their leaders, and those leaders stand for reelection at some regular interval. Thus citizens, voting for leaders who best represent their views, and holding those leaders (or their political parties) accountable for their performance in office at the next election, make democracy work. At least that is the theory.

Naturally enough, voting is a topic that has drawn quite a bit of attention in political science, and the classics of political behavior research have all focused, in one way or another, on the vote decision. Understanding how voters make their decisions is tantamount, at some very basic level, to understanding how democracy works. There can be no more important question in political science. Yet with all of our research over the past half century, and the numerous models of vote choice that have been proposed, how much do we really know about how voters decide?

If that question is understood to mean how well can we predict or explain the vote in a statistical sense, the answer is quite well indeed. The existing models do an excellent job of prediction, including appropriate voter, campaign, candidate, and political environment factors into a regression stew and "explaining" with high accuracy which voters choose Democrats and which choose Republicans. But such prediction is thin, supported as it is by post hoc mathematical modeling, and provides little in the way of true understanding of how voters in the real world gather campaign information about the candidates and use it to make a decision. Most of our existing models of the vote choice are relatively static, based in a very real sense on cross-sectional survey data, taking what little (typically) voters know about the candidates at the time of the survey as a given with almost no thought to how they went about obtaining that information in the first place. But campaigns are *dynamic* events that occur over time, and deciding whether and how to vote is a process that also occurs over time and that needs to be understood (and studied) as such.

Consider five hypothetical voters in the 2004 U.S. presidential election.

- William R is an accountant working for Xerox in Rochester, New York. He believes the only way to pick a president is to learn everything there is to know about the candidates' experience and policy proposals and to evaluate the likely consequences of those policies for his family and himself. He watches *News Hour with Jim Lehrer* on PBS and scours the newspapers daily for information about the candidates. He could tell you the minutest detail about George W. Bush's plans for post-war Iraq, his stand on immigration or the environment, John Kerry's record as Senator from Massachusetts, his policies on health care reform and national defense, Ralph Nader's feelings about corporate business practices, and so on. Aided by his photographic memory, he took the weekend before the election off so he could integrate what he learned about the strengths and weaknesses of each candidate into overall summary evaluations. George Bush came out with the highest total, and thus earned William's vote.
- Anne D is a business consultant in San Diego. "Time is money," she always says, and even though she believes that the candidates have to be evaluated according to the likely consequences of their winning, she feels it is simply "not worth the effort" to pay any attention to campaigns until near the end. She never votes in primary elections and considers only the Democratic and Republican candidates because "no other candidate has a chance of winning." She evaluates the candidates primarily in terms of how likely they are to have any tangible effect on her own pocketbook. She gladly accepted her $500 tax refund the year before the election, but business has been very poor since President Bush took office, and she has made much less from her consulting job since the 2000 election than she remembers making during the boom years under Clinton and Gore. Although she has voted Republican in the past, Kerry and the Democrats seem like the obvious choice to Anne this year.
- Warren M is a shift supervisor in an automobile factory living in a middle-class neighborhood in Detroit. A lifelong Democrat – as were his parents – Warren found the decision to vote for John Kerry an easy one. He believes that Kerry has superior political experience compared to George Bush, and he trusts him a lot more than any Republican. As a Democrat, he cares about a strong economy and believes Kerry has better plans for getting the economy going again

4

than does Bush. As a father with two teenage boys, he is delighted that his candidate will do everything he can to keep us out of war. And of course he is disgusted with how President Bush has been distorting Kerry's war record during the campaign. All of these concerns pushed him toward the Democratic ticket.

- Teresa C is a soccer mom living in the suburbs of Atlanta. With four kids at home, she has many more pressing things on her mind than politics. Nonetheless, she believes that a good citizen should vote. She cares about two issues, and two issues only: prayer in school and government vouchers for private education. George Bush shares her views on these two issues; John Kerry does not. Enough said, choice made – now back to the game and other more immediate family matters.
- Herbert S's approach to politics is just like his take on the weather: "It's going to be hot in the summer, cold in the winter, and pretty nice in the fall and spring. And if something different is going to happen, you'll hear about it." Democrats, he knows, are pretty much always "for the people a little out of the mainstream." They generally think government should try to help people get ahead. Republicans, on the other hand, are for a strong defense, "want the rich to get richer," and "don't want the government to do anything." Herbert checked out what people were saying about Bush and Kerry enough to know they both fit pretty well with their party stereotypes, and as an African American working for the Social Security Administration in Washington, he found it easy to support Kerry in the 2004 election.

Many of our readers will recognize these five hypothetical voters as caricatures of major political science views of the vote decision: classic economic rational choice (William R) and Downsian "constrained" rationality relying upon retrospective considerations (Anne D); the so-called social psychological or Michigan model of *The American Voter* (Warren M); single-issue voting (Teresa C); and cognitive psychological approaches of "bounded" or "low-information" rationality (Herbert S). These approaches have driven much of the voting research over the past fifty years, and they provide context for the process model of decision making we develop in this book. It is not our intention to provide a complete review of the voting behavior literature, which would require several books to do justice to the topic. But these same hypothetical voters also illustrate four largely distinct models or approaches to decision making that are implicitly assumed by these political science views of voting. We will therefore also use this brief review of previous voting models to introduce these more general models of decision making.

MODEL I: RATIONAL CHOICE

William R is the classic "rational" voter of economic theory as specified by von Newman and Morgenstern (1947) and Arrow (1951). The approach is explicitly normative in its orientation, describing how decision makers ought to behave to guarantee value-maximizing decisions.[1] To highlight the specifics of this model, William evaluates the candidates in terms of the expected consequences for his own self-interest of each of them winning the election.[2] Some of those consequences are uncertain, and thus the probabilities of the different consequences occurring must also be considered. William believes that the more information he has about all of the alternatives under consideration, the better the resulting decision will be, so he seeks out as much information about every possible alternative as he possibly can. William knows and cares a lot about politics, which makes the job of gathering information somewhat easier. With his photographic memory and accountant training, he has relatively little difficulty keeping track of this information, although even *he* must focus exclusively on the election for a period of time in order to integrate all of the information he has gathered and come up with an optimal decision.[3] This classic economic perspective on rationality views humans

---

[1] Applications of the economic approach in political science are too numerous to mention, but Davis, Hinich, and Ordeshook (1970) and Riker and Ordeshook (1968) are two of the early classics; Enelow and Hinich (1984) and Hinich and Munger (1997) provide more recent summaries and extensions of the general approach.

[2] "Self-interest" is one of those slippery terms that, if we are not careful, can be stretched to mean almost anything. Without denying that most people derive some benefit from larger considerations (e.g., the continuation of the human race), we will restrict our meaning of self-interest to relatively short-term tangible benefits to the individual and his or her immediate family.

[3] The rational choice approach also assumes that decision makers follow a number of formal mathematical principles in making their probability judgments and value assessments, including regularity, independence from irrelevant alternatives, transitivity, procedural invariance, dominance, and all the dictates of Bayes theorem. Hastie and Dawes (2001) summarizes these principles more simply by stating that a decision can be considered rational if it is (a) based on the status quo of current assets such that losses or foregone gains are equivalent; (b) based on all possible/plausible outcomes associated with the choice; and (c) does not violate any of the basic rules of probability where uncertainty is involved. Downs (1957) characterizes the rational actor as one who (1) can always make a decision when confronted with a range of alternatives; (2) ranks all the alternatives facing him or her in order of his or her preference in such as way that each is either preferred to, indifferent to, or inferior to each other; (3) has a transitive preference ranking; (4) always chooses from among the possible alternatives that which ranks highest in his or her preference ordering; and (5) always makes the same decision each time he or she is confronted with the same alternatives (p. 6).

(*Homo economicus*) as *omniscient calculators* (Lupia, McCubbins, and Popkin, 2000) or (a term we like even more) *ambulatory encyclopedias*, although it is difficult to imagine very many people being able to follow its dictates. Nevertheless, the image of a cold, dispassionate accountant carefully weighing the pluses and minuses associated with the different alternatives is an appropriate one to hold here.

Our second voter, Anne D, is just as rational in her orientation as our first voter, but she does not have the demonic cognitive abilities of William R. Although she would be pleased to consider all possible information about all possible alternatives if somebody else would gather and integrate that information for her, she recognizes quite logically that it takes time to gather this information, time she could spend doing more enjoyable and/or more productive things. She also believes that it is not going to make much of a difference in her life if the Republican or the Democrat wins the election. Hence, she learns a few easily obtainable bits of information about the two major candidates, mostly based on her experience with them, but once the marginal cost of new information exceeds the potential gain from that information, she stops paying attention to the campaign. We would call this procedure optimization under constraints[4] (Gigerenzer and Todd, 1999), and in broad strokes it is the procedure described by Anthony Downs (1957) and his followers.[5]

Both constrained and unconstrained rational choice models assume people consciously and explicitly consider the consequences (both positive

---

[4] The constraints must work with some stopping rule, which tells the decision maker to cease looking for additional information. It is interesting to consider exactly how a stopping rule would actually provide any cognitive savings, and if it does, how it could be considered rational. For example, how does the decision maker know that additional information will not prove to be especially valuable, without actually looking at it? Obviously there could be no cognitive savings here. Alternatively, if the decision maker were automatically forming some sort of on-line evaluation of every candidate (see the discussion of Milton L in Chapter 8, n. 1), then the stopping rule could involve some sort of variance indicator, and the rule could cut off the search for additional information once the evaluation stops varying very much with additional information. But then cognitive resources would have to be spent to monitor and calculate variance in some manner, and still the decision maker would have to assume that additional information would be similar to information already obtained about an alternative, a very questionable assumption in a dynamic situation such as a political campaign.

[5] Fiorina (1981) provides one of the best political science examples of this approach with his model of retrospective voting. According to Fiorina, voters normally prefer retrospective (i.e., based on past performance) evaluations over prospective considerations (balancing promises about future policy) because the information costs associated with the former are much less, and the reliability of that information much greater.

7

	Model 1 **Rational Choice:** *Dispassionate Decision Making*	Model 2 **Early Socialization and** **Cognitive Consistency:** *Confirmatory Decision Making*	Model 3 **Fast and Frugal** *Decision Making*	Model 4 **Bounded Rationality and** *Intuitive Decision Making*
Assumptions about Information Search	Decision makers should actively seek out as much information as possible, about every available alternative [until the cost of additional information exceeds its expected benefit].	Information gathering is basically passive, except party identification should be sought early. Most exposure to relevant information comes from the media and is largely inadvertent. Perception of media messages is often biased in favor of early-learned predispositions, and to the extent information search is purposeful, it too is biased toward those early-learned predispositions.	Decision makers should actively seek out only a very few attributes of judgment which they really care about or which they have found to be most diagnostic, and ignore everything else.	People actively seek out only enough information to allow them to reach a decision (although depth of search is conditioned by the perceived importance of the decision). Cognitive shortcuts and various decision heuristics are heavily (and almost automatically) utilized.
Method of Decision Making	Explicit, conscious, cognitively difficult memory-based consideration of the positive and negative consequences associated with each alternative	Memory-based evaluations of what is known (long-term) and has recently been learned (short-term) about the different alternatives	Explicit memory-based consideration of the one or two positive and negative consequences associated with each alternative	Satisficing or related methods which attempt to make choice relatively easy by restricting information search
Motivations for Choice	Self-Interest	Cognitive Consistency	Efficiency	Making the best possible decision with the least amount of effort; Avoiding value tradeoffs
Electoral Inputs to Decision	Mainly retrospective (e.g., job performance) and prospective (e.g., issue stands) judgments about candidates.	Primarily party identification, but also issue stands, economic evaluations, perceptions of the candidates, and evaluations of the incumbent's job performance.	Candidates' "stands" on the few attributes a voter considers (but certainly not limited to policy stands)	Cognitive shortcuts (stereotypes, schemas, etc.) and other political heuristics

Figure 1.1. Four models of individual decision making.

and negative) for their own self-interest associated with every alternative course of action. More information is always considered to be better than less information, although "constrained" rationality realizes that the cost of gathering all that information may exceed the marginal benefit from having it. People are not always right in their calculations – consider Anne D's limiting of alternatives to the two major party candidates because they are the only two who have a chance to win, as if her own single vote could make a difference in the outcome of the election – but the point is they presumably reach a decision based upon those calculations. Most importantly, to the extent that the dictates of rational choice are followed (see n. 2), the procedure promises to result in the best possible choice for each individual decision maker, which gives rational choice a strong normative component. This is classic rational decision making, and we will refer to it as *Model 1*.[6] Model 1 voters should be open to whichever party or candidate can make the most convincing appeals. Figure 1.1 highlights the model's most important features.

MODEL 2: EARLY SOCIALIZATION AND COGNITIVE CONSISTENCY

Warren M is exactly the type of person the authors of *The American Voter* (Campbell et al., 1960) were describing. Most citizens know little and care less about politics – one of the most far-reaching and well-documented findings of the Michigan model of voting – and by these standards, Warren seems fairly sophisticated. He is first and foremost a party voter – a long-term psychological attachment learned at his mother's knee – and his party identification colors his views of the personal characteristics, issue stands, and performance evaluations of the candidates, the three most important short-term factors affecting the vote decision. Warren believes, for example, that Democratic Senator John Kerry has the better political experience for the presidency – a position that would be hard to defend objectively against a sitting incumbent with almost four years on the job. Whereas our first two voters were presumed to be making explicit decisions based on rational calculations of the consequences of Bush or Kerry

---

[6] We also chose this label to celebrate Allison (1971), whose wonderful book about the Cuban Missile Crisis introduced the senior author to the decision-making literature. Allison presented three different models of governmental decision making, the first of which, Model I, is identical to our own Model 1. Allison's remaining two models are very explicitly models of *organizational* decision making, however, and are thus not very relevant to individual decisions like the vote choice. Allison used Roman numerals to label his models. To help avoid confusion, we will employ plain old (Arabic) numbers for ours.

winning the election, Warren's decision, if not quite predetermined by his party identification, is clearly strongly influenced by it. Most importantly, that party identification is something Warren essentially inherited at birth (rather than explicitly chose in some rational manner), much like racial, gender, class, and religious identifications.

The American Voter is one of the most influential books in all of political science, and its basic theory about long- and short-term forces and the "funnel of causality" is still the bible for many students of political behavior. Moreover, its theory guides one of the most extraordinary data collection efforts in all of the social sciences, the American National Election Studies (ANES) – biannual surveys conducted by the survey research center at the University of Michigan around every national U.S. election since 1952. These surveys have proved invaluable to learning most of what we know about American public opinion and voting behavior.[7]

The Michigan approach is a perfect illustration of what we call *Model 2* decision making. Whereas Model 1 decisions are based on explicit dispassionate calculations of self-interest, Model 2 decisions are strongly influenced by early-learned social identifications, which, like all such identifications, tend to be accepted with little or no consideration of alternatives.

---

[7] As a model of the vote, *The American Voter*, published in 1960, has survived amazingly well. Some of its findings have been challenged and revised, to be sure, but the basic structure of the model remains today. To briefly mention one of the major challenges, the 1950s in America may have been an unusually quiet, noncontentious period in our country's history, when politicians were centrists and few issues were publicly debated by opposing elites. Following the implicit lead of elites, few in the general public were much engaged by the political issues of the day. This changed by the mid 1960s. Civil rights, urban riots, the increasingly unpopular war in Vietnam, and the women's liberation movement brought the much more contentious issues of the day into the homes of the general public via the nightly news. Moreover, this period saw some of the most ideologically extreme candidates running in the presidential elections of the period, including Goldwater and Johnson in 1964, Humphrey and Wallace in 1968, and McGovern and Wallace in 1972. The general public, again following the lead of political elites, were much more involved with political issues, more consistent in their own views, and more likely to base their vote decision on perceived agreement with the candidates. Such is the story told by *The Changing American Voter* (Nie, Verba, and Petrocik, 1976). At the same time, parties were apparently becoming less important, and the media-dominated period of candidate-centered politics came to the fore (Wattenberg, 1981). Markus and Converse (1979) incorporate (and evaluate) most of these revisions in their updating of the basic Michigan model with data from the 1972 and 1976 presidential elections. Most recently, Miller and Shanks have specified more precisely in *The New American Voter* (1996) the important categories of variables in the funnel of causality. Still, these revisions were more of degree than kind and do not threaten the basic model laid out by Campbel et al. (1960).

That is, such identifications develop through simple conditioning rather than any calculation of self-interest (see Sears, 1975; Sears and Funk, 1991). To the extent the parties stay basically the same, there is no real need for continuous monitoring of party activity – a view that is very consistent with the general dearth of political information held by the American public. Thus, exposure to political information is generally viewed as haphazard and unintentional, and most citizens learn only the basic gist of the most prominent issues covered by the media. Moreover, perception of political information is often biased by prior predispositions, and voters are motivated to *maintain* their prior convictions. Hence, even though in theory it is easy to know how to change the minds of Model 1 decision makers – change the contingencies, and they should change their decisions – Model 2 decision makers have many psychological devices that work against change, making most of their decisions essentially standing decisions. Thus, we would not expect Model 2 voters to be strongly influenced by any political campaign. If Model 1 decision makers are trying to maximize self-interest, Model 2 decision makers are trying to confirm a prior (standing) predisposition.

The theory and empirical evidence for Model 2 voting is strongly shaped by the ANES surveys that have developed along with it. By their very nature, surveys are snapshots of public opinion at a particular point in time, and thus not well suited to explicating the process of information search and decision making that must occur over time. Thus, political scientists who have (implicitly, at least) adopted a Model 2 view of voter decision making have said little about how information is gathered, and it is up to us to flesh out the information search and decision making aspects of the model a bit more.

The information gathering of Model 2 voters is clearly envisioned as largely a passive (media-driven) process, but the one big exception is that voters should try to learn a candidate's party affiliation as soon as possible. Any subsequent purposeful or intentional political information seeking could have a partisan flavor to it as well – that is, party voters should be expected to disproportionately seek out information about their own party's candidate(s) rather than the opposition.[8] This contrasts

---

[8] The logic behind this prediction comes from *cognitive dissonance* theory (e.g., Festinger, 1957), an extremely important theory in social psychology at more or less the same time that *The American Voter* (1960) was in its heyday. The theory assumes people are strongly motivated to avoid experiencing cognitive dissonance, which could arise by knowing one supported a lousy candidate, for example. One way to avoid such unpleasant cognitions would be to change one's perceptions of the candidate (He really isn't so bad – or at least he is better than the other guy). This is what is meant by party identification "coloring" perceptions of other political

with Model 1 decision makers, who should seek out the *same* information about all alternatives. And even though the Michigan researchers do not say much about the degree or amount of information search, it is clear they expect many voters to *have* a reasonable amount of information about the major candidates in a presidential election. For example, Miller and Shanks (1996) describe a multistage decision process whereby partisan and policy-related (ideological) predispositions influence current policy preferences and perceptions of current (mostly economic) conditions, which in turn influence retrospective evaluations of the incumbent candidate's (or party's) job performance, all of which influence perceptions of the candidate's personal qualities, which influence prospective evaluations of the candidates and the parties, which combine to lead to the vote choice. This is a lot of information, even if we limit consideration to two candidates. Thus, information "gathering" (which sounds a little more passive than "searching") should be relatively deep, and quite possibly unequally distributed across the competing candidates. Again, the most important features of Model 2 are summarized in Figure 1.1.

MODEL 3: FAST AND FRUGAL DECISION MAKING

In certain ways, our fourth voter, Teresa C, is like our optimization under constraints voter, Anne D, in that they both seem to have limited time for politics. Anne's value judgments are based on her own self-interest, and her time constraints focus around the costs of information *gathering*. On the other hand, Teresa's values are not so narrowly tangible and economic, and her constraints seem more focused on the costs of processing information rather than on gathering it per se.

Political scientists have labeled decision makers like Teresa C single-issue voters (e.g., Conover, Gray, and Coombs, 1982), although in her case this would be a slight misnomer, as she clearly cares about two issues. Both of her concerns are what Carmines and Stimson (1980) would call "easy" issues, which they characterize as issues long on the political agenda,

---

information. But another way to avoid dissonance would be to seek out positive information about one's candidate, to counterbalance some initial negative impression. (Sure, Bill Clinton cheats on his wife and lied about it to the American public, but he has also done a fantastic job with the economy, he has eliminated the deficit and created millions of jobs, he has kept us out of war and brought some hope of a long-term peace in Ireland and the former Czech Republic.) This latter procedure leads to our prediction of biased information search. Lodge and Taber's (2000) recent work on motivated political reasoning might be another theoretical approach to justify the same basic predictions.

largely symbolic rather than technical, dealing with policy ends rather than means. "Hard" issues are more technical in nature, dealing more with the appropriate means to achieve a universally valued end. It does not take any great sophistication to vote on easy issues, whereas voting on hard issue has a more Model 1 ring to it. Easy issue voting could be called fast and frugal decision making (Gigerenzer and Todd, 1999); we will refer to it as *Model 3*. Our image is of what Joe Friday (from *Dragnet*) must have been like at the ballot box: "Just the facts, Ma'am."

MODEL 4: BOUNDED RATIONALITY AND INTUITIVE DECISION MAKING

Our last voter, Herbert S, like several of our earlier examples, reaches his decision based on very little information gathered during the campaign itself, but his motivations are somewhat different from any of our earlier voters. Indeed, it is hard to see much motivation at all in Herbert's behavior. There is no calculation of consequences associated with the different alternatives, no coloring of the information about them based on some early-learned political predisposition, no consideration of or conforming to the views of other people. Instead, the candidates are simply categorized as a Democrat and a Republican, and various stereotypic attributes of Democrats and Republicans are presumed to be true of Kerry and Bush. Because Kerry is assumed to share many more of his values than Bush, the decision to vote for him is almost automatic, although Herbert does seek out a few specific bits of information to confirm that Bush and Kerry really do hold the positions he expects them to hold. This is clearly an application of "low information rationality" (Popkin, 1991; see also Sniderman, Brody, and Tetlock, 1991), an approach that allows people to make decisions without too much effort.

A version of low information rationality is most consistent with our own view, which we will refer to as *Model 4*, intuitive decision making. This approach argues that most decisions (including most political decisions) are better understood as semiautomatic responses to frequently encountered situations than as carefully weighed probabilistic calculations of the consequences associated with the different alternatives.[9] Fifty plus years of survey research on voting has taught us that most people are not very interested in politics, and judging from basic textbook

[9] We could make the same statement about even the most consequential decisions made by political elites, although this would take us well beyond our own data. See Allison and Zelikow (1999), Jervis (1976), Levy (2003), or Mintz and Geva (1997) for evidence about elite decision making that is largely consistent with our general perspective.

knowledge, they do not know much about how government works or who the major players are below the level of president and vice president (Delli Carpini and Keeter, 1996). Few citizens have anything approaching an "ideology," and most do not have very stable or "real" attitudes toward even the major political issues of the day (Converse, 1964, 1975; Zaller, 1992).

Models 3 and 4 share a view of humans as cognitively limited information processors who make decisions in a much more "intuitive" (i.e., less formal and calculating) manner. We will have more to say about this view in the next chapter. For now let us simply point out that these last two models take as their starting point a perspective on human cognition diametrically opposed to that of Model 1 and classic rational choice.

Model 4 further holds that most of the time decision makers are guided by two competing motivations: the desire to make a *good* decision and the desire to make an *easy* decision. The consequences of the decision matter, but only in the broad sense of "How important is this decision to me?" rather than detailed Model 1 considerations of the consequences associated with every different attribute associated with each different alternative course of action. If a choice is very important to a person, getting it right should be the more important consideration. But for most decisions – and certainly most political decisions – "doing it easily" should be the primary concern. Indeed, according to Model 4, people's severe cognitive limits make the easy way often the only way that a decision can be reached.

But in one respect Models 1, 3, and 4 are quite similar to each other, and very different from Model 2: They assume information gathering is at least in part intentional and an integral part of a decision making strategy. Model 1 differs from Models 3 and 4 on how much information decision makers are assumed to want, but they all share the belief that decision makers actively seek out the desired amount. As with the other models, the crucial features of Models 3 and 4 are summarized in Figure 1.1.

We are certainly not the first political scientists to suggest that people employ different heuristics and cognitive shortcuts in making their political judgments, although no one has offered a full-blown voting model based on this approach. But even research that accepts the very real limitations of voters does not usually consider whether those limitations are consequential, brushing them aside under the assumption that gut rationality, for example, leads voters to do "well enough." As Bartels (1996) points out, however, it is not enough to simply assume that a lack of information can be easily overcome; it has to be demonstrated. We argue that because a vote decision is based on information – even if the amount of information collected is limited – the failure of existing models of the

vote decision to seriously consider how voters acquire and use information means we still do not have a very good understanding of *how* voters decide how to vote.

Voting Correctly

Why does all of this information processing matter? Isn't the only important question which candidate receives the most votes? We think not. We believe that the processes voters use in making their choices can lead to better or worse decisions – that is, votes. The normative questions asked by most voting research are usually quite limited. If they are addressed at all, the focus is typically on low voter turnout, or how far below the democratic ideal our ill-informed and uninterested public falls. These questions are certainly important, but they do not get to what we believe is the most critical question for a functioning democracy – the linkage between the vote and government accountability. If voters cast votes that fail to represent their interests, this linkage is severely damaged. The simple act of voting is not so simple if people fail to make good choices. So in this research we ask whether citizens are able to vote correctly.

At first glance, this may seem a strange question. Assuming people actually vote for the candidate they want to vote for, then of course they voted correctly. That is, according to some views, unless a person somehow messes up the mechanics of voting and invalidates their ballot (which, as we all now know, happens more frequently than we realized), everyone by definition votes correctly, and it makes no sense to even ask this question. Economists have a wonderfully vacuous notion of "revealed preferences," which perfectly captures this sense: All told, people *must* have preferred the candidate they voted for, or else why would they have voted that way in the first place? The notion of revealed preferences is based on economists' underlying assumption that people are rational actors, and thus their actions reveal what their values and preferences must have been.

We will not grant this assumption at the outset, not only because it eliminates one of the most fundamental and interesting questions of all, but also because Model 1 strikes us as a pretty unrealistic description of human behavior. Even the most Machiavellian political leaders or the most cost-conscious free-market consumers do not go around calculating their every move – nor even very many moves. There simply is not the time and boundless energy required for such decision making. Nonetheless, classic models of rationality do provide us with a behavioral method for evaluating the quality of decisions. A decision could be judged of high quality by the extent to which rational decision-making processes (seeking all possible information about all plausible alternatives, etc.) are followed.

These procedures are supposed to guarantee the highest probability of reaching the value-maximizing decision, and thus there is a theoretical reason to take these procedures as normative standards. At the very least, this gets us away from assuming that all decisions are correct by definition, although it does require some method for observing people's decision processes.

Such a procedural definition, although far better than assuming away the question, still does not get us very far toward understanding whether voters effectively translate their preferences into a vote for the candidate who best represents those interests. This, we believe, is the best standard for evaluating the quality of a decision: Did the voter, in the hurly-burly of an actual election campaign, with all the constraints imposed by real life, still manage to select the candidate that he or she would have chosen in the ideal world of fully informed preferences? This is a fundamental question that prior voting research has missed and that purely behavioral definitions fail to engage fully. A new approach to studying the vote decision is needed.

What We Can Add to the Understanding of the Vote Decision

This book makes three major contributions in defining one such new approach. First is the question of voting correctly. In Chapter 4 we will define new substantive criteria for judging if voters can and do vote their informed interests. These substantive criteria are independent of the procedures by which the decision is reached, thus transforming decision strategy (including Model 1 rationality) into a very important independent variable that could lead to more or less correct voting. For the moment, we simply want to make the point that this is a question that should interest political scientists of all stripes, a question that political science should be asking.

We began by arguing that voting is the institution through which the will of the people is expressed, the institution through which democracy works. In asking the normative question about correct voting, we will be focusing on the first step in judging the effectiveness of that institution, and for comparing alternative institutional arrangements for achieving the same end. Democracy works best, we would hold, when the will of the people is accurately expressed through vote decisions. Theorists have made the point that the aggregation of individual preferences into aggregate policy is often problematic (Arrow, 1951); however, if voters cannot correctly express their individual preferences in the first place, then there is nothing at all to constrain public officials. Said another way, the more people vote correctly, the better a democratic system of government is functioning. Thus, the first major advance we are making is to suggest a new way to look at the vote decision itself. One interesting question, to be sure, is whether the Democrat or the Republican receives a voter's support, but the more interesting question may well be whether that decision, whatever it was, is (from the voter's own perspective) a correct one.

Providing a criterion for addressing normative questions is one thing; developing empirically based models for understanding whether voters reach that criterion is something else again. To make significant advances in understanding how voters decide, we must devise a method for studying the vote process, a method that allows us to observe voters while they are making their vote decisions. Survey research just cannot do the trick. The second major advance of this book is presenting such a new method. The technique, which we call *dynamic process tracing*, is based on a standard method for studying decision making in psychology, but we have radically revised it to better match the realities of modern political campaigns. This method allows us to observe voting from up close, to dig below the surface and watch voters as they try to gather facts about candidates while negotiating the overwhelmingly mad rush of information that characterizes modern high-level election campaigns. And it allows voters an important role in shaping their own information environments. Using this methodology, we will observe, and attempt to understand, the rules or strategies voters follow as they selectively sample from the total pool of available information. We will see how the nature of the campaign, and the nature of the candidates running in it, affects information processing. And we will do this with an explicit awareness that voters know that they must do more than simply form evaluations of different candidates – they must also choose among them.

This last point relates to the third major advance of this book: the presentation and elaboration of a new framework for understanding voter decision making and the development of a new set of measures for studying it. We take no credit for the underlying psychological theory, as there is a well-developed literature on behavioral decision theory (BDT) upon which we rely. However, it is the application of this theory to voting that is at the core of our argument. Voting is about information, and thus understanding how people acquire and use information in making vote decisions is critical. Behavioral decision theory guides the process-oriented voting framework we present in the beginning of Chapter 2 and the new measures we will use to test it. Categorizing our own views (and those of our predecessors) on voter decision making into Models 1, 2, 3, and 4 is our attempt to recast the vast voting behavior literature into a new decision-making framework.

Overview of the Remainder of the Book

The next section of the book describes our theory and methods, as we devote a chapter to each of the three major contributions we hope to make to the study of voting behavior. Chapter 2 provides a brief overview of bounded rationality and the cognitive procedures people have developed to cope with their cognitive limits. This chapter presents several formal decision strategies that have been identified in the BDT literature, strategies that fall under one of the four major approaches to decision making introduced in the current chapter. Chapter 2 also discusses how information search can be measured, exploring procedures that in turn provide the key to determining which decision strategy is being followed. It concludes with a set of theoretically derived predictions or hypotheses that will guide much of the analysis to follow.

Chapter 3 presents our new dynamic process-tracing methodology. The shortcomings of traditional process-tracing techniques for studying an election campaign are discussed, as we illustrate how our new methodology overcomes those limitations. We describe the presidential election campaign simulation that we developed to go along with our new process-tracing methodology and discuss how this simulation captures what we consider to be the crucial aspects of modern political campaigns. The chapter also includes a discussion of the strengths and weaknesses of experiments as a research technique. Here we address the crucial issues of the internal and external validity of this research.

Chapter 4 then develops and justifies two measures of correct voting, two closely related ways of determining whether the voter actually supported the candidate he or she would have chosen under the best of all possible circumstances. In this chapter we go beyond our own experimental data and look at correct voting in recent American presidential elections using representative survey data.

The second section of the book focuses on information processing and generally treats it as the dependent variable. Chapter 5 sketches out the broad outlines of what voters actually "did" during our mock presidential election campaigns. Here we describe how much and what types of information people chose to look at during the campaigns, compared to what was available. We develop measures of the different information search variables (initially discussed in Chapter 2) that behavioral decision theorists have employed in studying decision making, including depth of search, comparability of search, and sequence of search, and translate these into our four broad categories or models of decision making. We also describe and summarize the different measures of memory available from our experiments.

Chapter 6 then begins looking at these basic results in more detail, focusing first on how characteristics of the voters themselves influenced what they did during the election campaigns. We look in particular at political sophistication or expertise, but we also consider broad political values or "identifications" – with parties, and with liberal–conservative ideologies – and the important background characteristics of age, education, and gender. We ask how (or whether) these important individual differences influenced information processing. One of them proves to be surprisingly strong. Chapter 7 then examines how the nature of the campaign influences information processing. Did the ideological distinctiveness of the candidates running in an election, their "fit" to common political stereotypes, or their very number influence how voters processed information about them? Did the campaign resources available to candidates, or how they chose to spend available resources, influence information processing?

The third section of the book turns more clearly to politics. Now we treat information processing as an independent variable and ask whether the various measures of information search and decision strategies have any detectable influence on the evaluation of candidates (Chapter 8), the direction of the vote (Chapter 9), and the quality or correctness of the vote choice (Chapter 10). Our theoretical approach leads us to ask a set of important questions about the vote choice that no previous researchers have addressed. In particular, we ask whether candidate evaluation is tantamount to the vote choice. More precisely, we will consider whether knowing that a *choice* must be made between several competing candidates affects how evaluations of them are formed, and how we in turn ought to model them. Chapters 10 and 11 then reconsider the contributions of what voters bring to any election, how the nature of the candidates and the campaigns sets the context of the election, and how all of these factors together influence information processing, not in terms of whether the Democrat or the Republican was supported but in terms of whether the correct choice was made. It is in providing at least a partial answer to this question – indeed, in posing the question in the first place – that we see the major contribution of our program of research.

In Part IV we conclude what we set out to accomplish in this book. We have established a new theoretical framework for studying voter decision making, developed a new research methodology ideally suited to studying that framework, and presented a number of empirical analyses testing (and largely confirming) predictions derived from our new theoretical framework. The concluding chapter briefly reviews what we have learned with an eye to the "so what" question. Although we think of ourselves as *political* psychologists, our approach to this research is primarily psychological, undeniably cognitive, and (to borrow a line from Reid Hastie,

1986) "unabashedly reductionistic" in digging much deeper below the surface of the vote choice than is common practice. We try throughout the book to convince our readers that the reductionism is worth the price, that the information processing variables that we have been considering throughout this book truly matter – and matter for the type of questions that political scientists want to address. We will try to make an overall assessment of the evidence for this point in the last chapter. And we will also try to sketch out a research agenda for the future – not just for ourselves, but we hope for many readers of this book.

2

A New Theory of Voter Decision Making

One of the expressed goals of this work is the development of a new process-oriented approach to voter decision making and the elaboration of a new set of measures for studying it. That is the task of this chapter. We begin with a very basic idea. Voter decision making *cannot* be much different from most other decisions people make in their daily lives. There is nothing special about the political environment that should cause people to overcome magically the limitations of human cognition. Indeed, everything we know about how citizens view politics suggests that for most people, most of the time, politics is usually a minor concern. Yet in certain high-profile situations such as presidential elections, citizens can hardly avoid exposure to politics and to the steady stream of political information that is made available. How can people cope with a potentially confusing and easily overwhelming information environment when they are motivated to pay at least some attention, but unable to devote superhuman cognitive resources to the task? Assuming one is going to make a choice,[1] some process for acquiring information and evaluating it is necessary.

As we argued in Chapter 1, however, most prior models of the vote choice tend to ignore the role of information acquisition and focus entirely on the end result. Virtually all political science models of the vote decision have adopted a Model 1 or a Model 2 view of decision making. Neither one of these models is well suited to answer questions about information acquisition and processing.

---

[1] We recognize that nearly half of the American public is apparently not particularly motivated to vote and thus would have no incentive to bother processing *any* information about a presidential campaign. Because this book is about voters, however, we will beg the question of information processing and decision making by those whose decision is to abstain.

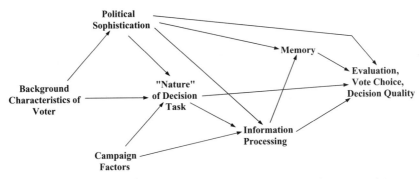

Figure 2.1. Process-oriented framework for studying voter decision making.

In contrast, behavioral decision theory takes as its primary goals both a description and an understanding of how people actually make decisions. Every study of real-world decision making has shown that rarely are all alternatives known, all outcomes considered, or all values evoked at the same time, as is presumed by the rational choice approach. People generally settle for alternatives that are "good enough" rather than seek out the value-maximizing alternative, no matter what constraints they are working under. Thus, behavioral decision theory provides a useful platform on which to build the new process-oriented approach to the vote decision we will detail in this chapter, an approach that is much more compatible with Model 3 and Model 4 decision making.

This new process-oriented approach is, first and foremost, about information and the processes voters use to acquire and evaluate it on the way to choosing a candidate. While still considering traditional antecedents of the vote – individual characteristics such as ideology and partisanship, economic status, political experience, personal characteristics, and the like – we focus our attention on understanding how those factors influence information acquisition and processing (rather than preferences themselves), crucial intervening variables that we believe, in turn, have a key (and totally underappreciated) influence on candidate evaluation and choice.

A broad schematic of our approach is set forth in Figure 2.1. It provides a general guide for the remainder of this chapter – and indeed for much of what follows in this book. This framework begins with four sets of factors that serve as the primary independent variables in our model: (1) demographic background characteristics of voters, including their partisan predispositions, which for us serve primarily as controls; along with two more directly germane to decision making, (2) political sophistication or expertise, and (3) what psychologists call "task demands" but what in our context is better labeled *campaign factors*. These three together determine (4) the subjective or perceived "nature" of the decision task.

What is new in our framework is the focus on a set of information processing variables, which along with memory play a crucial intervening role. Information processing and memory are hypothesized to have important direct effects on the nature and quality of the vote decision. But they are themselves hypothesized to be functions of prior decision-making variables in the model, including most prominently the perceived nature of the decision itself. Thus, we believe that the set of information processing variables included in our model are an important route by which individual voter differences, and institutional and campaign factors that determine the nature of the decision task, ultimately have their influence on the direction and quality of the vote choice itself. One cannot truly understand how the vote choice is made, we would argue, without explicating every step in this model.

We will begin by focusing on the information processing portion of the model. For most readers, this will be the least familiar portion of the model, and we will therefore spend the most time on it. We then much more briefly discuss the key decision-making concepts that precede information processing, political sophistication, and task demands. We also briefly discuss the role of memory in our model (itself often used as an indicator of information processing, but serving a conceptually more independent role here) and the nature of the ultimate dependent variable in our model, the vote choice itself.

HUMAN COGNITION AND ITS LIMITS

Behavioral decision theory is distinctly psychological in its orientation, beginning with the view of humans as limited information processors. The architecture of human cognition (Anderson, 1983) is designed with a number of important limitations. Our sense organs (eyes, ears, nose, etc.) are always being bombarded by stimuli, the vast majority of which are never actually processed by those organs (Zimmermann, 1989). That which does get processed almost immediately becomes subject to a very real bottleneck in short-term memory (STM – also known as working or active memory). Of the millions of bits of information that our sense organs are capable of processing in a brief period of time, STM can maintain only 7 ± 2 chunks of information at any given time (Miller, 1956). We all know the experience of looking up a phone number and then walking across the room to place the call, being distracted, and completely forgetting the number. Only if we attend to or "rehearse" the number can we maintain it long enough to dial the phone. Short-term memory is the part of memory that is currently activated, and the only part of memory where direct processing of information is possible.

Sometimes perceptions are activated strongly enough or rehearsed often enough that they become a part of our essentially unlimited long-term-memory structure. Memories, or nodes in long-term memory are linked together in an associative network so that when one node becomes activated – as we perceive an external stimulus or decide to search memory for some particular topic – other nodes that are linked to it have a potential to become activated as well, and thus also are available in STM. Again, despite our almost limitless long-term memory, only that small portion currently activated can actually be processed. Moreover, this active processing is serial, one item after another (rather that parallel – two or more items simultaneously), which presents another significant cognitive limitation.

Now, what does this have to do with voting? Paying attention and perceiving information to the point that short-term memory is activated, and then attending to it enough to build long-term-memory links, and finally recalling it from memory when it is needed, is time consuming, requires substantial processing effort, and is at best an imperfect procedure. The limitations of human cognition suggest that, to the extent deciding how to vote includes a memory-based process, it cannot be based on very many memories. Add to this the fact that politics is not very important to most people – even during a presidential election – and it becomes even less likely that voters will routinely make the cognitive effort necessary to support the processes assumed by many prior models of the vote. Thus, while economists and some political scientists have developed models of human behavior that require a significant investment of cognitive energy – classic Model 1 decision making – psychologists have become convinced that people act more as cognitive misers (Taylor, 1981; Fiske and Taylor, 1991) – or, perhaps more accurately, as "boundedly rational information processors" (Simon, 1956).

Even voters motivated to pay close attention to politics will find it impossible to learn everything about everyone. Highly motivated voters might well work harder to overcome their cognitive limits, though perhaps only if they are motivated toward accuracy rather than toward confirming preexisting beliefs (see Kunda, 1987, 1990). The potential irony here is that those most motivated to pay attention to politics are those most likely to be strongly partisan and therefore perhaps most likely to engage in motivated reasoning (Lodge and Taber, 2000), where confirming preexisting biases seems to be a priority. This is certainly a major presumption of Model 2. In the end, although we do not doubt that motivation plays a role in the processing of information, the architecture of human cognition creates very real limits no matter how motivated a decision maker may be.[2]

Coping with Cognitive Limits

If humans have so many information processing limitations, how do we cope with a world that can overwhelm the senses with information? This is not just a problem for politics; it confronts us in every aspect of life. People generally *want* to make good decisions – they just cannot do so in the idealized manner described by Model 1 rational processes.[3] The answer is that human beings have developed a large number of cognitive mechanisms for dealing with information overload. These mechanisms are generally employed automatically without any conscious forethought and can simplify both evaluation and choice processes. Most of these cognitive shortcuts are quite general and have ramifications for many aspects of human life.

The decision theory literature describes a wide range of approaches people use to cope with cognitive limits. We will quickly review the most important of them and then examine these strategies within the context of candidate evaluation and choice. Because we believe that evaluation and choice are distinct though interrelated processes, we will discuss simplifying strategies for each separately.

Simplifying Evaluations

Heuristics are problem-solving strategies (often employed automatically or unconsciously) that serve to "keep the information processing demands of the task within bounds" (Abelson and Levi, 1985, p. 255). They represent cognitive shortcuts, rules of thumb for making certain judgments or inferences with considerably less than the complete search for alternatives and their consequences that is dictated by rational choice.

Kahneman and Tversky (1972, 1973, 1984; Tversky and Kahneman, 1973, 1974) have identified three general cognitive heuristics that decision makers employ in lieu of detailed information gathering and analysis. These heuristics allow decision makers to simplify complex judgments

---

[2] The preceding discussion has been, admittedly, a very facile overview of cognitive architecture and processing and is informed by Anderson (1983), Anderson and Bower (1973), Anderson et al. (2004), Simon (1957, 1979), Smith (1998), and Wyer and Srull (1986), where the reader can find much more comprehensive discussions of cognitive limitations.

[3] See also Lupia and McCubbins (1998) on this point.

by focusing attention on a small subset of all possible information. They include *availability* – judging frequency, probability, and causality by how easily concrete examples come to mind, or how easy it is to generate a plausible scenario;[4] *representativeness* – assigning specific instances to broader categories (stereotypes, schemata) according to how well the particular instance fits or matches the essential properties of one category rather than another; and *anchoring and adjustment* – forming a tentative response and then adjusting by reviewing relevant data. We could refer to these three as forming judgments according to how accessible something is in memory, by how typical a particular example is, and by what comes first.

Categorization or grouping seems to be a basic property of human perception, such that when new stimuli are perceived, the first thing people try to do is categorize the stimuli as another instance of some familiar group (Cantor and Mischel, 1979; Rosch, 1978) that is already understood to have certain default characteristics. Such category- or "schema-based" processing is cognitively efficient because once a stimulus is perceived as another instance of some preexisting schema, the details of the new stimulus can be largely ignored, and default values associated with the schema assumed to hold. Ignoring the details allows for more efficient processing. Efficiency also results from being able to make category-based inferences about the particular stimulus even when the detailed information is *not* actually present in the information environment – thus avoiding additional information search.

Judgment heuristics and categorization have direct application to candidate evaluation. After all, what is partisanship, when applied to candidate evaluation, other than a cognitive shortcut? So in evaluating a candidate, a voter might apply *partisan and ideological schemata* (Conover and Feldman, 1986, 1989; Kuklinski and Hurley, 1994; Lau and Redlawsk, 2001a; Lodge and Hamill, 1986; Rahn, 1993; Sniderman et al., 1986). This is as simple as categorizing candidates in an election according to widely available political schemata, assuming schema-consistent detailed (default) information and applying category-based affect (Fiske and Pavelchak, 1986). The result is an evaluation "colored" by preexisting partisan preferences and the assumptions that come with them.

Likewise, one might apply *person stereotypes* concerning gender, race, age, appearance, and so on to flesh out an impression of the candidates (Fiske and Taylor, 1991; Miller, Wattenberg, and Malanchuk, 1986; Riggle et al., 1992; Rosenberg, Kahn, and Tran, 1991). Such stereotype- and/or schema-based inferences are applications of Kahneman and Tversky's

---

[4] The generation of possible causal scenarios is sometimes distinguished from availability as the simulation heuristic (Kahneman and Tversky, 1982).

(1972) representativeness heuristic and are certainly simpler than doing the careful, individualized information search necessary to be data-driven rather than schema-driven.

What comes to mind quickest is at the heart of availability. When a voter encounters a new candidate, for example, she may apply to that candidate the first things that come to mind. For a Democrat this might be the thought that Democrats like to raise taxes. Campaigns want to increase the availability of one set of attributes when their candidate is described, and a completely different – and opposite set – when their opponent is described. Thus, what comes to mind can have significant implications for how candidates are evaluated. Anchoring and adjustment works by establishing a starting point for making a judgment. Once established, evaluations may be potentially constrained by that starting point, rather than being fully updated by new information.

Simplifying Choice

The boundaries between evaluation and choice processes are fluid, but the two are certainly not identical, and we will typically treat them as distinct. Decision makers seem to simplify their task of making a choice in at least three fundamental ways: decomposition, editing, and using decision heuristics.

Decomposition refers to breaking a decision down into its component parts, each of which are presumably easier to evaluate than the entire decision. A candidate running for political office might try to devise a campaign strategy by making separate decisions about television advertising, personal appearances, and policy positions. Problem decomposition is closely related to specialization and division of labor that are essential in any successful organization.

Editing (or more aptly, *pruning*) refers to simplifying a decision by eliminating (i.e., ignoring) otherwise relevant aspects of the decision. Voters might simplify their decision task by restricting attention to familiar candidates, thus effectively removing one or more alternatives from the choice set. (This is probably the best explanation for the powerful "incumbency effects" observed in many electorates.) Single-issue voters limit the number of "outcomes" associated with each candidate that must be considered, thus also largely avoiding the need to resolve goal conflicts. A decision maker could simply count the number of pluses and minuses associated with each alternative rather than try to weigh them by importance or devise an evaluative scale with more than two levels. All of these procedures would greatly simplify any decision.

Decision heuristics are similar to the judgment heuristics described earlier, but they are more directly concerned with simplifying the choice between alternatives. Focusing more specifically on the vote decision, we can describe five common heuristics or cognitive shortcuts that people utilize in making vote choice. These heuristics provide great cognitive efficiency while probably still yielding reasonably accurate decisions most of the time. We say "probably" because there is in fact little empirical research addressing how people go about making a vote decision and how likely they are to choose the candidate who, for them, is best. Thus, the implications of the use of these five cognitive shortcuts should be considered testable hypotheses rather than statements of fact.

1. *Affect Referral* (Wright, 1975). If an election involves several candidates with whom you are already quite familiar, vote for the most highly evaluated candidate. This heuristic can be used only for candidates who have been around for multiple elections, but it could be used in any general election campaign if voters have already formed impressions of the candidates from a primary election.

2. *Endorsements*. Follow the recommendations of close acquaintances, trusted political elites (Carmines and Kuklinski, 1990; Mondak, 1993; Sniderman, Brody, and Tetlock, 1991), or social groups (Brady and Sniderman, 1985; Lau and Redlawsk, 2001a; Sniderman, Brody, and Tetlock, 1991) with whom you identify. In other words, let someone else do the hard work of figuring out how to vote.

3. *Familiarity* (Goldstein and Gigerenzer, 1999). If you have heard of one candidate but not any of the others, and your evaluation of that one candidate is neutral or better, vote for the candidate with whom you are already familiar. This heuristic is a variant of Tversky and Kahneman's availability heuristic. As noted earlier, familiarity works hand in hand with pruning as a method for simplifying choice.

4. *Habit*. Vote how you voted the last time. Make a "standing decision" (e.g., always vote Republican) and stick to it (Quadrel, Fischhoff, and Davis, 1993).

5. *Viability*. Only consider candidates that have a good chance of winning (Aldrich, 1980; Bartels, 1988; Lau and Redlawsk, 2001a).

Judgment and decision heuristics, and the simplification processes of pruning and decomposition, all help to solve the problems of bounded rationality. We can adopt an evolutionary perspective and conclude that these simplifications must in general "work," in the sense of producing choices that are, if not optimal, at least "good enough" most of the time to encourage their reproduction – and rarely bad enough to lead to the extinction of the decision maker!

A New Theory of Voter Decision Making

Nonetheless, all of these simplification mechanisms, whether focused on evaluation or choice, can at times lead to poor decisions. Decomposition, for example, can lead to very embarrassing choices if the components of a decision are treated as independent when in fact they are not. A voter who examines one set of candidate policies completely independently from another set may find he is unable to make a coherent decision, preferring different candidates on different policies. Editing can lead to poor decisions when the aspects of the decision that are ignored would result, cumulatively, in a new preference order across alternatives had they been considered. And heuristics can lead to systematic biases when the reason the heuristic is generally effective (e.g., more frequent occurrences really are easier to recall; numerical anchors provided by the decision context usually are reasonable) is not true in some particular instance.

Thus, decision makers are potentially faced with a real dilemma in coping with cognitive limitations. On the one hand, because we are not omniscient calculators, we simply need to use some cognitive shortcuts, some means of simplifying decisions so that a choice can be made. But on the other hand, whatever shortcuts and simplifications we adopt come with a potential cost: inaccurate judgments and something short of value-maximizing decisions. Behavioral decision theory research suggests that this dilemma occurs because people generally have two competing goals in decision making (see Hogarth, 1975; Lau, 2003; Payne, Bettman, and Johnson, 1993): (1) the desire to make a good decision and (2) the desire to reach a decision with minimal cognitive effort.

This leads to another important distinction between rational choice and behavioral decision theory approaches. Rational choice focuses attention on the structure or elements of a decision – the multiple alternatives, the relative importance of each criterion of judgment to the decision maker, and the value of the different outcomes that are associated, with some probability, with each alternative. Research guided by behavioral decision theories, in contrast, is much more likely to be concerned with the dynamic processes of *how decisions are made*, with information search, and with strategies for making choices. This will be our focus as well, although we will try to apply it to all four of the general models of decision making (including rational choice) presented in Chapter 1.

Not surprisingly, behavioral decision theory researchers have developed methodologies particularly suited to observing decision making, with the underlying assumption that the best way to study decision making is to observe it while the decision is being made (Svenson, 1979). Using process-tracing methodologies, decision researchers can keep track of what information is obtained and the order in which it is obtained, and thus make inferences about the strategies employed in making a choice.

We will have more to say about process tracing in Chapter 3 as we describe existing techniques and propose a new and better way to study the vote decision.

DECISION STRATEGIES

We have seen that decision makers are beset with cognitive limits, but armed with potentially useful tools to mitigate the effects of those limits. Now we turn to an examination of decision strategies that may combine several of these tools during the evaluation and choice process. Simply put, a decision strategy is a set of mental and physical operations that an individual uses to reach a decision. In the most general sense, it includes identifying alternatives, searching for information about them, and identifying a method for making a choice. Examining decision strategies brings our focus directly to the information processing section of our general framework for studying decision making shown in Figure 2.1.

What we called Models 1 through 4 in the previous chapter are actually broad categories of decision strategies. The behavioral decision theory literature has identified a number of distinct decision strategies that fall into each of these broader categories. These strategies differ in terms of how cognitively difficult they are to use, how much of the available information they consider, the order in which that information is considered, and their likelihood of reaching a best decision.

A major way to categorize decision strategies is by the extent to which they confront or avoid conflict (Billings and Marcus, 1983; Ford et al., 1989). If one alternative is preferred to all other alternatives on every dimension of judgment, it is said to dominate the other alternatives, and there should be no conflict in making a decision. But when one alternative is preferred on one dimension of judgment but a different alternative is preferred on another dimension of judgment, the potential for value conflict or tradeoffs exists. Decisions in such an environment – which we suspect is very common in an electoral setting – can be made in one of two ways:

- *Compensatory* strategies are cognitively complex information integration rules where decision makers are assumed to assign a value to every salient attribute associated with each alternative. Some of those values can be positive, and others negative, but when they are combined into an overall evaluation or decision, a positive value on one dimension can *compensate for* or trade off against a negative value on another dimension. Conflict is confronted and resolved in the process of integrating the positive and negative information or values associated with a choice. Compensatory strategies require commensurable outcomes or values: The only way the value associated with two different attributes can be traded off is if they both somehow can be compared on the same dimension. Generally, analysts assume the concept of "utility" in order to allow these tradeoffs to be made. Our Models 1 and 3[5] (and at least on the face of it, Model 2 as well) involve compensatory decision making.

- *Noncompensatory* strategies, on the other hand, rely on an incomplete information search to avoid conflicts. Negative values on one attribute or possible outcome do not trade off against positive values on another attribute or outcome; instead, alternatives are usually eliminated once negative information about them is obtained. Incommensurability is not a problem because no tradeoffs are made. A great deal of research has shown that most decision makers, most of the time, try to avoid value tradeoffs (Hogarth, 1987). They are time-consuming, cognitively difficult, at the extremes (e.g., *Sophie's Choice*), emotionally draining. But this avoidance has a potential cost: less accurate or ideal decisions. Noncompensatory decision strategies are at the heart of Model 4.

This simple dichotomy of compensatory and noncompensatory strategies is the tip of the decision strategy iceberg, but it provides a useful structure for our analyses of voter decision making. Voters may adopt any of a number of more specific strategies that fall under these broader categories, many of which operate to greatly simplify the evaluation and decision process. Appendix A details several of these strategies, three of which are well-known examples of Model 1 decision making, one of which is an example of Model 3, and two of which are well-known examples of Model 4 decision making. Model 2 is an unusual case, but we will specify a formal decision strategy for it as well. We have moved this somewhat detailed discussion to an appendix to keep from disrupting the general flow of our argument. Readers interested in the particulars of how different choice strategies "work" and can lead to different decisions should turn to this appendix and follow the adventures of a hypothetical voter Ralph as he employs several of these decision strategies. Here we will turn to the more immediate problem of determining which of the broad types or categories of strategies a decision maker is actually using.

---

[5] If a fast and frugal decision strategy were based on a *single* criterion of judgment, however – a "take the best" rule – it could not involve any compensatory tradeoffs, of course.

Theory and Methods

Any descriptions of specific decision strategies are idealized accounts, of course, and would rarely be observed in such pure states.[6] But it is very possible that somewhat "impure" variants of these strategies could be employed to actually reach a decision. One may well ask, then, how can we tell which strategy a decision maker is using? A very important finding of much behavioral decision theory research is that different patterns of information acquisition clearly reflect distinguishable choice strategies. Thus, a key to understanding any decision is observing how people acquire information because this in turn sheds light on the decision rules and heuristics that people follow in making their choice.

The Content of Information Search

Even while political scientists have never been particularly concerned with the search for information, the content of search – or rather, the content of memory, which presumably is a product of both intentional search and inadvertent exposure – has been an important focus of previous work on voting. Party affiliation, issue stands, candidate personalities and their experience/qualifications for the job, group attachments, and so on are the "stuff" of the vote decision, and some basic agreement or similarity between what a voter likes and what a candidate has (or is), must be the basis of any vote choice. Anyone trying to understand or predict the outcome of any decision must somehow link the preferences of the decision maker to the characteristics of the choice alternatives. These links are formed by (purposeful and inadvertent) information search.[7] We contend, however, that there is much more to understanding any decision.

---

[6] Taber and Steenbergen (1995) attempted to model several pure decision strategies with a procedure they called computational process tracing in order to predict the choices subjects made in a mock election study. No process-tracing data were gathered, but they did know the political beliefs of their subjects, and which of two hypothetical congressional candidates they preferred. In an indirect attempt to understand which strategy(ies) might have actually been employed, the authors asked the question "*Had* subjects used this strategy, what choice should they have made?" Unfortunately, all the rules Taber and Steenbergen considered did a good job of predicting subjects' actual vote choices, which make it difficult to use this procedure to determine which strategies were most likely to have been used.

[7] There is actually very little direct evidence for this assumption (Graber, 1984, would be a clear exception), although the indirect evidence – for example, that citizens who say they pay a lot of attention to politics generally know more facts about very current events and relatively new political candidates – is pretty convincing.

A New Theory of Voter Decision Making

The Process of Information Search

That much more is the process of decision making; that is, how information is gathered and combined to reach a decision. If decision makers were omniscient calculators with perfect memory who seek out and process all relevant information, the order in which information is acquired would be irrelevant. But if decision makers are limited information processors who will almost certainly make a decision before all possible information has been obtained, then the order of information acquisition can be crucially important. It should be obvious that how much information is obtained can influence choice. Somewhat less obviously, even controlling on amount of information, how information comes to a decision maker can also influence choice. Appendix A provides examples of how the order in which alternatives are examined or the completeness of search within alternatives can influence choice. Thus, if we can develop standard measures of each of the components of information search, they can be the key to knowing which decision strategy is being employed.

Depth of Search. Consider first the depth of information search. By depth of search, we mean how much of the available information is considered before a decision is reached. According to rational choice theory, all relevant information about every alternative should be obtained. In practice, though, it almost never is. Nonetheless, Model 1 decision strategies generally assume that as much relevant information about every alternative that can be reasonably gathered in the available time should be considered, and thus that search will be relatively deep. Likewise, Model 2 assumes that a good deal of information will be gathered, if only to bolster or justify a standing decision. In contrast, each of the noncompensatory strategies of Model 4 allows for much shallower search, although the choice set and target levels could be such that all information must be considered before a satisfactory alternative is found, or all but one alternative eliminated. And of course the entire raison d'être for Model 3 is very limited information search. Thus, the depth of search is one way to distinguish between strategies.

Comparability of Search Across Alternatives. The variance in the amount of information considered about each alternative is another way to distinguish between choice strategies. Compensatory strategies like those of Models 1 and 3 generally assume that the same information should be considered about every alternative, while the noncompensatory strategies of Model 4 allow for unequal search across alternatives. Thus, compensatory strategies dictate equal search across alternatives and small variance, while noncompensatory strategies often show high intercandidate

33

variance. As discussed in Appendix A, unequal search is also one of the ways Model 2 decision makers ensure that they make the right decision.[8] Variance measures are particularly useful in distinguishing between decision strategies when task constraints (e.g., time) make it impossible for all information to be considered.

The fact that information may vary by candidate means that voters may often be considering *noncomparable alternatives*: those with at least some attributes that are unique to each alternative (Johnson, 1984, 1986). Alternatives can be *inherently noncomparable* – guns vs. butter, say – or *de facto noncomparable* because of information about some alternatives that exists but is unknown to the decision maker. Elections often involve choices between inherently noncomparable alternatives, when an incumbent with a track record of performance in office is running against a challenger who has no prior experience in the office being contested.

According to classic rational choice, information that is available about some but not all alternatives should be ignored in making a choice – but we suspect it rarely is. Instead, people use what information they have and, whenever possible, make category-based inferences about the missing information.[9] More generally, however, the possibility (probability, in most instances) of incomplete search of available information means that virtually any decision in practice could involve (partially) noncomparable alternatives.

Sequence of Search. Finally, we can also have the sequence of information acquisition, which considers how decision makers move from learning about one candidate/attribute pair to another (known as transition analysis; see Jacoby et al., 1976). Four types of transitions are possible, which we further categorize as ordered and haphazard. Ordered search is of two types, alternative-based and attribute-based.

1. With *alternative-based* search (more formally, intra-alternative, inter-attribute), sometimes also called *holistic* search, decision makers consider the different alternatives sequentially. Voters following this search strategy would learn about the issue stands, political experience, personal values, and whatever else they considered

---

[8] With the added proviso that the disproportionate search goes toward the in-party candidate.

[9] For example, Fiorina's (1981) model formally allows both for retrospective evaluations of the incumbent's job performance and for comparison, hypothetical judgments about what the world would have been like had the other party won the last election, although even he expresses doubt that many voters would actually take this extra step.

important about one candidate in an election, before trying to learn the same information about a second candidate, and so on until they have explored all the competing candidates. If information were presented in a matrix format (similar to Figure A.1 of the Appendix), this would involve searching down the columns of the matrix.

2. With *attribute-based* search (intra-attribute, inter-alternative), sometimes also called *dimensional* search, a decision maker chooses one attribute for consideration and compares the values of all competing candidates, or sometimes pairs of alternatives, on that issue, before turning to another attribute and comparing all of the competing alternatives on it.

Haphazard search includes the other two logical possibilities:

3. *Inter-attribute, inter-alternative* transitions occur when the decision maker switches from learning about one attribute for a particular candidate to learning about a different attribute for a different candidate. Even decision makers following very ordered search sequences would engage in *some* inter-attribute, inter-alternative transitions as they switched from learning about the last attribute about Candidate A to learning about the first attribute of Candidate B, for example.

4. *Intra-attribute, intra-alternative* transitions occur when the same item of information is "reaccessed" before any other information is considered. Whenever this last type of transition occurs, it can usually be considered a random error.

An important point related to sequence of search is that it is far easier for cognitively limited decision makers to keep the relevant information in working memory if an *ordered* search sequence is followed. Ordered information can also be processed and stored in long-term memory more efficiently, which should be another important aid to decision making. Even when information acquisition is not entirely controllable, however, the sequence in which information becomes available, the structure of that information in the environment, and the decision maker's ability to at least partially restructure that sequence in some coherent manner can have important effects on decision making, even changing preferences among alternatives (Tversky and Sattath, 1979).

Matching Information Search to Decision Strategy

We have gone to some length to discuss the measures of depth, comparability, and sequence of search for one very important reason: Each of the

Decision Rule	Type	Depth of Search	Comparability of Search	Sequence of Search	Cognitive Effort
Model 1c:	Compensatory	Deep	Equal	Candidate-based	Very high
Model 1d:	Compensatory	Deep	Equal	Dimensional	Very high
Model 2:	Mixed	Relatively deep	Unequal	Candidate-based most likely, but either OK	Moderate
Model 3:	Compensatory	Relatively shallow	Equal	Either	Generally low
Model 4c:	Noncompensatory	Depends: typically shallow	Generally unequal	Candidate-based	Moderately low
Model 4d:	Noncompensatory	Generally shallow	Generally unequal	Dimensional	Low

Note: The suffix "c" refers to candidate-oriented search, while the suffix "d" refers to dimensional or attribute-focused search.

Figure 2.2. Characteristics of different decision rules.

decision strategies discussed in Appendix A specifies a unique combination of these three information processing variables. Figure 2.2 summarizes the crucial details. The various Model 1 decision strategies all assume deep information search, equally distributed across the alternatives, but they differ as to whether candidate- (alternative-)based or dimensional-(attribute-)based search should be followed. Model 2 also assumes relatively deep search, but it expects that search to be unequally distributed across the candidates. There are no clear guidelines in Model 2 for either candidate-based or dimensional search, however, as is also the case for Model 3 decision making. On the other hand, Model 3 assumes relatively shallow search, equally distributed across the alternatives. Finally, the different strategies falling under Model 4 all assume relatively shallow search, unequally distributed across the alternatives, but (as was the case with Model 1) differ in whether they suggest a predominance of candidate-based or dimensional search.

Because we suspect it will be easier for most of our readers to keep the gist of our four broad models of decision making in mind rather than the details of the more particularized labels that are used for decision strategies in the decision theory literature, we will try to refer to all decision strategies by their broader category labels. When we want to distinguish between variants that expect more candidate-based or dimensional search, we will adopt the convention that a trailing "c" will refer to a model assuming largely candidate-based search (e.g., Model 1c), while a trailing "d" will refer to a model assuming largely dimensional search (e.g., Model 4d).[10] This will be our own little cognitive heuristic for the readers of this book: "c" for candidate-based search, "d" for dimensional search. Models 2 and 3, which are agnostic about order of search, should never have a trailing "c" or "d."

REMAINING VARIABLES IN OUR FRAMEWORK FOR STUDYING THE VOTE DECISION

Our general framework for studying voting (shown in Figure 2.1) summarizes all of what we have discussed so far in this chapter into its information processing stage. It is this stage that is most unique to our approach, and we have spent most of this chapter providing the conceptual background to explicate it fully. Having done that, we can now take a step back through the model to have a quick look at the factors that are hypothesized to affect information processing directly. In particular, three sets of distinct factors – background characteristics of the voter, political expertise, and demands of the decision task itself – combine to create the voter's own subjective perception of the nature of the task at hand. The background characteristics – for example, cognitive ability, education, gender, ethnicity, party and ideological identifications – are fairly well studied in the voting literature, but they are usually conceived as having a direct impact on the vote. If one were concerned with the *direction* of the vote – that is, whether the Democrat or the Republican was chosen – that conceptualization may be adequate. But we are more concerned with how that vote decision is reached. For our purposes, these background characteristics are clearly antecedent to two more conceptually important factors, political expertise or sophistication, and task demands, the latter a shorthand for the context of the election environment.

Political Sophistication or Expertise

The amount of knowledge or experience or sophistication an individual has in a particular domain is the only individual difference generally found to affect information processing in decision making (Chase and Simon, 1973; Klayman, 1985; Reder and Anderson, 1980; Shanteau, 1988, 1992). By definition, experts have more knowledge in their area of expertise than nonexperts (or "novices"). One might think that experts

---

[10] Although candidate-based search should be pretty clear in an electoral context, the term "alternative-based" is more appropriate for many types of decisions. However, it is very common to refer to dimensional search as attribute-based search, and employing a trailing "a" to refer to either one of them could be misunderstood. Hence we will use "c" for candidate/alternative-based search, and "d" for dimensional/attribute-based search.

would consequently take much longer to make many decisions because it would take them longer to consider all of this additional information. However, just the opposite is generally true. This so-called paradox of the expert can be explained by the way experts structure and organize information in memory.

Experts learn how to group or "chunk" information together into meaningful wholes. They form cognitive schemas that allow them to make reasonable inferences without paying attention to all the details of every situation. And they learn to pay particular attention to specific "diagnostic" or heuristic information, which obviates the need to gather more elaborate, specific, and/or detailed information. That is, experts are better able to discriminate between relevant and irrelevant cues (Shanteau, 1992). Payne, Bettman, and Johnson (1993) suggest that experience in a decision domain affects the frequency and recency with which possible decision strategies have been used, thus making those strategies more accessible in memory. And according to Shanteau (1988), experts adjust their initial decisions more often than nonexperts, and they try to learn from the successes and failures of earlier decisions. Experts tend to accept small errors in decision making but avoid large mistakes.

Thus, we would not expect political experts, compared to nonexperts, to seek any more or less total information in making a vote decision, but instead to disproportionately seek certain particularly useful or diagnostic types of information – for example, they might be more likely to employ any of the political heuristics described earlier (Lau and Redlawsk, 2001b).

Campaign Factors

A second factor determining the perceived nature of the voting task in our model is the situational or contextual nature of the campaign itself, what psychologists would call task demands. Choice of decision strategy seems to be highly contingent on the nature of the decision task (Payne, Bettman, and Johnson, 1993). One very important set of factors involves the complexity or size of the decision task. *Task complexity* is usually defined in terms of the number of alternatives under consideration times the number of different attributes across which they vary. The general finding from research on task complexity is that people rely more heavily on simplifying decision heuristics as a task becomes more complex. This is true both for variation in the number of alternatives (Biggs et al., 1985; Billings and Marcus, 1983; Klayman, 1985; Lau and Redlawsk, 2001a; Olshavsky, 1979; Payne, 1976) and for the number of attributes under consideration (Jacoby, Kohn, and Speller, 1974; Keller and Staelin, 1987; Malhotra, 1982). Generally speaking, decision makers rely upon some noncompensatory decision strategy when there are more than two alternatives, while they may use more compensatory strategies if there are only two alternatives (Einhorn, 1970; Tversky, 1972).

Holding task size or complexity constant, additional factors can affect the difficulty of the choice facing decision makers. One such factor that can characterize many political decisions is *time pressure*. Time pressure may shift a decision maker's goals from accuracy to efficiency. Thus, decision makers faced with time pressure may accelerate processing (i.e., work faster); reduce the total amount of information considered, focusing on the most important factors; or change decision strategies, shifting from a compensatory to a noncompensatory strategy (Payne, Bettman, and Johnson, 1988).

Another factor affecting choice difficulty is the *similarity of the alternatives* to each other. When alternatives are very dissimilar, it is relatively easy to distinguish between them, so decision makers can rely on a relatively easy strategy with confidence that they will be making the correct choice. When alternatives are similar to each other, on the other hand, it is much more difficult to find the best alternative. Depth of search should increase (Bockenholt et al., 1991), and decision makers may be more likely to employ a compensatory decision strategy (Biggs et al., 1985). Of course, when alternatives are very similar to each other, it usually doesn't matter very much if one selects the second- or even third-best alternative.

Finally, there is a great deal of research in behavioral decision theory on *response mode* effects (i.e., whether a choice among, or a ranking of, or an evaluation of different alternatives is required). This topic has received so much focus because it has been found that changing response mode can lead to preference reversals, which violates one of the fundamental propositions of rational choice, that of *procedural invariance* – that strategically equivalent ways of eliciting a preference should reveal the same preference (Tversky, Sattath, and Slovic, 1988). The leading explanations for these observed preference reversals have to do with processing differences associated with the different response modes. The need to *evaluate* alternatives leads to alternative-based searching and more quantitative thinking, while *choosing* among alternatives leads to more attribute-based searching and more qualitative thinking (Fischer and Hawkins, 1993; Lichtenstein and Slovic, 1971; Tversky, 1969; Tversky, Sattath, and Slovic, 1988). This research suggests that we ought to distinguish between decision making and judgment, a task to which we will return shortly.

The Perceived "Nature" of the Decision Task

In our framework, we summarize all of this contextual material as the "campaign factors" involved in a particular election. But just how demanding those various contextual factors are is partially contingent on political expertise – experts should find certain environments less demanding than novices. So we suggest that expertise and campaign factors, along with the background characteristics of the voter, combine to form a subjective perception of the nature of the voting task. The subjective nature of the decision problem itself could vary along several dimensions. We will be primarily concerned with the perceived difficulty of the decision, but we could easily imagine the magnitude of the consequences associated with the outcome as another dimension of potential import. Clearly the more demanding the task, the more subjectively difficult the decision, while the more expert or experienced the decision maker, the easier the decision.

The subjective nature of the decision task should in turn affect information processing – the ways decision makers attempt to gather information, the type of information they collect, and the decision rules they employ to combine that information into a choice. Very easy decision tasks may allow certain information acquisition patterns or decision rules that are not possible with more difficult or more demanding decision tasks. And political sophisticates may be aware of certain ways of acquiring information or combining it into a choice with which novices are not familiar.

Similarly, it is reasonable to hypothesize that the more important the decision is to the decision maker, the more she will be motivated by decision accuracy rather than decision ease, and the greater the effort that will be expended in making the decision (Payne, Bettman, and Johnson, 1993). Thus, information search should be deeper, and compensatory decision strategies will be more likely to be employed (Lindberg, Garling, and Montgomery, 1989). This reasoning assumes that deeper information search leads to better decisions, a conclusion that is easy to accept granted omniscient rationality and unlimited cognitive abilities, but that may not actually hold in practice for limited information processors. Indeed, Gigerenzer and Goldstein (1999; Czerlinski, Gigerenzer, and Goldstein, 1999) have demonstrated at least some instances when additional information actually results in lower quality decisions, a possibility we will explore in Chapter 10.

Memory

In our framework, how information is processed has two primary sets of consequences. First, information acquisition patterns should influence both the *quantity* and *accuracy* of memory, although not always in the same way. Depth of search, for example, should be positively related to amount of memory, but it could be negatively related to accuracy of memory. Within-candidate search sequences may well result in more memory than within-attribute sequences, and either of the two ordered search sequences should make it easier to retrieve more (and more accurate) information from memory than more haphazard search.

Candidate Evaluation and the Vote Choice

Finally, both the information processing variables and memory combine to determine the evaluation of the candidates and the nature and quality of the decision that is reached. We will certainly look to see what factors lead to the vote for any particular candidate, which in a general election context in the United States translates into looking to see whether the Democrat or Republican receives any particular vote. We will look to see how well we can predict the vote choice from the affective implications of the information gathered by voters and whether memory plays an independent role in the vote choice.

But our larger concern will be with the normative issue of the extent to which the choice that is reached by a voter could be described as the correct one. Theoretically, our measures of the relative depth, sequence, and comparability of search across alternatives should be particularly important in predicting the quality of the decision reached. A priori, we would have to hypothesize that Model 1 decision strategies will be associated with the highest probability of voting correctly, as their very purpose is to maximize expected utility, and they seem to guarantee the highest probability of reaching such a decision. But previous behavioral research has found at least some instances where Model 3 produces better results than Model 1; and from an evolutionary perspective, in many situations Model 4 decisions ought to be almost as good as Model 1 decisions. We will look to see whether political campaigns and elections are among the situations where noncompensatory decision strategies can be effective. And in any case, our theory sees a clear role for memory in making a correct vote decision.

This last discussion assumes that we have some way to determine and measure the quality of the decision making. This is no easy task, we want to remind readers, and it is a task that previous researchers studying the vote decision have largely ignored. Such a measure is crucial, however, for our approach to studying the vote decision. We have put a good deal of time and effort into developing such a measure (Lau and Redlawsk, 1997), but we defer further discussion until Chapter 4. The point we want to make here is that focusing exclusively on whether the Democrat or the Republican gets any particular vote, or gets the most votes overall, precludes any consideration of the larger normative issues.

Theory and Methods

Distinguishing Evaluation and Choice

Before we go much further, we need to return to our very clear distinction between *evaluation* (or judgment) and *choice* (selecting from a set of alternative). Social scientists often treat judgment and decision making as if they are essentially the same thing so that decisions are considered as nothing more than selecting the most highly evaluated alternative. This is a mistake for at least three reasons. First, we can certainly distinguish between the two semantically. A judgment involves the evaluation of a single entity along some dimension: for example, how attractive/funny/likable/smart a person is. A decision, in contrast, involves a *choice* between two or more discrete alternatives: *whether* to take drugs, *who* to marry, *when* to retire, *which* candidate to support in the election. Making a choice implies more commitment to the chosen alternative than making a judgment suggests about the judged entity, and it may well also involve searching for reasons to justify the choice (Slovic, Fischhoff, and Lichtenstein, 1982). People make judgments all the time without necessarily putting those judgments into action.

Second, people make many decisions without first explicitly evaluating the alternatives on some global dimension. "Spur of the moment" decisions are certainly of this type, as are habitual or standing decisions, such as "always vote for the Democrat." Even though such decisions may be based in part on evaluations formed during prior and more elaborate decision processes, they are also based, in part, on a prior choice. If one always votes for Democrats – for whatever past reasons – no real evaluation of either the Republican or Democrat is necessary prior to making a choice in a new election.

We suspect that in most presidential elections voters make at least some global evaluations of the candidates prior to the vote no matter how preordained their vote might be. But a third reason it is wrong to equate judgment and choice is that global evaluations, even when they are made, do not necessarily dictate choice. People may vote strategically – that is, choose a less preferred alternative because their most preferred candidate has no chance of winning (Abramson et al., 1992). People may vote for a candidate they do not particularly like for some reason largely external to the decision itself (acting "against my better judgment"), such as to please a parent or girlfriend.

Having said all this, however, we suspect that the vote decision in particular – or any choice between different people – is rarely made without first forming some global evaluation of the different candidates for the position. Psychologists have recognized that forming an overall impression or evaluation of a person seems to be what people will naturally do, if left to their own devices (Hastie and Pennington, 1988). Hence candidate evaluation almost certainly occurs when a vote choice is made. The important point is that decision making and evaluating are two different procedures and should not be conflated. Evaluation need not precede choice, nor is choice inevitably based on a comparison of some global evaluations of the alternatives under consideration. We will expand upon this point in Chapter 8.

CONSEQUENCES OF DECISION STRATEGIES: THE "SO WHAT?" QUESTION

The information processing variables in our model are really the focus of this book. Although such considerations play a vital role in behavioral decision theory, they have largely been ignored by past researchers studying the vote decision. In theory, as we have laid out in this chapter, these considerations should be important. Demonstrating that they are is the primary challenge before us.

It should be obvious that whatever information citizens have about the candidates when they enter the voting booth is an important influence – no, *the* most important influence – on their vote choice. But voters must deal with cognitive limits, and consequently we contend that how voters go about gathering that information has an impact on the vote decision. Figures A.2 through A.5 of Appendix A illustrate how the application of different decision rules, given the same candidates and same voter preferences, can result in very different choices being made. For a book on decision making, there is no stronger consequence we can imagine.

But let us consider some additional consequences. Clearly different search strategies can result in different levels of knowledge about the candidates in the choice set. Model 1 rational choice strategies dictate complete search of all relevant information about every alternative, and even if we soften this unrealistic demand, rational strategies all employ some compensatory choice mechanism, which at the very least dictates that the same information be learned about every alternative. Model 4's noncompensatory strategies, on the other hand, suggest (a) that search will probably be much shallower than when employing a compensatory choice strategy and (b) that voters are likely to learn much more information about some alternatives than about others.

These facts have implications for evaluations of the competing alternatives. We argued earlier that decision makers may not form global or overall evaluations about every alternative in every choice set, but in an election, where the alternatives involve people, such global evaluations would most likely be formed. The depth of information search, and its comparability across candidates, could affect how candidates are evaluated. A voter using a compensatory decision strategy and relatively deep search should see the yin and yang of all candidates, both those ultimately chosen and those rejected, and should have relatively moderate global evaluations as a consequence. That is, confronting and trading off the good and bad points of a candidate should result in more moderate evaluations (assuming candidates *have* such good and bad points, of course), compared to a decision maker employing a noncompensatory decision strategy and relatively shallow search, who may learn only a few negative things about rejected candidates, and only a few universally positive things about the chosen alternative. Thus, depth of search should be inversely related to extremity of evaluation.

We would also argue that how information is gathered affects how it is stored in memory, which in turn affects the probability that it will be recalled (and what else will be recalled with it) at the time of a decision. Being exposed to certain information is not the same thing as "remembering it" for cognitively limited decision makers. Depth of search obviously affects the amount that can be recalled: You can only remember what you have been exposed to. But cognitive limits should place some cap on the magnitude of this effect so that any influence of depth of search on the amount of memory will level out after a while. Only slightly less obvious is our contention that sequence of search also influences memory, both in content and quantity. If memory is an associated network of interconnected nodes, as most cognitive psychologists believe, then how information is encountered will largely determine how it is stored in memory, and thus the ease with which it can be recalled. A voter relying primarily on intra-candidate search can establish a coherent person schema for each candidate in memory and do a fairly good job answering the question, "Tell me what you can recall about Candidate X." This same person might have a much more difficult time answering the question, "Which candidate is closest to you on issue Y?" A voter relying primarily on intra-attribute search, on the other hand, should find questions of the latter type easier to answer than the former.

This completes our discussion of the psychological theories underlying our process-oriented approach to studying the vote decision. We conclude this chapter with Figure 2.3, which summarizes many of the predictions that can be derived from our theory. Acceptance of the view of humans as boundedly rational information processors is tantamount to accepting the idea that those same humans will have developed a variety of different cognitive shortcuts or heuristics for easing the computational burden of decision making in a complex, information-rich environment like a modern presidential election campaign. The upshot of all of this is that

Basic Premises

* People have clear cognitive limitations that severely limit their information processing abilities.
* As a consequence, all people have developed cognitive heuristics or shortcuts that help them cope with their cognitive limits.
* Expertise in any area is not defined by fewer cognitive limitations, but rather by more effective coping strategies.
* In general, decision makers are guided by two often conflicting goals: the desire to make a *good* decision, and the desire to make an *easy* decision.

Factors that should lead to a priority on one of the goals over the other include:

Making a Good Decision	Making an Easy Decision
• Increasing perceived importance	• Competing obligations/interests
• Increasing stakes	• Familiarity/complacency
• Increasing anxiety	• Increasing task difficulty
• Novelty	• Time pressure

Factors That Affect Information Processing and Choice of Decision Strategy

Model 1 (Rational Choice): As the most cognitively difficult decision strategy, albeit one that promises a value-maximizing outcome, Model 1 is more likely to be chosen when there are only two alternatives in the choice set, by experts in any particular domain, and when decision makers are primarily motivated to make good decision.

Model 2 (Confirmatory Decision Making): Model 2 is most likely to be chosen by strong political partisans, and in situations of high anxiety or otherwise high perceived "importance" of an election. Model 2 decision makers should be motivated to learn candidates' party affiliations as soon as possible. And particularly when they are exposed to information that might lead them to question their standing decision, they should be motivated to seek disproportionate information about their in-party candidate that should serve to bolster or confirm their long-standing predispositions.

Model 3 (Fast and Frugal Decision Making): Model 3 is most likely when a decision is particularly difficult or when decision makers are working under severe time pressure.

Model 4 (Semiautomatic Intuitive Decision Making): Any factor that leads decision makers to be primarily motivated by desires to make an easy decision, particularly increasing task difficulty, should lead to great use of Model 4 decision strategies.

Figure 2.3. Theoretical assumptions and predictions derived from process-oriented framework for studying the vote decision.

Expected Consequences of Decision Strategies

Model 1: More moderate, less polarized candidate evaluations; higher quality decisions when decision tasks are relatively easy, or when the strategy is employed by a relative expert.

Model 2: Polarized candidate evaluations; lower quality of decision.

Model 3: More moderate, less polarized candidate evaluations; better quality decisions when decisions are – or are perceived to be – very difficult.

Model 4: Polarized candidate evaluations; better quality decisions when decisions are (perceived to be) relatively difficult.

Factors Affecting Memory

- *Depth of search* should be positively related to amount of recall, although the effect should be curvilinear due to cognitive limitations.
- *Ordered search sequences* should be positively related to accuracy of recall.
  - Holistic (within-candidate) search should be related to both amount and accuracy of recall when candidate-oriented memories are requested.
  - Dimensional (within-candidate) search should be related to both amount and accuracy of recall when attribute-oriented memories are requested.
- *Expertise* should be positively related to both amount and accuracy of recall.

Consequences of Memory

- There is no necessary, deterministic relationship between the affective nature of memory and candidate evaluation.
- But the affective nature of memory should be related to candidate choice.
- And accuracy of memory should be related to quality of decision making.

Figure 2.3. *(continued)*

Model 3 and Model 4 are far more likely to describe the actual decision processes of those less involved with politics, and that Model 2 is far more likely than Model 1 to describe the decision processes of those more interested and involved in politics.

We have now accomplished our first expressed goal of developing a new process-oriented approach for studying voter decision making and elaborating a new set of measures for studying it – at least at a conceptual level. Before we can try to operationalize those measures and provide some empirical evidence for many of the hypotheses that derive from this discussion, however, we must turn to another of our major goals, which is to develop a new method for observing voters while they are making their vote decision. That is the topic of Chapter 3.

3

Studying Voting as a Process

Presidential campaigns are inherently dynamic events that occur over a certain period of time. They have a defined beginning, around the time candidates throw their hats into the ring, along with a clear ending – Election Day. Throughout the campaign season, citizens are inundated with information about the candidates, whether they wish to pay attention to politics or not. One would have to read no newspapers or magazines, watch no television and listen to no radio, and have no contact with other people in order to avoid acquiring at least a little information about the candidates running for president.[1]

The amount of information available during a campaign varies, however, depending on the campaign cycle itself. During a contested primary season, for example, significant amounts of information are readily available, at least in those states holding contested primaries. On the other hand, once a candidate has locked up the nomination, the amount of information about the campaign may drop temporarily, only to be revived during the parties' conventions.

Similarly, both the *amount* of information and the *type* of information available vary. Before this series of experiments began, we examined a selection of newspapers during the 1988 presidential election season and found evidence that issue-oriented information becomes much more readily available as campaigns progress, while candidate background information (such as family, education, prior jobs, etc.) predominates early in the primaries and then again early in the general election season (Lau, 1992). Other types of information also appeared to differ in their availability

---

[1] Obviously, this is not true for every type of election. There is almost always much more information readily available during a presidential election campaign than, say, during township council campaigns. As this study focuses specifically on mimicking the presidential election season, any general comments regarding information availability are meant to refer to presidential campaigns.

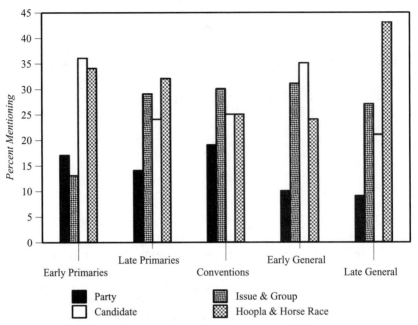

Note: Data display the percentage of paragraphs mentioning the particular content. Numbers can sum to more than 100% because a paragraph could receive multiple codes.

Figure 3.1. Content of media coverage of the 1988 U.S. presidential election campaign.

during the campaign, with "hoopla and horse race" (campaign events and polls) consistently declining in relative frequency until the last weeks of the campaign, when polls dominate all other information. Figure 3.1 summarizes these data. They are from only one campaign and are based only on the coverage of that campaign in four newspapers; nevertheless; these are the only data we know of that have attempted to objectively determine the actual content of a presidential election campaign.

Clearly, election campaigns are dynamic, information flows vary, and citizens can learn a little about the candidates without any effort at all, or they can learn much more by actively seeking out information. But how have political scientists normally studied this ever-changing environment? In general, elections have been studied using static techniques such as cross-sectional surveys administered shortly before or after the election (or sometimes both). The most ambitious panel surveys (where the same respondents are interviewed at multiple points in time) may begin earlier in the campaign, say before the primaries start, and interview the same voters three or four times before election day (e.g., Berelson, Lazarsfeld, and McPhee, 1954; Lazarsfeld, Berelson, and Gaudet, 1944; Patterson, 1980). Such designs have been mimicked more recently by Just et al. (1996), who used a series of in-depth interviews to follow a small number of voters over the course of an election (see also Graber, 1984). Other political scientists have used experiments to examine candidate evaluation (Lodge, McGraw, and Stroh, 1989; Lodge and Stroh, 1993; Lodge, Steenbergen, and Brau, 1995). None of these prior approaches is completely up to the task of understanding information acquisition and use during a campaign because none comes close to collecting the type of dynamic data needed to understand a campaign. Such research techniques do not have the ability to measure (or manipulate) the information environment in which respondents lived, and thus they have no direct knowledge of the particular campaign information their respondents have been exposed to.

If we wish to understand the cognitive processing of campaign information as voters make their decisions, typical survey and experimental methods employed by social scientists will not work. We need a methodology that can track voters as they encounter information and can record the ways in which that information is accessed, examined, and used. Fortunately, behavioral decision theory researchers have developed several methodologies for doing just that, with the underlying assumption that the best way to study decision making is to observe it while the decision is being made (Svenson, 1979). These process-tracing methodologies keep track of what information is obtained and the order in which it is obtained to make inferences about the strategies employed in making the choice.

PROCESS-TRACING METHODOLOGIES FOR STUDYING DECISION MAKING

Behavioral decision theorists have utilized two primary strategies for studying decisions "while they happen," verbal protocols, and information boards. With *verbal protocols*, the decision maker is asked to "think aloud" while he or she is making some decision, to vocalize "every passing thought" (Ericsson and Simon, 1980). The decision maker is thus assumed to be able to report on the contents of working memory as a decision is being made.[2] Verbal protocols are an excellent technique for exploratory

---

[2] It takes some practice to be able to vocalize "every passing thought" without noticeably interfering with the decision making itself. Ericsson and Simon distinguish between *concurrent* verbalizations, where decision makers try to report on their thoughts as they are making a decision, and *retrospective* verbal protocols, where decision makers try to describe cognitive processes that occurred earlier in time. The latter should not be considered a process-tracing methodology at all, for it must rely on long-term rather than short-term memory, and people are notoriously

research for developing models of how people go about making a particular type of decision. Because verbal reports are less easily quantifiable, however, verbal protocols are generally a less powerful technique for testing hypotheses.

The second major process-tracing technique for studying decision making is the *information board* (Carroll and Johnson, 1990). Information boards present subjects with a matrix of "learnable" information much like that in Figure A.1 in Appendix A, where the alternatives under consideration are the columns of the matrix, and the different attributes of choice (i.e., the different outcomes associated with every alternative) are the rows. Unlike Figure A.1, however, the actual information is hidden from view (i.e., the cells of the matrix are blank or only include a label), and decision makers must *actively* decide to learn any specific bit of information by physically selecting it.

The matrix is typically represented on a computer screen, and the decision maker selects information to learn by clicking on a particular cell of the matrix with the computer's mouse. The computer automatically records every action the decision maker takes, so that at the end there is a complete record of what the decision maker accessed, how long every bit of information was considered, and the order in which it was examined. Experimental procedure dictates that only one cell of the matrix can be open at a time. This gives the experimenter complete control over and knowledge about what information is available to the decision maker at every moment of the decision task.

Process-tracing techniques have been readily applied to decision making in a number of contexts, most notably consumer research. For example, Jacoby and colleagues (Jacoby, Kohn, and Speller, 1974; Jacoby, Speller, and Berning, 1974) used this classic approach to determine the effects of increasing information availability on the ability of consumers to choose among detergents, rice, or prepared dinners. Subjects chose the product-attribute pairs of interest and read the information on cards that described, for example, the whitening ability of a particular detergent brand.

The value of the information board methodology is its ability to provide the researcher with a controlled environment in which every action taken by the decision maker can be observed and recorded. This allows the researcher to get to the heart of information search and acquisition: the myriad of different ways decision makers can search for information, and

poor after-the-fact reporters on what has influenced their own behavior (Nisbett and Wilson, 1977). People can give plausible rationalizations for their behavior, but those explanations may have little association with why people actually did what they did.

how the use of different decision strategies drives what people learn about the choices facing them.

Process Tracing and the Study of Voting Behavior

The use of information boards[3] in consumer decision making seems natural. For many products, the process of making a decision entails examining the products as they are arranged on a grocery shelf, perhaps picking up some of them to read their labels. While political campaigns do not proceed in such an organized, easy-to-use fashion, information gathering during the campaign could be simulated on an information board, and a few prior studies have done just that.

Herstein (1981) used an information board to trace candidate evaluation. Two hypothetical candidates were created with forty-five attributes provided for each candidate. These attributes included candidate positions on issues, personal information, and party identification. Subjects were instructed to examine as much or as little information as they desired and were allowed to spend as much time as they wished making their decision. Herstein recorded the items subjects examined along with the order in which the attributes were chosen. In addition, subjects were instructed to talk aloud as they made their decisions to express verbally what they were thinking. The comments they made were recorded as part of the procedure.

Herstein's goal was to develop a process-oriented model of the vote, taking into account not only what information was considered but also the order in which it was considered and the ongoing evaluations made by voters during the process of information acquisition. In his resulting model, voters select pieces of information, evaluate the information, and make candidate comparisons on various attributes, much as they would do for any consumer product. Herstein found that subjects sought more information when the campaign consisted of two middle-of-the-road candidates of similar ideologies than when the race was between two clearly distinct ideologues. This finding makes a lot of sense. Faced with a more difficult decision in choosing between two candidates, it seems a reasonable approach to gather more information until the differences become clearer.[4] In an interesting anomaly, Herstein also claimed that

---

[3] See Mintz and Geva (1997) or Mintz et al. (1997) for an information board study of decision making in international relations.

[4] Herstein also found that his subjects made relatively few verbal comparisons between the two candidates as they examined information. Instead of indicating a general evaluation on a continuing basis, subjects tended to focus their evaluations on the particular item being examined at the moment. This seems to argue that voters wait

party identification did not seem to matter much to his subjects because the party attribute was chosen far less often than other types of information, and subjects typically chose party much later in the decision process than would be anticipated given the supposed importance of party in American presidential elections.

More recently, Riggle, Johnson, and Hickey (1996) employed a computerized information board to study age differences in political decision making, using a senatorial election as the decision task. They identify seven prototypical search patterns, finding that older subjects are much more likely to engage in searches within candidates, using a satisficing strategy (Simon, 1956) to determine final choices. Similarly, Huang (2000; Huang and Price, 2001) reports a study in which an information board was used to examine the depth of information search across several different experimental conditions. Subjects were placed into one of four groups, crossing impression formation goals (impression versus nonimpression) with the effort expended on search (effortful versus effortless). Subjects processing with a memorization goal evidenced the deepest search and accessed the most information. On the other hand, subjects motivated to form an impression showed significantly deeper search than did the remaining two groups. Huang also found sophistication effects, with sophisticated subjects more likely to engage in noncompensatory search strategies and to process information more efficiently than nonsophisticates.

Shortcomings of the Standard Methodology for Studying Election Campaigns

Even though these studies use process-tracing techniques effectively, they all rely on traditional static information boards in which all possible candidate-attribute pairs are always accessible to subjects. Further, subjects could spend as much time as they wished learning about candidates with no risk of missing any information – despite the fact that real political campaigns are dynamic events, where the information environment is constantly changing. Thus, particular results that may depend on easy access to information or unlimited processing time are suspect. For example, Herstein's finding that the party of the candidates in the simulation did not matter much seems likely to be attributable to the artificial nature of the standard information board. In a real general election, party matters

until a particular "moment-of-decision" in order to make their overall comparison between the candidates, much as Kelley and Mirer (1974) posit. Yet the Kelley and Mirer rule of voting for the candidate with the greatest net positive reasons in memory failed to do a very good job of predicting a subject's ultimate choice.

because it is a heuristic summarizing a large amount of information that is much more difficult to obtain and that few voters have the time or inclination to learn and reconsider with each succeeding election.[5] In Herstein's static information board study there were no constraints on the ability of subjects to learn as much as they wished about the candidates, and thus no particular need to use a party identification heuristic.

Most people learn about political candidates through the mass media. In some types of media – print media and, more recently, the internet – the information flow is relatively under the control of the voter. That is, the reader can choose to read some stories carefully, skim others, and totally ignore still others. The occasional photo or headline might be viewed almost involuntarily, but readers still have most of their information acquisition options fully under their own control.

Television and radio, on the other hand, are far less controllable. Where it is easy to jump around in a print story, skipping a part and paying attention to another part, it is generally impossible to do so with television and radio. Moreover, all media share the feature of transience. That is, stories that appear one day as "news" will often disappear the next, unless there is an ongoing story. But even stories that run over several days eventually die out. Thus, the voter who is not paying attention while the media cover allegations of misdirected campaign funds, for example, may find it hard to get that information once the story is over, or even to know that such a story existed. Clearly, a static information board approach to studying campaigns fails to take into account this transience. It is far superior to most other methodologies for keeping track of information search, but "voters" are still searching for information in a decision context far removed from a real political campaign. In many ways, the classic static information board represents an *ideal world* for making a decision – but one far removed from the context in which voters typically make their decisions. What is needed is a new process-tracing methodology that can model the dynamic flow of electoral information during a campaign.[6]

---

[5] See Fiorina (1981) on this point.

[6] Researchers employing traditional information boards are not the only ones to be led somewhat astray by thinking about politics in too static a manner. For example, Lupia and McCubbins (1998) argue that "If a stimulus does not cause an individual to change her actions . . . then the benefit derived from paying attention to the stimulus is zero" (p. 26). This statement is true only if this stimulus is the *last* thing the person learns before she must act, and all future actions are irrelevant. Just because information is not sufficient to change behavior at the moment it is learned does not mean that at some subsequent point, after new information is learned, the combined

Theory and Methods

We have revised the traditional static information board, modifying it into a dynamic, ever-changing design that better mimics the flow of information during a presidential campaign (Lau, 1995; Lau and Redlawsk, 1992, 1997, 2001a, 2001b; Redlawsk, 1992, 1995b, 2001a, 2001b, 2002, 2004; Redlawsk and Lau, 1995). Where the static board allows subjects to have access to all available information at all times, the revised dynamic board emulates the ebb and flow of a political campaign over time. The essential feature of the static information board – the ability to trace the decision-making process as it happens – is retained, but specific information comes and goes. Where standard information boards are static and easily managed by the subject, actual election campaigns are dynamic and unmanageable. It is easily possible with our revised methodology to overwhelm subjects with information. Where standard information boards allow all information to be available whenever a subject wants it, information during a real election campaign contains a "here today, gone tomorrow" quality, as does our new method. And, where the standard information board would make all types of information equally accessible, from positions on arcane issues to party identification and poll results, our simulation models the relative ease or difficulty of finding certain kinds of information at different times during a campaign.

We accomplished these goals by designing a radically revised information board in which the information (i.e., the boxes or attribute labels) scrolls down a computer screen, rather than remaining fixed in place. Figure 3.2 provides an example of the main screen employed for the election simulation in our experiments. There are only a limited number of attribute labels visible on the computer screen at any one time. Most include a candidate's name and the particular information that would be revealed if this label were accessed (e.g., "Martin's Basic Economic Philosophy"). The rate of scrolling is such that most people can read two or three labels before the position changes. Subjects access the information behind the label by using a mouse to click on the label. The scrolling continues in the background while the detailed information is read, however, creating a "cost" in terms of missed information and mimicking the dynamic nature of election information flow. This scrolling format allows only a small subset of a very large database of information to be available

---

weight of the new and the old information might be sufficient to change behavior (or to increase knowledge, in Lupia and McCubbins's terms). Because political campaigns – and politics in general – are ongoing, dynamic processes, it is impossible to judge at any point in time just how valuable any piece of information will prove to be.

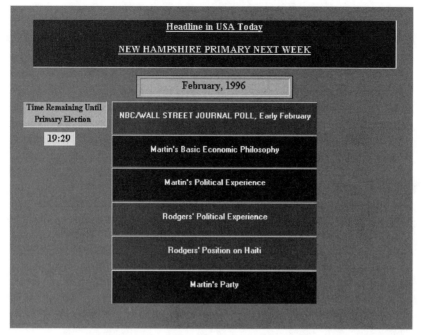

Figure 3.2. A dynamic information board.

at any one time, and it makes the task of processing campaign information much less manageable for the subject. In addition, the relative likelihood of any particular piece of information becoming available is controlled; consequently, some information (like party identification) is much easier to obtain (appears much more often) than other types of information (such as an obscure policy position). The actual probabilities or different types of information appearing at different points in the campaign are based on the data reported in Figure 3.1 from the actual 1988 U.S. presidential election.

The Campaign Simulation

Interested readers can turn to Appendix B for more details about how our dynamic process-tracing methodology actually works. The preceding brief description should be sufficient for most readers to have a pretty good idea what the decision task was like for subjects in our experiments. The methodology itself is agnostic about the particular content of the information being presented to decision makers, of course, although we certainly were not. We created a mock presidential election campaign including eight candidates (four Democrats and four Republicans), with a primary election campaign lasting about twenty minutes, followed by

The Democrats:	CANDIDATE D1 Terry Donald, Governor of Illinois	CANDIDATE D2 Gerry Singer, Governor of New Mexico	CANDIDATE D3 Gale Martin, Senator from Maryland	CANDIDATE D4 Andy Fischer, Senator from California
Background	56-year-old Lutheran; BA from Boston College, MPA from University of Chicago; no military experience; married with one daughter starting law school at Harvard	62-year-old Catholic; BA in political science and economics, later LD from University of New Mexico; served in the Navy during the Korean War; married with 3 sons and one granddaughter	58-year-old Baptist; BS in chemistry from Georgetown University, dropped out of John Hopkins medical school; served in the Army reserve; married with 3 daughters, the oldest of whom is a physician in Baltimore	49-year-old Catholic; BA in political science from UCLA, LD from Stanford University; served in the Air Force during the Vietnam War; divorced with two children now attending college in California
Basic Social/Political Philosophy	"Usually considered a strong liberal on most issues"	"Usually considered a liberal on most issues"	"Usually considered a moderate on most issues"	"It is difficult to label Fischer as a traditional liberal or conservative."
Specific Policy Stands [a] (Objective Ratings)	Mean = 1.27 Std Dev = .61	Mean = 2.13 Std Dev = 1.14	Mean = 4.02 Std Dev = .97	Mean = 4.10 Std Dev = 1.63
Descriptions from a Family Friend	"Generous, personable, learned"	"Likeable and hardworking; a real good neighbor"	"Tough, but thoughtful and considerate"	"Personable, witty, captivating"
And a Political Opponent	"Wants to be the bride at every wedding and the corpse at every funeral"	"Calculating and cunning; determined to get elected at any cost"	"Egotistical; strives for success no matter what the price"	"A head-in-the-clouds idealist with little sense of what is possible"
Campaign Slogan	"The 80s were the decade of the rich; the 90s are the time for the rest of us."	"Good jobs and affordable health care for all Americans!"	"Let's make the American dream achievable to all who work for it"	"Safe streets, good jobs, and a better tomorrow"

56

Background	47-year-old Baptist; BS in biology from the University of Kentucky, LD from Duke University, and MBA from University of Miami; no political experience; married to a lawyer, no children.	56-year-old Methodist; engineering and law degrees from Cornell University; no military experience; married with no children.	64-year-old Presbyterian from Nebraska; BS in economics from Yale, LD from Harvard; served in the Army during the Korean War; married with 3 children and 7 grandchildren	60-year-old born-again Christian; BA in communications from the University of Southern California; served in Air Force during the Korean War; married with 5 children and 9 grandchildren.
Basic Social/Political Philosophy	"Takes stands that vary along the ideological spectrum from left to right"	"Usually considered a moderate on most issues."	"Usually considered a conservative on most issues"	"Usually considered a strong conservative on most issues"
Specific Policy Stands (Objective Ratings)	Mean = 4.25 Std Dev = 1.85	Mean = 4.44 Std Dev = 1.04	Mean = 5.83 Std Dev = 1.16	Mean = 6.67 Std Dev = .70
Descriptions from a Family Friend	"Distinguished, intelligent, and fun-loving"	"Refreshingly honest, dependable, and trustworthy"	"Approachable; listens, and follows through"	"Amiable, compassionate, sympathetic"
And a Political Opponent	"Obstinate and unyielding once mind is made up"	"Unoriginal; implements others' ideas with only minor expansions"	"Quick tempered; demands immediate implementation of chosen course of action"	"Impatient; unwilling to wait for gradual change"
Campaign Slogan	"Let's make America better than it's ever been!"	"Working together for a better tomorrow"	"Less government is almost always better government"	"First in war, first in peace, and first in the future world!"

Figure 3.3 Brief description of mock presidential candidates.

[a] The candidates' issue stands were rated rated by a panel of political experts on the same 7-point issue scales used to measure subjects' political beliefs. Point 1 on these scales was always the most liberal response, while point 7 was always the most conservative response.

a general election campaign involving the winners of the two parties' primaries, lasting about twelve minutes.

Subjects in our experiments were asked to imagine that they were voting in the upcoming U.S. presidential election (the 1996 election, for subjects in our first experiments, the 2000 election, for later experiments), that President Clinton was not running for reelection, and thus both parties had tightly contested primary elections to choose their standard-bearers for the fall campaign. Subjects were told that even though none of the candidates in our experimental campaign were real, they were designed to be very much like the type of people who have run in recent presidential elections. After practicing acquiring information with our scrolling format, subjects were required to "register" as a Democrat or Republican and were told that at the end of the primary campaign they would only be able to vote in their party's primary. The general election campaign, which followed, always involved one of the Democrats and one of the Republicans from the primaries.

Each candidate was described by forty-six distinct attributes that appeared and could be examined at least once during either the primary or general election campaign,[7] including twenty-three issue stands, party affiliation, general political philosophy (i.e., ideology), seven items with personal background information, six personality descriptions, a picture, several performance evaluations, and several items about campaign strategy. The campaigns also involved endorsements from fourteen interest groups and the results from fifteen to twenty different polls conducted at various points during each campaign. In the primary, the endorsements and polls were specific to either the Democratic or Republican primary campaign, in practice doubling the number of such items available for access, although only half of them were relevant to the decision most immediately at hand.

Figures 3.3 and 3.4 describe the eight mock candidates we created for our presidential campaign simulation. The figures list the names the candidates were given for the simulation, and these names are how our subjects knew them. But it will be far easier for our (cognitively limited) readers to refer to them by a shorthand mnemonic. Thus henceforth when we need to distinguish between them, we will refer to the four Democrats

---

[7] Almost all of this information appeared at least once during *both* the primary and (for the two remaining candidates) general election campaigns. The only exceptions were a few items that were specific to the primary or the general election campaigns. For example, "Walker's Primary Election Strategy" was different from "Walker's General Election Strategy"; the former was only available during the primary, the latter could be accessed only during the general election.

Terry Donald (D1)/Jackie Walker (R4)	Gerry Singer (D2)/Chris Rodgers (R3)
Gale Martin (D3)/Pat Thomas (R2)	Andy Fischer (D4)/Sam Green (R1)

Figure 3.4 Images of mock presidential candidates.

as candidates D_1, D_2, D_3, and D_4 and to the four Republicans as R_1, R_2, R_3, and R_4. (These shorthands are also listed in Figures 3.3 and 3.4.) Generally speaking, for both parties the lower numbered candidates are the most liberal, and the higher numbered candidates are the most conservative. Keep in mind that this translates for the Democrats into ideologies ranging from very liberal to moderate and for the Republicans into ideologies ranging from moderate to very conservative.[8]

WHY CONDUCT EXPERIMENTS?

Having introduced our new dynamic process-tracing methodology, it makes sense to stop for a moment and consider the strengths and weaknesses of experiments as a research technique. Twenty years ago experiments in political science were extremely rare. The common explanation was that much of what political scientists study (governments, legislatures, elections, international conflict and war, etc.) were not amenable to experimentation. This explanation does not hold up to closer scrutiny, for it

---

[8] There are actually two moderate Democrats (candidates D_3 and D_4) and two moderate Republicans (candidates R_1 and R_2), which on average have indistinguishable ideologies. These candidates differ in another interesting way, however, which will be discussed in Chapter 7.

implies that the topics that other disciplines study where experimentation is much more the norm (e.g., psychology's interest in stereotypes, cultural norms, or human nature, or physic's interest in time, relativity, and quantum mechanics) are somehow more amenable to experimentation. When the great German social psychologist Kurt Lewin immigrated to this country in the early 1930s, he brought with him the conviction that *anything* about human society could be operationalized and studied experimentally (Lewin, 1939, 1946, 1951). To truly understand something, Lewin believed, you had to be able to *change* it, and to change something you had to know about causality. Lewin was the father of experimental social psychology in this country, and his influence (conveyed by his students after his premature death) made experimentation the dominant methodology in that discipline.

Political science also experienced a behavioral revolution around Word War II, but the shape the revolution took in that discipline was guided much more by survey research than experimentation (Dahl, 1961; Wahlke, 1979). Representative surveys around real elections are a research design ideally suited to description: How many Democrats and Republicans are there, and what do they think about their leaders and representatives, and the policies they propose? Which candidate has the most support as the election approaches, and how have relative preferences changed since the last survey? While experiments in political science are more common today than they once were,[9] still experiments in general, and experimental studies of campaigns and voting in particular, are much more the exception than the rule.

Fuller discussion of the crucial features of experiments are available in any research methods textbook, and need not be repeated here. We only mention their primary advantage: the ability to make causal inferences. With an experiment, the researcher typically creates a simplified version of some phenomenon of interest and then randomly confronts subjects with slightly different versions of that experimental situation, varying only in some critical feature (the *manipulated* independent variable) the experimenter believes affects a behavior of interest. With careful experimental procedures and random assignment of subjects to conditions, we are in a very good position to conclude that any observed difference in the behavior of interest across conditions of the experiment have been *caused* by the manipulated independent variable(s). The details of our own experimental procedures are presented in Appendix C.

---

[9] In no small part because of the influence of political psychologists trained in social psychology; see Kinder and Palfrey (1993) or McDermott (2002) for recent reviews. Experimentation also came to political science through economics.

Studying Voting as a Process

Experimental Manipulations

The big advantage of creating our own mock presidential election campaign is that we have complete control over every aspect of it. Thus, we can be certain that all the candidates were completely new to all our voters. We do not have to worry about (or control for) the fact that more politically sophisticated or experienced voters, say, may already be familiar with some of the candidates before the election campaign even begins. Consequently, we can observe everything subjects are exposed to about the candidates and track everything they try to learn in deciding how to vote.

In fact, complete control over the campaign gives us the ability to manipulate virtually every aspect of it. For example, in all but one of our studies, we randomly manipulated the number of candidates running in each party's primary, such that half the time there were four Democrats but only two Republicans competing for their respective party's nomination, while the other half of the time, there were two Democrats and four Republicans running. Thus, the total number of candidates was held constant at six. As detailed in Appendix C, we required every subject to register to vote in either the Democratic or Republican primary. We had no control over how individual subjects registered, of course, but by varying the number of candidates running in the two primaries, we effectively randomly manipulated the number of alternatives in the voter's choice set. This number-of-candidates manipulation is one of our most important because, by varying the number of alternatives a voter much choose among, we are manipulating the objective difficulty of the decision.

We will describe many of our other experimental manipulations in more detail as their results are examined in the following chapters. To give the reader a hint of what is to follow, our studies involved additional manipulations of the difficulty of the choice, including the ideological distinctiveness of the competing general election candidates, their conformity to partisan stereotypes, and whether the party's candidate in the general election had been supported or rejected by the voter in the earlier primary election. We manipulated the timing, number, and nature (or positive or negative "tone") of the campaign advertisements aired by the different candidates. And we manipulated the attractiveness and gender of the candidates themselves. In some cases, these manipulations were designed to test various aspects of our general framework for decision making; in other cases, the manipulations were designed to learn something about important real-world questions of today's politics. As we shall see, not all of these manipulations "worked" in the sense of producing the hypothesized differences we expected to find. But because we have carefully controlled the experimental situation and randomly assigned subjects to the different levels of our manipulated factors, we can learn a great deal about how various situational or institutional factors in campaigns cause people to process information differently, and we can observe the consequences of those information processing differences as they subsequently shape the nature and quality of the decisions that are reached.

INTERNAL VERSUS EXTERNAL VALIDITY

If experiments are so good for allowing causal inference, why would anyone conduct any other type of research? Unfortunately all research designs, like most things in life, involve tradeoffs, tradeoffs that, in this context, are usually expressed in terms of internal and external validity. *Internal validity* refers to the extent to which the conclusions about causality that one wishes to draw from the study are valid. Experiments with manipulation, control, and random assignment are very high in interval validity. To achieve the required level of control, however, it is usually necessary to conduct experiments in a laboratory – and thus away from the environment in which the behavior usually occurs.

External validity refers to generalizability – the extent to which the conclusions reached in the laboratory apply in other settings. Surveys of citizens concerning real elections have one big advantage: They concern a real event. The indisputable logic of experimentation is that changes in the dependent variable were due to differences in the independent variable in this experiment (read: this experimental setting). Although the qualifying phrase rarely appears in print, all scientists are very aware of the qualification. The crucial question for external validity is how similar is the laboratory setting to a situation people would face outside of the laboratory? The more complicated the phenomenon one is trying to study, the more necessary it usually is to simplify that phenomenon – but then the laboratory setting becomes further from reality.

Internal and external validity are not either/or propositions; they differ by degrees. An experiment conducted in a field setting would almost inevitably be less controlled than an experiment conducted in a laboratory, and therefore would have somewhat lower internal, but somewhat higher external, validity. The two are not the opposite of each other, but they tend to be inversely related, such that designs with high internal validity often have low external validity, and vice versa. Surveys conducted around real elections are even weaker than field experiments in their ability to shed light on the *causes* of a particular vote decision, but of course they are much higher in external validity. There is no ideal solution or one best research design for all problems, and the best research, ultimately, employs multiple research designs and multiple research settings, such that the shortcomings and qualifications of any particular design can be overcome by another design in another research setting.

External Validity of the Dynamic Information Board

It should be quite clear that the dynamic information board as described in this chapter differs substantively from a real election campaign. All of our voters start with no information whatsoever about the candidates and learn whatever they can in a brief twenty-minute primary and an even briefer twelve-minute general election. Obviously, real presidential election campaigns occur over a much more extended period of time. Much of what subjects in our experiments learn they get from reading text, although we do have some video information. And there is a very limited social element – voters in our studies sit in front of a computer and do not interact with other voters, except for the implicit social cues they receive by accessing items such as endorsements and polls.

A final major difference between our experiments and the way information is normally presented during campaigns involves the relatively narrow focus of every discrete bit of information that was available about the different candidates. For example, a voter could choose to learn a candidate's stand on gun control without necessarily being exposed to any of the candidate's other related policy positions, say toward crime or capital punishment. Similarly, information about a candidate's background came in fairly discrete "chunks" (their family, education, religion, military experience, etc.), whereas in actual campaigns one is more likely to come across all of this information together. The breaking down or "unitizing" of information about the candidates was necessary because of our desire to know exactly what each voter learned – or at least was exposed to – about each candidate. If a voter accesses "Singer's Age," we can be pretty confident that the voter read that "Gerry Singer is 62 years old." If we provided much longer statements about that candidate's background, we would be much less confident that a voter actually processed any distinct fact in that longer description.

Moreover, longer statements mean longer reading time, and thus – because of the continual scrolling of the dynamic information board – more information that voters are never exposed to even once. Both of these factors would combine to add much more "noise" (and less control) to the experimental setting. We chose less realism for greater control. And of course voters could learn all of a candidate's stands in any particular policy area, and/or many facets of their backgrounds, by selecting to read all the discrete items. Still, we make no claims that our mock campaign environment is a faithful analog of a real presidential election campaign.

Nonetheless, our experimental setting does connect nicely to real-world campaigns in certain respects. The candidates used are very realistic, taking positions on issues appropriate for their ideologies and party affiliations and having the type of political experience typical of major presidential candidates. The type of information presented mirrors what would be found in a real campaign. The candidates took positions on current national problems, and the types of solutions they offered all came from proposals discussed in leading newspapers such as the *New York Times* or *Washington Post*. The campaign videos were created from actual campaign ads, and the candidates were given realistic political histories. Every effort was made to create a decision environment in which subjects make a real choice among candidates.

We could have taken further steps to give our experiments more "mundane" realism (i.e., to make them more like the actual situation in which the phenomenon of interest – a vote decision – actually occurs), but we would never get away from the necessity of conducting the research in a very controlled (and thus inevitably artificial) setting. At the very least, all of our subjects knew they were in an experiment.[10] For the purposes of this research, however, it was most important to create a decision task that confronted subjects with certain key features of modern political campaigns: They are dynamic; they overwhelm voters with far more information than they can possibly process; some information is much easier to obtain than others; and some information (political ads) comes to voters "free of charge," without any effort on the voter's party, whereas other information is only available to those voters who choose to look at it.

In this goal, we have certainly succeeded. Our subjects have to devise some methods for overcoming their information processing limitations, just as voters in actual presidential campaigns must devise procedures for overcoming these same problems. Subjects are faced with a task of collecting information, evaluating it, and making a choice. They are placed in a particular decision-making environment, and the results of the experiments certainly tell us something about what happens in such environments. It is perfectly reasonable then, to conclude that the results also tell us something about voting, to the extent that it is a decision-making task in an information-rich environment. Are the procedures our subjects devise the same as those employed by voters in real elections? We have no way of knowing for sure. Yet it certainly is plausible that our subjects would first try to use the same procedures with which they are already familiar from similar situations – for instance, actual election campaigns.

---

[10] Of course, all survey respondents are also aware that they are being "observed" and face subtle social pressure to give socially desirable responses (see Kinder and Sanders, 1990).

Studying Voting as a Process

Experimental Realism

A different standard that experiments can achieve is *experimental realism*, not how similar the experimental setting is to the real-world situation it is attempting to simulate but how psychologically compelling the experimental task is. We have no hard data on this point, but, anecdotally, our subjects did take our mock election campaigns quite seriously. We provided a two-minute break between the primary and general election campaigns, during which time the two parties would apparently hold their primaries, and subjects would learn which candidates were running in the general election campaign. Many subjects cheered if their favorite candidate "won" the party's nomination, and jeered if he or she did not.[11] We had no reason (nor any method) for determining the "winner" of the general election campaign, however, and did not announce any winner. But the most frequently asked question by far during our debriefing was "Who won?" The vast majority of our subjects took this decision very seriously and acted as if they cared about the mock election campaigns we created for our studies.

Subjects

Most experiments in the social sciences employ the pervasive college sophomore as subjects (Sears, 1986). This is a convenient, inexpensive, and usually very compliant population, and their availability has been institutionalized in most psychology (and a few political science) departments in larger universities across the country. For some topics of study, college sophomores are perfectly appropriate subjects. There is no reason to think that the basic perceptual processes of college students operate any differently from any other group of people. But for other topics – and political decision making is one of them – college students provide a particularly inappropriate subject population. College students generally come from a very narrow age range, and of course an even narrower range of educational obtainment. Age and education are two of the demographic characteristics that typically have the strongest impact on political attitudes and behavior, effects that cannot be replicated with subjects lacking variance in those characteristics. Sears (1986) argues college students will have less crystallized social and political attitudes than people later in life, yet these attitudes provide the crucial inputs to political perception and judgment. Younger people almost by definition will have less experience with political matters, and, in virtually every domain, expertise develops

---

[11] The "winners" of our primaries were always a product of experimental manipulations and thus unrelated to vote totals, although no subject knew this.

65

with greater experience. Expertise is one of the most important factors to consider in studying decision making, and the typical college student, who will have had the opportunity to vote in at most a single major national election, will not have had the opportunity to develop very much of it.

We therefore targeted a much broader population of subjects. Our requirements were only two: (1) that subjects be eligible to register and vote in U.S. elections (i.e., they be U.S. citizens at least 18 years of age), and (2) that they *not* be currently enrolled in a college or university. Our resulting subject pool, while certainly not meant to be representative of anything, is broadly similar to the type of people living in central New Jersey where our experiments were run. Table C.1 in Appendix C presents summary statistics describing these subjects and provides further details on subject recruitment. The crucial point is that our subjects, ranging in age from 18 to 84 with a mean of over 45, have as a group had far more opportunity to be involved in politics than the typical 19- or 20-year-old college sophomore. Indeed, our typical subject has been eligible to vote for longer than most college students have been alive!

Of course, having the opportunity to be involved in politics does not necessarily mean that all of our subjects took those opportunities. Indeed, if they had, we would face the same restricted variance problem that confronts anyone using college students as subjects, albeit now at the upper range of political involvement rather than the lower range. This is a realistic fear because even though we took pains to explain in recruiting subjects that we did not just want people who were interested in and knew a lot about politics, still the study was described as being about how people make vote choices, and it is not unreasonable to fear that our volunteers would be inordinately interested in politics.

Table 3.1 compares the political interest and experience of our subjects to responses to very similar questions from respondents in the 1994 to 2000 ANES surveys – the period bracketing when our experiments were run. As can be seen, our subjects were on average clearly more active in politics than a random sample of their fellow citizens, although few of these people would be considered "activists." One the other hand, our subjects claim to be only a little more interested in and knowledgeable about politics than the average voter. Overall, these numbers are definitely higher than we would expect from a representative survey of the American public. But the important point is that our subjects ran the full gamut from the most politically involved to the least politically interested.

Evidence of the Generalizability of Our Experimental Data

We can also provide evidence for the external validity of our experimental data by comparing some of our experimental results with survey

Table 3.1. *Indicators of Political Sophistication*

	Campaign-Oriented Political Behavior[a]		Community-Oriented Political Behavior[b]		Frequency of Following Politics in the Media[c]	
	Experiment	ANES	Experiment	ANES	Experiment	ANES
Range	0–5	0–5	0–3	0–3	0–4	0–4
Mean	2.5	1.3	1.5	0.7	2.1	1.9
Median	2.0	1.0	2.0	1.0	2.2	2.0
Std Dev	1.6	1.0	1.1	1.0	0.7	1.1

	General (Factual) Political Knowledge[d]		Correct Ideological Placement of Politicians[e]	
	Experiment	ANES	Experiment	ANES
Range	0–11	0–11	0–7	0–6
Mean	6.5	5.7	5.3	3.9
Median	6.0	6.0	6.0	4.0
Std Dev	2.6	2.5	1.8	2.0

	Frequency of Talking to Others about Politics			General Interest in Politics	
	Experiment	ANES		Experiment	ANES
Never	4%	22%	Little or None	22%	24%
Rarely	33%	26%	Moderate	34%	48%
Once/twice a week	33%	26%	Good or Great Deal	44%	28%
3 or 4 times a week	16%	20%			
Daily or almost daily	13%	10%			

Note: ANES data average across the 1994, 1996, 1998, and 2000 studies, whenever similar questions are available.

[a] Includes voting in the last presidential election, ever working for a candidate, wearing a campaign button, contributing money to a candidate or political party, and trying to convince others how to vote.

[b] Includes working with others on some community project, writing to a newspaper or representative to express an opinion, and writing to a political representative to seek some service.

[c] Average frequency of watching the national and business news on television and watching all-news networks like CNN; reading about national news in a newspaper, and reading a national news magazine like *Time* or *Newsweek*; and listening to national news programs on the radio. 0 = Never, 4 = Daily or almost daily.

[d] Number of correct answers to 11 factual items, including length of representative's and senator's terms, party in control of the House and Senate, identifying the Secretary of State, Secretary of Defense, and leader of Russia; knowing that the federal deficit is smaller than it was in 1988; ball-parking the size of the defense budget; knowing how a bill becomes a law; and knowing who nominates judges for the federal courts.

[e] Placing George H. Bush, Bill Clinton, Bob Dole, Dan Quayle, Al Gore, Jessie Jackson, and Ronald Reagan on the correct half of the ideological spectrum.

data gathered from actual elections. The top half of Figure 3.5 presents the proportion of voters defecting from their party in five recent U.S. presidential elections, by strength of party identification.[12] At least two well-known points about party identification can be seen in this survey data. First, the stronger the party identification, the stronger the tendency to vote for the party's candidate; and second, this tendency is greater among Republicans than Democrats, which is why Republican candidates win many elections even though there are more Democrats than Republicans among the mass public.[13] Now look at the bottom panel of Figure 3.5, which presents the rate of defection in our experimental elections. Note that the pattern tracks quite closely to the ANES studies.

Figure 3.6 reports defection rates not by strength of party identification but by which candidate the respondent supported in the primary – the one ultimately *chosen* by the party and thus running in the general election or the one who was *rejected* by the party in favor of some other candidate. Again the top panel presents the ANES data, which shows the same two trends seen in Figure 3.5. First, if a respondent's candidate in the primaries wins the party's nomination, voters are extremely likely to support that same candidate during the general election, particularly when compared to fellow party members who supported some other candidate during the primary. The figures fall between those of strong and weak party identifiers and are substantially nearer to the former than the latter. And second, we again see the greater tendency for Democrats to defect from their party than Republicans, irrespective of who they supported during the primaries.

But the point we want to make here is shown in the bottom panel of Figure 3.6, which presents the same analysis for our subjects, some of whom faced a candidate in the general election that they had already rejected in the primary. The results from the experiments are astonishingly close to the ANES results. We believe both of these analyses (and several others to be presented later in this book) provide clear support for our contention that subjects not only took the experiments seriously but actually behaved as if engaged in a real political campaign. What more could we ask?

---

[12] In 1972, 1976, 1980, 1988, and 1992, the ANES asked respondents if they had voted in a primary election, and if so, which candidate they had supported. The data in Figures 3.5 and 3.6 come from these five election studies.

[13] Another not-quite-so-well-known point is also evident in this data: a nonmonotonic relationship between party identification and the vote choice. Independents "leaning" Democratic appear to be stronger Democrats than "weak" identifiers with the party, at least judging by the tendency to support the party's candidate.

Studying Voting as a Process

National Election Studies

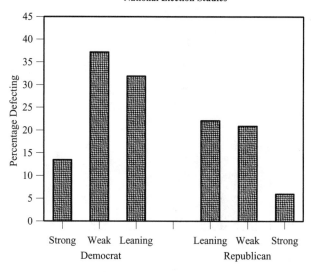

Our Subjects

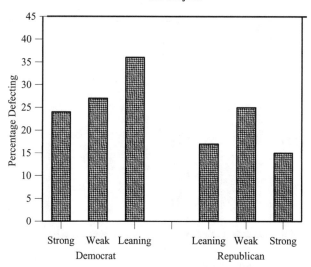

Figure 3.5. Defection from party in presidential voting by strength of party identification.

National Election Studies

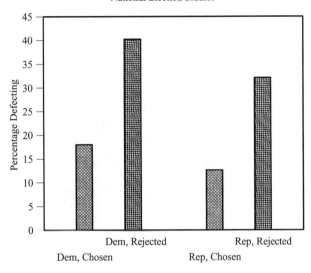

Our Subjects

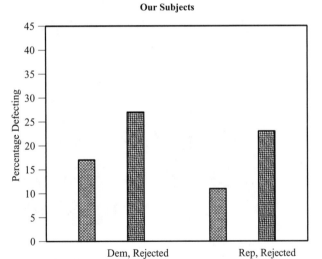

Figure 3.6. Defection from party in presidential voting by vote in party primary.

CONCLUSION

This chapter has described – probably in excruciating detail for some readers – a new technique for studying the vote decision, a technique that allows us to collect information on voter decision making no other researchers interested in this topic have ever had. These experiments were time-consuming to conduct and somewhat complicated to design, but their strength lies in our ability to "get inside" voters' heads, to better understand the role information processing plays in voter decision making. Our procedure supplies the detailed process-tracing information upon which previous research in behavioral decision theory relies, but in an experimental setting that better approximates the hurdles voters face in real elections. Our experiments thus provide a broad test of the general framework for studying voter decision making presented at the beginning of Chapter 2.

We are about to begin looking at the results of those experiments. But before we begin looking in detail at voters' information processing during an election campaign, we must address one remaining question. How can we determine or evaluate the quality of voters' decisions? We have argued that this should be a fundamental question of voting behavior research, but we have not yet discussed how this question can be addressed empirically. That is the topic of Chapter 4.

4

What Is Correct Voting?

The classic texts of democratic theory assume that for a democracy to function properly, citizens should be interested in, pay attention to, discuss, and actively participate in politics. The attention and discussion provide information about political affairs, which allows citizens to make political decisions (e.g., a vote) based on carefully considered principles reflecting their own self-interest and the common good. All citizens may not be able to live up to these standards – some may be too disinterested, or lack sufficient information, or lack the skills to understand politics, and as a consequence vote by habit or narrow prejudices, or not vote at all – but as long as a clear majority of citizens do live up to these standards, the collective wisdom of the people will prevail.

As discussed in earlier chapters, however, five decades of behavioral research in political science have left no doubt that only a tiny minority of the citizens in any democracy actually live up to these ideals. Interest in politics is generally weak, discussion is rare, political knowledge on the average is pitifully low, and few people actively participate in politics beyond voting (e.g., Berelson, Lazarsfeld, and McPhee, 1954; Campbell et al., 1960; Converse, 1964; Delli Carpini and Keeter, 1996).

The wide divergence between classic normative theory and political reality has led to two widely divergent responses. On the one hand, there are those who accept both the normative theory and the empirical data, and conclude as a consequence that governments calling themselves "democracies" are not truly democratic. An apathetic public cannot possibly constrain government officials, this line of argument goes;

This chapter relies heavily upon a previously published article [Lau and Redlawsk, 1997]. The analyses in Table 4.3 have been updated to include data from the 1992, 1996, and 2000 American presidential elections, which were not previously available to us. Somewhat miraculously, the story we have to tell has not changed at all with the inclusion of these three additional election years.

instead, some capitalist power elite, military-industrial complex, and/or giant media conglomerate have used democratic institutions and a complacent citizenry to manipulate government policy toward their own ends (e.g., Bennett, 1988, 1992; Burnham, 1965, 1974; Fishman, 1980; Gans, 1979; Mills, 1971).

On the other hand, there are those who accept the empirical evidence but revise downward the requirements of normative theory so that modern governments can still be considered mostly "democratic." For instance, Page and Shapiro (1992) argue that *aggregate* public opinion can be fairly stable and rational – and even, perhaps, guide public policy – while based on mostly ill-formed "nonattitudes" among individual citizens. Fiorina (1981) shows the advantages of basing vote decisions on retrospective judgments of the party's past performances rather than spending the time to learn about the candidates' future policy proposals. Others argue that the widespread ignorance of and indifference toward politics typically seen in Western democracies is in fact a good thing, for it reduces social conflict and contributes to greater system stability (Berelson, Lazarsfeld, and McPhee, 1954; McClosky, 1964; Mueller, 1992; Prothro and Grigg, 1960). In other words, democracy still "works" – and in fact may even work better – if only some *minority* of the population are attentive to politics, ideological in their thinking, and so on (see also Dahl, 1961, 1989; Huntington, 1968; Lindblom, 1965; Schattschneider, 1960).

Although we are somewhat in sympathy with each of these divergent responses, we take issue with the very point on which they both agree: Do the empirical data in fact require so drastic a revision of classic democratic theory? True, if modern citizens paid the type of attention to public affairs that Rousseau prescribed several centuries ago, they would do little else but follow politics. Such standards are unrealistically high and, we would argue, not necessary for the average citizen. Classic democratic theory prescribes active attention to and close scrutiny of government policy because, logically, it seemed the only way that citizens could make correct decisions. If A (an active, attentive public) is necessary for B (democracy), and A is not true, then logically B cannot be true.

This syllogism holds only if we accept the premise that close attention to politics and the actions of government officials and the promises of competing candidates are necessary for correct voting decisions. But what if they are not? What if people can make reasonably good decisions, most of the time, without all the motivation and attention and knowledge that is required by classic theory?

As already discussed in Chapter 2, cognitive psychology teaches us that humans are limited information processors (Fiske and Taylor, 1991; Lau and Sears, 1986). People can process only a small fraction of the information to which they are exposed. Citizens do not have all the information about politics that is required of them by classic democratic theory; neither do they process that information in as logical a way as those theorists hoped, in large part because of strict cognitive limitations. It is not so much that people do a particularly bad job of processing political information, of course, but rather that we do an equally bad job of processing any other type of complex information. If the same standards that classic democratic theory holds up for citizens were to be applied to any other area of human life, such as finding mates or buying cars or choosing colleges, people would be judged to be just as inept in those areas.

Most people nonetheless seem to make adequate marriages, get decent educations, and make reasonably good automobile purchases. We have already seen how this is possible: Human beings have adaptively developed a large series of cognitive heuristics or shortcuts that allow them to make pretty good judgments most of the time (Kahneman, Slovic, and Tversky, 1982; Nisbett and Ross, 1980; Tversky and Kahneman, 1974). These heuristics "do sometimes lead people astray when they are overextended or misapplied ... but] people's intuitive inferential strategies are probably used appropriately and effectively in the great majority of cases" (Nisbett and Ross, 1980, p. 255).

As a consequence, if we are going to make judgments about the "democratic" nature of different forms of government, we should do so at least initially on the basis of the quality or correctness of the political decisions that citizens make within that system of government rather than on the basis of the ways in which those decisions are reached. Democracy is not a simple form of government, and judgments about the nature of different governments that claim to be democratic should not be made in a simplistic, either-or manner. Certainly degrees of democracy are possible, and we would argue that a crucial criterion is the proportion of citizens voting correctly at any particular point in time rather than the manner in which those vote decisions are reached. That is, if most people, most of the time, vote correctly, then we should not be too concerned if those vote decisions are reached on the basis of something less than full information about the different policies espoused by different candidates, much less knowledge of how government actually carries out policy decisions or who the important players are.

But What Is a "Correct" Voting Decision?

Determining the quality or "correctness" of a vote decision is not an easy task, however. Who is to decide what is correct? One approach is for the writer's or researcher's values to determine what is correct. This approach is exemplified by the recent popular book *What's the Matter with Kansas?*

(Frank, 2004), whose author believes people's votes ought to be consistent with their economic interests (and thus presumably ignoring their noneconomic interests), but there are many additional examples we could cite. We are reluctant to define what is good for everyone, however, and even if we were not, we doubt that many people would be willing to accept our judgments. Instead, we begin by defining "correctness" *based on the values and beliefs of the individual voter*, not on any particular ideology that presumes the values and preferences that ought to be held by members of different social classes, for instance, and not on any larger social goods or universal values. Given the limitations of human cognitive abilities discussed earlier, however, we are equally reluctant to accept as correct any individual vote just because it was freely chosen by that individual, as Downs (1957) and his followers might. Instead, we adopt a theoretical middle ground by defining correctness based on the fully informed interests of individual voters. As Dahl writes, "A person's interest or good is whatever that person would choose with fullest attainable understanding of the experiences resulting from that choice and its most relevant alternatives" (1989, pp. 180–1; see also Connolly, 1972; Delli Carpini and Keeter, 1996; Lippmann, 1955; Mansbridge, 1983). Thus, we will define a correct vote decision as one that is the same as the choice that would have been made under conditions of full information. Ideally, this determination can best be made subjectively, by the voter him- or herself, on an individual basis.

This chapter has several purposes. We will first describe our attempt to operationalize, in the context of our mock election studies, this ideal of fully informed voters determining for themselves the correct vote decision. This measure is the easiest to defend theoretically, but it is very costly (in terms of subjects' time) to obtain, and it would be essentially impossible to employ with any nonexperimental study of a real election. But we then use this operationalization as a means of validating a second and more easily obtainable measure of correct voting. In so doing, we move from a completely subjective, individually determined definition to a more objective, expert-determined judgment of which candidate best matches the voter's own stated preferences.

The experimental data are crucial for what we are attempting to accomplish in this book but also for providing a justification and validation for using an objective, externally determined measure. Having obtained it, we then briefly illustrate the use of such measures with the 1972–2000 American National Election Studies. These latter results provide important construct validity for this measure. Relatively few researchers will follow our lead in devising their own mock elections where they might be able to employ an analog to our initial measure, but they certainly can employ our second, more objective measure of correct voting. Indeed, we were so happy with this alternative measure that we dropped the correct voting determination from Studies 3 and 4 and used the experimental time for other purposes. This more objective measure of correct voting is the only one available to us in Studies 3 and 4.

Finally at the end of the chapter, we return to the question of what ought to be required of citizens by democratic theory, after we have a better idea of just how well our disinterested, apathetic, uninformed citizens actually do in making their vote decisions.

Determining "Correct" Vote Choices in Our Mock Election Studies

Most of the experimental procedure is described in Chapter 3 and Appendix C, but it seemed best to defer a description of our method for determining a correct vote choice until now. After the mock election campaign was over and the debriefing began, subjects in our first two studies were questioned about their impressions of the experiment, and they were asked to complete one final task. The experimenter commiserated with subjects about how difficult it had been to obtain all the information they would have liked, but explained it was very important for us to know if the subjects thought they had voted "correctly." The pictures of two of the candidates from the primary election were shown on the computer screen, the one the subject had voted for, and another candidate from that same party. Recall that the number of candidates running in each party's primary was randomly manipulated in these studies. If there were only two in-party candidates running in the primary, then those two candidates were chosen. In the four-candidate primary condition, there was some discretion, however, and to make this choice as difficult as possible, the computer was programmed to select the candidate (from the three available) who was closest to the subject on the issues.

The experimenter brought out a notebook where all the information about these two candidates was laid out side by side, so that it was very easy to compare. Most pairwise comparisons involved roughly ten pages of single-spaced text. The experimenter explained that he or she knew it was impossible to learn everything about any of the candidates during the experiment, but as one last task we wanted the subjects to look this material over carefully and decide if they still would have voted the way they did if they had been able to learn all of the available information about these two candidates. These instructions were designed to get subjects to take this final task seriously and to set up a context in which they would feel free to change their minds about their initial vote choice in the primary election in light of full information about the candidates without feeling defensive or foolish about their original choice.

What Is Correct Voting?

If after carefully considering all information available about these two candidates, subjects decided they still would have voted for the candidate they actually did vote for, we consider that they voted correctly. If after receiving full information, subjects decided that they would have changed their initial vote, however, then we say they voted incorrectly. This is our first, and probably most defensible, measure of correct voting.[1]

An Alternative "Normative-Naive" Measure of Correct Voting

Unfortunately, none of us have the opportunity to learn everything there is to know about the candidates in a real election, and few people have the motivation to even learn everything that is readily available about them. Nonetheless, we believe that almost everyone tries to vote correctly, given whatever they have learned about the candidates (and parties) by Election Day. We now attempt to model how people could "naively" or "intuitively" go about making these decisions.

From the preelection questionnaire, we know subjects' political preferences and policy stands; likewise, we know where the candidates stand on those issues, and by employing expert judges can reasonably express candidates' stands on the same scales used by subjects. Most importantly, we know exactly what information a voter was exposed to about the different candidates. We do not know precisely how that information was evaluated by each individual voter, but we can make very informed guesses based on our knowledge of the voter's preferences. Thus, we are in an excellent position to try to model the vote decisions that people actually made in our elections.

In fact, assuming that people do indeed *try* to vote correctly, this in essence is a second measure of correct voting – a normative measure

---

[1] Besides random error, there are at least three plausible reasons why subjects may not be completely accurate in their own assessment of the correctness of their initial vote choice. One is self-presentation: Despite our efforts to make it acceptable to admit that one had not made the optimal decision – and we were careful to avoid words like "mistake" and "incorrect" – some subjects still might have been reluctant to do so. A closely related reason is avoiding postdecisional dissonance – or any unpleasant internal state resulting from learning one has made a bad decision. A third reason is fatigue: This final task was presented to subjects after an average of 126 minutes of prior effort in the experiment (the range was 93 to 160, with a standard deviation of about 13 minutes), and the material they were given to examine carefully about the two candidates was almost twelve pages long, single-spaced. It would only be human for people to give this material less careful consideration than they would have if they had been presented with this task at the beginning of the experiment rather than at the end. Nonetheless, we stressed to subjects how important this final task was, and most subjects put forth a very serious effort.

of naive vote preferences – one that is based on the voter's own values, to be sure, but one that ultimately is determined by the authors rather than the voter him- or herself. We consciously juxtapose the terms "normative" and "naive" in the description of what we are trying to model. This measure is naive or intuitive in that it is based on the voter's actual information-gathering strategies rather than on any ideal, logical, or expert-determined process, but it is normative in that it is based on an objective evaluation of that information, and thus an objective determination of which candidate the subject should have voted for, given their own political preferences and the differential candidate information to which they were exposed.

In Chapter 8 we describe how we compute an on-line evaluation of the candidates, using an additive combination of information learned about a candidate, weighted by the importance of that information to the voter. Readers seeking more detail on this measure can look ahead to Chapter 8. The information incorporated into this on-line evaluation includes party identification, issues, candidate personality, and group endorsements, with all considerations scaled to have a one-point range. The evaluation counters developed in Chapter 8 are based only on what was viewed about each individual candidate; however, here we explicitly incorporate the normative perspective by calculating the on-line evaluation based not only on what was looked at, but also including what *should* have been looked at. We determine subjectively for each voter what should have been looked at according to the voter's own behavior. That is, if a voter looked at a piece of information for at least two candidates, we take it as evidence he cares about that dimension of judgment, and therefore believe he should have examined the same information for all candidates in the choice set, and we calculate the evaluation counter as if he did. On the other hand, any attribute that was never considered or only accessed once is assumed to be unimportant to the voter and is therefore dropped from the calculation of correct voting. Thus, the version of the evaluation counters used in Chapter 8 are candidate-specific, but the counters used in this chapter are explicitly comparative, as elections are in the real world.

RESULTS

Vote Choice

The first analytic task is to see how well this simple method of determining differential candidate preference can predict the actual vote choice of our subjects. We specified a very simple logistic regression in which vote choice in the primary election was regressed on the difference between the candidate evaluation measures calculated for the two candidates offered to subjects for closer inspection after completion of the main experiment. This single variable (which of course incorporates issue voting, group endorsements, and candidate appearance and personalities) was highly significant ($p < .001$), correctly predicting over 60% of the actual vote choices against a baseline of 50% – about as good as could be expected in a primary election campaign where party cannot be used as a voting cue.

Predicting Correct Voting

Survey designs of actual elections are far better vehicles for learning why one particular candidate won an election or for building models to predict the direction of the vote choice. In contrast, we are primarily interested in understanding whether people voted correctly according to their fully informed interests, not which candidate they voted for. Seventy percent of the subjects (206 out of 293) would not have changed their vote after learning everything there was to learn about the two candidates, and thus by this definition voted correctly. The remainder, by their own determination, voted incorrectly.[2] This is our first important finding, although it is impossible to say how generalizable this 70% correct figure is, given that it is based on voting in a mock election study, albeit one designed to simulate the crucial aspects of real campaigns.

The first major question we pose is how well our normative measure of naive or intuitive candidate preference predicts fully informed correct voting. If the prediction is good, we are justified in referring to it as a normative measure and in using it as an alternative measure of correct voting, a surrogate for the more complete, but much more difficult to obtain, fully informed correct vote determination.

Thus, we specified a second logistic regression in which the subject's fully informed determination of which candidate was correct was regressed on the normative candidate differential variable described earlier. This single variable is again highly significant ($p < .001$) and correctly predicts almost 66% of the correct vote choices – better than this same variable predicts the actual vote choice! This is strong validation of our normative candidate differential variable as another measure of correct voting. Just as importantly, our normative method of determining candidate preferences does almost as well in determining correct voting

---

[2] That fully 30% of the subjects were willing to say they would change their vote, and thus implicitly to admit that they had initially voted incorrectly, is evidence that self-presentation concerns were probably not a very big issue to most subjects (see note 1).

decisions as voters themselves did (who voted for the correct candidate 70% of the time).

This finding is the crux of our argument, and we want to put it in clear perspective. We have good, but certainly incomplete, knowledge of voters' preferences. Based on this knowledge, we can make reasonable (but again far from perfect) inferences about how subjects evaluated the information they learned about the candidates, and knowing nothing about how voters actually combine these evaluations into a vote choice but modeling a plausible alternative, we can do almost as well in determining correct vote decisions as can voters themselves, who have perfect knowledge of their own preferences and perfect knowledge of how favorably they responded to the candidate information to which they were exposed.

The reason our normative measure of naive candidate preference predicts a fully informed vote choice better than it predicts an actual vote choice is that voters, under normal information processing circumstances, cannot possibly achieve the care and objectivity that would be possible to achieve given more time and the opportunity to become fully informed about two opposing candidates. On the other hand, with the aid of a powerful computer to help keep track of what has been learned about the multiple candidates, we can reasonably approximate that care and objectivity. In other words, under normal circumstances, the vote decision is most likely an intuitive, global judgment, and people with limited cognitive resources have a very hard time combining complex sets of information to make such judgments. Only when given the time and presented with the information in a very focused (only two candidates, not all six) and easy-to-compare format (information about the two candidates presented side by side) can people approach the objectivity of our simple linear algorithm.[3]

Thus, our results suggest (1) that voters in our experiment, confronted with the same type of time constraints and information overload that voters in actual elections face, nevertheless do a pretty good job of selecting the candidate they would have voted for had there been no constraints on their information-gathering capabilities (i.e., if they have full information) but (2) that they could clearly do better than they do under

---

[3] Although it is always hard for people to accept, the finding that fairly simple but objective algorithms for combining multiple criteria for judgment outperform naive (or expert) decision makers who rely on a global judgment is fairly common in the decision-making literature. Perhaps the classic example is Meehl's (1954) summary of twenty different studies comparing what he called "clinical" judgment to a statistical summary of objective information available to the decision maker. In no case was the global judgment found to be superior to the statistical summary. Dawes (1988) reviews many subsequent studies, all of which reach the same conclusion.

current circumstances, given more time or presented with information in a more easily "digestible" manner, and (3) that we as researchers or external observers can determine fairly accurately who individual voters, given full information, would want to pick as their best choice.

Further Validation of the Normative–Naive Candidate Preference Measure

We can provide further evidence that our normative candidate differential measure is a reasonable approximation of a fully informed correct vote decision and is in fact what voters are trying to achieve during the correct vote determination stage of our experiment. First, we can ask whether the additional information subjects learn about the candidates during the final correct-voting determination task can predict their wanting to change their initial vote choice. If we cannot understand how additional information might *change* decisions, then we probably do not have a very good understanding of how those decisions are reached in the first place.

To answer this question, we put subjects' actual vote choices into three categories, according to our normative measure of candidate preference: Had subjects voted for the best possible alternative, the worst possible alternative, or (in the four-candidate condition) a candidate that fell between these two extremes? If our measure reasonably captures voters' fully informed preferences, then we should observe a much higher percentage of voters wanting to change their vote who (according to our measure) had originally voted for the worst possible candidate than the best possible candidate. The data, shown in Table 4.1, reflect just this pattern of results: Almost 44% of those we thought picked the worst alternative were willing to admit a mistake after examining more information about the candidates, while less than 17% of those who we believed picked the best possible candidate wanted to change their minds.

As a final check that our normative–naive measure of differential candidate preference is a good approximation of how voters would try to process information and decide who is their best choice if they had the opportunity, we can use the same procedures to model the additional

Table 4.1. *Willingness to Change Original Vote as a Function of the Quality of the Original Choice*

	Would Not Change	Would Change	Total (N)
Worst candidate chosen	56%	44%	100% (82)
Intermediate candidate	62%	38%	100% (58)
Best candidate chosen	83%	17%	100% (148)

Tau c = .26, $p < .001$

information subjects gained about the candidates during the full-information correct vote determination task – that is, information that was not available to them when they made their actual vote choice. If our method is a good one, then this new variable – which incorporates all the new information presumably gained only after the campaign was over, during the correct vote determination task – should predict which of the two candidates was chosen by subjects as their correct choice, after controlling for the actual vote choice.

To address this question we recoded the dependent variable to represent whether Candidate A or Candidate B (an arbitrary distinction) was determined by the subject to be the correct choice, and use as predictors whether subjects had originally voted for Candidate A or Candidate B, and a new variable reflecting an evaluation of the new information learned about the two candidates during the final correct voting determination that was not known at the time of the original vote. The original vote choice reflects the intuitive or naive candidate choice. Whatever information was actually learned about the candidates during the primary election (plus whatever inferences people were willing to make) are reflected in this vote choice. We already know this will be a highly significant predictor because we have seen that, after being presented with more information, 70% of subjects report that they voted correctly in the first place – a big improvement over a chance level of 50%.

The more substantively interesting variable is the second in the equation, the effect of the additional information gained from the fully informed correct voting task. If we as outside observers, knowing only the voter's preferences and the stands of the candidates, can predict fully informed choices better than voters with their own intuitive methods can – that is, if we do indeed have a good handle on what it is that voters will believe is their best choice – then our information-gained variable should add significantly to the predictive power of the equation. As shown in Table 4.2, the information-gained variable does add significantly to the predictive power of the equation. Indeed, we go from just under 62% correct when we only consider the vote choice itself – that is, when we only consider how well subjects themselves did during the election campaign in selecting the correct candidate – to an almost perfect ability (95%) to make the correct choice once we consider the new information subjects saw before making their own choice about which candidate was the correct one for them. As a consequence, we are now even more confident that we understand how voters are determining their correct vote choice because we can predict how additional information about the alternatives influences that decision. Thus, we are reasonably confident in offering our naive normative method for determining candidate preference as an alternative criterion for correct voting.

Table 4.2. *Effect of New Information on Decision to Change Vote*

	B	S.E.	Increase in Probability
Constant	−1.24***	.21	.22
Direction of actual vote	1.76***	.27	.39
Effect of new information	.28**	.12	.33

** $p < .01$; *** $p < .001$.

Note: Data come from a logistic regression analysis that also included a constant. For this analysis, −2 times the log likelihood was 330.48; the model Chi-Square with 2 df was 54.31 ($p < .000$). The last column indicates the increase in probability of making a correct prediction (of which candidate subjects believed was correct for them) from the full range of each variable. We estimate the effect of the new information on voters with the direction of the actual vote variable (and the constant) already in the equation. $N = 292$.

An Application to American Presidential Elections

The results from our experiments are quite impressive. Confronted by an information environment that in some ways is even harder to deal with than an actual campaign, our subjects nevertheless voted correctly 70% of the time. The skeptical reader may still doubt that this would ever generalize to an actual election, however. Any experimental study of the vote choice, no matter how realistic it attempts to be, is going to be a far cry from an actual election campaign. In this section, we illustrate how our method can be applied to American National Election Study data – the mainstay of behavioral research in American politics.

It is certainly possible to construct a measure analogous to the normative method of determining naive or intuitive candidate preference used in our experimental data with the information in the typical ANES survey. There is no analog to our importance weights, but in analyses not reported here, an equal-weights version of the normative measure of naive candidate preference performed almost as well as the weighted version. Likewise, we have no direct measure of what information about a candidate a voter has been exposed to. However, we can use willingness to answer survey questions about the candidates (e.g., willingness to attribute an issue stand to a candidate) as a reasonable indirect measure of information exposure. Using this analog to our normative measure of naive candidate preference as a surrogate measure of correct voting, we can determine (with many more qualifications than are necessary for our experimental data, of course), the percentage of voters in different American presidential elections voting correctly.

We pose three simple macro-level hypotheses about differences across elections in the percentage of voters who should have voted "correctly" in these elections. To the extent that these hypotheses are supported, they provide important predictive validity for our surrogate measure of correct voting as it can be operationalized from survey data. Thus, we offer the following hypotheses as predictive validity tests:

1. Given limited cognitive resources, voters are more likely to make correct decision when there are fewer candidates to choose from than when there are more alternatives in the choice set. This hypothesis suggests that voters were more likely to make correct choices in 1972, 1976, 1984, and 1988, and 2000, than when there was a reasonably successful third-party candidates running in the general election, as was the case in 1980, 1992, or 1996.[4]

2. Holding the number of candidates constant, voters will be more likely to make correct decisions when the candidates are easy to distinguish than when they are difficult to distinguish. This would suggest higher rates of correct voting in 1972, 1984, and 1988, when more ideologically extreme candidates captured the two parties' nominations, than in 1976 or 2000, when more centrist candidates opposed each other.[5]

3. All else equal, voters will be more likely to make correct decisions when campaign resources are reasonably balanced, giving all candidates an equal opportunity to get their cases across, than when resources are imbalanced. Phrased more cynically, this hypothesis suggests that candidates blessed with relatively greater campaign resources than their opponents can buy greater support than they should have received had everyone voted correctly.

---

[4] When we originally published these results, we could not include data from the 1992 election. The on-again off-again nature of Ross Perot's candidacy in 1992 was "off-again" when the ANES staff made its final decisions about their preelection survey, which resulted in a dearth of questions about Perot in that survey, and precluded our including that election in the analyses. This was particularly unfortunate for testing Hypothesis 1, as the Perot candidacy in 1992 was by far the most successful third-party candidacy in the prior eighty years. Perot was also a candidate in the 1996 election, however, and even though his candidacy did not attract nearly as many votes from the public that year, it did attract many more questions from the ANES staff. The 1996 data (and of course the 2000 data as well) were not available when we published our original article, but if we make the assumption that Perot held the same positions in 1992 as he did in 1996, we can use experts' perceptions of where Perot stood on the issues in 1996, and plug them into the 1992 analyses. This assumption strikes us as a reasonable one, but we would certainly agree that the data from 1992 should be considered as more tentative than the data from any of the other election years. We replicated all of the analyses reported in Table 4.3 with and without 1992, and the general pattern and statistical significance levels of the results are the same either way.

[5] George W. Bush has turned out to be one of our most conservative presidents, but he campaigned in 2000 very much as a centrist (see Pomper, 2001).

Table 4.3 presents the results of a test of these hypotheses. Without going into all the details (which are available in an appendix to Lau and Redlawsk, 1997), we have replicated as nearly as possible with ANES data an equal-weights version of our normative measure of naive candidate preference. With the ANES surveys, we have the same type of information about voters' own preferences as we have in our experiments. The trick is getting decent "objective" measures of where the candidates actually stand on those considerations, and we achieve this by looking at the mean perceptions of political experts – those above the median on a political knowledge scale in each survey. In addition to party identification, every policy issue and candidate-group linkage that could be objectively estimated was included in the analysis. Taking this measure as our criterion of correct voting, we can determine the proportion of voters in recent American presidential elections who voted correctly.

Table 4.3 is broken into eight sections, one for each presidential election between 1972 and 2000. The first column displays the proportion of voters for each candidate who, by our determination, voted correctly. The overall proportion for each election year is shown in the last column of the table. These numbers range between a low of 37% for Ross Perot in 1992, to a high of 89% for Walter Mondale in 1984. Overall accuracy of voting across these eight elections ranges from 58 to 80%, with a mean of 72%. These data conform very nicely to our experimental results.

Consistent with Hypothesis 1, the mean number of correct votes in those years with only two major presidential candidates, 77.2%, is significantly higher than the mean number of correct votes in the three elections in our data with an important third-party candidate, 62.3% ($z = 15.9$, $p < .001$).[6]

Hypothesis 2 predicts that, holding the number of candidates constant, the percentage of correct votes in elections with ideologically distinct candidates should be greater than the percentage of correct votes in elections with ideologically similar candidates. If we consider only those elections

---

[6] One could make the case that the appropriate comparison for testing Hypothesis 1 is the proportion of correct votes for the Democratic and Republican candidates across these two types of elections, ignoring the third-party candidates themselves, who typically suffer from numerous impediments to electoral success beyond the lack of a major party affiliation. The percentage of correct voters in the three elections with strong third-party candidates rises to 65.5% by this measure, but the difference is still highly significant, $z = 12.1$, $p < .001$. One might also argue that this hypothesis is confounded by strategic vote considerations (e.g., Abramson et al., 1992); for example, some voters believed that Perot was their "best" choice but they also realized that he could not win and so voted for their "second best" choice who had a much better chance of winning. Such considerations should not affect the

Table 4.3. *Correct Voting in American Presidential Elections, 1972–2000*

Presidential Candidate	% Supporters Voting Correctly	% Reported Vote	% Predicted Correct Vote	Deviation, % Reported − % Predicted	% General Election Spending	Deviation of Spending from Proportional Share	Overall Accuracy
1972							79.0%
McGovern	74.5	35.7	38.5	−2.8	33.7	−16.3	
Nixon	81.5	64.3	61.5	2.8	66.3	16.3	
1976							75.5%
Carter	72.2	51.1	47.1	4.0	52.4	2.4	
Ford	78.9	48.9	52.8	−3.9	47.6	−2.4	
1980							67.8%
Carter	64.0	40.0	34.6	5.4	40.0	6.7	
Reagan	73.7	51.6	46.5	5.1	47.7	14.3	
Anderson	50.6	8.5	19.0	−10.5	12.3	−21.0	
1984							76.8%
Mondale	89.0	41.8	55.7	−13.9	40.5	−9.5	
Reagan	68.0	58.2	44.2	14.0	59.5[a]	9.5	
1988[b]							80.2%
Dukakis	83.8	47.1	51.7	−4.6	53.0	3.0	
Bush	76.7	52.9	48.2	4.7	47.0	−3.0	
1992							58.2%
Clinton	65.6	47.4	42.3	5.1	38.6	5.3	
Bush	59.9	33.7	33.7	0.0	44.4	11.1	
Perot	36.5	18.9	24.0	−5.1	17.1	−16.2	
1996							63.6%
Clinton	72.9	52.7	46.2	6.5	45.9[a]	12.6	
Dole	55.1	39.7	25.5	14.2	45.8	12.5	
Perot	43.5	7.6	28.3	−20.7	8.3	−25.0	
2000							74.5%
Gore	80.4	52.0	57.1	−5.1	49.5	−0.5	
Bush	68.1	48.0	42.9	5.1	50.5	0.5	

[a] Figures include spending during the primary because Reagan and Clinton were unchallenged during their party's primary.

[b] These 1988 figures correct a slight coding error in our original presentation of these data.

without strong third-party candidates (who muck up the conceptual clarity of this hypothesis), 1972, 1984, and 1988 were years with ideologically distinct candidates, while 1976 and 2000 were years with more centrist candidates, based on the perceived placement of the major party candidates on a standard liberal–conservative scale by the most informed survey respondents. Consistent with our prediction, the mean number of correct voters in the three years with ideologically distinct candidates, 78.6%, is greater than the number of correct votes in the two years with more centrist candidates running, 75.1% ($z = 3.33$, $p < .001$).

The data necessary for testing Hypothesis 3 is less straightforward. Each section of Table 4.3 includes five additional columns of data: the percentage of voters in the survey who reported voting for one of the major presidential candidates that year; the percentage of votes each candidate would have received if all voters, by our calculations, had voted correctly; the difference between the two (a positive difference indicates the candidate received more votes than he should have, while a negative difference means he received fewer votes than he should have); the percentage of all money actually spent by each candidate (or on behalf of each candidate) during the general election campaign;[7] and finally the difference between that percentage and a fair or proportional share of the money (i.e., $100\%/c$, where c is the number of candidates).

The crucial data for Hypothesis 3 are in the two rows of deviation or difference scores. If Hypothesis 3 is correct, then candidates with a disproportionate share of campaign resources (i.e., a positive difference in the sixth column of the table) should be able to win more votes than they correctly should have (i.e., a positive difference in the fourth column of the table); candidates with disproportionately fewer campaign resources should, all else being equal, receive fewer votes than they should have. Thus, Hypothesis 3 predicts a positive correlation between disproportionate spending and disproportionate votes. The Spearman rank-order correlation between these two difference scores is .73 [$t(17) = 4.43$, $p < .001$], providing strong confirmation of the third hypothesis.

---

relative *rankings* of the three candidates on feeling thermometer evaluations, however. We therefore repeated this analysis, substituting the relative ranking measure for the actual vote choice. With this alternative criterion, the overall percentage of correct votes (i.e., rankings) actually falls to 61.8%. If we limit the analysis to voters who evaluated the Democrat or Republican highest (our equivalent to major party voters), the percentage correct rises to 66.5%. In neither case would it appear that strategic voting considerations provide an alternative explanation for these results.

[7] These spending figures are reported in great detail in Alexander (1975, 1979, 1983); Alexander and Haggerty (1987); Alexander and Bauer (1991); Alexander and Corrado (1995); Corrado (1997, 2001).

IMPLICATIONS

Any political philosophy presumes a view, a psychological theory, of human behavior. Classic democratic theory sets unrealistic standards for ideal citizens at least in part because it holds unrealistic expectations about the very nature of human cognition. Beginning with a more circumscribed human psychology, we can set more realistic goals for democratic citizens – and still judge how readily those goals are met.

We offer a very simple standard: Irrespective of how the vote decision is actually reached, how frequently do voters vote correctly? To ask this question implies that one has an answer to it, or at least a method for obtaining the answer. Relying on notions of fully informed interests, we have suggested one such method. Our analysis of both experimental and survey data show that our method does a reasonably good job of measuring correct voting. Had we relied only on the experimental data and its rather artificial full-information correct-voting determination, our findings would have been of more limited value. But the second measure of correct voting, available in both experiments and surveys, should prove to be much more useful because it is much more widely applicable. Moreover, that we have found corroborating evidence from two very different research designs lends much credence to either set of findings alone.

Taking our results at face value, we can return to the question with which we started this chapter: Is 72% of voters voting correctly in a typical presidential election "good enough" for a system of government to be considered truly democratic? We are pleasantly surprised by these results: This high a level of correct voting certainly validates the efficiency of heuristic-based information processing that underlies our view of human nature. Moreover, it challenges those critics who hold that democracies' problems stem primarily from people not having the motivation to gather the information to be able to figure out what is in their best interest. Most people, most of the time, can make this calculation, at least in presidential elections.

But is this level high enough for us to consider that (at least) the American version of democracy works at some minimal level? It is certainly too soon to draw any firm conclusions to this question in any case, and we should mention several very important caveats to our findings.

1. If 72% of voters are voting correctly in the typical presidential election, then 28% are voting incorrectly. If this 28% were distributed randomly it would not be much of a problem, but our test of Hypothesis 3 above demonstrates that it is not randomly distributed: Candidates with more money have an advantage. Here is yet one more

argument (as if another is needed) for the importance of serious campaign reform for American elections.

2. The analyses in Table 4.3 only consider voters – but barely 50% of the American public votes. The interests of nonvoters is beyond the scope of our analysis, but it certainly is not beyond the scope of theoretical concern.

3. We have examined presidential elections only, but our federal system ensures that much of what is important in politics happens at lower levels of government. Unfortunately, we would expect lower levels of correct voting at lower levels of government – or at least for elections with less media attention than presidential elections, which is to say, all other elections. If 72% of voters vote correctly for president and 62% vote correctly for mayor, we would be quite happy. If 72% vote correctly for president and 32% vote correctly for mayor, we would not.

Political science as a field has only begun to map out the correct-voting landscape. A great deal more research must be conducted before empirical political science can be of much help to normative theorists struggling with this question.

Whatever may ultimately prove to be the answer to the question of the extent to which any system of government can be considered truly democratic, no one would argue that things cannot be improved. Given a metric of correct voting, we can turn to the equally important question of what leads people to make more or less optimal decisions. This question can be addressed at both the individual and institutional levels. For example, we could ask if particular information search tactics or different decision or choice strategies lead some individuals to make better decisions than others. We cannot simply assume that all voters use heuristics and other information shortcuts equally effectively (see Bartels, 1996). We will have much more to say about this in subsequent chapters. We could also ask whether different practices the media have developed for covering campaigns encourage or discourage the more effective information processing strategies. We could ask whether institutional arrangements that favor two-party systems or that separate the fates of executives and legislators change the probability of correct voting. And we could study whether certain campaign tactics are particularly effective in distorting the correct outcome of an election, and if so consider means of discouraging those tactics. All of these questions – which we believe a "relevant" political science ought to be asking – can only be addressed with a defensible measure of correct voting.[8]

---

[8] Lau et al., 2005, provide preliminary answers to some of these questions.

This concludes the first major section of the book. The next section presents the initial results of our experiments, focusing on information processing and memory. Chapter 5 illustrates, in very broad outlines, what voters in our mock elections actually *did*. Most importantly, in Chapter 5 we describe how the information processing variables and choice strategies discussed earlier were actually measured or operationalized in our studies. With these basic measurement concerns out of the way, Chapter 6 is the first of two chapters focusing on different predictors of information processing and memory. Chapter 6 considers what voters bring with them to any election – a general level of political sophistication or expertise, long-standing political preferences, and (more speculatively) a gendered perspective on voting. Chapter 7 then brings in campaign factors: the number of candidates running in an election, their familiarity, their ideological distinctiveness, their stereotypic nature, the resources available to candidates to air campaign ads, the timing and nature of those ads, and so on. Each of these sets of predictors must be examined if we are to fully understand information processing during an election campaign.

This is a lot of ground to cover, but it will make us much better prepared to begin understanding how people decide how to vote.

Part II. Information Processing

5

What Voters Do – A First Cut

We have two goals for this chapter. First and foremost, we want to describe, in broad outlines, what voters in our mock election campaigns actually did. Now, our "broad outlines" may seem like the minutest details to many students of politics, who typically are primarily concerned with which candidate – or even which party's candidate – won the election. But remember that our purpose is to get inside the heads of ordinary citizens while they are making their vote decisions. To accomplish this goal, we must dig much deeper than simply observing the vote choice and trying to explain it from preelection political attitudes and values.

Second, we must describe the actual measures and operationalizations of the information processing and search variables described at a more conceptual level in Chapter 2, which provide the windows for looking (if not actually getting) inside the heads of our voters. It is precisely these data that no previous students of the vote decision have had, and because they are unique to our study, we must carefully describe how the crucial variables are constructed.

Because most of the measures we rely upon will be unfamiliar to most of our readers, we must spend sufficient time describing them. These measures are so central to our undertaking that this discussion cannot be relegated to appendices. Thus, a full understanding of what is to follow requires the reader to work through this chapter carefully. If on the other hand one is willing to take our word that we are measuring what we say we are, you can probably get by with just skimming this chapter to briefly acquaint yourself with what it contains. Then if when reading subsequent chapters you find yourself wondering how we actually measured one of the concepts we are talking about, you can return to this chapter and read more carefully.

All of our studies included a primary election campaign, with multiple Democrats and Republicans competing for their party's nomination, and most of our studies also included a general election campaign, where one of the Democrats faced off against one of the Republicans. These two types of campaigns, even though they involve some of the same candidates, provide radically different decision contexts for two important reasons. First, party affiliation, the most important predictor of vote outcomes, and probably the most informative cue one can get about any politician, is absent as a distinguishing factor in a primary election because all of the relevant candidates in a choice set (that is, in the Democratic or Republican primaries) share the same party affiliation. We are not the first political scientists to notice this difference, although primary elections have drawn far less scholarly interest than general election campaigns (see Aldrich, 1980, and Bartels, 1988, for rare exceptions). The absence of party affiliation as a distinguishing factor makes the vote choice in a primary election more difficult to reach than a decision involving candidates from different parties, and it may be reached in a very different manner. Furthermore, the general election campaign always follows the primaries so that the candidates themselves – at least those who make it to the general election campaign – are much more familiar to voters. For these reasons, we will present the data separately for these two types of election campaigns.

Even more radically different are the dynamic and static information boards that we used in one of our experiments. Most of our data come from the more realistic dynamic format, and we will focus on that. Indeed, unless we explicitly say otherwise, all the information we provide in this chapter was gathered with the dynamic information board format. Later in the book, we will use the static information board data to compare how the use of cognitive shortcuts (heuristics) might work in a perfect world, but otherwise we analyze the dynamic information board results.

HOW MUCH INFORMATION DID VOTERS GATHER?

Primary Campaign

Figure 5.1 displays the number of items voters chose to learn during the primary election campaign of our experiments. The mean is just under seventy-four items, with a standard deviation of almost twenty-seven. This works out to accessing four or five new things about the candidates every minute of the campaign when a political advertisement was not disrupting the voter's ability to access what he or she wanted to learn.[1] Most of this mean is comprised of voters learning information about

---

[1] Another way to look at this data would be to add ten to twelve items to each observation, one for each political advertisement a voter was exposed to. We have chosen to limit this discussion to the information voters chose to learn about the candidates, but the reader should not forget that in our experiments, as in actual

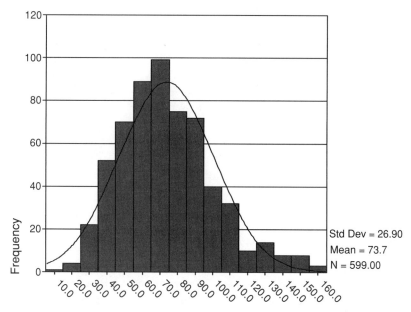

Figure 5.1. Number of items accessed, primary election.

individual candidates, although some of it (about seventeen items, on average) was comprised of group endorsements or poll results that, by their nature, applied to multiple candidates – all the Democrats or all the Republicans – and some of it (about fourteen items, on average) was comprised of the voter reaccessing something previously examined.

It is more instructive to look at how voters distributed their information seeking across the different candidates in the campaign. Recall that all voters had to register to vote in the Democratic or Republican primary before the primary campaign began, and that they all subsequently experienced a primary campaign with two or four Democrats and two or four Republicans.[2] We limit the analysis here to the three experiments

campaigns, voters are exposed to some political information they have not actively chosen to learn.

[2] We allowed voters to register with any party they wished, and we would have to expect that a few self-identified Democrats would register to vote in the Republican primary, and vice versa, just as in real life partisans sometimes "cross-register." In fact, 24 of the 556 voters expressing some partisan leanings (4%) registered to vote in the opposite party's primary. Whether this was done in error, or for some strategic purpose, we do not know. We have never seen any figures about how many partisans in real life cross-register, but our figures do not strike us as too far out of line. Forty-nine of the 79 pure independents (62%) registered to vote in the Democratic primary, with the remainder in the Republican primary. Throughout the following chapters,

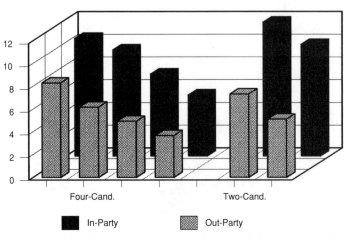

Figure 5.2. Number of unique items accessed per candidate, primary election.

with a total of six candidates in the primary election (our other study always had two candidates in each primary) so that whenever there were two Democrats there were four Republicans, and vice versa. We have no reason to think that Democrats are any different from Republicans when it comes to basic information processing (in the next chapter, we will look to make sure), but it does seem plausible that voters will treat candidates from their own party ("in-party" candidates) differently from candidates from the other party ("out-party" candidates). Indeed, if voters were acting in a purely rational Model 1 manner, they would figure out the party affiliation of the different candidates early and restrict search entirely to in-party candidates, at least until they had made up their minds how to vote. It also seems reasonable that the number of in-party candidates should affect the amount of information search per candidate, if only because there is only so much time available, and it must be divided between two in-party candidates in some conditions, and four in-party candidates in the other. Of course another possibility is that information search is random, in which case none of these differences will occur, and we will simply observe an approximately equal number of items accessed about each of the six available candidates.

Figure 5.2 presents the mean number of unique items learned about each in-party and each out-party candidate, separately for the four- and two-candidate conditions.[3] The in-party candidates are represented by

when we refer to the "in-party" and the "out-party," our reference is to the party in whose primary the subject registered to vote, not to any self-professed partisanship.
[3] This manipulation always refers to the number of candidates in the in-party, in the voter's actual choice set, although it simultaneously indicates the number of

dark bars in the back of the figure, while the out-party candidates are represented by light bars in the front. For the in-party, for each condition, we single out the candidate subjects voted for and place the number of items accessed about him or her to the left, arranging the number of items accessed about the remaining in-party candidates in descending order. There is no chosen out-party candidate, so for each condition we sort the number of items accessed about the different candidates, and list them in descending order.

Three patterns are clear in the data. First, holding the number of candidates running in a party's primary constant, there is more search devoted to in-party candidates than to out-party candidates, although the amount of search devoted to the out-party is far greater than would be expected if voters were acting in a purely rational manner and focusing only on candidates within the choice set. Second, for both the in-party and the out-party, search per candidate is greater when there are only two candidates (rather than four) running in a party's primary, but total search for all candidates in the party is greater when there are four candidates to sum across rather than two. And third, even within the party, search is not equal across candidates; it is graded such that voters choose to learn much more about some candidates than others. For the in-party, it is the candidate for whom subjects voted (the leftmost in the figure) who gets the most attention. Search goes down about two items per candidate as we move to the right in Figure 5.2. The same general pattern holds for the out-party, although none of them can be singled out as the chosen candidate.

Even at this early stage in our analyses, we feel very safe in concluding that information search in our experiments was not random. There is some method to the madness of how voters cope with the overwhelming demands of a high-level political campaign. Making sense of that method is the challenge before us.

These data from the entire primary campaign could be obscuring more subtle patterns of search occurring at different times during the campaign. For example, it would be surprising if early in the campaign voters were devoting more search to the candidate they would ultimately chose, before they had had much of a chance to make that determination. Likewise, search could be largely limited to in-party candidates during the first part of the campaign, with voters turning to learning about the out-party candidates only after they have decided whom to pick among their own

candidates in the out-party. By "unique" items, we mean we are excluding (or counting only once) instances where the same item was examined more than once. We are also not considering here group endorsements and polls, which present information about multiple candidates.

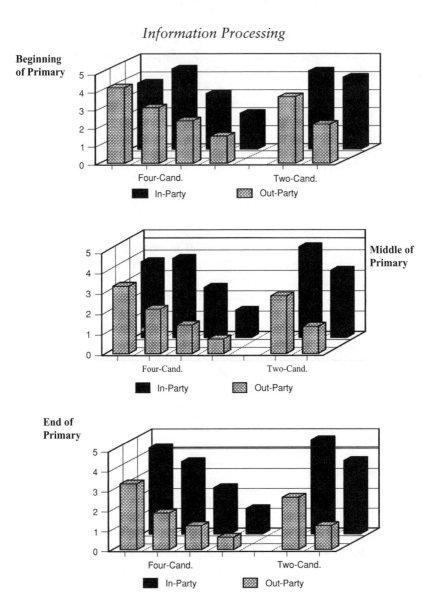

Figure 5.3. Unique items accessed per candidate, each third of primary campaign.

party's alternatives. To examine these possibilities, we divided the primary campaign into thirds and repeated the preceding analysis for each third of the campaign.

Figure 5.3 presents the results. Starting with the in-party, there is no clear differentiation between the chosen candidate and the others in the four-candidate condition until the final third of the campaign, when the chosen candidate receives the most attention. In the first two thirds of the campaign, however, one of the other candidates received as much search (slightly more, actually) as the candidate the voters ultimately selected in the voting booth. In the two-candidate condition, on the other hand, this determination was made earlier, by the middle of the primary, when we can clearly observe more search being devoted to the candidate who will ultimately receive their vote. This makes perfect sense, and it is yet another indication that it is harder to choose among four alternatives than among two.

Turning to the out-party, the pattern of search looks pretty much the same at the beginning, middle, and end of the primary. We cannot observe a growing shift toward any particular candidate, as we did for the in-party, nor is there any reason that we should. People are not choosing among the out-party candidates. It does seem clear that there is no shift toward greater attention to the out-party later in the campaign, however. In fact, contrary to our speculations, if anything there is slightly more search going to out-party candidates at the beginning of the campaign compared to later. Whatever voters are doing learning about the out-party candidates during the primary, there is no detectable "rational" shifting of attention to the potential candidates in the general election once the in-party primary vote choice has been made.

General Election Campaign

Figure 5.4 presents the total number of items accessed by voters during the general election campaign of all four of our experiments. The distribution is again approximately normal, with a slight skew to the right. The mean is a little more than forty-eight items accessed, almost precisely two thirds of the mean number of items accessed during the primary, which is not surprising given that the length of the general election campaign was approximately two thirds of the length of the primary campaign. Evidently voters continued to access information at about the same rate as during the primary – four to five new items per minute. This is divided between two candidates rather than six, however, so average information searched per candidate was greater in the general election than the primary.

On the other hand, not all the information accessed during the general election campaign was new. Virtually all the candidate-specific information available during the general election campaign could also have been accessed during the primary. Only candidates' "General Election Campaign Strategy" and their "Debate Performance" were entirely new to the general election campaign. If we look at only new information accessed during the general election – the candidate-specific information that had not been accessed during the primary campaign, plus new group

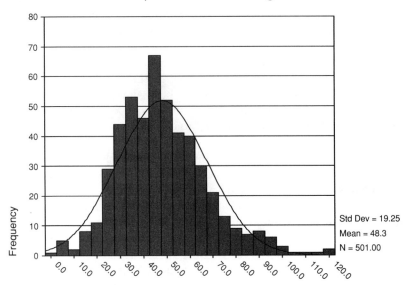

Figure 5.4. Number of items accessed, general election.

endorsements and poll results pertaining to the general election – and ignore any reaccessing of the same information already examined at least once during the general election campaign, the total drops to a little over thirty-five.

Figure 5.5 breaks this down by the in-party and out-party candidates, where again "in-party" and "out-party" refers to the party in whose primary the subject registered to vote. The in-party candidate enters the general election campaign of our mock election being better known by most voters than the out-party candidate, judging by the amount that had been learned about these two candidates during the primary. This disadvantage to the out-party candidate would have been worse, had we not designed most of our experiments to make the general election choice as difficult as possible by preventing the candidate the voter supported in the primary from making it to the general election. (In other words, our voters' choice usually lost the primary election.) The average number of accessed items about the in-party candidate running in the general election was 8.5 (comparted to 6.1 for the out-party candidate), significantly less than the 10–12 items voters had learned about the candidate they had supported in the primary. The informational imbalance between the two candidates running in the general election at the outset of the campaign is exacerbated by voters' actions during the general election campaign itself, however, when voters on average learn two more things about the in-party

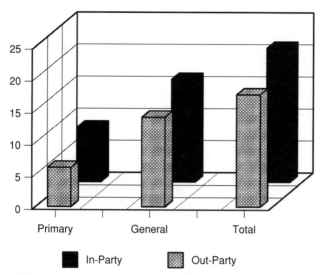

Figure 5.5. Unique items accessed per candidate running in each election campaign.

candidate than the out-party candidate (16 vs. 14). This results in an overall information advantage to the in-party candidate of about 3.4 items.

This difference, we should note, is exactly what is predicted by Model 2, which suggests that search will be biased toward the in-party candidate and counter to the demands of Model 1 and Model 3, which dictate equal search across candidates.[4] Of course, our electorate could still be comprised of a mix of Model 1 and Model 3 voters, on the one hand, who consider pretty equal amounts of information about the two candidates, and Model 2 and Model 4 voters, on the other hand, for whom the disparity is much greater than the four-item mean difference suggested by the data in Figure 5.5. We will defer that question until later in this chapter. For now, all we can say for sure is that there are a lot of voters who are not utilizing a compensatory decision strategy.

The number of items accessed about the two candidates during the primary and general election campaigns do not add up to the totals reported to the right of Figure 5.5 because the numbers from the general election

---

[4] In fact, to the extent voters directed the bulk of their search during the primary toward the in-party candidates who were actually in their choice set – which is rational, and which in practice we know they did – compensatory decision strategies like Model 1 would predict disproportionate search directed toward the out-party candidate during the general election to compensate for this earlier imbalance. This clearly did not happen.

campaign include items that had previously been accessed during the primary election campaign. On average, about three of the fourteen to sixteen candidate-specific items voters looked at about each candidate running in the general election campaign were items they had previously examined during the primary. If we assume that all the items that were reaccessed had been effectively forgotten (reasonable), and that all of the items that were not reaccessed had been remembered (dubious), this would put memory at about 80% of what had been learned during the primary, *at most thirty minutes earlier*. This is an upper-bound figure; we have a good deal of evidence, to be presented later, that forgetting is much greater than this. For now let us just state that the effects of voters' cognitive limits can be seen, even in the context of our brief experimental mock campaign.

WHAT KINDS OF INFORMATION DID VOTERS GATHER? THE CONTENT OF SEARCH

We have now painted a reasonably clear picture of how much information our voters chose to learn about the candidates in our campaigns. But what was its content? That is, what types of information did voters want to learn? Here we must remind readers that all information was not equally available. As we noted in the previous chapter, the availability of different types of information differed widely, modeled after the actual availability of that same type of information during the 1988 presidential election. If our subjects were randomly selecting information, they would have selected it in about the same proportion as its availability.

The data, from the primary campaign, are shown in Figure 5.6. We group the information into five general categories: *Person* information, including each candidate's background, personality, their pictures, and judgments about his or her current job performance; *Hoopla and Horse Race,* including poll results, campaign slogans, and reports on each candidate's campaign strategies; *Issues,* including each candidate's stand on economic, foreign policy, and a variety of social issues; *Party,* consisting solely of reports of each candidate's party affiliations; and *Endorsements,* reports of each candidate's endorsements of twelve to fourteen political interest groups. The percentage of actual items accessed falling into each of these categories are displayed in the front row of Figure 5.6; the percentage of that same type of information available is shown in the back row of the figure. The two sets of data are not exactly the same. Our voters accessed a little less person information than would be expected by chance (35.6% observed vs. 40.7% available), and a little more issue information (23.0% vs. 18.5%) and group endorsements (10.4% vs. 7.4%). Still, the overall impression one gets from the figure is that the content of the campaign strongly determined the content of information search. If we

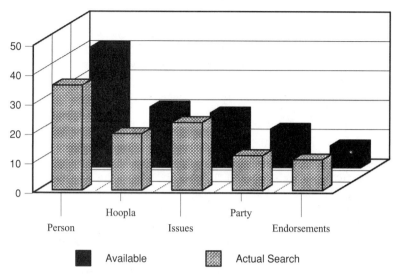

Figure 5.6. Content of search, primary election campaign.

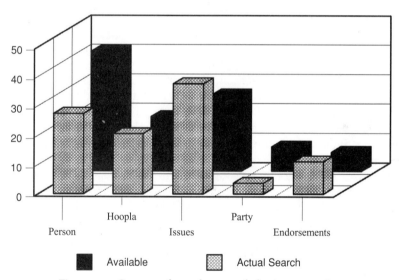

Figure 5.7. Content of search, general election campaign.

correlate these two measures, treating each category equally, the overall rank-order association between the two is a very respectable .80 ($p < .05$).

In contrast, look at the comparable data from the general election campaign, presented in Figure 5.7. Now it is easy to see clear distinctions between what was available and what voters actually examined. Voters looked at more issue information (37.5% vs. 25.9%), endorsements (11.1% vs. 6.5%), and hoopla (20.5% vs. 18.5%) and less person (27.3% vs 40.7%) and party information (3.7% vs. 8.3%) than would be expected by chance. The overall rank-order correlation between these two measures drops to a nonsignificant .60.

How can we explain the difference between these two observed patterns of information search? We cannot give a definitive answer, but we would speculate that because there are so many candidates running during the primary campaign – all of whom are totally new and unfamiliar – people have a relatively difficult time executing coherent search strategies. In such a context, the information environment (i.e., what is available) has a relatively large effect. Voters can shape the amount of information they learn about different candidates, but only grossly, particularly during the first two thirds of the primary campaign. By the time the general election campaign comes around, however, there are only two candidates still running, voters already know a little about them, and they have a pretty decent idea of the type of information that will become available. In such a context, it is much easier for voters to influence significantly the type of information they learn about the candidates.

MEMORY

So far we have been focusing exclusively on information search or acquisition. But what about the retention of that information – that is, memory? We previously looked indirectly at memory, when we took the reaccessing of information as a sign of forgetting. But we have more direct measures of memory than that. The content and structure of memory are standard (indirect) indicators in the psychological literature of information processing, where the type of detailed information search provided by our process-tracing methodology is often absent. In that case, it is quite reasonable to assume, for example, that quantity of memory is a good indication of depth of processing. Memory does not play that same role for us, however, because we have much more precise data available. Instead, memory in our model is a function of, a consequence of, prior information processing. It is common sense to assume that the more information about a particular object one is exposed to, the greater the contents of memory about that object will be. Given cognitive limits, the relationship should flatten out eventually, but at relatively low levels of information exposure, the relationship to memory should be mostly linear. We will also hypothesize that the greater the structure to the information search is – the more candidate-based and/or attribute-based search a person utilizes – the greater the memory becomes.

The role that memory plays in decision making is another question. The on-line processing model (Lodge, McGraw, and Stroh, 1989; Lodge, Steenbergen, and Brau, 1995) argues that memory plays little or no role in the vote choice, or rather the only role for memory is retrieving the running tally evaluations of the competing candidates. Memory for the bases of those evaluations is irrelevant. We see a much more important role for memory. But before we can explore any of these questions – and we will look at them all in subsequent chapters – we need to describe our measures of memory.

First, a little background information is necessary. Memory has been studied a great deal in psychology (see Norman, 1976, 1982, for reviews), and one of the most common findings is that people process information differently if you tell them ahead of time that you are going to ask them to recall the stimuli they are exposed to.[5] Even with the explosion of public opinion polling, people do not normally walk around processing political information with the understanding that someone will eventually ask them to recall any of it, so it is important that the voters in our experiments were similarly blissfully ignorant. Thus, we were careful to never mention anything about memory until near the end of our experiments, after subjects had been exposed to and voted in the various campaigns, when we unexpectedly asked our subjects to recall as much as they could about the two candidates running in the general election. Voters were given two sheets of paper, one for each of the general election candidates (in random order), and asked to jot down "everything they could remember" about the two candidates.[6] After at least several minutes, when subjects said they could not remember anything more, we asked them to go back and look at what they had written down and to tell us whether, when they

---

[5] Somewhat paradoxically, people typically have a harder time remembering things when they have been forewarned that they will subsequently be asked to recall them, compared to when they have been instructed ahead of time to try to "form an impression" of a hypothetical person being described. The typical experimental paradigm is to present lists of traits that could be used to describe a person. The common explanation for this finding is that, in forming an impression of a hypothetical person, people will form a schema-like memory structure with links to the different traits learned about the hypothetical person, which aids subsequent recall. People trying to remember specific trait information may not link the different items together, making subsequent recall much more difficult.

[6] In Study 2 there was no general election. Subjects were given the memory test for all six candidates in the primary. For half of those subjects, the memory test was expected; for the other half, it was not. Redlawsk (2001a) describes these data, but in this book we will generally limit our attention to memory of the two candidates involved in the general election campaign, except where we otherwise indicate.

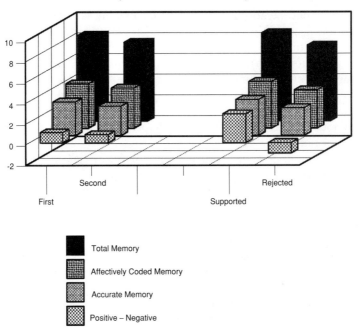

Figure 5.8. Memory for general election candidates.

learned this particular bit of information, it made them like this candidate more, like the candidate less, or did not really change their opinion of the candidate. In other words, we asked voters to code their own memories as positive, negative, or neutral about each candidate.[7]

The left-hand side of Figure 5.8 displays the basic information. On average, subjects could recall about eight things about each of the two candidates, somewhat more about the candidate randomly listed first rather than second (8.3 vs. 7.6 items). This difference was expected[8] and was the reason for the random ordering. About half of that information for each

[7] This method contrasts with that used by the ANES, who ask respondents to provide their memories already categorized into positive and negative (i.e., reasons to vote for and against each candidate). If people have affectively neutral memories about a candidate – that he is from Texas, say – they presumably would not bother reporting them to the ANES. Thus, all else being equal, one might expect more memories reported with our question than with the ANES's method. All else is certainly not equal, however, so any comparisons between our results and the ANES's are confounded by many factors in addition to question wording.

[8] Randomizing the order of recall is important because we would expect that searching through memory about one candidate would make memories about any other candidate slightly more difficult to retrieve. The difference, though relatively slight, is highly significant: $t(496) = 5.24, p < .001$.

candidate (4.3 items for the first candidate, 3.9 items for the second) was affectively coded – that is, it made the voter like the candidate more or less. To put these numbers in some perspective, ANES respondents typically report between 2.5 and 3.0 reasons to vote for and against each of the major party candidates in actual presidential elections.

A more telling way to present this information is to rearrange it by the candidates the subjects voted for and against. The right-hand side of Figure 5.8 presents this information. Voters could recall significantly more information about the candidate they supported in the election than the one they did not support (8.5 vs. 7.3 items; $t(449) = 10.03$, $p < .001$); they could also remember more affectively coded information (4.5 vs. 3.7 items; $t(437) = 8.93$, $p < .001$) for the candidate they supported. Moreover, the *affective implications* of that memory – (i.e., positive memories minus negative memories) is much more favorable to the candidate the person voted for (+2.8 vs. −1.0; $t(437) = 19.24$, $p < .001$). This pattern still appears in our data, even without specifically asking for reasons to vote for and against each candidate, which as we argue in note 7 in this chapter, partially "builds in" such a correlation.

In our first and fourth studies, we were able to code the general election memories for their accuracy. We had no way of judging the accuracy of about half of the reported memories, almost all of which mentioned a personal reaction to something about one of the candidates (e.g., "I liked his issue stands," "He would ruin the economy," "I just didn't like him"). But the remaining memories mentioned something more clearly about the candidates themselves, and these memories could usually be judged for their accuracy. Statements such as "He was liberal," "He was pro-life," or "The cops liked him" (which we translated into "He was endorsed by the American Association of Police Officers") could all be judged as true or false. We certainly did not expect verbatim reporting of any of the information, so we adopted a fairly lenient "gist" criterion for judging the accuracy of any statement. Still, this proved to be an extremely time-consuming task, as each memory had to be linked to one or more specific items that had been accessed or to some text contained in one of the ads the voter had been exposed to.[9] We would not count a memory as "accurate," even if it were in fact true about the candidate in question, if we could not identify some specific source for this information.

On average, three of the four reported memories about each candidate that could be coded for accuracy, were judged as being accurate. And once again, there was an advantage for the candidate the person voted for in the general election (4.3 vs. 3.4 accurate memories; $t(283) = 7.01$, $p < .001$).

---

[9] Coding reliability varied between .86 and .97, depending upon the task.

Information Processing

DECISION STRATEGIES

Chapter 2 presented a number of formal decision strategies associated with our four different models of decision making. We want to determine which of these rules best describes the decision making of voters during political campaigns. As described in Chapter 2, the various decision strategies can be differentiated by the depth of search, the comparability of search across alternatives, and the sequence of information gathering. Before turning to decision strategies, we first must develop measures of these different concepts.

Depth of Search

Several different measures of the depth of information search are available to us. The first two come from imagining an attributes by alternatives matrix of the classic static decision board. One measure is the number of alternatives (columns) that were considered, that is, did the voter examine at least something about every candidate? A second measure is the number of attributes (rows) that were considered, that is, the number of "considerations" by which the alternatives were compared. These two measures are easy to compute: They simply involve counting the number of candidates, and then attributes, which were considered at least once. It makes sense to limit consideration to information relevant to candidates in the voter's choice set, which eliminates any information gathered during the primary campaign about the out-party candidates. This also means that in the primary we should not look simply at the number of in-party candidates that were considered; instead, we should look at the proportion because the number of candidates running in the primary was manipulated and thus differed randomly across voters.

It turns out that the number of alternatives considered has too little variance to be of much use to us, no matter how it is measured. Only 8 of our 656 subjects did not access at least one candidate-specific bit of information about every in-party candidate running in the primary, and if we consider looking at group endorsements or poll results as gathering information relevant to all candidates in the campaign, then all voters in our experiments considered every alternative in the primary. The same is true for the general election campaign. It could be that, unlike buying a car or choosing an apartment, the norms of elections dictate that all alternatives on the ballot be considered. This is certainly true, although another explanation for our failure to find much variance in this measure is the relatively small number of candidates running in our elections compared to the number of different models of cars, say, that would basically suit a car buyer's needs. Had we been modeling an Israeli election, for example, with twenty or more parties running candidates, we undoubtedly would have seen more variance in this measure. In any case, the number of alternatives considered does not provide us with any useful information.

The number of attributes considered does provide us with useful information, however. Even though we had a relatively small number of candidates running in our campaigns, there was a large number of attributes across which those candidates differed – forty-five candidate-specific items (forty-six items in the general election campaign), twelve to fourteen endorsements, and fifteen to twenty polls. Each of these could have been considered by voters, and many of them were: an average of almost thirty-six in the primary, with a range of thirteen to fifty-five, and a mean of almost thirty-four in the general election (with a range of two to sixty-three). So here is a measure with a good deal of variance across voters.

The most intuitive measure of depth of search, of course, is the total amount of information that was accessed. This is what comes first to our minds. Again, we limit consideration to information relevant to candidates in the voter's choice set, so we exclude information accessed about out-party candidates during the primary. But our readers should already see a possible problem with this simple, intuitive measure of depth of search – it is affected by the number of alternatives in the choice set. Look back at Figure 5.2. There is more total search devoted to a party when there are four rather that two candidates running in that party's primary – and this is true for both the in-party and the out-party. But there is more search per candidate when there are only two candidates running in a party's primary. Which of these two measures, then, better captures what we commonly understand "depth of search" to mean? Holding the number of candidates constant, it won't matter, and either measure will do equally well. But when the number of candidates vary, as they do in most of our primary election campaigns, it makes a clear difference. Defined in terms of the total number of unique items devoted to in-party candidates, there is deeper search in the four-candidate condition. Defined in terms of average number of unique items per in-party candidate, there is deeper search in the two-party condition.

We could make a case for either measure, and have gone back and forth in our own thinking. Ultimately we decided to sit on the fence and use both of them, along with the number of attributes considered, in a summary measure of depth of search. This somewhat inelegant solution has the advantage of removing any built-in relationship between our number-of-candidates manipulation and depth of search. Thus in the end, we have three distinct measures of the depth of search from both the primary and general election campaigns, the number of attributes considered during the campaign, the total number of unique items considered about candidates in the choice set, and the average number of unique items selected

Depth of Search   **Comparability of Search**

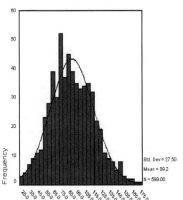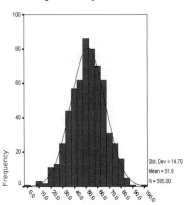

% Attribute-Base ÷ %Candidate-Based Search   **Systematic Search**

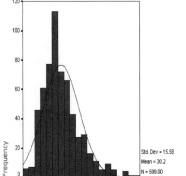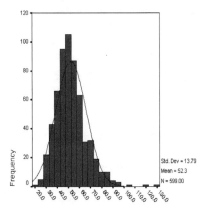

Figure 5.9. Distribution of different measures of information search, primary election campaign.

per candidate (per in-party candidate for the primary). This summary scale has a reliability (coefficient alpha) of .92 in the primary and .98 in the general election. The distribution of this summary variable (from the primary) is shown in the upper left panel of Figure 5.9.

Comparability of Search Across Candidates

A rational decision maker utilizing a compensatory decision strategy must seek out the same information about every alternative. Noncompensatory decision strategies, on the other hand, generally result in very different levels of information seeking across alternatives. The standard indicator of the equality of information search across alternative is the variance of the amount of information gathered across alternatives. If the same number of attributes is considered about every candidate, the inter-alternative variance will be very small; if the amount of information gathered about the candidates differs widely, however, that variance will be relatively high. High variance is associated with low equality across alternatives, and vice versa.

This measure works well when information search is under the decision maker's control, as it is in the ideal world represented by a static information board. But when the number of attributes that could be considered is large, decision time is limited, and information search is much more difficult to control, as is the case in a presidential election campaign (and our experiments), this measure could be quite misleading. Voters in our four-candidate primary could have considered ten different candidate-specific items about every in-party candidate – thus producing zero inter-alternative variance – and still have absolutely no overlap between candidates in the information examined!

We therefore devised a much more direct measure of the comparability of search across alternatives: the percentage of all attributes considered about any relevant candidate compared to that considered about all relevant candidates.[10] This hypothetical example would have 40 in the denominator and 0 in the numerator, resulting in a comparability score of 0, reflecting the low comparability across alternatives that is appropriate in this instance.

Our new measure of the comparability of search across alternatives ranges from 0 to 98% in the primary, with a mean of 51.8%, and ranges from 31 to 90% for the general election, with a mean of 59%. Its correlation with the standard variance score is only −.18 in the primary (−.29 in the general election), reflecting our belief that the variance is a poor indicator of the concept we are trying to measure.[11] We will rely on our direct measure as the indicator of choice. Its distribution from the primary election is shown in the upper right-hand panel of Figure 5.9.

[10] With this definition, it is much more difficult to have a high comparability-of-search score with four alternatives to consider, compared to only two. The likelihood of not even seeing some desired information about one of four candidates (because it scrolled down the screen when a political ad hid what was available) was pretty high. To compensate for this difficulty, in the four-candidate condition of the primary election, we increased the numerator whenever information was examined about three or four candidates. Note that group endorsements and polls are relevant to every alternative in the choice set, so they increase both the numerator and the denominator equally.

[11] The negative correlations are expected because variance translates into low comparability. But the low magnitude of the correlation (i.e., that it is fairly close to 0) indicates that the two are not measuring the same thing.

Sequence of search refers primarily to whether search was largely candidate-based (intra-alternative, inter-attribute) or attribute-based (intra-attribute, inter-alternative). The standard measure is the ratio of intra-alternative to intra-attribute transitions. In our studies, however, when there were relatively few alternatives compared to the attributes, it was much more difficult to make intra-attribute transitions. Indeed, with our dynamic information board and only six different items available for access at any point in time, it was relatively difficult to make either intra-attribute or intra-candidate transitions, at least in the primary when there were six alternatives to choose from. With a static information board, it is always possible to make either an intra-attribute or an intra-alternative transition, so a straightforward count of the number of intra-attribute transitions divided by the total number of transitions[12] is a good indicator of the prevalence of intra-attribute transitions. In practice in our studies, however, while a decision maker trying to conduct an intra-candidate search would rarely have to wait too long for another item about the candidate in question to come along, the wait would typically be much greater for a decision maker trying to conduct intra-attribute search.

We therefore created new measures of the sequence of search, the percentage of all possible intra-alternative and intra-attribute transitions that were made. The realm of the possible was defined over the period of time between accessing any two items. Suppose a voter examines Thomas's stand on abortion during one of our campaigns. He finishes reading about this stand, returns to the campaign, and then accesses Thomas's family background. This is an intra-candidate transition and is counted as such. Both the number of intra-candidate transitions and the number of possible intra-candidate transitions increases by one. It is quite conceivable, however, that it was not possible to make an intra-attribute transition because no other candidate's stand on abortion was ever available for access before the next item was chosen. In that case, the number of possible intra-attribute transitions would not increase. Now, if it were possible to select another candidate's stand on abortion, but the voter had nonetheless decided to select a different item about Thomas, then the number of possible intra-attribute transitions would increase by one.

These measures were more difficult to compute than they are to describe, although little more than brute computer power is required to keep track of everything. The percentage of possible intra-candidate transitions ranged from 10 to 100% in the primary, with a mean of 38.9%. Intra-candidate transitions ranged from 32 to 100% in the general

---

[12] The total number of transitions equals the number of items examined, minus one.

election, with a mean of 76.5%. The percentage of possible intra-attribute transitions ranged from 0 to 100% in the primary, with a mean of 13.6%. The full 0 to 100% range was observed for this measure in the general election campaigns as well, where the mean was 44%.

We then created two summary measures from these variables for both the primary and general election campaigns: the log of the ratio of possible intra-attribute to possible intra-candidate transitions, to represent the relative prevalence of these two major types of transitions, and the sum of the two variables, to represent the amount of *systematic* search – either intra-candidate or intra-attribute. The former is needed to help distinguish between decision strategies; the latter could prove useful in indicating the extent to which a voter was able to examine information in the context of our dynamic information board systematically. The distributions of these two variables from the primary campaign are displayed in the bottom two panels of Figure 5.9.

Operationalizing Decision Strategies

These measures of depth, comparability, and sequence of search provide a great deal of information about how voters decided how to vote. The best way to summarize this information is to use these measures to see if we can match up individual voters with any of the decision strategies described in Chapter 2. Consider the information in Figure 5.10, which is a simplified version of Figure 2.2. Depth and comparability of search completely discriminate among our four models of voter decision making. Model 1 assumes relatively deep search, equally distributed across the candidates; Model 2 also assumes relatively deep search, but unequally distributed across the candidates. Model 3 assumes relatively shallow search, equally distributed across the candidates, and Model 4 assumes relatively shallow search, unequally distributed across the candidates.

	Depth of Search	*Comparability of Search*	*Sequence of Search*
Model 1c	Deep	Equal	Candidate-based
Model 1d	Deep	Equal	Dimensional
Model 2	Moderately deep	Unequal	Candidate-based most likely, but either acceptable
Model 3	Relatively shallow	Equal	Either
Model 4c	Depends: Typically shallow	Generally unequal	Candidate-based
Model 4d	Generally shallow	Generally unequal	Dimensional

Figure 5.10. Characteristics of different types of decision strategies.

Sequence of search comes into play if we make the finer distinctions between more specific decision strategies discussed in the behavioral decision theory literature, which are subsumed under are broader models. As described more fully in Appendix A, satisficing (Model 4c) and the Weighted Additive Rule (Model 1c) assume a more alternative-based than attribute-based search; Elimination-by-Aspects (Model 4d) and Additive Difference Rule (Model 1d) assume a relatively more dimensional or attribute-based than alternative-based search.

There are no absolute standards as to what constitutes deep or shallow search, equal or unequal distribution across candidates, alternative- or attribute-based sequences, however. What is reasonable in one context may be next to impossible in another. Decision makers can only adapt to the constraints of any particular decision context – and the whole point of our mock election campaigns was to design a decision context with a lot of constraints. It would be physically impossible for a voter to consider anywhere close to all possible information about all possible alternatives in our experiments, even in a two-candidate primary campaign, and it therefore would be foolish for us to adopt such a standard for categorizing someone as a Model 1 voter. Such unrealistic straw men are of little use to anyone.

But we can take these three measures, all gathered within the constraints of our mock election campaigns, and perform simple median splits on the data so that half of all voters are categorized as conducting relatively shallow search, and half are categorized as conducting relatively deep search; half of all voters are categorized as distributing their search equally across candidates, and half are categorized as distributing search unequally across candidates; and half of all voters are categorized as performing relatively more alternative-based search, and half are categorized as performing relatively more attribute-based search. This procedure allows the actual decision-making context to determine what is feasible. Within that context, some voters engaged in relatively deep search, some engaged in relatively shallow search; some in relatively comparable search across candidates, some in much less comparable search; and so on. Focusing just on depth and comparability of search, the two median splits combined result in four categories, corresponding to our Models 1 through 4. As a first and inevitably rough cut, this strategy will categorize our voters as using one of these four broad models of decision making. The median split on sequence of search can further subdivide Models 1 and 4 into the theoretically defined subcategories, if we want to do that as well.

The data from the primary and general election campaigns are shown in Figure 5.11. (At this stage, we won't bother distinguishing between the candidate-based and dimensional variants of Models 1 and 4.) This is

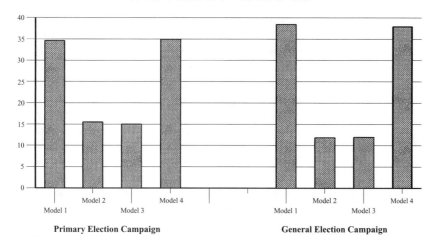

Note: Data are the percentage of all voters employing each of the different types of decision strategies based on a simple median split of the depth of search measures from the primary and general elections campaigns,respectively.

Figure 5.11. Prevalence of different decision strategies: a first cut.

actually a pretty interesting analysis, even at a descriptive level, because virtually all previous research on decision strategies has been conducted in comparatively simple decision environments. We know of no other study in a controlled environment that has attempted to identify decision strategies in a situation as complex as ours.

The median splits force some voters to fall into all of our four categories, of course, and by chance we would expect 25% in each. Clearly this is not the case – roughly 35% of our voters fall into each of Models 1 and 4, with only 15% in the remaining two categories. In general, these initial figures strike us as being reasonably plausible, with one exception: the small number of voters who are categorized as using Model 2 during the general election campaign. There is extensive prior research in political science on the vote decision from a Model 2 perspective, and this model works best in a general election context when a Democrat is facing off against a Republican. In fact, our initial procedure probably does a particularly bad job of capturing Model 2 voters, in that we are totally ignoring the prominent role of party affiliation in Model 2.

So we made a second cut at categorizing voters into our four broad models, this time also considering the priority of accessing party affiliation, particularly during the primary election campaign.[13] Model 2 voters ought

---

[13] Although Model 2 most clearly applies to a general election context where candidates differ by party, there is actually no need to go out and learn the general election candidates' party affiliations because they should already have been learned during

to learn candidates' party affiliation, and they ought to learn it soon. Of course, there is nothing inconsistent about accessing party identification in any of the other models – they just do not grant it the preordained status that Model 2 does. Hence, we must continue to consider both depth and comparability of search in categorizing even Model 2 voters.

This requirement of seeking party affiliation early sets up another hurdle for being categorized as Model 2, which can only reduce the number of Model 2 voters. To compensate for this additional hurdle, we lowered the percentile for being considered relatively "deep" search from 50% to 40% for Model 2 voters. This has the effect of transferring a few voters who were initially categorized into one of the other models, but who also accessed party affiliation pretty quickly, into Model 2. It also has the effect of leaving uncategorized some voters – those who looked at party affiliation relatively late in the campaign and who were otherwise solidly Model 2 (i.e., those who conducted such a deep search, unequally distributed across the candidates, that they could not slip into one of the other categories). Our initial median-split categorization procedure has the advantage of placing everyone into one of the four categories. After we include another consideration for one of those categories but not the others, we have the possibility of leaving some people out. This can cause statistical difficulties if the excluded group is fairly small, as it was here.

There are at least two solutions to this statistical problem. The first is to exclude the unclassified voters from all analyses; this solution has the obvious cost of eliminating subjects. The second solution is to increase the size of the unclassified group. We followed this latter solution by lowering the upper limit for shallow search to the 45th percentile, and raising the lower limit for relatively deep search to the 55th percentile, throwing all voters in the middle 10% of the measures of depth of search into an unclassified or undifferentiated category. In the following analyses, we will be able to estimate separate coefficients for each decision strategy, which will all be compared to these unclassified voters.

The revised data are shown in Figure 5.12. We can think of the unclassified voters as insufficiently exhibiting any of our four a priori types of decision strategies to unambiguously be categorized as a Model 1 or

the primary election. Indeed, almost everyone accessed party affiliation at least once during the primary election campaign; however, a large minority of voters (28%) never accessed it during the general election campaign, presumably because they were very confident about which of the general election candidates was a Democrat and which was a Republican. Hence, we consider how soon party affiliation was accessed during the primary campaign even for our categorization of Model 2 voters in the general election.

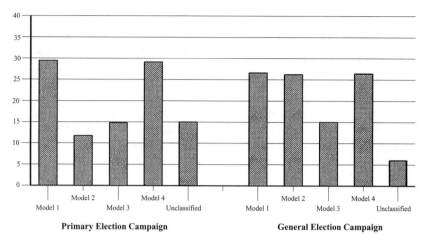

Primary Election Campaign   **General Election Campaign**

Note: Data are the percentage of all voters employing each of the different types of decision strategies in the primary and general election campaigns, respectively.

Figure 5.12. Prevalence of different decision strategies: revised measure.

Model 2 or Model 3 or Model 4 voter. More importantly, the data – particularly for the general election – look much more as we would expect. Our revised coding scheme has taken about 5% of the voters initially placed into Models 1 and 4 and moved them into Model 2. Now Models 1, 2, and 4 are all very comparable in size and a bit bigger than Model 3. This is an excellent result, because our revised coding scheme also does a significantly better job of representing the conceptual definitions of the different models.

SUMMARY

This concludes our initial pass through the data. We have covered a lot of ground in this chapter. With one or two exceptions, we have developed all of the measures we will be using in the remainder of the book. We have also established how we determine the information search strategy each voter is using. Readers who would like to see the step-by-step search process of some of our voters, are directed to Appendix D, where several of these are presented. This is a more concrete way to see what voters did, although it is one that is inevitably so idiosyncratic that it makes abstraction and empirical analysis – the hallmarks of science – next to impossible. We will rely on the summary measures of theoretical concepts developed in this chapter in the remainder of the book.

It is now time to begin testing the various parts of our process-oriented framework for studying the vote decision presented in Chapter 2 and to demonstrate that all this information processing data can teach us something interesting about voting. Following the logic of this framework, the next two chapters treat information processing as a dependent variable. Chapter 6 considers the impact of individual background characteristics and of political sophistication on information processing. This is followed by a chapter examining the effects of the political context – the nature of the candidates and their campaign strategies – on information processing. Only after we have thoroughly examined the intermediate steps in our model will we begin considering the effects of information processing on the most interesting political variables.

6

Individual Differences in Information Processing

The previous chapter presented, with moderately broad brush strokes, the decision processes people used in trying to make their vote choices in our mock presidential election. In that initial presentation of our data, we ignored, for the most part, differences between voters, differences among candidates, and (with the major exception of presenting information from the primary and general election campaigns separately) differences across campaigns. But all voters are not the same, candidates oftentimes do have very significant differences, and campaigns – even limiting consideration to presidential campaigns – come in many different flavors. More importantly, theory tells us that certain variations among decision makers (i.e., voters), alternatives (candidates), and decision contexts (campaigns) are particularly interesting to examine. Of course, that same theory guided the design of our research in the first place in that it suggested interesting experimental factors to manipulate and important individual difference variables to measure.

In this chapter and the next, we will provide much more focused explorations of our data. First we consider individual differences among decision makers. We will look in particular at three categories of individual differences: basic background demographic characteristics (including age, education, and gender), political sophistication or expertise, and two presumably long-standing political preferences – partisanship and ideology. The goal in these two chapters is still to understand information processing, decision strategies, and memory – the crucial intervening variables in our model. We do not have strong a priori expectations of finding much in this chapter because the decision theory literature has generally found that situational factors are far stronger predictors of the type of variables we are considering here than any differences between decision makers. As will soon become evident, however, the results prove to be more interesting than we had anticipated.

POLITICAL SOPHISTICATION

Of these three categories, the most theoretically important, by far, is political sophistication or expertise. As discussed in Chapter 2, almost by definition experts in any domain should have more knowledge about that domain. But they should also have more experience thinking about and making judgments and decisions in that domain. This experience should give the expert several advantage in making decisions in his or her area of expertise – and provides us with a number of testable hypotheses.

Sophistication is an extremely important theoretical variable in decision making, and we went to great lengths to measure it, including a count of the number of campaign-related and more community-oriented political behaviors our subjects had engaged in; a fairly stringent political knowledge test, which asked respondents to answer a number of factual questions about how American government works and to identify a number of important political actors; and measures of following politics in the media, frequency of talking about politics, and self-proclaimed interest in politics. Our subjects on average had engaged in two or three (of five) campaign-oriented behaviors, and one or two noncampaign-oriented political behaviors; they talked about politics and paid attention to national news a little more than once or twice a week in the media; they knew the correct answer to about seven of eleven basic knowledge questions about politics,[1] and could correctly locate five of seven prominent politicians on the ideological spectrum; and, in general, they claimed to be "moderately" interested in politics.

As most would expect, these different indicators of political sophistication all correlate positively with each other, and for simplicity we combined them into an overall measure of sophistication or expertise.[2] As seen in Figure 6.1, this summary scale has the usual bell-shaped or normal distribution, with relatively few subjects at either end of the distribution, and the great bulk of the subjects clustered around the overall mean. For current purposes, the important point is that our subject population contains a great deal of variation in the variables that ought to be important in studying political decision making. Our summary measure of political sophistication clearly captures both the knowledge and experience associated with expertise.

---

[1] This number in particular seems quite high. However, for easier "grading" all eleven factual knowledge questions were multiple-choice with four response items, so just by chance the proverbial monkey at the keyboard would be expected to get about three of the eleven questions correct – which puts our subjects' somewhat higher mean knowledge score in proper perspective.

[2] Cronbach's alpha, a measure of the reliability or internal consistency of a summary scale, was .83 for the seven-item summary measure.

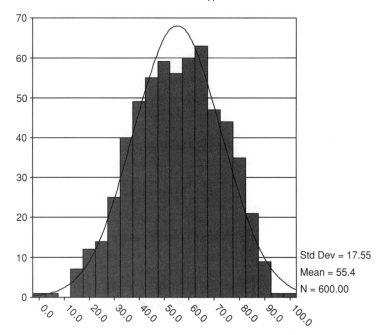

Figure 6.1. Distribution of subject political expertise.

First, through their experience, experts should have learned that certain types of information are particularly useful or diagnostic for making a decision. Thus, we would not in general expect experts to seek out more information when trying to reach a decision, but they may well seek out different types of particularly helpful information. We will reserve a closer consideration of political heuristics for Chapter 11. But we would also expect political experts to be more interested in explicitly political topics – particularly candidates' policy stands and the endorsements of political lobbying groups – while nonexperts or novices might be relatively more interested in familiar (but not particularly political) social information about candidates' backgrounds, families, and personalities.

Second, experts may have found particular decision strategies to be especially helpful in reaching a decision. One very good possibility is that experts will have sufficient cognitive resources to allow them to employ a rational Model 1 decision strategy, which relies on a relatively deep information search that is fairly equally distributed across the alternative candidates. Another equally good possibility is that, armed with their superior knowledge of particularly diagnostic information, experts may believe that they can make very good decisions with relatively little information. Their experience and well-established partisan and ideological schemas may allow them to very confidently infer a great deal of information about the candidates without actually seeking it out. This would be Model 3 or Model 4 decision making. Our predilections are more toward the latter possibility, but there are good reasons to expect the former as well, and we will not prejudge the issue.

Third, because the expert has thought about problems in his or her area of expertise more than nonexperts, he or she should have more highly developed schemas in memory for processing and retrieving relevant information. Thus all else being equal, experts should be able to remember more political information than novices, and probably be more accurate in their memories. This advantage should be particularly important, and perhaps exaggerated, when the conditions under which the decision maker is trying to reach a decision are particularly trying or stressful, as they are in our dynamic campaign environment.

All of these advantages should result in "better" decision making by experts. We will defer this question until Chapter 10 and focus here on the information gathering and processing that lead up to a decision. In doing that, we want to make sure that we are isolating the effects of political expertise from related variables that could have similar effects. This is the role played by the other two categories of predictors considered in this chapter.

Control Variables

Education. For theoretical reasons, the "expertise" that we care about is domain-specific (i.e., it is political knowledge and political experience that should be important in making a vote decision). However, expertise in one domain could well be related to expertise in another, and most experts share basic intelligence and a good deal of education. We want to isolate the effects of political sophistication from intelligence and the broader intellectual experience that comes with education, and we can do both of those reasonably well statistically by including education in our analyses. Education should have much the same effects as political expertise; to make sure that whatever power we are attributing to expertise is in fact attributable to political knowledge and experience, and not just greater intelligence and learning, we must include both variables in our analyses.

Political Predispositions. Long-standing political predispositions such as partisan and ideological identifications provide another complicating factor. Most studies of political behavior include party and ideological identifications as major predictors. Now, those studies are usually looking at political evaluations of one type or another, and rarely the type of information processing variables that concern us in this chapter. When we turn to candidate evaluation and the vote decision in Chapters 8 and 9, these two political predispositions will play a major role in our analyses as well. We have no reason to suspect that Democrats and Republicans, however, or liberals and conservatives, process political information or make political decisions in fundamentally different ways.

Nonetheless, we will include these political predispositions as controls in our early analyses for the simple reason that these variables will play an important role when we turn to predicting political outcomes – candidate evaluations and the vote choice – and we want to make sure that any influences on information search and processing variables that we want to attribute to factors such as expertise are independent of these political predispositions. The problem is that both partisanship and ideology are related to political expertise, in the sense that as people become more knowledgeable and interested in politics, their political predispositions become stronger (more extreme). This relationship is not with direction of identification – experts are no more likely to be Republican than Democrat, liberal than conservative – but with strength of identification. In theory, there is no reason why someone strongly interested in and highly knowledgeable of politics could not be an ideologically moderate political independent, but in practice they rarely are. Ideological moderation and political independence are oftentimes the resting place of those with little or no interest in politics.

Thus, even though we have no a priori reason to expect political predispositions to be related to information processing, we want to include them as controls in our analyses so that we can be confident that the effects we expect to attribute to political expertise are completely independent of these predispositions. Because we have two of them available to us, and they are strongly correlated with each other in contemporary American politics ($r = .60$ in our data), we will keep ideological identification in its original, left–right evaluative nature, but "fold" partisan identification at its midpoint so that the measure taps strength of identification.[3] All of this will make our examination of the effects of political expertise extremely conservative, in that any reported effects will be *independent of* education, direction, and strength of political predispositions.

Age. There are several reasons to think that older people might have a harder time using our computer program than younger people. First, a reasonable amount of manual dexterity is required to access the information scrolling down the computer screen. Such fine motor coordination

---

[3] Pure independents received the lowest score on our measure of strength of partisanship; strong Democrats and strong Republicans both received the highest score. Independent "leaners" and weak partisans receive intermediate scores on this variable.

becomes more difficult with age.[4] Second, older people would probably have had less experience with a computer than younger people. Unfortunately, we did not think to ask such a question, but it is quite likely to be true. We began our studies just as computers were becoming pervasive in the workplace, but a goodly number of our subjects were already retired (25%), and another subset of subjects were homemakers, and it is reasonable to believe that many of these two groups of subjects would have had relatively little prior experience using computers. Finally, there is the possibility that mental capacity is shrinking in the elderly, and that this could affect decision making. Riggle, Johnson, and Hickey (1996) find that age does have effects on information search, as older subjects accessed less information in their study but spent a longer time studying what they did access.

Gender. Finally, as with political predispositions, we have no a priori reason to expect any information processing differences between males and females (although we might expect women to be particularly concerned with one set of issues, and men with another). But much has been made in recent years of a "gender gap," of women voting disproportionately for Democratic candidates. This fact alone would lead us to pay particular attention to gender differences. But in addition, some of our own candidates were female; thus we will also examine gender differences among voters on information search and processing.

RESULTS

Content of Information Search

To explore these various individual-difference or voter effects, we regressed a series of information search and information processing variables on six independent variables: our summary scale of political expertise, age, years of education, gender, strength of party identification, and liberal–conservative identification. Figure 6.2 presents the results from

---

[4] We gathered informal impressions from our experimenters which confirmed this possibility. Subjects in their 80s seemed to have much more difficulty getting the "hang" of accessing the scrolling information on the computer, such that they required noticeably more practice during the practice session before they felt ready to start the experiment. Further evidence comes from our second study, when we asked subjects at the end of the experiment to go through a list of everything they had looked at during the primary election campaign and to tell us, in their own words, why they had selected this particular item. Some of these items were accessed "by mistake" (about 5–6% overall). The correlation between age and number of such mistakes was $r = .30$, suggesting even more directly that older people had more trouble using the mouse to access the information they desired.

Individual Differences

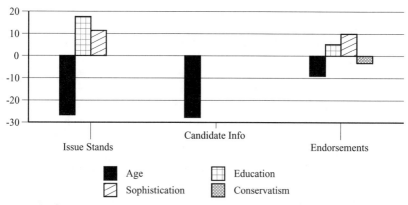

Note: The figure compares the estimated effect of 67 years of age, 20 years of education, gender (being female), and the full range of our ideological identification and political sophistication scales. Data come from regression equations, which also controlled for gender and strength of party identification. Only effects statistically significant at the $p < .05$ level or better are displayed.

Figure 6.2. Effects of background characteristics on content of search.

three different analyses of various measures of the content of information search, specifically candidates' issue stands, more personal or social background and personality characteristics, and group endorsements. There is a separate section in the figure devoted to each dependent variable. So that one can appreciate the relative magnitude of the different effects, Figure 6.2 shows the predicted effect of a reasonably full dose of each of our independent variables: 67 years of age, 20 years of education, gender (being female), and the full range of our political sophistication, strength of party identification, and political ideology scales. For simplicity, only variables that achieve conventional levels of statistical significance (i.e., $p < .05$) are shown in the figure.

Consider the first analysis, which explained the number of candidate issue stands voters accessed across the two campaigns and is displayed on the left-hand side of Figure 6.2.[5] Three variables had effects that are significantly different from zero. Age had the biggest effect: an 80-year-old voter is predicted to access twenty-five fewer candidate issue stands than a 20-year-old voter, holding all other variables constant. But education and sophistication also had noteworthy effects, both in a positive direction. A voter with a graduate degree is predicted to access about eighteen more

[5] When a dependent variable is a discrete count of some phenomenon, as it is here, it is more appropriate statistically to use the Poisson distribution in performing the analysis. A Poisson regression provides very similar results to those presented here, however, and for simplicity we rely upon a more familiar OLS regression.

issue stands than a person with no education; and a political expert – again, controlling on age, education, gender, and political predisposi- tions – is predicted to access about eleven more issue stands than a com- plete political novice, on top of any effects of education.

We had predicted the effect of sophistication on seeking out issue stands. The same general pattern of effects holds when we consider another type of explicitly political information, the endorsements of different lobbying groups. Again, education and sophistication are both positively related to seeking out such endorsements, but age – and surprisingly, conservatives – are somewhat less likely to seek out these endorsements.[6]

The converse of that prediction is that sophistication would be neg- atively related to seeking out standard personal information about the candidates. This prediction was not supported: Sophistication was totally unrelated to seeking out personal information. As shown in the middle of Figure 6.2, only age is significantly related to accessing person-related information, and its effect is estimated to be slightly stronger than the effect of age on examining issue-rated information.

Clearly, the most consistent and strongest individual difference effect on the content of search is one of our control variables, age. Indeed, when we look more finely at content (breaking down the broad variables reported in Figure 6.2 into finer categories, in analyses not reported here), this age effect is so pervasive that it would seem to have little to do with content, but rather much to do with amount. The older our voters were, the less information of all types they considered.

This age effect is so strong that it clearly deserves further analysis, particularly because the three different possible explanations for them offered earlier have very different implications for how we would think about these results. Such an analysis would take us too far afield from our present purpose, however, and we will have to defer a more thorough exploration of age effects to another time. Let us just assert here that there is clear empirical support for all three of those explanations. Thus, some of the age effect is artifactual, but some of it – roughly half, we would estimate – is due to declining cognitive abilities of older people, and thus has very real implications for voter decision making outside of our laboratory.

Information Search

Figure 6.3 presents the results of a series of regressions of our various mea- sures of information processing, including depth of search, comparability

---

[6] Note that this effect is not a product of the nature of the groups offering endorse- ments; these groups were comprised of an equal number of liberal and conservative groups. We will have much more to say about group endorsements in Chapter 11.

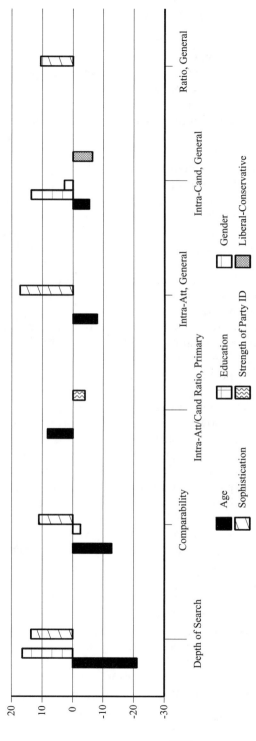

Figure 6.3. Effects of background characteristics of information processing.

Note: The figure compares the estimated effect of 50 years of age, 16 years of education, gender (being female), and the full range of our political sophistication scale. Data come from regression equation, which also controlled for ideology and strength of party identification. Only effects statistically significant at the $p < .10$ level or better are displayed. Dependent variables do not all have the same scale so it is not appropriate to compare the magnitude of effects across dependent variables clusters. That is, we can conclude from the figure that 50 years of age has a greater effect on accessing issue stands than 16 years of education, but it would not be correct to conclude from the figure that age has a greater effect on accessing issue stands than it does on accessing group endorsements.

of search across candidates, and sequence of search. We considered these variables separately for the primary and general election campaigns. The results for depth of search and comparability of search were very similar across campaigns, so the results we present in Figure 6.3 average across the two campaigns. Beginning with the depth of search, which combines the number of items accessed with the number of attributes considered, we already know from our previous analyses that age will have a strong and negative effect on depth of search. Indeed it does: 70-year-olds score almost 21 points lower on our depth of search scale compared to 20-year-olds. But both education and sophistication are strongly positively associated with greater depth of search. We had resisted the seemingly obvious prediction that sophistication would be associated with greater depth of search, offering instead the more subtle hypothesis that expertise would be related to seeking only certain types of particularly useful information. As presented earlier, we did detect a strong effect of sophistication on seeking group endorsements in particular. Nonetheless, as the results in Figure 6.3 clearly show, sophistication is strongly related to greater depth of search across the board.

Expertise is also strongly related to greater comparability of search across candidates. As can be seen in the second section of the figure, the effect of expertise is about equal in magnitude but opposite in direction to the effect of age. Older people are less likely to seek out comparable information across candidates, but experts are more likely to seek such comparable information. This age effect is distinct, however, from a lesser amount of search. No matter how little or much total information a voter looks at, that information can be distributed evenly across candidates, or not. In fact, given time constraints, it is probably easier to look at the same information across candidates when there is less information overall considered. If this reasoning is correct, then the negative effect of age on the comparability of search across candidates occurs despite the lesser total search conducted by older people.

Turning to our measures of sequence of search, we considered both the percentage of intra-attribute and the percentage of intra-candidate transitions separately, along with the summary measure of the ratio of the two. For the primary election, the summary measure accurately represents the separate results for the two constituent parts, so we only show it. Older voters exhibit a higher percentage of intra-attribute (i.e., dimensional) to intra-candidate transitions; strong partisans exhibit just the opposite pattern, a higher proportion of intra-candidate rather than intra-attribute transitions. We certainly did not predict either of these results, and the effect of strength of party identification in this analysis is particularly intriguing, given that we are considering a primary election where party does not help distinguish among the alternative choices.

In the general election, the various measures of sequence of search show different patterns, which are obscured by the summary measure, so we present the results for intra-attribute and intra-candidate search by themselves, along with the combined ratio measure. Two variables influenced the percentage of intra-attribute search sequences: age, negatively, and expertise, positively. The most sophisticated voters engaged in 17% more intra-attribute search compared to rank novices, all else being equal. The negative effect of age on intra-attribute search in the general election contrasts with the positive effect it had on the relative degree of intra-attribute search in the primary election, a difference for which we have no good explanation.

Age continues to have a small negative effect on the percentage of intra-candidate search, an effect now joined by ideology. Strong conservatives engage in about 6% less intra-candidate search than strong liberals. Because this is the only time, in seventeen different analyses, where ideology proved to have a significant effect – and as we had no theoretical reason to expect that it might have an effect – we remain skeptical that this is anything more than a stray random result. Both education and being female (though not political expertise) had positive effects on the percentage of intra-candidate transitions. Voters with a college education engaged in about 10% more intra-candidate search than voters with no education; females engaged in about 3% more intra-candidate search than did males. When putting these two constituent variables together and looking at the ratio of intra-attribute to intra-candidate search, the only variable that proves to have a significant effect is sophistication. Again, experts engage in about 10 percent more intra-attribute relative to intra-candidate search, all else equal.

Decision Strategies

We also looked at the effects of expertise and the various control variables on choice of decision strategy. Because the dependent variable here is nominal – that is, it has five (or seven, if we differentiate between the two subcategories of Model 1 and Model 4 voters) categories that do not have any inherent order – the statistics involved in conducting a multivariate analysis are fairly complex.[7] But the pattern of results can

---

[7] The appropriate analysis involves a nominal logistic regression. Again, the point of a multivariate analysis is to see the unique effect of each variable after controlling the others. It is quite reasonable, for example, to expect political experts to generally have

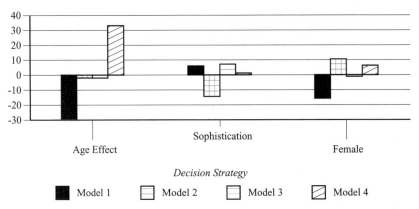

Decision Strategy

■ Model 1   ☐ Model 2   ☐ Model 3   ▨ Model 4

Note: The figure compares the percentage employing each decision strategy in the extreme groups of each independent variable. In the case of gender, where there are only two categories, it is the percentage of females employing each strategy minus the percentage males employing that strategy. So 42.7% of all males employed Model 1 during the primary, compared to 27.0% of all females, for a difference of −15.7%. For age, the percentage of the youngest quartile is subtracted from the percentage of the oldest quartile. For political sophistication, the percentage for novices is subtracted from the percentage for experts.

Figure 6.4. Effects of background characteristics on choice of decision strategy in the primary election.

be illustrated more simply by showing the simple bivariate relationships between the control variables and decision strategy. We took a further step to simplify the analysis by collapsing the two subcategories of Model 1 and Model 4 into their larger group, after assuring ourselves the basic results did not change. We will present only those bivariate results that also proved to be statistically significant in a multivariate analysis.

First, just by eye-balling the results in Figure 6.3, we get a good idea that older people were less likely to employ either of the two more "rational" strategies, in that they were lower on depth of search and comparability of search across candidates, the two hallmarks of the rational decision strategies. This impression is confirmed by a significant relationship between age (in quartiles) and choice of decision strategy during both the primary $(\chi^2(9) = 54.6, p < .001)$ and general election $(\chi^2(9) = 46.5, p < .001)$ campaigns. The results from the primary election are shown in Figure 6.4,

quite a bit of education and to be strong partisans. Only with a multivariate analysis can we be certain that a simple bivariate relationship between political sophistication and choice of decision strategy, say, is not really a function of education. The simpler bivariate results we present in the text were all also significant in the multivariate analysis, which is available from the authors upon request.

which contrasts the proportion of the youngest voters (those 25 or younger) employing each decision strategy to the proportion of the oldest voters (63 and older). Over 47% of the youngest voters employed a Model 1 strategy, compared to less than 18% of the oldest voters. In contrast, almost 52% of the oldest voters employed Model 4, compared to less than 19% of the youngest voters. There were no major age differences with the other two decision strategies. The pattern is exactly the same in the general election, and it is a huge effect. Whether we are observing the high point of a special cohort who are particularly drawn to Model 4 decision making – but who will soon disappear from the political scene – or a pattern of results that will replicate itself as subsequent generations age is a question we cannot answer here.

We had predicted a significant relationship between political sophistication and use of decision strategy, and as shown in the middle section of Figure 6.4, that is exactly what we see during the primary ($\chi^2(9) = 17.0$, $p < .05$). As expected, experts (top quartile of the political sophistication scale) were 6% more likely to choose Model 1 than were novices (bottom quartile). Experts were also about 7% more like to employ Model 3, but more than 14% less likely to employ Model 2. No real differences can be seen for Model 4. Thus, what distinguishes experts is not so much the amount of information they consider in making their choice (although there is a clear relationship between sophistication and depth of search), but a preference for a compensatory decision strategy (Model 1 or Model 3). However, we do not observe a similar effect of political sophistication on choice of decision strategy in the general election campaign ($\chi^2(9) = 9.1, p > .42$). There, novices are slightly more likely (about 3%) to choose Model 1 or Model 2, while experts are slightly more likely (3 or 4%) to choose Model 3 or Model 4. But again, these differences are no more than would be expected by chance.

The one other effect we see in our data, observable in both the primary and general election campaigns, is a gender effect. Males are more likely to prefer Model 1, and females are more likely to prefer the noncompensatory Model 2 or Model 4 decision making. This sounds a bit like (a lack of) political sophistication, except that this effect clearly replicates in the multivariate analysis that controls for sophistication (and education and age and partisan predispositions), and there is almost no relationship between gender and sophistication. So whatever the effect we are observing here, it is not a function of political sophistication, nor any of the other background variables that are part of the multivariate analysis. This effect is, however, consistent with research on gender differences in rhetoric and preferred communications patterns (e.g., Brystrom, 2004; Crawford, 1995; Tannen, 1990).

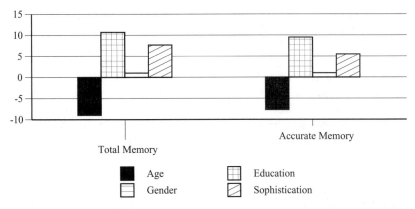

Note: The figure compares the estimated effect of 50 years of age, 16 years of education, gender (being female), and the full range of our political sophistication scale. Data come from regression equation, which also controlled for ideology and strength of party identification. Only effects statistically significant at the $p < .10$ level or better are displayed. Dependent variables do not all have the same scale, so it is not appropriate to compare the magnitude of effects across dependent variable clusters.

Figure 6.5. Effects of background characteristics on memory.

MEMORY

It is becoming more and more apparent that age is the most important individual difference. Older people clearly chose to look at less information during our election campaigns. Unfortunately, this effect could be explained by less experience with computers, declining fine-motor ability, or declining cognitive abilities. The first two explanations should have nothing to do with memory, however. Even our oldest voters looked at far more information about the candidates than anyone could remember. So if we do observe a significant effect of age on memory – and it is negative – declining cognitive ability becomes the most likely explanation.

Figure 6.5 presents the results both for total memories of the two candidates involved in the general election campaign and for accurate memories about them. Age has a significant negative effect in both equations. An 80-year-old voter remembers nine fewer things overall, and about seven fewer accurate facts about each of the two candidates, compared to a 20-year-old voter. In contrast, both education and political expertise are associated with more and more accurate memories. The effects are about equal in magnitude but opposite in direction to that of age. Gender also has a significant (but smaller) effect, with females reporting about one more memory (and one more accurate memory) about the candidates than males.

We also hypothesized that both depth of search and sequence of search would affect amount and accuracy of memory. We expected that either ordered search sequence (i.e., candidate-based or attribute-based) would lead to greater memory. Our expectations were strongly confirmed in terms of depth of search, but not sequence of search. In fact, both relatively high intra-attribute search sequences and relatively high intra-candidate search sequences were negatively related to total memory and total accurate memory, although neither effect was statistically significant.[8]

SUMMARY

Summarizing what has been learned in this chapter, political sophistication did have a significant effect on many, but by no means all, of the cognitive variables considered in this chapter. Education also frequently proved to be important, and as a rough approximation we would say about as important, as expertise. As education and expertise always had similar effects in our equations (i.e., their coefficients always had the same sign), had we excluded education from the equations we would have observed much stronger, and more consistently significant, expertise effects. But we can confidently conclude that whenever we did detect a significant effect for expertise, it was *political* sophistication, and not wider learning in general or greater intelligence, that is the determining factor. We will continue to include a control for education in any subsequent analysis where political sophistication is predicted to have an important effect.

We have had little to say about gender, which accords with our expectations. We detected significant gender effects in seven of fifteen analyses – clearly more than would be expected by chance – but even when a gender effect was statistically significant, it was pretty small in magnitude relative to other variables in the equations. The two political predisposition variables were significant even less often (strength of party identification twice, ideology only once) and like gender had relatively small effects even when they were significant, although we did see males focus more on Model 1 decision making, while females were more oriented toward Models 2 and 3.

The big surprise in the analyses reported in this chapter was the strong and fairly consistent effect of voter age. We simply had not thought about age as an important intervening factor in the vote decision. As already discussed, part of the effect of age is probably an artifact of our experimental procedure – that voters had to access information about candidates

---

[8] These analyses also included a control for total search. The more items one looks at, the more it is possible to remember. But depth of search (and age) were significantly related to search controlling on total number of items accessed during the experiment.

that was scrolling down a computer screen – but part of it might also be attributed to declining cognitive abilities with age. We want to eliminate the artifactual age effects from our experiments because these will have no analog to decision making during a real election, while retaining any residual effects of age, which probably do affect voters in actual elections in much the way they affected voters in our experiments.

We can do this statistically by including measures of a lack of computer experience and poor manual dexterity in every equation, or equivalently by first regressing each of our cognitive variables on these two predictors and then using the residuals from these initial equations as our variables of interest. We will take the latter course because, once implemented, it makes life (or at least the analysis) much easier from then on. We will not have to have additional variables of no substantive interest floating around in our equations.

It is not yet clear whether age will influence the nature or quality of the vote decision, however. We certainly expect older people to have somewhat different concerns than younger voters, and these different concerns or priorities could result in different candidate evaluations and vote choices. But that is not what we are talking about. Some of the biggest effects of age on cognitive processes concern memory, yet some models of the vote decision (e.g., the on-line model; see Lodge, Steenbergen, and Brau, 1995) hold that memory is irrelevant to the accuracy with which candidate evaluations are formed, and vote choices are reached. We disagree; our theory clearly holds that memory is important to the vote decision, at least when it comes to voting correctly. Likewise Model 1 decision making would seem to require a strong role for memory. Thus, we would predict now that age will continue to have strong effects as we proceed through the various steps of our decision making framework. What is clear at this point is that we should continue to examine age (and education) as two background characteristics whose effects must be accounted for.

7

Campaign Effects on Information Processing

The previous chapter looked at how differences among voters – their general political sophistication, their political predispositions, and their education, gender, and age – affect information processing and choice strategies. All these characteristics are things voters carry around with them, as they live through actual political campaigns, and as they showed up to participate in our experiments. In this chapter, we turn to exploring how differences between campaigns influence those same variables. In particular, we will examine how the number of candidates running in an election, their ideological distinctiveness, the candidates' fit with partisan stereotypes, whether the candidate supported during the primary is running in the general election, the resources they have available to buy television advertising, and the timing of their ads during the campaign, all affect information processing and choice strategies.[1] The first three of these factors clearly involve the difficulty of the choice facing the voter, *the* instantiation of the "nature of the decision task," which completes the initial stage of our framework for studying decision making (Figure 2.1).

---

[1] Our experiments ignore several other very important considerations that could fall under this same topic – in particular, differences between candidates' qualifications for the job (Jacobson, 1987; Jacobson and Kernell, 1981; Squire, 1992), voters' familiarity with them, and agreement with the candidate on policy issues. As has already been seen in Chapter 3, our mock candidates are all pretty well qualified for the job of president, as is typically the case among the serious contenders for the presidency, but voters were totally unfamiliar with all of them. Thus, our experiments provided no variance on these important factors. There is a clear difference in familiarity across the primary and general election campaigns, of course, but it is confounded with every other difference between those two types of campaigns and is thus impossible to study by itself. Agreement on policy issues will figure prominently when we turn to candidate evaluation and the vote choice in Chapters 8 and 9, and we will reserve a more thorough discussion of it until then (see also Redlawsk and Lau, 2003).

Information Processing

NUMBER OF CANDIDATES RUNNING IN AN ELECTION

Three of our studies manipulated the number of candidates running in a primary election campaign. And we have already seen in Chapter 5, one of the important consequences of this manipulation is the amount of search devoted to each candidate. Look back at Figure 5.2. It is easy to see that voters' information processing is strongly affected by this manipulation. Indeed, we could infer from this figure that voters' information seeking is guided by at least three motivations: (1) learn something about every candidate in each party; (2) devote disproportionate attention to the candidates from your own party; and (3) within each party devote more attention to the candidates you like best.[2] The latter sounds much more like Model 2 or 4 and counter to the demands of compensatory decision making that is Model 1 and Model 3. Let us now consider whether the content, along with the amount of search, is affected by this manipulation before we draw out some of the implications of these search patterns.

We looked first at whether there were any distinctive patterns of search for person- or issue-related information. There were not; the data for either of these two major categories of information look very much like the pattern shown in Figure 5.2, although of course each bar, each mean, is only about half as large. But other variables provide more interesting results. Figure 7.1 presents the mean value of our three crucial information processing scales (depth, equality, sequence), separately for the two- and four-candidate conditions. All of these variables except the sequence of search measures are defined exclusively in terms of in-party search. Depth of search is significantly greater in the four-candidate condition ($t(371) = 1.98$, $p < .05$), but the strongest effect by far is a much greater tendency for there to be comparability of search across alternatives in the two-candidate condition than in the four-candidate condition ($t(397) = 12.18$, $p < .001$). There is no difference between conditions in the proportion of intra-attribute versus intra-candidate search, the standard indicator of search sequence. As seen to the right of Figure 7.1, there is a significant effect of the manipulation on the overall proportion of systematic (i.e., intra-attribute plus intra-candidate) search ($t(399) = 2.64$, $p < .01$).

Figure 7.2 shows how the various measures of information search translate into decision strategies. For simplicity, we only show the four broad models because the subtypes of Model 1 and Model 4 exhibit the same patterns as the broader categories do. The number of candidates

[2] We are less sure of this last point because we have not actually linked evaluations of the candidates to information search, knowing only that voters devoted the most search, among the in-party alternatives, to the candidate they supported in the primary.

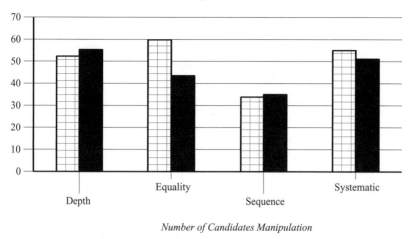

Number of Candidates Manipulation

☐ Two-Candidate   ■ Four-Candidate

Figure 7.1. Effect of number of candidates running in the primary on information search.

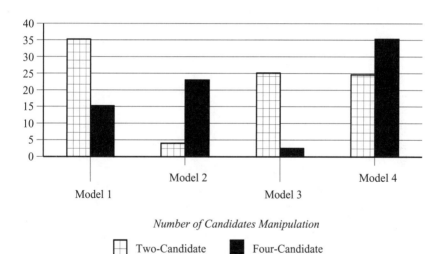

Number of Candidates Manipulation

☐ Two-Candidate   ■ Four-Candidate

Figure 7.2. Effect of number of candidates running in the primary on decision strategy.

manipulation has a very significant effect on decision strategy ($\chi^2(4) = 94.1$, $p < .001$), with voters much more likely to employ one of the two compensatory strategies (Model 1 or Model 3) in the two-candidate condition than in the four-candidate condition. In contrast, voters in the four-candidate condition were much more likely to employ one of the more intuitive strategies (Model 4) or the confirmatory Model 2 strategy. This one manipulation on decision strategy has a huge effect. The one distinguishing feature of all the compensatory strategies is that they require comparable search across candidates. Clearly, our voters found it very difficult to gather comparable information about four different alternatives. We will see how this effect plays out on the nature and quality of the vote choice in the following chapters.

IDEOLOGICAL DISTINCTIVENESS OF CANDIDATES IN AN ELECTION

One of our studies manipulated the ideological distinctiveness of the two candidates running in the general election campaign. Two ideologically distinct candidates provide an easier decision task than two ideologically similar candidates. But does this manipulation also result in any observable effects on the amount or content or nature of the resulting information search? On its face, there is no effect of this manipulation on the amount of search, nor is there any effect on search strategies, at least when we limit analysis to this one study where ideological distinctiveness was manipulated.

The effect of manipulating the number of candidates on the use of decision strategy in the primary election was so dramatic that we wanted to push this analysis a little bit further. Therefore, we turned to voters from other studies who, for reasons other than a random manipulation, experienced the same candidate pairings in the general election as subjects in either our distinct or similar ideology conditions when this factor was manipulated. This more than doubles the sample available for analysis, providing us with much more power to detect significant effects.

This effort paid off because we now have sufficient statistical power to detect significant differences for depth and equality of search across alternatives. Figures 7.3 and 7.4 present the relevant data. As was the case for the number of candidates manipulation, our voters engaged in deeper search ($t(257) = 2.07, p < .05$), which was more equally distributed across alternatives ($t(255) = 2.34, p < .05$) in the easier distinct candidate ideologies "condition" compared to the more difficult similar ideologies condition. (There were no differences across conditions for either measure of sequence of search.) These information search differences translate into a marginally significant effect on choice of decision strategy ($\chi^2(4) = 9.0$, $p < .06$). Voters are more likely to employ Model 1 in the simpler distinct candidates condition but more likely to employ Model 2 or Model 4 in the similar ideology condition.

The differences between conditions are not as stark as those for the number of candidates manipulation – in part because all voters in the

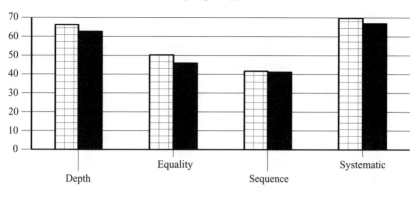

Figure 7.3. Effect of ideological distinctiveness on information search, general election campaign.

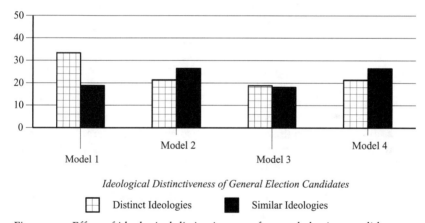

Figure 7.4. Effect of ideological distinctiveness of general election candidates on decision strategy.

general election campaign were in a two-candidate condition – but they are entirely consistent with them. Voters comparing two ideologically distinct general election candidates were more likely to employ one of the compensatory decision strategies (52.1%) than voters making the more difficult decision between two ideologically similar candidates (36.9%), who in turn were much more likely to utilize one of the noncompensatory decision strategies. As was the case with the number of candidates running in the primary, voters were more likely to employ one of the more rational strategies when the decision was relatively easy, but they were more likely to rely upon a more intuitive strategy when the decision was more difficult. Here we see the two competing goals of making a good decision and making an easy decision playing off against each other. Holding the desire to make a good decision constant, a more difficult decision context – one involving two ideologically similar candidates – would seem to require a more careful, compensatory strategy like Model 1. But this same decision context also makes Model 1 exceedingly difficult to apply because the payoff (in terms of large issue-based candidate differentials) is small. As we have predicted, when push comes to shove, easy will almost always trump good.

We remember that old saying from our high school sports days, "When the going gets tough, the tough get going." We attribute this quote (probably incorrectly) to the legendary coach Vince Lombardi. We must not have had any former Green Bay Packers in our subject pool, however, because in our experiments, when the choice became difficult, our voters did everything they could to simplify the task for themselves. This is undoubtedly a much more common human response to task difficulty, although it would not have made Coach Lombardi happy.

FIT WITH PARTISAN STEREOTYPES

Our first study manipulated the stereotypic nature of the out-party candidate running in the general election campaign. Half of all voters experienced a campaign where the out-party candidate (D3 or R2) fit the mold of a stereotypic moderate from their respective parties. Their "Basic Social and Political Philosophy" described them as moderates, and they took consistently moderate policy stands, verging only occasionally to the left (for the Democrat) or the right (for the Republican). The remaining voters experienced a campaign where the out-party candidate (D4 or R1) took policy stands that were, on average, moderate (and indistinguishable from the average stands of the two stereotypic moderate candidates) but that in fact ranged from the most liberal extreme to the most conservative extreme. Thus, these candidates took a number of policy stands that were very counternormative for their party. Their "Basic Social and Political Philosophy" was described as "difficult to label as a traditional liberal or conservative." We refer to D4 and R1 as the nonstereotypic candidates. The question we ask here is: Did this manipulation affect voter's information processing?

The answer is yes, although it is in somewhat subtle ways. The top half of Figure 7.5 shows the content of information search for these two types

Content of Search, General Election Only

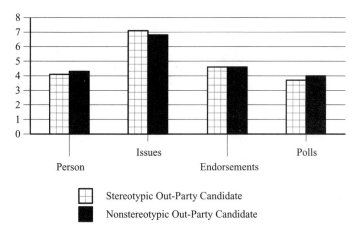

Stereotypic Out-Party Candidate
Nonstereotypic Out-Party Candidate

Re-accessing Information Previously Learned in Primary, and Memory

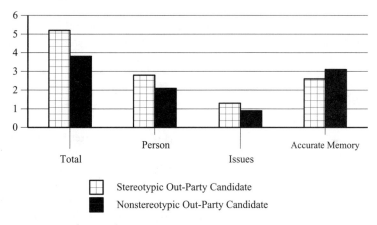

Stereotypic Out-Party Candidate
Nonstereotypic Out-Party Candidate

Note: Data come from study 1. N = 192.

Figure 7.5. Effect of stereotypic nature of out-party candidate manipulation on information search.

of out-party candidates during the general election campaign. There are absolutely no differences in the content of search during the general election campaign, nor (if you add across all of those columns) in the total amount of search directed to the out-party candidate. Look, however, at the bottom of the figure, which singles out information accessed during the general election that had previously been accessed during the

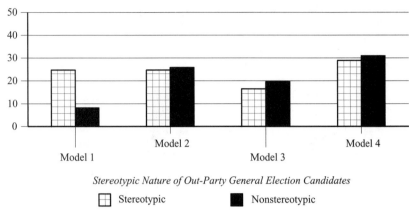

Stereotypic Nature of Out-Party General Election Candidates

☐ Stereotypic   ■ Nonstereotypic

Figure 7.6. Effect of stereotypic nature of out-party candidate manipulation on decision strategy.

primary campaign – in other words, information that was looked at initially, possibly forgotten, but then reaccessed during the general election campaign.[3] There is less reaccessing of personal information ($p < .06$) and policy stands ($p < .01$) – and if you add these two, total information ($p < .01$) – about the nonstereotypic candidate than the stereotypic candidate.[4] Thus, it would appear that the somewhat unusual nature of the nonstereotypic candidate made this person a little more memorable in the voters' eyes – a nontrivial advantage, in most elections.

There were no differences in any of our crucial measures of depth, comparability, or sequence of search attributable to this manipulation. All of these measures are defined in terms of all candidates in the choice set, of course; consequently, any differences in these measures due to the manipulation of the nature of one of those two candidates would tend to be suppressed. But look at Figure 7.6, which presents the percentage of voters employing the four broad types of decision strategies. Choice of decision strategy differs significantly depending on whether the out-party candidate is stereotypic ($\chi^2(4) = 13.3, p < .01$). Voters are noticeably less likely to employ one of the rational strategies (8.2% vs. 24.7%) when the out-party candidate is counterstereotypic, once again following the pattern of avoiding cognitively difficult rational choice procedures when

[3] Because the group endorsements and poll results available during the general election campaign refer to a different pairing of candidates and of course were not available during the primary, it is not possible to reaccess either of these two types of information.

[4] There is no significant difference in total reported memory about the out-party candidate across this manipulation, but the data on accurate memories approaches conventional levels of significance ($p < .11$).

the choice itself is fairly difficult.[5] But voters are commensurably more likely to utilize one of the various noncompensatory strategies when the out-party candidate is nonstereotypic. It would seem that many voters are flummoxed by having the nonstereotypic candidate in the mix, or they want to avoid the value tradeoffs that a serious consideration of the nonstereotypic candidate would probably engender, and they consequently found it very difficult to employ a "rational" strategy that requires relatively deep information search and frequent value tradeoffs. Notice that we cannot attribute this difference to a little payoff from employing a Model 1 strategy, as we could with ideologically similar candidates, because here the issue differential should be much larger, on average, in the nonstereotypic condition.

IS THE CANDIDATE SUPPORTED IN THE PRIMARY RUNNING IN THE GENERAL ELECTION?

A different study manipulated whether the candidate the voter supported in the primary election captured the party's nomination, and thus was running again in the general election campaign. Although we expected most people to vote for their party's candidate in the general election, this tendency should be exacerbated if the party's nominee was the voter's first choice among the competing primary candidates. We can quickly report here that indeed it was, although not as strongly as one might expect (87% of all voters supported their party's candidate in the general election if they had previously voted for that candidate in the primary, while 85% of those who voted for some other candidate in the primary pulled the party's lever in the general election campaign). This may be an instance where ceiling effects left little room for even stronger partisan behavior. In any case, the question we focus on here is: Did any information search or processing differences accompany this rather obvious (although, as it turns out, not that powerful) effect on the vote choice? There is no past research to rely on, but we would speculate that voters would conduct a shallower information search in a race where they have a clear favorite, compared to an election in which the voter's favorite candidate is not running.

The quick answer, however, is: "No, they did not." There are absolutely no differences in the total amount of search, or the content of search, or the sequence of search, or the comparability of search across candidates,

---

[5] This result is counter to predictions of the theory of affective intelligence (Marcus, Neuman, and MacKuen, 2000), which clearly predicts that unusual, unexpected situations should produce anxiety, engage the surveillance system, and lead to more rational decision processes.

or memory, or the decision strategy employed to reach a decision, that can be attributed to this manipulation. Even our speculation about shallower information search when a voter's favorite horse was in the race proved to be flat out wrong, as voters engaged in slightly deeper (although not significantly so) information search in elections where their choice from the primary was running. Evidently learning one's fellow party members do not share one's opinion about the relative merits of the party's candidates did not upset information search process and decision making during the general election campaign to the same degree as the presence of a nonstereotypic out-party candidate in the election!

CAMPAIGN RESOURCES

In the primary election campaign of one study, we manipulated the campaign resources available to the candidate who was farthest away from the voter on the issues. We selected this "farthest away" candidate to get the extra resources – that is, political advertisements – because we wanted to see if voters would be more attracted to candidates they wouldn't otherwise like simply because they have more resources, and we could identify the farthest away candidate as a likely target before the campaign actually began. Unequal campaign resources is a very common situation in American elections, particularly during the primaries. Those resources do not always translate into votes (John Connoly, Phil Gramm, and Steve Forbes come immediately to mind), although often they do. The question we ask here is: Do more ads result in differential information processing, which in turn might help explain the electoral effects (or the lack thereof) of those resources?

In the equal resources condition, each in-party candidate had one (if there were four of them) or two (if there were only two of them) campaign ads. In the unequal resources condition, however, the candidate who was farthest away from the subject on the issues was given two additional ads. In the two-candidate condition, we simply shifted one of the two ads each candidate was supposed to get to the farthest away candidate, so that the closer candidate had only one ad, while the farther away candidate had three ads. In the four-candidate condition, when each candidate was only scheduled to have one ad to begin with, we had to create two additional time slots for the extra ads for the farthest away candidate.[6]

---

[6] Out-party candidates always had two ads apiece, if there were only two of them, or one ad apiece, if there were four of them. We did this to keep television advertising as balanced as possible across the two parties. Thus, there was usually a total of eight ads during the primary, four for each party, except in the four-candidate primary, unequal resources condition, when there was a total of ten ads – six from in-party candidates, four from out-party candidates.

This design complicates the analysis. To begin with, we must include the two- versus four-candidate manipulation in all our analyses; we have already seen how it affects information processing. There will always be one in-party candidate with the extra ads, but the number-of-candidates manipulation means that there will be either one or three alternative in-party candidates with fewer ads; however, the real complication comes from our decision to give the farthest-away-on-the-issues candidate the extra ads. Voters do *not* distribute their information search equally across the candidates in the choice set, as we saw in Chapter 5. They have favorites, and one of the bases for picking favorites is, in all likelihood, agreement with the candidate on the issues. Thus, we would expect the candidate farthest away on the issues to get less search to begin with. To address this point, in our analysis we will ultimately examine the amount of search directed to the farthest-away candidate who has extra ads, compared to how much search a comparable farthest-away candidate gets when he or she is not blessed with additional campaign resources.

This is a lot to keep track of. Combine all of this with the basic procedure for determining which candidate is the farthest away (based upon each voter's own particular combination of issue stands), which makes it possible for any of the eight candidates to be selected as farthest away, and there is a great deal of random noise in the analysis.[7] This stacks the deck pretty strongly against our being able to detect any significant information processing consequences, and we won't look for anything too subtle. But how about simply the amount of information search that is directed toward the candidate who has more television advertisements than the other candidates running in the primary? Ads are meant ultimately to attract votes, but they ought to do that by getting voters to pay more attention to the candidate sponsoring the ads – and that means more information seeking about this particular candidate.

We therefore conducted a repeated measures analysis of variance (ANOVA), where the between-subjects factors were the number-of-candidates manipulation and the campaign-resources manipulation, and the repeated measure contrasted the amount of search directed toward the candidate who was farthest away from the voter on the issues – who would thus get the two extra campaign ads, in the unequal resources condition of the campaign-resources manipulation – to the average amount of search directed toward the remaining in-party candidates. In the two-candidate condition, this was simply the other in-party candidate, but in

---

[7] We might also remember that there are two distinct parties here. By ignoring party, we are assuming that Democrats and Republicans react in similar ways to one candidate in their party's primary having a lot more money than the others to buy television advertising.

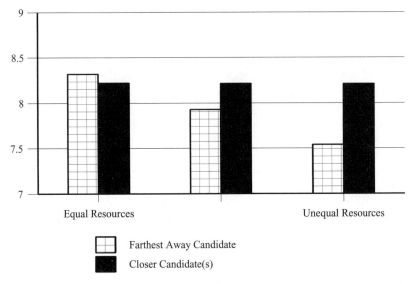

Note: Means for the "closer" candidate average across the three remaining in-party candidates in the four-candidate primary condition.

Figure 7.7. Effect of differential campaign resources on amount of information search directed toward primary candidates.

the four-candidate condition, this was the mean search across the three remaining candidates. We also included age and expertise as covariates in this analysis.

This is a complicated test, but the part of the analysis that concerns us is fairly simple.[8] We are predicting an interaction between the campaign-resources manipulation and the repeated measure. This effect does not quite reach conventional levels of statistical significance ($F_{(1,186)} = 2.51$, $p < .12$), a result at least in part of the inevitable random noise associated with this analysis. But the results are quite interesting, and they deserve some discussion, although we should keep in mind that we have a little less confidence in them compared to most of the other findings discussed in this book.

Figure 7.7 presents the nature of the interaction between the campaign-resources manipulation and the amount of search directed toward the farthest-away candidate and the remaining candidate(s). The campaign-resources manipulation has absolutely no effect on the amount of search directed toward the candidates who were closer to the voter on the issues and whose campaign resources were therefore not affected by

[8] The full ANOVA table is available from the authors for interested readers.

the manipulation. But look what happens to search directed toward the farthest-away candidate, whose campaign resources are in fact manipulated. In the equal resources condition, the farthest-away candidate gets essentially the same amount of search as all the remaining in-party candidates.[9] But when this candidate has two more televised ads than the remaining candidates, voters compensate by actually *seeking less information about this candidate* on their own accord. This is certainly not what the sponsoring candidate would have hoped to achieve; in fact, it is exactly the opposite. And it is yet another reason why "campaign effects" are difficult to produce: Voter's own information search tendencies may work to balance the information available across the candidates, and thus work against the efforts of any candidate blessed with superior campaign resources.

TIMING OF POLITICAL ADVERTISING

We attempted another manipulation of campaign advertising during the primary election in a later study, this time involving the timing of a candidate's ads. Some candidates choose to spend their resources early, getting their name before the public before their opponents. These candidates are hoping for *primacy effects*, to borrow a term from memory research. They hope the public will find out about them early and decide they like them; they would like to see this early favorable impression last until Election Day. Voters who satisfice in their decision making, who look for an acceptable alternative and then, essentially, stop searching, would make this first group of candidates happy. Other candidates hoard their resources until late in the campaign, assuming perhaps that most people are not paying attention until close to the election and/or hoping for *recency effects* such that the last information voters learn before the election comes most easily to mind, and is thus most influential. These candidates are certainly hoping that all voters keep an open mind until Election Day.

The logic of timing campaign advertisements during particular points in a campaign is to get one's name and, perhaps, a particular message before the voters at a given time. Either of those goals would be facilitated if voters, on their own accord, sought out additional information about the sponsor of the ads. Thus, we looked once again at the amount

---

[9] It would seem, then, that we were mistaken in our belief that agreement with a candidate on the issues is one of the factors that would determine the amount of search directed toward a candidate. There is, however, a near-significant interaction between the number-of-candidates manipulation and the repeated measure. All in-party candidates get essentially the same amount of search in the four-candidate condition, but the candidate closer to the voter on the issues receives significantly more search in the two-candidate condition. So we were half right.

of information selected about each of the candidates in the targeted (two-candidate) primary, not only across the entire primary campaign but also separately for each third of the primary campaign. We have no a priori hypotheses about whether airing ads early versus late will result in more total unique search directed toward a candidate, but we would expect relatively greater search early in the campaign directed toward the candidate who aired his or her ads early in the campaign and relatively greater search late in the campaign toward the candidate who aired his or her ads late.

There are undoubtedly a variety of factors that would lead a candidate to choose to air most of his or her ads early or late in a campaign, factors that make it difficult to evaluate the effectiveness of either strategy. We can ignore these subtleties in our mock election campaigns and randomly assign one candidate to air ads early in the campaign and another candidate to wait until the end of the campaign. We assigned this manipulation to whichever party's primary had only two candidates, regardless of whether it was the in-party or the out-party.

Without going into all of the details, there is a statistically significant advantage to airing one's ads early compared to late, at least in terms of the total amount of information that voters seek out about the sponsoring candidate. But the difference was so slight (9.9 vs. 9.7 items selected) that it is difficult to imagine it has any practical significance. Moreover, we could find no evidence that voters timed their information seeking in accordance with when the designated candidates were airing their ads. This nonfinding is somewhat disappointing because a more direct relationship between the timing of ads and information seeking would have had much more interesting implications, given that the availability of different types of information (both in our experiments and in reality) varies over time.

CONCLUSION

In summary, the collection of candidate factors considered here provides a somewhat mixed picture of the influence of such factors on information processing during an election. The two- versus four-candidate manipulation in the primary election is proving to be our strongest experimental manipulation. It had a huge effect on decision strategies. The ideological distinctiveness manipulation and stereotypic nature of the out-party candidate manipulation, both conducted in general election campaigns, had similar though less striking effects. In every case, voters seemed to shy away from Model 1 decision strategies in just those situations where they might be expected to do the most good, when the choice itself was fairly complex. But this is exactly what out theory predicts. Given greater incentives for making the best possible decision – incentives that rarely if ever exist during even presidential elections – we might expect to see voters shifting strategies toward those they believe would most likely yield the best decision. Here we are presuming that voters would believe that Model 1 strategies are actually most likely to produce the best choice, and we have no direct evidence on this point. But it is very plausible to us that the typical person would believe that difficult decision strategies should work best when the choice itself is difficult. This is the type of simplistic, semantic reasoning in which people often engage.

There was also an interesting effect of campaign resources on information search directed toward the candidate with superior resources. We found, counter to our expectations (and certainly counter to the desires of any candidate blessed with superior campaign resources), that voters compensate in their discretionary information search by actually seeking out more information about the candidates with fewer resources in situations where one candidate can afford to air many more ads than the others. Now, two caveats should be mentioned about this result. One is that our finding comes from a mock election study experiment, and it is unclear how generalizable this finding will prove to be to actual campaigns. This is a problem with any experiment. The second is that the candidate blessed with the extra resources was always the candidate farthest away from the voter on the issues. Voters may well try to counter the resource advantage of a candidate they do not particularly like by going out of their way to learn even more about his or her opponents, while operating in an opposite manner if a candidate they like has the resource advantage. We cannot say, for we have not run this manipulation. We hope to have more to say about this question in the future.

A RECONSIDERATION OF WHAT WE HAVE LEARNED SO FAR

We have now finished our exploration of the "cognitive underbelly" of the vote decision. Chapter 6 considered differences between voters, particularly their political sophistication, while Chapter 7 explored the influence of campaign factors, the candidates running in the election and the way they utilize their campaign resources – all on the amount and content and nature of information search, processing, and memory. We are now ready to turn to the outcome of the campaign in terms of evaluations of the candidates and the nature and quality of the vote decision. Before doing that, however, we want to summarize our findings so far in terms of our general framework for the vote decision presented at the end of Chapter 2. Figure 7.8 provides such a summary.

It begins with the same conceptual framework presented in Figure 2.1 but fleshes out the model by breaking the information processing variables

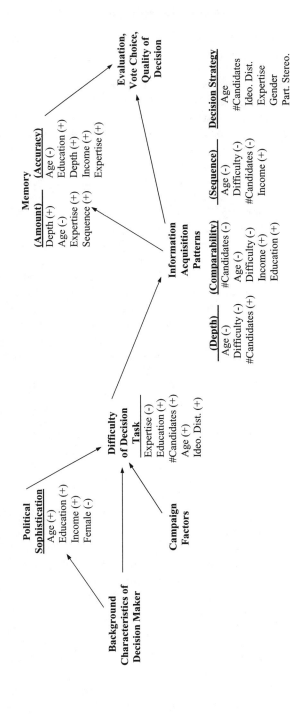

Figure 7.8. The cognitive underbelly of the vote decision.

(Information Acquisition Patterns, Memory) into their component parts and then listing, under each dependent variable in the model, the prior variables that have proven to be statistically significant predictors of that conceptual variable. In most cases, the diagram summarizes across several analyses, as particular manipulations were available only in certain studies and/or as the same basic analysis was repeated across the primary and general election campaigns. The direction of the relationship is listed in parentheses after each significant predictor, and we have listed them in decreasing order of importance.

To start with an analysis we have not actually presented earlier, *political sophistication* is a function of age, education, income, and gender. Race and frequency of church attendance have not been significant predictors in these analyses and were not included in subsequent analyses of information search. Similarly, the perceived difficulty of the decision task was a function of the experimental manipulations meant to influence it,[10] along with expertise, education, and age. Notice the importance of distinguishing between political sophistication and education in this analysis. As we would expect, political experts generally found the vote choice to be less difficult than novices; but controlling on expertise, education is actually positively related to perceived difficulty – that is, holding political sophistication constant, the more educated generally found the vote decisions to be more difficult than those with less education.

We will not repeat the various significant predictors of information acquisition patterns, which are all listed in the figure and have been discussed previously. Notice that at least some background characteristics, manipulations of campaign factors, and perceived difficulty are significant predictors of every category of the information processing variables. We will, however, point the reader's attention to our summary of a complete analysis of memory, reported here for the first time in the book. In particular, none of our previous examinations of memory have included any of the information processing variables as predictors, yet this link is very important theoretically. Two of the information search measures prove to be important predictors of total amount of memory (controlling on all prior variables in the model), depth and sequence of search. Depth of search also had a significant effect on accuracy of memory.

The effect of depth of search on the total amount of recall needs no deep explanation: The more that is accessed, the more it is possible to recall. Of course, virtually everyone looked at far more information than

---

[10] In Chapter 5, we reported that the manipulation of whether the party's candidate in the general election had been previously chosen or rejected by voters was also significantly related to perceived difficulty. This relationship did not survive controls for background demographics and political sophistication, however.

they could possibly recall, and it is conceivable that memory would "fill up" after the first few items that are learned about a candidate, and that any subsequent deeper search after this point would "go in one ear and out the other," as our mothers would say. But that is not the way memory works. Every item accessed has some probability of being recalled, and the net effect is more memory with more information considered.

Depth of search also has a positive effect on the accuracy of memory, and this effect is not quite so obvious. One could imagine depth of search having a negative effect on accuracy of recall, if more and more information confuses a voter, say. If we had measured accuracy in terms of what had been considered, then certainly depth of search would be negatively related to accuracy. But based just on what was recalled, greater depth leads to greater accuracy.

The sequence of search had a weaker effect on memory. Use of either of the more systematic search sequences, intra-candidate or intra-attribute, was associated with greater total memory. This makes perfect sense to us, as either of these search patterns should have contributed to more "coherent" memory structures for our two candidates, and thus greater ease of recall. We also hypothesized that more systematic search sequences would be associated with more accurate memory as well, but this proved not to be the case. In fact the effect of systematic search sequences was slightly negative, controlling on all the other variables in the equation, although never approaching significance.

Together, the analyses summarized in Figure 7.8 present an informal test of our general model. This theoretical model has held up quite well so far. All the hypothesized causal paths in Figure 2.1 have found empirical support, save for the direct influence of the perceived difficulty of the decision task on memory. Any influence of perceived task difficulty on memory must work through one or more types of information processing.

But all this prior analysis will be of only academic interest (and not very much of that) if these variables do not also influence the nature and quality of the vote decision. That is the primary question to be addressed in the remainder of the book. Chapters 8 and 9 consider what our model has to say about candidate evaluation and the vote choice. The chief purpose of political campaigns, after all, is to give citizens an opportunity to learn about the competing candidates in an election and to choose among them. Although we do not have a representative sample of the public nor an actual election of that public's political leaders, we do have a reasonably compelling experimental approximation of such an election. Moreover, we have much more detailed measures of information search, processing, and decision strategies than anyone before us has had. Chapters 8 and

9 will illustrate what all this "psychological nonsense" (as a skeptical colleague once put it) buys us.

Chapter 10 then turns to the two normative measures of the quality of the vote decision presented in Chapter 4. Along with those who have studied the vote decision before us, we retain an avid interest in who wins an election and in trying to understand why one candidate succeeded while others failed. But as citizens of the world, as lovers of democracy, we are also concerned with whether (or how many) people voted correctly in an election. Campaigns that result in the "wrong" candidate being elected – wrong from the perspective of the collected polity – cannot be good for any political system. Thus, Chapter 10 asks whether we can identify any individual or institutional factors that are associated with a greater or lesser probability of a correct vote, with the ultimate aim of starting a dialogue about how a political system might encourage the former and discourage the latter.

Part III. Politics

8

Evaluating Candidates

In discussing the results of our experiments so far, we have focused on information – how voters search for it, what type and how much of it they consider – and how information search in turn is affected by the decision environment, such as the number of candidates and the type of election. For a book about what voters do, up until this point we have actually talked very little about politics and voting. Beginning with this chapter, that changes. With what we have now learned about the importance of information processing as a background, we can turn to what, for most voting research, is the *raison d'etre* – candidate evaluation and choice. In this chapter and the next, we examine how voters evaluate candidates and how they choose among them. But we will not be content with just these traditional concerns. In Chapter 10, we will also consider just how good a job our voters did, and what factors affected their ability to vote correctly. And in Chapter 11 we will turn our attention to political heuristics, a very important topic for a book focusing on information processing. These four chapters will complete our study of the process-oriented framework established in Chapter 2 (and Figure 2.1) for examining the vote choice.

This chapter focuses specifically on candidate evaluation. We have three goals here. First, we want to examine the question of on-line versus memory-based evaluation. This will require a brief review of the relevant psychological and political science literatures. As we will soon argue, even though the evaluation of political figures outside of a campaign probably proceeds on-line, as does most person perception, the unique environment of a campaign, where voters need to *compare* candidates directly on the attributes (policy stands, personal qualities, etc.) they care about, creates an important role for memory. Second, we will show that just because we might know which candidate a voter evaluates most highly, we do not necessarily know which candidate that voter will choose in an election.

This point stems directly from our argument that evaluation and choice are not the same thing. Finally, we will consider the effects of decision strategy on global candidate evaluation. Our framework suggests that how voters learn about candidates – the information search and acquisition strategies they employ – has implications for how positive or negative they feel about the candidates at the end.

ON-LINE VERSUS MEMORY-BASED EVALUATION

There is a great deal of research in social psychology on person perception (e.g., Gilbert, 1998; Hastie and Park, 1986), which suggests that whenever people come across information about another person in their social environment, they form an immediate on-line impression of the person. That impression – an efficient summary of the information – is remembered, but the specific information upon which it is based is much less important to retain. When additional information about this same person is encountered, this "evaluative counter" or "running tally" is retrieved from memory and updated based on the new information, with the resulting new summary evaluation stored in memory. Again, however, there is no need for the specifics upon which the new evaluation was based to be remembered.

This theory has been applied in political science most directly by Milton Lodge and his colleagues at SUNY Stony Brook (e.g., Lodge, 1995; Lodge, McGraw, and Stroh, 1989; Lodge and Stroh, 1993; Lodge, Stroh, and Wahlke, 1990; McGraw, Lodge, and Stroh, 1990) who, in a series of clever experiments, have found evaluations of a (hypothetical) Congressman Williams to conform to the predictions of the on-line model. Applied to voting, the model suggests that people evaluate political candidates as they do other people, and that the vote is simply a matter of comparing the running tally for each candidate and choosing the one more positively evaluated (Lodge, Steenbergen, and Brau, 1995).[1]

---

[1] We can easily provide an example of on-line voting in the 2004 election analogous to our five hypothetical voters from Chapter 1 who were illustrating other voting models. Consider Milton L, a bus driver living on Long Island, taking commuters into lower Manhattan every morning and then back again in the afternoon. He is not very interested in politics, but he always hears about what is going on in the country from his passengers, who are usually reading the *Wall Street Journal* on their way into work. Every time he hears something positive or negative about one of the candidates, it makes him think about how he feels about that candidate at that moment, and he adjusts his evaluation accordingly. But by the next day, his riders are typically talking about something new, and he rarely remembers what they were talking about the day before. As the election approaches, Milton has a decidedly more favorable impression of George Bush than of John Kerry, although he would

Although this theory may seem innocuous enough, the on-line model is actually diametrically opposed to one of the few political science models of the vote choice that explicitly considers the process of decision making, Kelley and Mirer's "simple act of voting" (1974). According to Kelley and Mirer, when it comes time for voters to figure out how they are going to vote, they simply canvass their memories for reasons to vote for and against each candidate and then vote for the candidate with the highest net positive score. Likewise, although they do not describe it as such, the authors of *The American Voter* (Campbell et al., 1960) clearly presumed memory-based processing, as much of their most direct evidence on voter decision making comes from a series of open-ended questions designed to tap survey respondents' memories about the two major candidates (Stokes, Campbell, and Miller, 1958). And once we recognize the limitations of short-term (or working) memory, any rational choice theory of voting in practice must also rely heavily upon memory. Thus, both Model 1 and Model 2 clearly presume memory-based information processing and, were they to turn to this question, candidate evaluation.

But according to the on-line model, once the running tally is updated, there is no reason for the detailed information upon which the updating was based to be retained in memory. Some information might be retained, but memory for candidate-specific information is driven by the same factors that influence memory for anything else (e.g., saliency, recency, and frequency of exposure), and there is no reason to expect what is in memory at any point in time to be representative of the information upon which the running tally is based. Thus, the tally may be summarizing a vast amount of information encountered by a voter, even if the voter is unable after the fact to detail what actually went into his or her judgment. Memory, according to the on-line model, is irrelevant – except for memory of the on-line tally itself. This fact has important normative implications because it means that candidate evaluations can be based upon a lot more information than what a voter is able to recall when asked by a survey interviewer (Lodge, Steenbergen, and Brau, 1995). But when we put those candidate evaluations to the task of making a vote choice, it is also very clear that the evaluations of multiple competing candidates will quite likely be based upon very noncomparable information sets. Thus, on-line processing fits very comfortably within our Model 4 category of decision making, but it is clearly incompatible with any compensatory decision theory that assumes that decisions are based on comparable information about the alternatives under consideration.

be hard pressed to tell anyone why. He doesn't always bother to vote, but this year it seems like a tight election, and he stops at the polls on his way home and pulls the lever for the Republican candidate.

EVALUATION VERSUS CHOICE

It seems pretty clear that in order to cast a vote, people must spend at least some time evaluating the choices they face and making judgments about them.[2] Of course, one can make a judgment even when no choice is involved. The evaluation of an incumbent between elections represents one such "choiceless" judgment in politics. People can usually provide a ready assessment of the president's job performance without resorting to a comparison of the president with potential challengers.[3] This evaluation, we suspect, is probably on-line, generated as information is encountered, though it may be memory-based and drawn from whatever information is readily accessible from memories retained about the president. Whichever it is – and we will have much more to say about this shortly – the process of evaluation is not synonymous with choice.

In Chapter 2 we made our initial case that evaluation and choice are not the same thing. Evaluation is about making a judgment on some dimension of interest about an object regardless of how many objects are being evaluated, while choice is inherently about selecting from a set of alternatives. Choice is about commitment, choosing between two or more objects (candidates), and often carries with it a (conscious or unconscious) justification of why one is chosen over the other(s). In this sense, choice is about taking an action, that of deciding. Judgment, on the other hand, does not imply action per se, nor does it suggest a need to justify one option over another. Judgment is simpler than choice, a matter of evaluating an object on some scale. We also pointed out that decisions are often made without much judgment. Spur of the moment decisions, for example, or standing decisions (such as a vote based primarily on partisanship) require no real evaluation before they are made. Finally, it seems quite clear that global evaluations – at least in elections – do not have to translate directly into a vote. Strategic voting, for example, might lead to a choice of a candidate with a lower overall evaluation if the voter believes that candidate has a better chance of winning, as might a vote

---

[2] Throughout this chapter, we follow typical practice in the decision literature in using the words "evaluation" and "judgment" as synonyms for the process of determining how much a person (or object) is liked or disliked, based upon some assessment, no matter how limited, of the known attributes of the person or object being considered.

[3] It is conceivable that in evaluating a president's job performance, citizens are implicitly comparing the sitting president to past presidents. If so, the time horizon of those comparisons would be very short. Past analyses of presidential approval (e.g., Mueller, 1970; Kernell, 1977) assume the process pretty much starts over with a honeymoon period for each new president, after which each president is judged against his own past performance – just as the on-line model would suggest.

made for other external reasons, such as based on group affiliation or to please someone else.

That evaluation and choice are independent has been suggested by others (Fischer and Johnson, 1986; Hogarth, 1987), but as Billings and Scherer (1988) note, the two "have not always been clearly distinguished." Johnson and Russo (1984), studying consumer evaluation and choice behavior, argue that "*choosing* one alternative from a set can invoke different psychological processes than *judging* alternatives, which are presumably evaluated one at a time" [emphasis in original]. And, as we have demonstrated in earlier chapters, in more complex choice environments, people often use strategies that simplify decision making, including strategies that can eliminate alternatives from consideration quite early in the process. On the other hand, when asked to evaluate all options (but not make a choice), people must consider all available alternatives rather than abandoning one or more before the end of the information search process (Johnson and Russo, 1984). Billings and Scherer (1988) find that subjects charged with making a choice between alternatives without explicitly being told to make evaluations search for less information overall and show more variability in information search than those told to make judgments.

We can conduct a simple test of this particular difference between judgment and choice using data from our primary elections. In the primaries, voters learned about candidates from their own party – between whom they would ultimately make a choice – and from the other party, where no choice was needed. We have already shown that there is much *more* search directed toward in-party candidates, but to replicate Billings and Scherer, we need to examine the variance in search across the sets of in-party and out-party candidates. To do this, we examined the number of unique items chosen for each candidate in the primary election. These data have already been summarized in Figure 5.2. As expected, whether voters faced an easy choice between two candidates or a harder choice among four, they conducted an uneven search across candidates within their party (where a choice had to be made) and a much more even search across out-party candidates where no choice was required. In a two-candidate primary, the mean variance across the in-party candidates is 10.11, while across the out-party candidates the mean is 5.80 ($p < .002$). The same pattern holds in a four-candidate primary, where in-party variance is 9.52 versus out-party variance of 4.26 ($p < .001$). This simple test provides clear evidence consistent with the findings of Billings and Scherer that there are important differences between choice and evaluation, justifying our skepticism that they can be considered one and the same even in voting.

So what? Why bother making such a distinction in voter decision making, which obviously culminates in a choice? Can't we simply adopt the assumption of most political science models that voters first evaluate and then choose the most highly evaluated candidate? This assumption is a hallmark of the Model 1 approaches we have considered, it has been frequently applied in certain renditions of Model 2 (e.g., Markus and Converse, 1979), and of course it also underlies the on-line model of the vote choice discussed earlier (Lodge, Steenbergen, and Brau, 1995). Even though we are quite willing to accept that people do, in fact, make many of their candidate evaluations on-line, we disagree with the radical premise that only the on-line evaluation matters, and that candidate memories – needed, we believe, to effectively compare candidates when information is learned asymmetrically – play no role in determining the vote. The problem is that the studies that form the bedrock of the on-line model have required only the evaluation of a political figure, yet the findings have been assumed to apply to candidate choice as well.[4] Some hint that this assumption is untenable has been found in our earlier research (Redlawsk, 2001a). Thus, we must now wade into the on-line versus memory debate, which we believe is important to specifying accurate models of evaluation and the voting.

IS CANDIDATE EVALUATION PURELY ON-LINE?

We need to take several steps to determine whether our thinking about the role of memory in candidate evaluation is accurate, or whether an on-line model sans any role for memory fully specifies the process. First and most importantly, we must specify the content of the on-line evaluation counter. This is a key point. If the counter does not take into account the full range of information that a voter examines in learning about candidates, it cannot properly specify how that voter evaluates the candidate. So we will pay particular attention to the question of just what goes into the evaluation counter. Second, we must also specify a memory measure that can

---

[4] Lodge, Steenbergen, and Brau (1995) explicitly consider the vote choice, but in a situation where all information about the two competing candidates is provided on a single sheet of paper in side-by-side, easy-to-compare fashion, as often appears in newspapers near Election Day. If all voters know about candidates is obtained in such a manner, there is no variability across candidates in information search, and no need for memory. But when voters obtain their information about the competing candidates in a more haphazard manner during the course of an entire election campaign, it is very possible for memory to play a much larger role. In fact the role of memory in the on-line model is now coming under some revision. Lodge, Taber, and Weber (2006) have recently suggested that the vote decision process may be more hybrid than pure on-line, and that what people remember about candidates may influence not only the updating of the on-line evaluation but also the vote itself, a position we strongly endorse (Redlawsk, 2001a).

be contrasted with the on-line evaluation counter. Because the evaluation counter is affective – it is about how people feel about candidates – we will also look at the affective content of candidate memories, derived by asking our voters how each memory they recorded made them feel about the relevant candidate. Finally, we need to assess the general level of familiarity a voter has with a candidate. The old saying is that "familiarity breeds contempt," but there is also the distinct possibility that familiarity breeds "contentment" as Zajonc (1968) put it many years ago. In either case, familiarity may have an independent effect on evaluation and, thus, is an important control. We can easily measure familiarity because we know exactly what and how much information voters examined about each candidate. Obviously, familiarity increases as more information is examined. Note, however, that this is not an "affective" measure as such; that is, we are not assessing whether people like or dislike what they look at (that is done by the evaluation counter and memory affect) but just how much "stuff" they may have learned about each candidate.

We will approach the on-line/memory test two ways. First, we will see the extent to which each variable predicts the *global* evaluation of candidates (controlling for other factors). At the end of the campaign, and immediately after voting, subjects rated each candidate on a 0–100 feeling thermometer scale. If the on-line model is accurate, these global evaluations should be primarily conditioned by the on-line evaluation counter, with little role for memory. On the other hand, if we are right in our belief that memory matters in a choice situation such as an election campaign, we should see effects of it here. Of course, as Rahn and colleagues (1994) have argued, it is possible that reported memories are more in the nature of justifications than independent predictors of global evaluation. After all, we collect the memories after the vote choice and global evaluation has been made, so perhaps they are contaminated by the vote choice itself.[5]

---

[5] While Rahn and her colleagues (1994) show that the responses to memory questions asked in the American National Election Studies appear to be justifications, we believe this comes from how the questions are asked. McGraw, Fischle, and Stenner (2000) argue that the method the ANES uses to gather memories about the candidates produces distortions in recall in a way that serves to rationalize existing preferences, and thus build in correlations between memory and evaluation. Different memory probes, like free recall, produce memory that is more representative and accurate in terms of the underlying information base. By asking our subjects to simply recall as much as they could about the different candidates, we employed a type of free recall probe that should be relatively free from justification biases. In ANES studies, participants are asked to tell what they like and dislike about candidates and parties. This stimulates affective memory, which is likely to be conditioned by global affect for the candidates or parties themselves. Our memory questions are less directive. We tell subjects to "list everything you can remember about [candidate name] no

Our second approach will address this problem with an unusual analysis in which we will assess the extent to which voters actually vote for the candidate they "should" based on their on-line evaluation counter. If memory works to predict what we call defection from the most highly (on-line) evaluated candidate, then we will have shown that memory has independent effects on evaluation that cannot be explained simply as justification. Of course, before we can begin, we need to be clear in how we specify the on-line evaluation counter.

Building an On-line Evaluation Counter

The simple idea behind the on-line evaluation counter is that it incorporates the affective assessment of each and every piece of information about a candidate that the voter encounters during information search. The practical difficulty of implementing this simple idea is that these affective assessments happen within voters' heads, in a process not especially visible to the researcher. Thus, we (and anyone else doing similar research) must infer the value of the on-line evaluation counter by specifying what information is part of it, how that information might be weighed by the voter, and how different (and potentially noncomparable) kinds of information are integrated. To date it appears that only Lodge and his colleagues and we have actually tried to calculate an on-line tally in published work in political science. In Lodge's case, this calculation was not very difficult. Subjects saw only forty simple issue stands for a single Congressman. Lodge generally asks subjects for their positions on each of the issues ahead of time and calculates the evaluation counter as a simple, unweighted, averaged summary of likes and dislikes.

In contrast, our studies include six different presidential candidates, each with forty-five distinct items (issues and other attributes) available (forty-six in the general election), as well as thirty-eight different endorsements by a variety of interest groups. It was not practical to ask subjects ahead of time for their preferences on every item, nor did we know ahead of time which items any given subject would choose to examine. Further, it seems to us that the approach taken by Lodge fails to account for the wide range of information that actually goes into any evaluation. Where previous studies only looked at issue positions, we added group endorsements, candidate personality factors, performance evaluations, and party

matter how trivial." From this we get a wide range of memories, including many that subjects indicate made them feel neither good nor bad about a candidate. So we believe that our means of collecting memory is less likely to result in contamination by the global evaluation already given, but we recognize we must establish this rather than to just assume it.

identification. This means that we have a much more complex job to do in building a counter, but that our counter will also be much more comprehensive in accounting for the information that does drive candidate preference.

The details of how we calculate our evaluation counter are laid out in Appendix E. What is important here is to know that we had to consider the questions of what "counts," how and whether to use some weighting scheme to reflect subjects' own perceived importance for different pieces of information, and whether to build an averaging (à la Lodge) or additive counter. As it turns out, while theoretically important, the choice of weighting and integration schemes has little practical implication for our analyses. We considered six possible approaches for each candidate (three weighting schemes by two integration approaches) and all turn out to be highly correlated.[6] In the end, for reasons explained in the appendix, we chose to weight the information voters examined by the subjective importance they attached to the same type of information in a real-world election, and to use an additive approach to integrating the evaluations on each attribute examined. In short, the on-line evaluation counter we will use throughout these analyses takes into account nearly all the information our voters examined, weights it for the subjective importance of each item, and adds the resulting positive or negative affect together to get a summary for each candidate.[7] It is important to note that these evaluation counters are asymmetric. That is, each is based solely on what was actually examined for the particular candidate. Thus, if subject A looked at "Position on Abortion" for candidate 1, but not for candidate 2, then the evaluation counter for candidate 1 will include this issue stand, but the counter for candidate 2 will not.

Memory

Since memory is also important to our models, a quick reprise of how we collected our memory measures might be useful. Following the general election (the primary in Study 2) and after voting and evaluating candidates, subjects were given sheets of paper headed by the name of each candidate in the election. They were then instructed to list "everything

---

[6] Mean $r = .65$, ranging from .20 to .93.

[7] One additional point worth noting is that our choice of an additive approach for the on-line evaluation counter will mean that both it and our affective memory measure will be on the same relative scale and will both incorporate only information that resulted in an affective response (positive or negative) since neutral information will neither increment nor decrement either measure. Thus, we are quite comfortable that we can readily compare the two.

you can remember about [candidate name], no matter how trivial it seems to you." The experimenter allowed the subject as much time as needed for the memory listing. Following this free recall task, the experimenter reviewed each memory listed by the subject and asked: "For this memory, did it make you feel good about [the candidate name], bad about [the candidate name], or neutral?" The experimenter recorded the reported affect on the form next to the memory to which it referred. Our affective memory measure is simply the sum of all negative memories subtracted from the sum of all positive memories, resulting in a net positive memory measure for each candidate.

Assessing Global Candidate Evaluation

Following each election, our subjects gave 0–100 feeling thermometer ratings to all the candidates running in the election, first in the primary and then in the general election. These feeling thermometer ratings are our basic measure of global candidate evaluation, and parallel the feeling thermometer approach used in survey research, such as the ANES.[8]

Before we look directly at our on-line versus memory question, it is useful to look at a summary of the global candidate evaluations given by our subjects, which we display in Figure 8.1. Recall that we had eight possible candidates, although no subject saw all eight. These eight are arrayed across the ideological spectrum as detailed in Chapter 3 (Figure 3.3). Because managing analyses with eight different candidates is somewhat unwieldy and because we have no reason to believe that partisanship correlates with the evaluation process, for primary election analyses we will combine candidates across partisan and ideological lines.[9] Thus, we will consider the most extreme Democrat and Republican together, and so on, labeling these combined candidates as Extreme (candidates D1 & R4, to use the labeling in Figure 3.3), Modal (D2 & R3), Moderate (D3 & R2), and Mixed (D4 & R1). We will definitely contrast in-party from

---

[8] Feeling thermometers have at least one serious problem, however. Even when labeled, as ours were, different people use different places on the thermometer as their starting point. For some people, a rating of 60 is pretty good, especially if their average rating is 40. For others, 60 might be actually below average. The result is that we must make adjustment for these differences within our subjects (Brady, 1985). Our general approach will be to account for each subject's personal average rating by using that mean as a variable in multivariate analyses, thus controlling for subjects' propensities to rate everyone (and every group) higher or lower. We calculate this control variable by taking the mean of all thirteen feeling thermometer ratings provided by subjects in the preexperiment questionnaire.

[9] Across all candidate evaluations, Democrats had a mean of 60.9, and Republicans had a mean of 60.6.

Evaluating Candidates

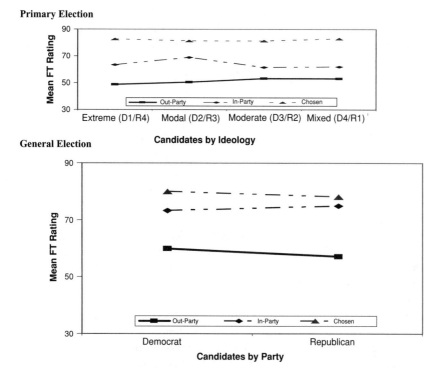

Figure 8.1. Global candidate evaluations.

out-party candidates in the primary but, for the most part, will not worry about whether the in-party is Democratic or Republican. For the general election, we will look at candidates by party, combining all of our Democratic candidates and all Republicans, since any given subject saw only one of each in that election.

Our voters were quite ready to give ratings to all of the candidates, whether in- or out-party. In the primary, the mean in-party candidate rating ranges from 61.5 for the moderate candidate to 68.8 for the modal candidate. We would, of course, expect the candidate who represents the mainstream of the party (as the modal is meant to do) to get higher ratings, on average, from the partisans in that party (who should themselves on average be closer to the modal party position). And while the difference is not large, that is exactly what we find. As expected, when the candidate was the one the voter chose in the primary, the rating was substantially higher, just under 82 on average, with no significant difference between candidates. Finally, when these same candidates are from the out-party, ratings drop quite a bit, about 8–15 points below the rating for them when they are from the in-party. Voters are also far more likely to rate out-party candidates at 50, neither warm nor cold. All of these patterns are quite reasonable and provide additional comfort that subjects in our experiments evaluated the candidates in the same manner as would be expected for real-world candidates.

The general election patterns shown in the bottom part of Figure 8.1 roughly match the primary election but with one interesting difference. Ratings in the general election are higher than those in the primary. In-party candidates are rated at nearly 75, compared to the low 60s in the primary. Out-party candidates are also rated higher in the general election, around 60, compared to around 50 in the primary. These generally higher ratings probably reflect the greater amount of information that most subjects had about the candidates in the general election, since they had potentially learned about the candidates not only during the current campaign but also during the primary.[10]

The usual way global feeling thermometer evaluations are used as a dependent variable is to assess the factors that predict either its direction (high or low) for a single candidate or the relative difference between two candidates (for example, ratings of Bush minus Kerry). Unfortunately, the complexity of our experimental campaigns makes this typical approach difficult. We could look at the ratings for each candidate individually, but this seems not only like overkill but also potentially confusing given that every one of our candidates was for some voters an in-party candidate and for others an out-party candidate, while the electoral context (i.e., which other candidates were running) varied widely. Alternatively, we could examine all our candidates together, pooling all evaluations into a single analysis. But this seems like too strong a reaction in the opposite direction, and it would undoubtedly obscure some importance differences. Or we could try to take relative differences between candidates, but in some elections we have two candidates – making this easy to do – while in others we have four, making such comparisons confusing at best. And, of course, we have both a primary election where partisanship is not a factor in the decision and a general election in which it is.

Ultimately for the primary, we decided to look at two classes of candidates from within the voter's own party (ignoring the candidates from the out-party), the candidate selected by the voter and the candidate(s) that the voter rejected.[11] In the general election, we can do something

---

[10] The increased general election rating of the in-party candidate is particularly noteworthy, given that this candidate was most often not the candidate supported in the primary election.

[11] Obviously, in making this choice, we forgo the ability to identify more traditional effects – such as that of ideology – on evaluation. Because we lump together all preferred candidates and all rejected candidates, regardless of the candidate's

Evaluating Candidates

Table 8.1. *On-line versus Memory-Based Global Evaluations*

	Primary Election		General Election	
	Preferred Candidate	Rejected Candidates	In-Party Candidate	Out-Party Candidate
Familiarity with candidate	.078	.519@	−.027	.216**
	(.122)	(.362)	−(.084)	(.101)
On-line evaluation counter	1.152*	.556	1.628***	−.865
	(.639)	(1.880)	(.603)	−865 (1.017)
Affective memory	1.896***	2.792**	2.422***	3.187***
	(.464)	(1.054)	(.249)	(.327)

@ $p < .10$, * $p < .05$, ** $p < .01$, *** $p < .001$.

Note: Table entries are unstandardized regression coefficients, standard errors in parentheses. Dependent variable is global feeling thermometer evaluations.

closer to a "typical" analysis that considers partisanship by looking at the evaluations for the in-party and the out-party candidates, once again combining Republican and Democratic voters. Because most voters voted for the candidate of their party in the general election, this is quite similar to looking at the chosen and rejected candidates and should also allow us to test decision strategy implications.

Evaluating Primary Election Candidates

We build a model that incorporates standard voter, candidate, and election factors but that also includes the effects of memory and the on-line evaluation counter on global evaluation. Table 8.1 describes the key variables of interest in these analyses.[12] Because we are conducting analyses that include memory, we are limited to using only Study 2 data for the primary elections, since that was the only study where memory measures were available from the primary. This means our results will of necessity be more tentative than most we present in this book because the sample size is much more limited. When we look at the general election model, we will be able to use the rest of our dataset.

It is important to point out that we are not building traditional voting models here (e.g., a model that predicts the ideological direction of the

ideology, we do not expect to find significant effects for voter ideology. An analysis that looked at a single candidate at a single ideological point would show significant effects for voter ideology, something we think is not particularly interesting for our work, and thus not a great loss in our analytical approach.

[12] Details on the full models and the operationalization of predictors are available from the authors upon request.

vote based on demographic differences and involvement with politics), and we are not substantively interested in the standard variables that most such models include. We certainly consider issue distance, partisanship, candidates factors, and so on, but we incorporate them all into the on-line evaluation rather than considering their individual effects. This allows us to focus on the two variables of real theoretical interest – the relative impact of memory and the on-line evaluation counter. We also include our measure of familiarity with the candidates as discussed earlier. Simply learning more information overall, of any kind and any valence, might have some effect on evaluation, and we want to control for that possibility.

When we enter all three of these variables into our primary candidate analyses, we find a strong role for memory, as we expected, whether for the preferred or rejected candidate. Each additional net positive memory adds two points to the evaluation of the preferred candidate and nearly three points to the evaluations of rejected candidates. And, as we also expected, we see some significant effects for the on-line evaluation counter, but surprisingly only for the preferred candidate. It would seem that, for the preferred candidate, global evaluation is conditioned on both an on-line process and a memory process. Each additional piece of information positively evaluated on-line increases the global evaluation by about 1.5 points. But there is no equivalent effect for rejected candidates. For them, memory and familiarity matter, but the on-line evaluation does not.

While we may have some difficulty building strong models for the evaluation of primary candidates, it does seem quite clear that there is a memory process involved. These results must be considered somewhat tentative because we have a relatively small number of cases available. Thus, we turn to our general elections to further investigate the roles of memory and the on-line evaluation.

Evaluating General Election Candidates

Before we begin, we should remember that subjects never entered the general election until they were already through the primary. Thus, they started the general election with some existing knowledge about the candidates, which was never the case in the primary. Further, unlike the primary, in the general election differences in the amount of information subjects learned about the two candidates are not very large. At the same time, analysis of the general election is, in a sense, far easier than the primary, if only because there are always only two candidates in the election who differ by party. So whereas in the primary we focused only on the set of in-party candidates, in the general election we must look at candidates from both parties. We will do this by analyzing in-party and out-party candidates separately, which has the effect of eliminating partisanship as a major factor in any model, although we retain it as a control variable.[13]

We built the same series of models for the general election as we did for the primary, making small adjustments as needed to recognize differences in the design of the elections. Once again, Table 8.1 reports the critical findings from this analysis. For our variables of interest, the results look very much like those for the primary. Memory matters for both in-party and out-party candidates. Each additional net positive memory results in a rating increase of two and a half points for the in-party candidate and more than three points for the out-party. And the on-line evaluation counter predicts the global evaluation of the in-party, but not the out-party candidate. Finally, out-party candidates look like the rejected primary candidates in another way – greater familiarity results in higher ratings, something that does not happen for the in-party candidate.[14]

Given the dramatic similarity of the results across two very different types of elections and with slightly different operationalizations of the nature of the candidates being evaluated, we feel very comfortable in our assertion that memory matters in candidate evaluation in the context of an election campaign. Although we also accept a role for on-line evaluation, it seems clear that any model of evaluation (and the vote) that fails to account for the role of candidate memories is underspecified.

We expected memory to be important in the comparative context of an election campaign. What is much more surprising to us is the failure of the on-line evaluation counter to predict evaluation of rejected candidates once memory and familiarity are controlled. This is not a function of any peculiarities of the individual candidates running in our elections, because all eight of them were "preferred" by some voters and "rejected" by others. Thus, the results presented in Table 8.1 actually generalize across eight different individual candidates, each of which show the same general pattern. This is a bit of a puzzle because there seems to be no particular reason why the on-line evaluation would be different in kind for rejected candidates compared to preferred ones. A closer look, however, reveals that the evaluations are not really different. In fact, the zero-order

---

[13] We do this because we do not find much interest in the role of partisanship in evaluating candidates. We know that partisans will evaluate their own party significantly more positively than the out-party, and we wish to avoid needing to consider this difference where possible. The effect of partisanship does not disappear, of course; it is represented by the difference between the constant terms associated with comparable models of evaluation of in- and out-party candidates.

[14] It may be worth noting here that we do see strong effects for partisanship in these analyses. But it is partisan strength that matters – stronger partisans rate their own party candidate much higher than weak partisans, while rating the out-party candidate significantly lower.

correlation between the on-line evaluation and the feeling thermometer rating is actually stronger for rejected candidates ($r = .153$, $p < .001$ compared to $r = .088$, $p < .05$). And when we do not include memory in our models, the evaluation counter for both types of candidates is significant and in the expected direction. The explanation may be that memory is particularly important in the evaluation of a rejected candidate and when entered into the model overwhelms the effects of the on-line evaluation. This could occur because as voters reject a candidate they become less likely to learn new things about him or her. Thus, by the time they are asked to make a global evaluation, the on-line evaluation may simply have faded and our voters find themselves evaluating based primarily on what they actually remember about those candidates. Preferred and in-party candidates, however, are most likely fresher in the mind, and their on-line evaluations are more easily accessed. Even so, memory still matters for these candidates as well, evidence that some hybrid process is clearly taking place (Redlawsk, 2001a; Steenbergen and Lodge, 1998).

DECISION STRATEGIES AND GLOBAL EVALUATION

We suggested in Chapter 2 that the particular decision strategies chosen by voters could affect how they evaluate candidates at the end of the election. In particular, we hypothesized that voters who use strategies that entail careful consideration of information for all candidates in the choice set (i.e., Model 1 compensatory strategies) might show an attenuation of differences in evaluating preferred and rejected (or in-party and out-party) candidates. Such voters spend a good deal of time learning things they both like and dislike about the whole set of candidates. This process might well result in a somewhat lower evaluation of a preferred candidate and a higher evaluation of rejected ones. On the other hand, strategies that suggest limited information search, such as Model 3 fast and frugal or Model 4 intuitive strategies, should accentuate differences in evaluation because little is learned about rejected candidates, and what is learned is probably negative. To complete the scenario, we frankly are not sure what to expect with Model 2 confirmatory strategies in a primary election because partisanship is not a factor, but in a general election, we expect such voters to give relatively higher ratings to their own party and lower to the other party. Thus, all three "nonrational" strategies should result in a larger net difference between preferred and rejected candidates in both the primary and the general election compared to Model 1 approaches.

We build on our memory model of evaluation to test these predictions. For both the primary and general election analyses, we add indicators of the type of search undertaken by each voter. The full models[15] test the effects of using any of our defined strategies compared to a voter using a Model 1 rational strategy. Because we are now examining a comparison process – that is, voters using a strategy in an election to compare candidates – we modify our earlier models to consider the net difference in global evaluation between the two types of candidates examined (preferred and rejected in the primary; in- and out-party in the general election). Of course this means our other measures – on-line evaluation, memory, and familiarity – are also recalculated as comparative measures.

Our expectations about search strategies are met in the primary election, where we find statistically significant effects for two of our three nonrational strategies, as well as for voters using an undifferentiated strategy. The results are summarized in the top of Figure 8.2 where we graphically display the net global evaluation by decision strategy. The combined effect of search on the preferred and rejected candidates shows something close to what we might expect, in that Models 3 and 4 both result in greater net difference in the evaluations of preferred and rejected candidates, compared to Model 1. Interestingly, Model 2 shows the smallest difference of all of the "non-rational" strategies, a difference which is quite similar to that produced by Model 1 itself. In retrospect that might make some sense, since such voters are very party-oriented, and might be less likely to see strong differences between party candidates within a primary election.

Turning to the general election, we continue to see a strong difference in evaluation for Model 3 – fast and frugal – searchers, compared to rational approaches, shown in the bottom panel of Figure 8.2. These voters, who limit their information search to only a few attributes across all candidates, show a much greater difference between evaluations of their in- and out-party candidates. The other three strategies, however, are relatively indistinguishable when we examine the net global evaluation as we have done here. Model 2 and Model 4 voters seem to have slightly greater polarization between the two candidates than do Model 1 voters, but the net difference is not statistically significant. However, if we examine the ratings of in- and out-party candidates separately, we find that Model 2 and Model 4 voters rate their own party's candidates significantly higher than do Model 1 voters (at about 75.5, compared to 71 for Model 1). This effect is the same for both Model 2 and Model 4; however, the reasons might be different. Model 2 voters, with their partisan screen, should simply see their own party in a more positive light. Model 4 voters, on the other hand, probably give a benefit to the in-party candidate because they

---

[15] The full models are available from the authors upon request.

Primary Election: Net Difference between Preferred and Rejected Candidates

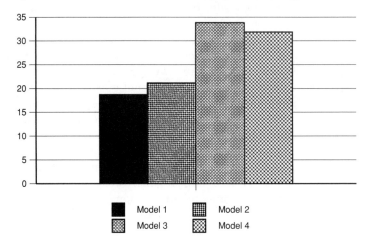

General Election: Net Difference between In-Party and Out-Party Candidates

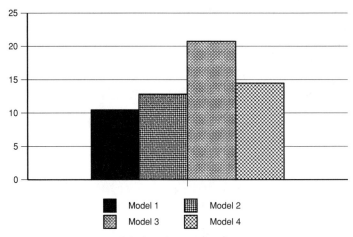

Figure 8.2. Global evaluation by decision strategy.

focus more directly on that candidate in their limited information search. Thus, as we expected, information search strategies do condition global evaluations, both for the primary and general elections. In particular, Model 1 rational voters are less likely to generate polarized evaluations, seeing more of the good and bad in all candidates. Other search strategies, however, do not show this same result.

Evaluating Candidates

IS EVALUATION THE SAME AS THE VOTE?

Because we have already built a statistical model of global candidate evaluation, it may seem that our intent to build an actual vote model in the next chapter will be an exercise in redundancy. After all, if the on-line model is to be believed, choosing which candidate to support is a simple matter of comparing on-line evaluations and selecting the candidate with the highest score. But of course, we have already shown that memory matters (and the on-line evaluation does not matter for rejected candidates). So we know that the basic predictions of the on-line voting model do not seem to be working as expected in our campaign setting.

Even so, how does memory matter? In particular, can memories for the candidates predict when voters do not vote for the most highly evaluated candidate? The answer may seem moot given that well over 90% of our voters gave their highest global evaluation to the candidate they voted for. As we have noted, we measure global evaluation with a feeling thermometer, which is usually the only evaluation available in survey-based voting research. The feeling thermometer always correlates highly with the vote. But it is not really an independent measure of candidate evaluation, coming as it does (in our study and in any postelection survey) after the vote is cast. The feeling thermometer is contaminated by the vote decision, something that does not matter when we want to assess global evaluation following the election, but that is a serious problem when a goal is to predict the vote itself. We need a measure uncontaminated by the actual vote, and our on-line evaluation counter fulfills this requirement quite well.

Although the vast majority of our voters gave their highest global evaluation to the candidate they voted for, using the on-line counter as a measure of candidate evaluation shows something very different. Recall that the on-line counter includes only information that has been encountered about each specific candidate. It does not assume any comparison between candidates and is not influenced by information actually examined for any of the other candidates. In this sense, it is a pure on-line evaluation. In accordance with the on-line model, we would expect our voters to give their highest feeling thermometer evaluation to the candidate generating the most positive affect (and also to vote for that candidate). But as it turns out, and contrary to the on-line model, a large percentage of our subjects did not vote for the candidate with the highest on-line evaluation. In the two-candidate primary, over a third of our voters chose the candidate with the *lower* on-line evaluation. In the four-candidate primary, only 35% of all voters selected the candidate with the highest on-line evaluation! In both cases, voters selected the candidate with the highest on-line evaluation more often than chance (50% in the two-candidate primary, 25%

Table 8.2. *Liking of Presidential Candidates and the Vote Choice*

	Voted Democratic	Voted Republican	Voted for Third Party
Liked candidate *more than* any other	78.1%	77.9%	51.3%
Liked candidate *as much as* any other	12.2%	11.3%	16.1%
Liked some *other viable candidate* more	9.6%	10.8%	32.7%

Note: Data are from the 1972–2000 ANES, using weighted samples, feeling thermometer evaluations of the candidates from the preelection wave of interviews, and reported vote choice from the postelection wave of interviews.

in the four-candidate primary), but clearly something more is driving the vote than a simple comparison of on-line evaluations.[16]

Lest this be seen as simply an artifact of our experimental design, we can take a look at ANES data to illustrate this point. We examined the relationship between liking presidential candidates, as measured in preelection feeling thermometers asked on surveys conducted by the American National Election Studies from 1972 through 2000, and the reported vote choice from the postelection interview. Here we use the preelection feeling thermometer as a surrogate for the on-line tally. Although most of these surveys also obtained evaluations of the candidates in the postelection survey, we restrict our analysis to evaluations from the preelection wave of interviews to minimize the problem of postelection rationalization. This global evaluation is, we believe, not as clean as our on-line evaluation counter, but it will do for our purposes here.

Table 8.2 presents the ANES data. About 78% of the voters for both the Democratic or Republican candidates reporting liking that candidate more than any other viable candidate. If we ignore the possibility of post decision rationalization,[17] we could readily explain these voters' decisions in terms of candidate evaluations. But another 20% or so of major party voters still must have based their ultimate decision on something besides their greater liking of one of the candidates. Eleven to 12% of major

[16] It is possible, of course, that our measure of the on-line evaluation is weak, that it fails to pick up important information that clearly matters to voters. If so, then we should expect that any attempt to find substantive reasons for the defections will go for naught. As we will see later, this does not prove to be the case. Undoubtedly, our evaluation measure contains a certain amount of error, but we believe that the process voters use to compare candidates in many cases overrides the values of the individual on-line counters.

[17] The great majority of voters in ANES surveys report having already decided how to vote by the time of the preelection interview, so postdecisional rationalization must remain a very viable possibility. See Lau (1982).

party voters liked their candidate as much as (but not more than) any other candidate, while about 10% of major party voters reported voting for a candidate who was not their most highly evaluated candidate shortly before the election. Now, some of these latter two groups of voters could have learned something about one or another of the candidates that was sufficient to shift their evaluations in line with the vote choice. (If we look at evaluations of the candidates gathered after the election, the number of Democrats and Republicans who voted for their most preferred candidate rises to about 82%.) But still, there is a goodly number of voters remaining.

Third-party voters are a somewhat different case because, during the period under consideration here, no third-party candidate ever had any chance of actually winning the election. Hence we would expect to observe a great deal of strategic voting (Abramson et al., 1992). Indeed, if we organize the data by candidate preference rather than vote choice, these expectations are born out: Only 38.8% of voters who liked a third-party candidate more than either of the major party candidates reported voting for that candidate. (The comparable figures for the two major party candidates are about 90%.) Hence, if evaluation tempered by strategic considerations is guiding the vote choice, we would certainly expect the people who actually voted for a third-party candidate (even though he or she could not possibly win) to have really liked that person – and certainly liked him more than either of the major party candidates. But the data in the last column of Table 8.2 belie this reasoning. Barely half of all third-party voters actually liked their candidate more than both of the two major party alternatives, and almost a third of them actually reported liking at least one of the major party candidates more than their own choice. Clearly there is a lot more going on than simply selecting the most highly evaluated candidate!

That "something else" may be the kinds of information search processes voters use, the rules they use for comparing candidates, and – we would hold – memory. The pure on-line model has no room for direct comparison of candidates when information is actually encountered. Instead, the evaluation for every candidate is updated independently of every other candidate. Thus, each candidate's on-line evaluation is a summary only of the actual information encountered for that candidate as it happened. This process seems very unlikely to us in an election environment where there is (or should be) substantial motivation to compare candidates on issues and traits that matter to the voter. It may be that this comparison process, as indicated by information search and memory measures, can at least partly explain why subjects did not always vote for the candidate with the highest on-line evaluation. Put another way, some information gathered about every individual candidate – which should be part of the on-line evaluation (and is, in our operationalization of it) – may be ignored when making a vote decision if that same information is not also available about other candidates in the choice set. Thus, the on-line evaluations associated with different candidates may be an incomplete indicator of the type of information that goes into the vote decision if those tallies are even partially based on noncomparable sets of information – as they most likely would be in any real election.

We might be able to get some sense of whether we are on the right track by reconceptualizing our measure of the on-line counter to be explicitly comparative. That is, we could choose to "count" only the information that our voters examined for multiple candidates in calculating an on-line evaluation counter – ignoring information that is uniquely learned about any candidate – and then see whether memory matters in the face of such an evaluation counter. This counter would ignore any information not examined for more than one candidate and would assume that voters consistently make comparisons. Although this is clearly not how the literature about on-line processing conceptualizes the evaluation counter, constructing such a measure using our data is fairly easy. But this seems like a poor strategy to pursue for the simple reason that this scenario is based on a highly unlikely presumption that all information that is not comparative is completely ignored. In a dynamic environment, voters would not know, when they learned a particular policy stand by one candidate, say, whether they would eventually be able to learn that same information about other candidates. It is simply inconceivable to us that such information would not be incorporated into some sort of on-line evaluation at the time of exposure, and/or that it would later be "subtracted out" because it was never learned about the other alternatives. This seems just as unlikely to us as the idea that no comparison happens at all. Instead, we need to allow for the possibility that the on-line evaluation process occurs in conjunction within a comparative process.

PREDICTING DEFECTION FROM ON-LINE EVALUATION

A better way to get some purchase on what is going on here is to try to explain "defections" from the candidate with the highest on-line evaluation. If, as we have argued, voters in an election are trying to make comparisons among candidates and, in making those comparisons, may override on-line evaluations, we should see evidence of this. In particular, if process matters, we would expect that voters showing a greater degree of deep comparative search (Model 1) might be more likely to defect as they learn more information about all the alternatives in the choice set and dig below the most easily available information. Positive and negative information is likely to be obtained about all candidates, and the resulting conflicts or value tradeoffs must be reconciled. In contrast, those engaging in any of the limited search strategies that either result in limited knowledge about all candidates (Model 3) or avoid tradeoffs entirely (Model 4) – and thus also limit comparison – may be less likely to have any reason to defect from the candidate with the highest on-line evaluation. As for Model 2 voters, in the general election we would expect them to be relatively less likely to defect if their preferred candidate is of the same party, and more likely if not. Because expectations are uncertain for Model 2 (particularly in the primary), we will use it as our reference point in the analyses to come. Finally, if memory matters when making a vote choice, then the more positive the memories of the most highly evaluated candidate are compared to others in the choice set, the less we should expect a voter to defect from the on-line evaluation.

We tested these propositions by building logistic regression models predicting the likelihood of a defection from the candidate with the highest on-line evaluation. The key independent variables are again comparative: relative on-line evaluation (of the mostly highly evaluated candidate minus the lower evaluated candidate), relative net positive memories (of the candidate with the highest on-line tally compared to alternatives with lower tallies), and relative familiarity.[18] We detail graphically the key findings in Figure 8.3 plotting the probability of a voter defecting from his or her most highly (on-line) evaluated candidate for each decision strategy.[19] While the differences in the primary election do not reach conventional levels of significance, the patterns are quite suggestive. Model 1 voters clearly stand out as more likely to defect from their most highly on-line evaluated candidate, compared to Model 2 voters. And those using the nonrational strategies appear to be somewhat less likely to defect. The general election shows the same basic pattern, only even more strongly for Model 1. Those who take the time to compare the in- and out-party

[18] As with our other large analyses, the full details are available from the authors upon request.

[19] Logistic regression analysis predicts the likelihood of an event happening (or not happening). Our analyses are coded so that the event we test for is a defection from the candidate with the highest on-line evaluation. In order to plot the probabilities, we must set values for each of the independent variables in the model and then vary the variables of interest (here we vary memory affect and search strategy). Thus, the graphs we show presume a female political novice at mean levels of education, age, candidate familiarity, and on-line evaluation. In the primary election we also set the number of candidates to two, while in the general election we assume that the in-party candidate was one that was rejected by the voter in the primary. Setting the primary to four candidates, or the in-party candidate to the preferred primary candidate does not change the pattern of the results, but it does change the probability of defection at all levels of memory to be greater in the primary, and lower in the general election.

Primary Election

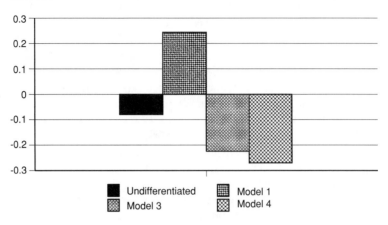

General Election

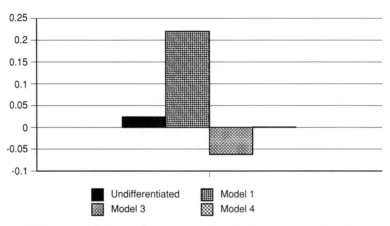

Note: Probabilities are from logistic regression models. Calculations assume a female political novice at mean levels of education, age, candidate familiarity, memory, and on-line evaluation.

Figure 8.3. Relative probability of defection from on-line candidate evaluation compared to Model 2.

candidates on a wide range of attributes are much more likely to end up voting against their on-line evaluation.

We should also point out that, as before, memory stands out as a significant predictor of whether a voter defects from his or her on-line evaluation. In effect, the affect associated with candidate memories overrides the affect associated with the on-line evaluation. Controlling for all other variables in the model (including the relative on-line evaluations), memory matters. Memory, in fact, has quite dramatic effects. Voters who have fewer positive net memories about the candidate with the highest on-line evaluation compared to other candidates are virtually certain not to vote for that candidate, regardless of search strategy. On the other hand, having even just a little more positive net memory about a candidate dramatically cuts down on the chances of defecting from that candidate. The same effect occurs for both the primary and general elections. On the other hand, the on-line evaluation itself does not significantly predict defection. That is, defection from that candidate is no more or less likely regardless of how net positive the on-line evaluation actually is.

The upshot of all of this is that the on-line evaluation does not automatically equal the vote, and it is possible to find systematic information-related differences between those who vote for the more highly evaluated candidates and those who do not. Simply put, having memories about the candidates matters a lot. The more positive the memories of the most highly evaluated candidate are, the less likely – by far – the voter is to defect from that candidate, while the the probability of defection increases dramatically when memory affect favors some other candidate. Clearly when it comes time to make a choice, voters – at least in these experiments – take into account much more than a simple comparison of their on-line evaluations.

WHY MEMORY MATTERS

Throughout the analyses in this chapter, we find consistent evidence that memory matters in candidate evaluation. Having more positive memories about a candidate results in a higher evaluation and lower likelihood of defecting from that candidate in the vote decision. We find this even when accounting for the on-line evaluation and for familiarity with the candidates. The strength of these findings, combined with the comprehensiveness of our election environment, convinces us that the pure on-line model underspecifies evaluation when it is embedded into an election environment that requires a choice between candidates. On-line evaluation may describe what happens when a pure evaluation task is at hand, but something more is needed to explain candidate evaluation during an election. That something more is the positive and negative memories of the candidates maintained by citizens as a product of their information search. We do not argue that these memories necessarily accurately represent everything voters encounter (Lodge, McGraw, and Stroh, 1989; Redlawsk, 2001a), nor do we argue that voters maintain large memory stores for all candidates. What we do argue is that whatever the memories maintained and then recalled, they have a profound effect on how voters evaluate candidates.

Why is this the case? What is it about a campaign that makes memory important? We think it is a fairly simple matter. When people evaluate candidates for the purposes of voting, they are interested not only in how each candidate stacks up against their own personal preferences (which is what the on-line model assumes) but also in how each candidate stacks up against the others in the choice set. The process of assessing the first part of this formula is simple: On-line evaluation of candidate information based on one's own preferences is cognitively easy. But when information flows in a relatively chaotic environment and is not easily managed by the decision maker, the task of comparing candidates to one another is not so simple. It is easy if you have the information in a handy to use, side-by-side format, and the amount of information is limited (à la most studies of on-line processing and any static information board study). But what if information flow is asymmetric? What if you learn about candidate A's position on abortion today but don't learn candidate B's position until a week from now? How do you compare them? By recalling A's position from memory, of course.[20] And that is why memory matters, and why, in a more realistic campaign environment, we find that it does.[21]

CONCLUSION

Our experimental election contests give us important insights into the role of information processing in candidate evaluation. We have found repeatedly that information search and memory play important roles in evaluation and choice. Evaluation in an election campaign is different from evaluation when no choice is involved. This comports well with studies that show on-line evaluation takes place only when the task at hand is impression formation. But even for those presumably using some on-line candidate evaluation, we find that memory for the candidates also plays a role. We believe there is a simple reason for this that has

---

[20] Of course, one might also compare them by ascribing a position on abortion to a candidate based on partisan stereotypes rather than on real information. In this chapter, we focus on information actually acquired (by accessing the particular item) during the campaign. We will expand our view of the information going into the evaluation counter to consider partisan default values when we look at correct voting in Chapters 10.

[21] For the moment, we are begging the question of whether the accuracy of those memories matters to the vote. From the perspective of the vote direction, accuracy should not matter; whether the memory is objectively accurate, if it is believed to be true by the voter, then it is true. We will take up the question of the role memory accuracy plays in Chapter 10 when our dependent variable is the quality of the vote, rather than its direction.

not been tested in previous studies of on-line evaluation. Subjects in our studies were actually voters. That is, they needed not only to form an impression but also to make a choice. In making a choice, most voters wish to make comparisons among the candidates, comparisons that have to be facilitated by memory. Thus, we find that when voters are comparing candidates, often both the on-line evaluation and memory matter.

9

Voting

Finally we turn our attention to the vote decision itself and the outcome of our election campaigns. This is usually the ultimate goal of voting studies, but for us it is simply a way station along the path. We are fully aware that our campaigns existed only within the confines of our laboratory, and that as a consequence the actual results of the elections (i.e., which candidates received the most votes) are not particularly interesting. We certainly believe the direction of the vote choice matters in actual elections, but as we will argue in the next chapter, the quality of that choice matters, too, and arguably matters more. In any case, our goal in this chapter is quite modest: to simply examine the extent to which knowing about our voters' information processing improves our understanding of how they made their vote choice. We will begin by replicating the kind of voting models that have become standard in the literature, and then we will see if we can do any better by building an explicitly information processing-based model focused on the role of actual information search and acquisition, along with on-line evaluation and (where possible) memory.

WHO WON?

In virtually every extant study of the vote decision, the researcher (and the reader) knows who won the election before the data gathering is complete. Such is not the case for us, and providing that information is actually more complicated than it sounds. Even though each subject voted in only one primary and one general election, in fact we had six different primary elections – that is, combinations of candidates on the ballot – and twelve (of the sixteen possible) different general election races. Recall that to present data on our candidates, we have adopted a convention of numbering the candidates from most liberal to most conservative within each party. The figures in this chapter that refer to candidates will use this scheme, along with the names we assigned to the candidates.

Figure 9.1 provides the best overall picture for the primaries, describing the number of subjects voting for each candidate in the four-candidate condition only (when all of the possible in-party candidates were on the ballot), separately for the Democratic and Republican primaries. As in real elections, our voters chose whether to vote in the Democratic or Republican primary. Democrats gave the least support to candidate D3 (Martin), their moderately conservative alternative, and divided their support fairly evenly between the remaining three candidates. Republicans, on the other hand, had a clear favorite, giving almost twice as much support to their mainstream conservative alternative, R3 (Rodgers), as any other candidate, and dividing their support for the remaining three candidates fairly evenly.[1] In general, voters within each party tended toward the available candidate in any given election most like the "modal" candidate of that party.

It is a bit trickier to show the general election results because they are completely dependent on which candidates were available in a particular election. Figure 9.2 displays the propensity to vote for each candidate whenever that candidate is running (implicitly averaging across all the various opponents). Our two mixed or nonstereotypic candidates, Democrat D4 and Republican R1, were the least likely to be chosen when they were running. On the other hand, in the few cases (only seven) where extremely conservative Republican R4 (Walker) was a candidate, he was chosen most of the time. But other than the Walker case, the pattern shows what might be expected – the modal candidates from each party, D2 (Singer) and R3 (Rodgers), were chosen more often than the others, when they were running.

VOTE CHOICE IN THE PRIMARY ELECTION

We begin by specifying a fairly standard or traditional model of the vote choice. Unfortunately there is not an overabundance of "traditional" literature on the vote choice in a primary (compared to general election) to rely upon, but we would expect all the usual suspects to be important in a primary election, with the exception of party ID, of course, as party does not vary across candidates in the choice set.[2] Usually the best data

---

[1] These patterns of relative support are replicated in the various two-candidate conditions. Democrats preferred candidate D2 (Singer) to D3 (Martin), 61 to 39%, and preferred candidate D1 (Donald) to D3 (Martin), 63 to 37%; Republicans preferred R3 (Rodgers) over R2 (Thomas), 64 to 36%, but divided their support evenly between R2 (Thomas) and R4 (Walker).

[2] Party identification typically determines which party's primary one will vote in, just as it did in our experiments. Much of the political science literature on primary

Democrats

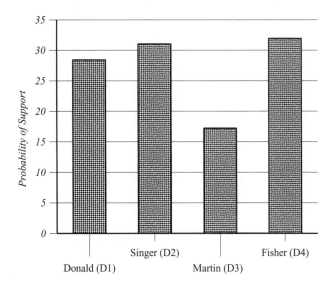

Republicans

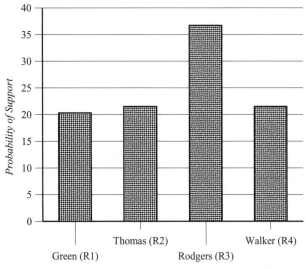

Figure 9.1. Vote choice, primary election campaigns, four-candidate condition.

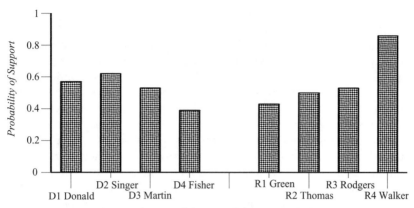

Figure 9.2. Vote choice when candidate available, general election campaigns.

researchers have comes from surveys, which provide an excellent reading on citizen preferences shortly before an election. We have the equivalent, from our preelection questionnaire. Researchers try to match the issue preferences, group identifications, and candidate judgments of the voters to the attributes of the candidates running in an election. We can do the same because we know the issue stands, group endorsements, and personal qualitites of all our candidates.

But our detailed examination of information processing to this point should make obvious some of the limitations of this traditional approach. With standard surveys, we do not know what campaign information voters have been exposed to and what they have actually learned about the candidates in an election. At best, we can get at this indirectly, through respondents' willingness to attribute issue stands or personality traits to individual candidates or to report on the contents of their memory. But such judgments, while arguably accurate in the aggregate, show tremendous individual variation. In the 2000 ANES study, for example, on average 41% of all respondents either admitted they did not know where Bush and Gore stood on each of the ten major issues of the campaign, or

elections focuses on various institutional factors, such as their number and timing, how winning leads to subsequent media attention and fund-raising success, and so on (e.g., Aldrich, 1980; Bartels, 1988). Aldrich and Alvarez (1994) looked at vote choice in primaries, suggesting that issues matter as well as voters' expectations about which candidate can win. Abramowitz (1989) also considered how primary voters factor in electability and viability. Williams and his colleagues (1976) anticipated to some degree the kind of work we are doing here in their investigation of a few different information integration strategies that primary voters might employ in coming to a decision. But with these few exceptions, little light has been shined on voter decision making in primaries.

attributed to them a position that was more than two points away from the modal response on traditional seven-point issue scales. If we take the modal response as an indication of where the candidates actually stand on each issue, and with our pretty lenient definition of "correct," the ANES responses were correct 59% of the time. If respondents randomly picked one of the seven legitimate responses, they would have been counted as "correct" over 53% of the time.[3] As a result, these data do not paint a very pretty picture about how many respondents have actually learned the candidates' stands on these issues. Responses to such questions probably tell us as much about the responder as they do about the candidate. In the end, the analyst is forced either to throw out the great majority of available cases because of missing data or (through variable construction) to assume that all respondents have been exposed to all aspects of the campaign and have reasonably accurate readings on the candidates. We know this assumption is not true, but we can normally do little about it other than shrug our shoulders and accept less precise coefficient estimates and greater overall residual variance in our statistical models.

We will follow this general procedure in estimating our traditional model of the vote choice. We devised measures of closeness to each candidate on the issues (by comparing the candidate's stand to that of the respondent), the attractiveness of each candidate's personality and job qualifications (based on ratings of our pretest subjects), and group-based attachments to each candidate (based on which candidate received different interest groups' endorsements and whether the endorsing group was liked or disliked). All these considerations went into the on-line evaluations presented in Chapter 8, and we followed the same procedures described in Appendix E except that here we assumed that every subject considered every bit of information available about every candidate. Rather than combining these considerations into a single evaluation of each candidate, as we did in approximating the on-line evaluation, we keep distinct issue, candidate, and group-based scales for tradition's sake.

Now comes the tricky part. Three of our four studies varied the number of candidates running in the primary election, which results in a little

---

[3] If the modal responses, which we are taking here as the "true" candidate position, are a 1 or a 7, then there are only three responses (1, 2, and 3 in the first case, 5, 6, or 7, in the second) that fall within the two-point range, and four that would be counted as clearly "wrong." But if the modal response is a 2 or a 6, four responses count as "close" (1–4 or 4–7), leaving only three as clearly wrong; and if the modal response is a 3, 4, or 5, five different responses would count as close, and only two as wrong. When we look at the actual data, 75 out of a total of 140 possible responses to the 20 questions – or 53.6% – would be counted as close.

over a third of all subjects voting in a four-candidate primary. There are two such primaries, one for the Democrats and one for the Republicans. For both the Democrats and the Republicans, moreover, the candidates paired against each other in the two-candidate condition were not always the same, although the most common pairing was the modal candidate running against the moderate candidate. We have to simplify this somehow, and chose the following procedure.

First, as in the previous chapter, because we have no reason to believe that Democrats and Republicans make their vote choices in different ways (they certainly make different choices, but the procedures should be pretty much the same), we combine voters from the two primaries. Now, whenever the modal candidate (D2 and R3) was not in his or her party's two-candidate primary, the extreme candidate (D1 and R4) was; and whenever the moderate candidate (D3 and R2) was not in the two-candidate primary, the nonstereotypic mixed candidate (D4 and R1) was. We therefore decided to treat our primary elections as if they always involved only two candidates – the moderate and the modal candidate from each party – with two exceptions. In the two-candidate condition when the moderate and/or modal candidates were not available, we substituted the mixed and extreme candidates, respectively. And in the four-candidate condition, if a subject actually voted for either the mixed or extreme candidate, we replaced the moderate or modal candidate with the one actually chosen, following these same substitution patterns. Thus, we model the primary election as if it always involved only two candidates, a moderate (or occasionally mixed) versus the modal (or occasionally an ideologically more extreme) candidate from the party. The candidate a subject actually chose is always one of the two candidates considered.

We made our candidate-specific measures of issue, person, and group-based considerations comparative by subtracting each measure for the moderate candidate from the comparable measure for the modal candidate. We then regressed the vote choice on these three comparative measures of preference for the modal over the moderate candidate, along with controls for age, education, income, gender, race,[4] party, strength of party identification, and strength of ideological identification. The party dummy variable is included to test our basic assumption that Democrats

---

[4] Earlier we noted that race had shown no effects on information processing in any of our analyses, and we were dropping race from further models. At this point, however, we need to include race as a factor in predicting the vote because it has been routinely shown to matter in voting models. Note that we do not believe race affects information processing per se; instead, we recognize that nonwhites in our sample are unlikely to vote Republican, independent of any other factors, in a partisan general election.

and Republicans make decisions in basically the same way. We specified the last two control variables as strength of identification rather than their full partisan range because we collapsed the Democratic and Republican primaries together. If strong partisans and strong ideologues generally prefer a modal candidate to a more moderate one, these variables will have positive signs in the analyses. Because of the way we constructed our variables, each of the issue, person, and group-based variables should be positively related to vote for the modal candidate. We have no particular reason to think any of the control variables will be significant, although the two strength variables should, if anything, be positively related to the modal candidates (and thus also have positive signs).

The results for this pretty traditional analysis of the vote choice are shown in the first two columns of Table 9.1. Each of our three candidate-preference variables has the expected positive sign and is highly statistically significant. The full model has a pseudo R^2 of .15 and correctly predicts over 64% of all vote choices (against a baseline of 50%, remember) – it's not great, but it is not unreasonable either for a primary election where party identification plays little role.[5] And it is not unreasonable when the three most important predictors all assume voters know a lot more about the candidates than is actually the case. But let's see if we can do any better.

We now construct a much more refined information processing model of the vote choice, guided by our general framework for voter decision making from Chapter 2. We would hold that the information actually examined and processed – as represented by the on-line evaluation of the candidates, general familiarity with them, and memory – should do a much better job of predicting the vote choice. Recall that we only have memory data from the primary election in one study, so for the moment we will ignore it. The more traditional factors – strength of party identification and ideology, perceptions of candidates' personalities and qualifications, their issue stands, and so on – become subsumed into the on-line evaluation. We again specify our crucial predictors as comparative measures by subtracting the on-line evaluation and total familiarity for the moderate candidate from the comparable measures for the modal

---

[5] To change the logistic regression coefficients into something more interpretable, compared to a median voter who is predicted to have only a slight preference for the modal candidate, a voter who is at the extreme value of comparative preference for the modal candidate on the issues would have a 33% greater probability of voting for the modal candidate. If we go through the same exercise for the comparative candidate and group-based variables, they would increase the probability of voting for the modal candidate by 13 and 30%, respectively.

Table 9.1. *Vote for the Modal Candidate in the Primary Election*

	Traditional Model		Information Processing Model	
Age	.160	(.392)	−.023	(.455)
Education	−.111	(.405)	−.378	(.453)
Income	−.114	(.291)	.237	(.332)
Female	.111	(.186)	.099	(.218)
Nonwhite	−.793**	(.315)	−.163	(.355)
Strength of party ID	.163	(.292)		
Strength of ideological ID	.345	(.350)		
Party	.299	(.209)	.221	(.222)
Four-candidate primary			.080	(.271)
Relative closeness of issues	2.914***	(.893)		
Relative personality/qualifications	1.422**	(.473)		
Relative group-based evaluations	2.667***	(.678)		
Comparative on-line evaluation			5.194***	(1.054)
Comparative candidate familiarity			8.809***	(.941)
Decision Strategy				
Model 1			−.038	(.354)
Model 2			−.121	(.414)
Model 3			.022	(.401)
Model 4			.145	(.334)
Model χ^2	67.99***	(15 df)	201.50***	(17 df)
Nagelkerke Pseudo R^2	.15		.40	
% Correctly classified	64.3		74.5	

*$p < .05$, ** $p < .01$, ***$p < .001$

Note: Table entries are logistic regression coefficients, with standard errors in parentheses. A vote for the modal candidate is scored high on the dependent variable. Analyses include controls for the different experiments, and a constant, not shown. $N = 569$.

candidate. We will also enter dummy variables representing the different decision strategies into these analyses, although we have no a priori reason to expect them to have any direct effect on the vote choice. As we saw in the previous chapter, these strategies help determine the comparative values of the evaluation counter, memory, and familiarity, and thus may not have any additional effect on the vote choice once these other variables are included in the analysis. We again include age, education, income, gender, and race, along with dummy variables representing the different experiments, as controls.

The results are shown in the last two columns of Table 9.1. As expected, both the comparative on-line evaluation and familiarity strongly affect the likelihood of voting for the modal candidate. The greater the positive difference in on-line evaluation between the modal candidate and his or her challenger(s), the greater the chance that the modal candidate will get the vote. The same is true of familiarity. As anticipated, however, the particular decision strategy chosen by a voter seems to have no direct effect on the vote choice; none of our four decision strategies shows any significant effects. Thus, whatever influence the particular decision strategies have seems to be indirect, through their influence on evaluation counters and candidate familiarity.

But the most important difference between the traditional model of the vote choice and our information processing model is their relative predictive power. As hypothesized, knowing what information voters choose to learn about the candidates greatly increases our ability to predict their vote choices. The pseudo R^2 associated with the analysis increases from .15 to almost .41, and the number of correctly classified cases increases from 64 to over 74%. These are big increases, and they are due entirely to (1) respecifying the candidate closeness variables (which are kept as three separate predictors in the traditional model, and combined into a single measure in the information processing model) to only count information that voters actually considered and (2) including our measure of the relative familiarity of the two candidates.

Does memory also matter to the vote choice in a primary election? To find out, we restricted analysis to the one study that included a measure of memory for the primary candidates and ran both our traditional and information processing models again, adding a comparative measure of affective memories to the latter.[6] With only ninety-eight cases available we have much less power to detect significant results – and to be fair, we compare it to a traditional model based on those same ninety-eight cases. Nonetheless, the new comparative affective memory measure has a highly significant effect. And as we saw in the previous chapter, when memory is included in a model of choice, the on-line evaluation loses its predictive power. Once again, our information processing model does a much better job of correctly predicting the vote choice, compared to the traditional model, as the pseudo R^2 increases from .30 to .85, and the number of correctly classified cases increases from 71% to 94%.

So what have we learned about primary voters? First, we can build pretty good models predicting the vote choice if we actually know what information voters learn about the candidates and how they evaluate that information. But, it appears at least in the one study where we have memory measures that, as we saw with candidate evaluation when embedded in an election, choosing between candidates implicates memory more than the on-line evaluation.

---

[6] These results are available from the authors upon request.

VOTE CHOICE IN THE GENERAL ELECTION

Clearly, we can do a good job of predicting the direction of the vote in our primary elections by accounting for information search and acquisition. But what about the general election? Given the acknowledged power of partisanship to predict the vote, can we still expect our measures of on-line evaluation, memory, and information search to make any difference? As we have already seen, not all voters vote for their party's candidate; perhaps information search can help explain defection from party. Certainly we expect "agreement" with the candidates (i.e., the on-line evaluations and memory affect) to matter, if they are anything more than partisan rationalizations.

It is much easier to analyze the vote choice in the general election because we always have only two candidates, one Democrat and one Republican. We will start by examining partisan choice. We conceptually replicate our traditional and information processing models from the primary election, subtracting the various candidate evaluation measures for the Democrat from the comparable measure for the Republican. We employ party and ideological identifications in their full partisan directional mode rather than the "folded" format to indicate strength of identification we had used in the primary (when there were no partisan differences between the candidates). The traditional model assumes the voters have been exposed to all information about the candidates, whereas the information processing model only considers the items that respondents actually looked at.

The results are shown in Table 9.2, and they are remarkably similar to those from the primary election. The traditional model does a good job predicting the vote choice in the general election, a noticeably better job than in the primary – which is only to be expected, given that the candidates in the general election differ by party. Indeed, the two most important predictors are party identification and relative closeness to the candidates on the issues. Group-based evaluations of the candidates are also important, and nonwhites are a little less likely to vote Republican. There is nothing particularly exciting or surprising here, which we take to be a good sign. We would be concerned, for example, if partisanship were not the key predictor in this equation. The fact that it is gives us more assurance that our voters were acting as they would in a real-world election. The pseudo R^2 for the traditional model is .32, and it correctly classifies 75.6% of the voters.

But our information processing model, which considers only information actually encountered by the voter, does an even better job, correctly classifying over 82% of the voters, with a pseudo R^2 of almost .60. All three of our comparative information processing measures are significant

Table 9.2. *Vote for the Republican Candidate in the General Election*

	Traditional Model		Information Processing Model	
Age	−.288	(.451)	.564	(.565)
Education	.712	(.468)	.250	(.587)
Income	−.258	(.327)	−.065	(.422)
Female	−.011	(.211)	−.125	(.264)
Nonwhite	−.369	(.367)	−.281	(.436)
Party ID (Republican)	2.805***	(.412)		
Ideological ID (conservative)	−.137	(.612)		
Relative closeness of issues	3.397**	(1.200)		
Relative personality/qualifications	−.449	(.519)		
Relative group-based evaluations	.985@	(.665)		
Comparative on-line evaluation			3.411**	(1.403)
Comparative candidate familiarity			6.332***	(1.157)
Comparative memory affect			9.496***	(1.184)
Decision strategy				
Model 1			.617	(.599)
Model 2			.404	(.589)
Model 3			.177	(.635)
Model 4			.070	(.594)
Model χ^2	136.95***	(13 df)	284.47***	(14 df)
Nagelkerke Pseudo R^2	.32		.60	
% Correctly classified	75.6		82.1	

$@p < .07, *p < .05 **p < .01, ***p < .001$

Note: Table entries are logistic regression coefficients, with standard errors in parentheses. Vote for the Republican candidate is scored high on the depend variable. Model 3 is the excluded decision strategy in the information processing model, and thus is estimated by the constant term. Analyses include controls for the different experiments, not shown. $N = 481$.

and correctly signed, although memory is clearly the strongest predictor of the vote. Comparatively more positive memory for the Republican predicts a vote in that direction, as does comparatively more familiarity with the Republican. The on-line evaluation counter is also positive and significant, although it is of a much smaller magnitude than memory. The decision process, then, appears to be a hybrid of on-line evaluation and memory-based processing, at least in predicting the partisan direction of the vote. Once again, decision strategies have no direct effect on the vote choice.

To give the reader a better feel for the relative importance of the different information processing measures, Figure 9.3 illustrates their relative power of increasing the probability of a Republican vote for a median voter who has average values on all the other variables in the equation, but

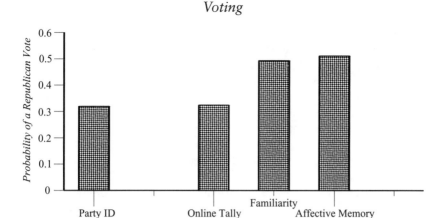

Note: Figure shows increase in probability of a Republican vote for the most extreme Republican-learning value of each variable (e.g., strong Republican party identification), over a baseline probability of .473 for a Republican vote by a median voter who has a neutral score on each variable.

Figure 9.3. Relative power of party identification and information processing measures on increased probability of a vote for the Republican candidate.

the most Republican-favorable value on each of the comparative information processing variables, in turn. Figure 9.3 also shows the contribution of a strong Republican party identification from the traditional model for a similar median voter. As can be seen, party identification and the comparative on-line tally are of comparable strength and each one, by itself, increases the probability of a Republican vote by a median voter by over 30%. But both relative candidate familiarity and relative affective memories are even stronger, by themselves increasing the probability of a Republican vote from a slightly less than even proposition to an almost sure thing.

PREDICTING PARTISAN DEFECTION

If there is any effect at all for decision strategies, we would expect it to show up not in the partisan direction of the vote choice but rather as voter defection from party affiliation to the other side. Our reasoning is simple: Decision strategies are indicators of (among other things) how much information voters learn about the two candidates. When learning is imbalanced – for example, a shallow search focused mostly on the in-party candidate – voters will not be able to make effective comparisons between the candidates and should tend to default to their own party. But when making a deeper, more comparable search across alternative, voters may learn more things they like about the opposition and some things they don't like about their own candidate, thereby increasing the likelihood of crossing over to the dark side. This should be most likely to be true of rational Model 1 voters, we would hypothesize, and least likely to be true of confirmatory Model 2 voters.

We examine this possibility by changing our dependent variable from a vote for the Republican or Democrat to a vote for one's own party or the other party. Recall that a voter's party is defined by the primary in which he or she registered to vote, rather than by the standard party identification measure, which allows all voters – even pure independents – to be included in the analysis. Of course, all directional predictors must be revised as well, so that now our information variables will be coded for in- and out-party, rather than Republican and Democrat. Otherwise, we will include the same predictors as in the general election vote choice analysis.

The results of this new analysis are shown in Table 9.3. To be consistent with earlier analyses, we also estimate a more traditional model predicting voter defection, but we will not comment on it here other than to note, as with our earlier analyses, that the information processing model does a far better job of predicting defection than the traditional model. All three comparative information processing variables are statistically significant (the comparative on-line evaluation marginally so) and have their expected positive sign. But what is most interesting in the analysis is that the decision strategies voters employ also have a direct and significant impact on the probability of defection. As hypothesized, the voters who are most likely to defect from their party affiliation are those who utilize a rational Model 1 decision strategy. As Figure 9.4 shows, a median voter employing Model 1 has a probability of defecting from party of almost .39, compared to a probability of defection by Model 2 voters just over .27. Interestingly, Model 3 voters are even less likely to defect than Model 2 voters, with a probability of defection of little more than 1 in 5. Clearly, the fast and frugal decision – unchallenged by detailed information search – is to vote party.

Also of interest is the pattern for our intuitive Model 4 voters. They seem about as likely to defect as Model 1 voters. This is somewhat unexpected and is worth considering further. A little deeper investigation (not shown here) reveals that the entire effect is located in the candidate-oriented Model 4c search – that is, those using a satisficing strategy. This strategy entails randomly starting with one alternative, one candidate, and searching until that alternative either satisfies all requirements at a minimal aspiration level or the voter finds that candidate fails to meet a requirement. If the former happens, there is no need to even look at any other alternative. The starting point can be a candidate of either party; consequently, if the out-party candidate is considered first and meets

Table 9.3. *Defection from the Party's Candidate in the General Election*

	Traditional Model		Information Processing Model	
Age	−1.249**	(.470)	−.748	(.585)
Education	.584	(.479)	1.189*	(.600)
Income	−.464	(.345)	−.710	(.445)
Female	−.003	(.222)	−.023	(.273)
Nonwhite	−.591	(.389)	−.472	(.445)
Party ID (Republican)	1.610**	(.575)		
Ideological ID (conservative)	−.358	(.629)		
Relative closeness of issues	3.095**	(1.086)		
Relative personality/qualifications	−.387	(.573)		
Relative group-based evaluations	1.050@	(.695)		
Comparative on-line evaluation			1.990@	(1.286)
Comparative candidate familiarity			4.215***	(1.000)
Comparative memory affect			9.929***	(1.242)
Decision strategy				
Model 1			.923**	(.408)
Model 2			.332	(.418)
Model 3			−1.281**	(.449)
Model 4			.853*	(.415)
Model χ^2	61.96***	(13 df)	215.17***	(14 df)
Nagelkerke Pseudo R^2	.17		.52	
% Correctly classified	73.2		84.2	

$@p < .07, *p < .05, **p < .01, ***p < .001$

Note: Table entries are logistic regression coefficients, with standard errors in parentheses. Defection from party affiliation is scored high on the dependent variable. Model 3 is the excluded decision strategy in the information processing model, and thus is estimated by the constant term. Analyses include controls for the different experiments, not shown. $N = 481$.

the aspiration levels, a voter using this strategy might be very likely to defect.

Of course, we are talking about a general election campaign here, a campaign that most voters would enter with partisan prejudices. Furthermore, voters will already be at least somewhat familiar with their own party's candidate, perhaps less so with the out-party's candidate. But recall one of the peculiarities of our experiments, that the great majority of our general election voters faced a campaign involving a candidate from their own party who was not their favorite among the competing candidates in the primary. In such a context, it seems not at all unreasonable to us to think that many party voters would actually start their information gathering by looking much more closely at the out-party candidate. If that candidate seems pretty reasonable, why not take a chance and vote for him?

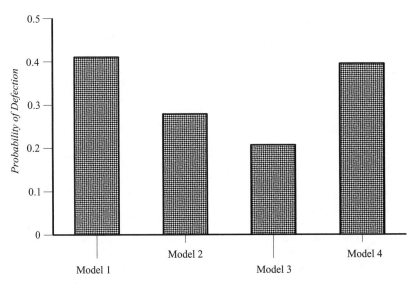

Note: Predicted probabilities are based on the model described in Table 9.3, setting all other predictors at their median values.

Figure 9.4. Probability of defection from in-party candidate in general election by search strategy.

This is one instance where a detailed knowledge of how a voter goes about making a decision provides a great deal of insight into explaining that decision. Model 1 and Model 4 voters display an almost identical probability of defecting from their party affiliation. Model 1 voters learn roughly the same amount about the same attributes for both candidates, and thus know the good and bad of their own party's candidate and the opponent. Here a vote choice is clearly based on a detailed comparison of the two competing candidates running in the general election; if in the aggregate these defections were to clearly favor one candidate over the other, we could fairly interpret the outcome of the election as resulting from the majority of voters finding one of the candidates to be truly superior to the other. But if our previous interpretation of Model 4 defectors is right, then the locus of their defection is in the primary, not the general election. Presumably most of these Model 4 defectors would not have defected had their party been smart enough to pick a different candidate. Indeed, in that case they might not have been Model 4 voters at all, but rather fast and frugal Model 3 (party-line) voters.

As with our other memory models, affective memory for the in- and out-party candidates plays a key role in determining whether or not a voter

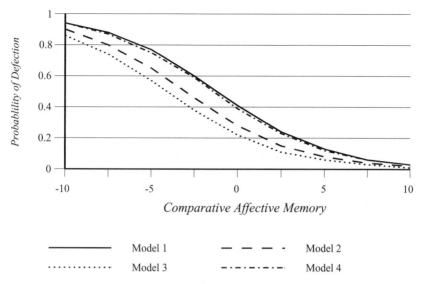

Note: Predicted probabilities for a median voter employing each of the different decesion stragegies, based on the analysis described in Table 9.3.

Figure 9.5. Probability of defection from in-party candidate in general election by memory and search strategy.

will defect from the party. Figure 9.5 illustrates this graphically. We have plotted our four search strategies against different levels of comparative memory affect, setting on-line evaluation and familiarity at their means. It becomes immediately clear that both the memory effects and the search strategies matter. Voters who have a net negative comparative memory – in other words, they have more positive memory about the out-party than the in-party candidate – are highly likely to defect, anywhere from 75–90% likely, depending on search strategy. Voters who are essentially ambivalent in their memories are still relatively likely to defect, with Model 1 and Model 4 voters as likely to defect as not. When voters have greater positive memory about their own party's candidate than the other, they are more likely to stay with their party, though Model 1 and Model 4 voters still show a significant propensity to defect.

CONCLUSION

We have certainly spent a lot of pages on something we initially said might not be very interesting, given that our elections are among invented candidates who mean nothing themselves to the real world of politics. But as it turns out, even these mock contests give us important insights into the role of information processing in the vote decision, and the results are more interesting than we first anticipated. We have built statistical models of the vote choice that incorporate information search and memory, and have shown that those models add substantially to our traditional understanding of the vote decision. Knowing what specific information voters were actually exposed to about the candidates and the campaign (rather than assuming that all voters were exposed to the same information) makes a big difference in our ability to understand and predict how citizens will vote. We reinforce the message that on-line evaluation matters in some cases, but we also show that memory plays a more important role. Clearly, when voters choose among candidates, they may consider their (independent) running tally evaluation of each those candidates, but they definitely compare candidates as well, and must use memory to do so.

We doubted that information search strategies would matter in determining vote direction, and for the most part they did not. On the other hand, we do know that search strategies have implications for memory and evaluation, which do factor into the vote choice. We did find some statistically significant direct effects for Model 1 rational search in the general election, as voters who examined more information about both of their options were more likely to abandon their own party and to vote for the opposition. This is an important finding. It suggests that by examining a larger amount of information for both candidates, a voter may well overcome any partisan default and cross party lines. In many ways this reinforces prior research on the importance of partisanship – especially when voters seem to know little about the candidates – however, it also clearly points to the value of information processing. Partisan predispositions can be overcome, but generally only by providing a great deal of information to voters and making it attractive and interesting enough that they will pay attention. And even if a great deal of information is available, some people simply will not make use of it, instead employing simplifying strategies that result in a less than complete search.

An interesting question remains, however. We have just shown that information processing has important effects on the direction of the vote, but does it also influence how good a job voters do in making that choice? Rational (Model 1) voters presumably do the best job (or at least as good a job as possible) because they learn a great deal about all their choices and are thus prepared to choose the ideal candidate – if they can process all that information. This is an important caveat. Less rational, intuitive voters, on the other hand, seem more likely to tend toward partisan defaults; consequently, they might not do as good a job – unless, of course, additional information confuses as much as it enlightens. Thus, we return to the vote choice in the next chapter, where we assess the extent to which our voters are actually voting *correctly*, and look at the roles information search, processing, and acquisition play in improving the chances that they do so.

10

Voting Correctly

In the past two chapters, we have considered two important topics in the study of voting behavior, candidate evaluation, and vote choice. We have seen how our information processing approach provides valuable insights in these traditional political science topics. Now we turn to another inherently political topic, one that gets at the very heart of democracy. In Chapter 4, we described two related measures of correct voting, the first determined subjectively by voters themselves after a good deal of additional consideration of two of the candidates from the primary, the second a "normative-naive" measure, based on an objective determination of a match between the candidates and the voter's own attitudes and revealed information preferences during the campaigns. Although our first subjective measure is easier to defend normatively, in practice we must rely primarily on the second objectively determined measure, for the simple reason that we have it for all elections in all experiments; the first, voter-determined criterion is available only in the first two studies, and then only for two of the candidates from the primary election. Either one of these measures allows us to address questions that heretofore have been almost completely ignored by the scientific study of voting behavior: "How regularly do voters 'get it right'?" and "What factors can we identify that lead to more or less correct voting?"

HOW OFTEN DO VOTERS GET IT RIGHT?

We reported in Chapter 4 that 70% of our primary voters voted correctly, by their own subjective determination. But this number was based on an effective choice between only two candidates because all subjects were asked to reconsider their decision by comparing the candidate they chose to one other candidate we chose – the one remaining candidate, in the two-candidate condition, or the remaining candidate closest to the voter on the issues, in the four-candidate condition. If we limit consideration to the two-candidate condition of our experiments, however, the figures are actually somewhat higher than this – 76% correct, by the subjective criterion, or 69% correct by our objectively determined measure. On the other hand, we calculate using our normative naive measure that only 31% of our subjects voted correctly in the four-candidate primary elections, when all four candidates are included in the mix. This does not strike us as a very high number – indeed, it is not much above the 25% level we would expect by chance. Thus, the optimistic note with which we concluded Chapter 4 about surprisingly high levels of correct voting must be qualified and restricted to campaigns with only two candidates. There is clearly less reason for optimism, based on the evidence provided here, when the choice set expands beyond two candidates.

Looking across the general election campaign of all studies – which always involved only two candidates – and ignoring various experimental manipulations, we find that 63% of our subjects voted correctly (by our normative-naive criterion, the only one we have available). This is clearly much better than the 50% we would expect by chance, but no better (indeed, slightly worse) than in the two-candidate condition from the primary, despite the fact that voters have the additional cue of party affiliation available to them in the general election, which we would expect to be a big aid. It should be remembered, however, that the great majority of our subjects were voting in a general election campaign with a candidate from their own party that they had rejected during the primary election. This could help explain the lower levels of correct voting in our general election campaigns compared to two-candidate primary elections. Whatever the case, this figure does seem to accord nicely with the data on correct voting in recent U.S. presidential elections presented earlier in Chapter 4. All of these finding for levels of correct voting are summarized in Figure 10.1.

But there is much more to be learned about correct voting than can be appreciated simply from overall levels. Our analysis of correct voting will proceed in several stages, following the general framework of the vote decision shown in Figure 2.1. We first introduce our set of background characteristics and general political attitudes, along with the triumvirate of political sophistication, manipulations of task difficulty, and the resulting perceived difficulty of the decision task. Although no one before us has even asked the question of what leads citizens to vote more or less correctly, a standard political analysis, we would imagine, would stop here – with a set of demographic indicators, general political predispositions, a focused measure of political sophistication or expertise, and – commonsensically – any variations in the objective and/or perceived difficulty of the choice voters must make. This will be our baseline model. We will also

Politics

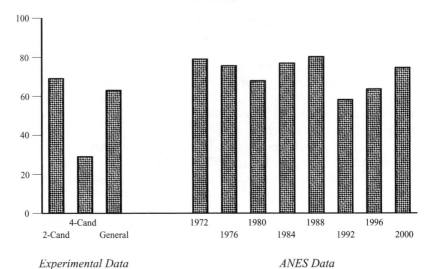

Experimental Data   *ANES Data*

Note: Data are based on the normative-naive criterion for correct voting.

Figure 10.1. Estimated levels of correct voting in experiments and recent U.S. presidential elections.

take a brief detour to see how well this same model works with voters in recent ANES surveys.

Our information processing theory leads us to dig much deeper in trying to understand correct voting, however. Thus, in the second stage of the analysis, we introduce our measures of information search, first as direct indicators and then as specific decision strategies. In each case, theory leads us to consider interactions between information processing and our measures of political sophistication and task difficulty.

In the final stage of analysis, we add a measure of memory. This last step is certainly contrary to the on-line evaluation model discussed earlier, but in the previous two chapters we have shown that both the on-line tally and memory contribute to candidate evaluation and the vote choice *in the context of an election campaign.* We believe that voters implicitly understand that memory matters enough to put some effort into remembering what is important to them about the candidates in an election. We are led to this conclusion by the underlying assumption that voters, like all decision makers, want to make a good decision with as little cognitive effort as possible. We do not say the best possible decision, because motivation in politics is rarely that high. But we do strongly believe that voters want to make good decisions, that at the very least they want to find a good-enough alternative who meets some minimum standards. If memory is needed to make such a good-enough decision, then voters will make the effort to remember as much as is required about the candidates in an election. Once again, making a choice is not the same thing as forming an evaluation.

BASELINE MODEL

The only demographic control variables we would expect to be correlated with correct voting are education and age. As college teachers, we certainly hope that education will be positively related to correct voting (and feel compelled to hypothesize that it will be!). And we have already seen that age is associated with shallower search, less memory, and so on, and we would therefore expect age to be negatively related to correct voting. We do not expect political orientation, represented in our model by liberalism-conservatism, to have any effect, although strength of party identification should be related to correct voting. But we do have clear theoretical expectations about the remaining variables in the baseline model.

Political sophistication is based on interest, experience, and knowledge, all of which ought to contribute positively to correct voting, on top of any influence of education or strength of partisanship. Indeed, we would expect the roles of education and strength of partisanship to be largely mediated by political sophistication in a multivariate model. We have several experimental manipulations of the difficulty of the decision task, any of which should reduce the probability of a correct vote. And we also have the subjective perceived difficulty of the vote choice, which is a function of both the decision maker's expertise (the more expert the decision maker is, the less difficult the choice should seem, all else being equal) and the manipulated nature of the decision. The more difficult the choice, the lower the probability of a correct vote. The predictions for sophistication, task manipulations, and perceived difficulty are all based on common sense, but they can help determine at a very basic level whether our results for correct voting make sense.

We begin with an examination of the simple bivariate relationships between correct voting and each of these independent variables. Figure 10.2 shows the four theoretically most important predictors in the baseline model. In the primary election (shown in the top half of the figure), all four of these commonsense predictors have exactly the type of relationship with correct voting that we would expect. The percentage of subjects voting correctly increases from 42% for independent independents (i.e., those without any partisan leaning at all, even when pressed) to 56% for partisan identifier (either weak or strong). Similarly,

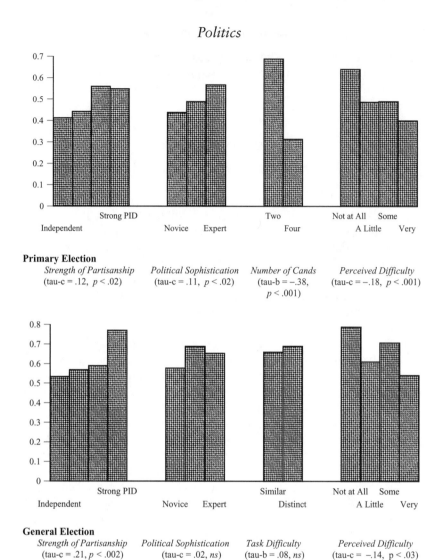

Figure 10.2. Effect of strength of partisanship, political sophistication, task demands, and perceived difficulty on correct voting.

barely 46% of novices vote correctly compared to almost 58% of political experts. Over 67% of those who thought the choice was not at all difficult voted correctly, compared to 44% of those who perceived the decision to be very difficult. But the strongest factor is the number of candidates manipulation. As reported previously, 69% of our subjects voted correctly in the two-candidate primary condition (much better than the 50% we would expect by chance), but only a little more than 31% voted correctly in the four-candidate condition (a little better than the 25% one would expect by chance alone).

Strength of partisanship, political sophistication, and the perceived difficulty of the choice all have the same basic relationship with correct voting in the general election, although the associations are usually somewhat weaker. As shown in the bottom half of Figure 10.2, the percentage of subjects voting correctly increases from 53% for independents to 77% among strong partisans, increases from 58% to 65% as a function of political sophistication, while the percentage of correct voting drops from 79% to 54% as a function of the perceived difficulty of the choice.

None of the different manipulations of the difficulty of the decision task in the general election proved to have a significant bivariate relationship with correct voting, however. The strongest effect was for the ideological distinctiveness of the two competing candidates, with 66% voting correctly when the two have similar ideologies, compared to 69% correct voting when they are fairly distinct ideologies. This is the one shown in Figure 10.2. One of our studies manipulated the stereotypic nature of the out-party candidate in the general election. Almost 63% voted correctly when the out-party candidate was a stereotypic moderate candidate, but 68% voted correctly when the out-party candidate took very nonstereotypic policy stands. This difference is not significant, and it is opposite what we expected a priori.

A different study manipulated whether the in-party candidate was one the voter had supported or rejected in the primary. Turning to the accept-reject manipulation, 63% of those whose in-party candidate in the general election was the one they had supported in the primary voted correctly, compared to almost 72% voting correctly when the in-party candidate was one they had rejected in the primary. We might speculate that voters, whose favorite party candidate won the nomination and therefore made it to the general election, simply pulled the party lever in the general election without seriously considering the out-party candidate, whereas voters who had a less-than-ideal in-party candidate in the general election more carefully weighed the merits and demerits of both general election candidates, leading to a greater likelihood of voting correctly. But again, these differences, although interesting, are not statistically significant.

Notice that overall levels of correct voting are higher in the general election campaign than in the primary, which reflects both the limited number of candidates and the fact that they differ by party, an important heuristic cue that was absent in the primary election. Manipulating task difficulty within the easier general election framework was a more difficult task than we had anticipated!

Table 10.1. *Baseline Model of Correct Voting*

| | Experimental Data | | | | ANES | |
| | Primary Election | | General Election | | General Election | |
	B	S.E.	B	S.E.	B	S.E.
Age	−.780	(.495)	.165	(.498)	−.164	(.132)
Education	−.506	(.532)	−.149	(.519)	.431*	(.223)
Income	−.067	(.343)	.145	(.345)	.119	(.130)
Female	−.061	(.231)	.181	(.225)	.002	(.054)
Nonwhite					.227**	(.080)
Strength of party ID	.057	(.347)	.930**	(.332)	1.433***	(.085)
Conservative ID	−.498	(.521)	.674	(.521)	−.317**	(.121)
Political sophistication	1.468*	(.809)	.133	(.283)	1.956***	(.202)
Number of candidates	−1.558***	(.224)			−.222*	(.103)
Ideological distinctiveness			.033	(.257)	.405***	(.105)
Perceived difficulty of choice	−.533	(.432)	−.326	(.437)		
Constant	1.034***	(.300)	.501	(.382)	−.076	(.092)
Correctly classified	68.4%		68.9%		69.9%	
Nagelkerke Pseudo R^2	.23		.06		.14	
Model χ^2 (df)	76.44 (11)		17.05 (11)		763.25 (13)	
Significance	$p < .000$		$p < .11$		$p < .000$	

$*p < .05, **p < .01, ***p < .001$

Note: Table entries are logistic regression coefficients. The models for the experimental data include dummy variables representing the different studies. Significance tests for directional hypotheses are one-tailed. For the experiments, $N = 402$. ANES data come from the 1980–2000 U.S. presidential elections, and also include dummy variables representing election year; $N = 7510$.

The bivariate results are mirrored, but of course weakened, in a full multivariate analysis when all four of these variables are entered simultaneously into a logistic regression, along with the remaining controls. These results are shown in the first four columns of Table 10.1, which report the results of the full analysis.[1] Interested readers can look directly at all of the statistics; we will describe the theoretically important results here. In the primary election, both political sophistication and the

---

[1] Although we have generally tried to avoid reporting complicated regression tables in this book, we make an exception in this chapter because its topic is so central to the story we want to tell, and because (we suspect) its conclusions will be the most controversial in the book.

number of candidates manipulation remain statistically significant, controlling on the other variables in the equation. As expected, the effect of strength of party identification is subsumed in the multivariate model by political sophistication. But the perceived difficulty of the choice did not have a similar "subsuming" statistical effect on political sophistication and task difficulty, as these two prior variables carried the statistical power in our primary election equation. Nonetheless, perceived difficulty does have its expected negative effect, and the estimate is noticeably larger that its standard error. Overall, the model from the primary is clearly a significantly better predictor of correct voting than chance.

The weaker bivariate results found in the general election reappear in the multivariate analysis. These data are shown in the middle columns of Table 10.1. Of our most relevant predictors, only the strength of party identification is clearly statistically significant. The other variables from Figure 10.2 all have their expected signs, but none of the estimates are ever larger than their standard errors. Overall, the baseline model for the general election does not perform much better than chance.

What we have from our baseline model then, considering both the control variables and the most obvious predictors of correct voting, is a pretty decent equation from the primary election campaign and a somewhat weaker one for the general election. This is just a commonsense starting point before we try to dig deeper in understanding correct voting. But before we consider what our information processing measures can add, let us take a brief detour into real politics to see if this commonsense baseline model can be replicated with survey data.

A SLIGHT ASIDE: CORRECT VOTING IN RECENT U.S. PRESIDENTIAL ELECTIONS

Most of the variables in our baseline model are also available in the ANES surveys. We have the standard array of demographic controls and can create as broad of a measure of political sophistication as we employ in our own experiments. The ANES data are from representative surveys, and we therefore should be able to say something much more generalizable about the effects of these control variables. There are no manipulations of task difficulty, of course, but by considering multiple election years, we can take advantage of naturally occurring variation across campaigns to approximate both our number-of-candidates manipulation from the primary campaign (contrasting campaigns with strong third-party candidates to those without them) and the ideological distinctiveness of the competing major-party candidates manipulation from the general election. We have already seen in Chapter 4 that these two naturally occurring

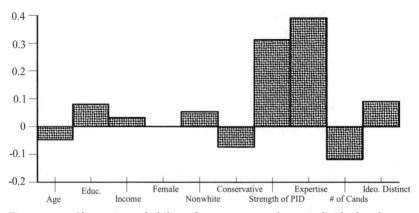

Figure 10.3. Change in probability of a correct vote due to individual and campaign factors, U.S. presidential elections, 1980–2000.

"manipulations" have the expected effect on correct voting, at least at the bivariate level. But will these relationships continue to hold up with a variety of controls? The only variable from our experiments that we cannot approximate with the surveys is any measure of how difficult the vote choice was perceived to be.

The last two columns of Table 10.1 present the results of a logistic regression predicting correct voting with data from six recent U.S. presidential elections, from 1980 through 2000. We have added a dummy variable for race because we have enough nonwhites in our combined samples to feel confident about our estimates. All of our hypothesized differences have their predicted effects in the survey data. Strength of partisanship and political sophistication are both positively related to correct voting, as is the ideological distinctiveness "manipulation," which should make the choice easier. On the other hand, age (marginally) and the number-of-major-candidates-running manipulation (strongly) were negatively related to correct voting.[2]

To make the logistic coefficients easier to understand and compare to each other, we have translated them into the increased probability of a correct vote resulting from a full dose of each independent variable in the equation, holding the remaining variables at their medians. These probabilities are displayed in Figure 10.3. As can be seen, the strongest factors influencing correct voting in the ANES data are two individual differences, strength of partisanship and political sophistication. All else equal,

---

[2] We define a major third-party candidate in the same way the Federal Election Commission does – one receiving at least 7% of the popular vote. Thus, John Anderson in 1980 and Ross Perot in 1992 and 1996 were major third-party candidates.

a strong partisan is 31% more likely to vote correctly than a pure independent; a political expert is 39% more likely to vote correctly than a total novice. These are both huge effects. We have never seen any demonstration of the importance of political involvement and sophistication more stark than this.

The two campaign factors also had noticeable effects, although much more modest than these two individual differences. Having two ideologically distinct major party candidates running against each other increased the probability of a correct vote a good 9% across the board, while a major third-party candidate running in the election decreased the probability of a correct vote by almost 12%.

There were two unexpected effects as well. Nonwhites were significantly (about 6%) more likely to vote correctly than whites; conservatives were significantly (about 8%) less likely to vote correctly compared to liberals. We had no theoretical reason to predict either of these effects. We might speculate that nonwhites would have strong group-based cues that could help them vote correctly that would be absent (or weaker) for many mainstream whites. And we are reminded of Tetlock's (1993) finding that conservatives are generally less "integratively complex" than liberals, which might be expected to translate into correct voting. But we will not pretend that this is anything other than post hoc speculation.

The inconsistent (and unpredicted) effect of voter's ideological identification aside (which runs in the opposite direction in some of our experiments), there is very impressive consistency in the results for our baseline model across two very different data sets. Education, income, and gender seem to have little to do with correct voting. Age might, but its effect does not consistently appear across analyses. Strength of party identification is strongly related to correct voting in a general election, but it is totally unrelated to correct voting in a primary campaign – which makes perfect sense because it is unclear how partisanship should help voters choose among their own party's candidates, as they must in a primary election.

Political sophistication is positively related to correct voting, as is the ideological distinctiveness of the two major-party candidates running in a general election campaign. The greater the number of candidates running in an election, on the other hand, the less correct voting there will be, whether in a primary or a general election campaign. The coefficient for the number of candidates running in the campaign is much stronger in the experimental data than the survey data. But again this makes perfect sense because the "manipulation" is also much stronger in the experimental data – two versus four candidates, in our experiments, compared to two versus three candidates, in the ANES data. And finally, the more difficult a choice is perceived to be by voters, the less likely they are to vote correctly, although this effect does not seem to be very strong, controlling on other variables in the equation.

We turn now to the information processing stage of our general decision-making framework, examining the effects of information search (and patterns of information search – i.e., the decision strategies those patterns indicate) on correct voting. The logic of why rational choice decision strategies are often considered normative strategies with the highest probability of the best possible decision now comes to the fore. Rational choice strategies assume that information search should be reasonably deep and spread equally across the different alternatives. This logic assumes that decision makers are able to process and comprehend all this information. Cognitive limits are very real, however, and the amount of information gathered by even our laziest and least interested voters would certainly exceed those limits. So now the question becomes: What happens with the information that is gathered but cannot be accurately processed and stored? One possibility is that it essentially disappears, more or less randomly, and therefore should not help decision making – but then it should not hurt it either. In this case, the maximum benefits of a rational choice strategy might occur well below the actual levels of information acquisition by our more active voters. But by this logic, we would still expect these Model 1 patterns to be associated with the best decision making.

Another possibility is that the extra information (beyond one's cognitive capacity to handle it) actually hurts decision making – that is, bad (excess) information crowding out good (processable) – by *confusing* voters and making them less likely to remember crucial information. It is here that the more intuitive noncompensatory Model 4 decision strategies may actually have some normative appeal. Several prior studies in marketing research have suggested the potential for information overload is very real, resulting in lower quality decisions (Bargh and Thein, 1985; Jacoby, Kohn, and Speller, 1974; Jacoby, Speller, and Berning, 1974; Kerstholt, 1992). If too much information results in poorer quality decisions, limiting search either by focusing on a subset of the alternatives or a subset of the attributes could in practice actually result in higher quality decisions. Almost the same logic applies to our fast and frugal Model 3 strategy, although we see added benefits from striving for comparability of (limited) search across alternatives without a direct effort to compare options. It is just too easy to imagine situations where a randomly chosen alternative could prove to be acceptable to a satisficing decision maker but also be clearly inferior to another alternative. (See Appendix A for an example.) Likewise, it is easy to imagine situations where the first attribute considered results in a single preferred alternative but where a little more additional search across a few more attributes could change preferences. In such cases, a Model 3 strategy would prove superior to either variety of Model 4 strategy (relying on alternative-based or attribute-based search). In practice, such situations may not occur that frequently, of course, but in our imaginations they do. We readily admit to utilizing the availability heuristic in mentioning this possibility here.

Different decision strategies and information search patterns undoubtedly work best in different situations, but in contexts where decision makers are overwhelmed by information, as in presidential election campaigns, we would be very surprised if any type of rational Model 1 strategy, which relies on relatively deep information search, were associated with higher quality decision making. We expect decision strategies that rely on relatively shallow search to generally result in higher quality decisions, although there could be particular voters (e.g., experts) or situations (when the decision is perceived to be particularly easy) when procedurally rational Model 1 strategies could prove to be efficacious.

We can think of few situations, however, when confirmatory Model 2 decision strategies should result in particularly high-quality decisions. Any strategy that relies on biased information search or biased perception will rarely be associated with any objective measure of quality, as our normative naive measure of correct voting is meant to be. We do not expect every Model 2 voter to engage in such biased search and perception, but enough will that overall levels of correct voting for people utilizing this strategy should suffer.

Let us make an important distinction here about how we think about correct voting. We believe, as social scientists, as supporters of democracy as a system of government, as concerned citizens who care about the quality of their own government, that correct voting is good, that it helps our system of government, and that, to the extent possible, we should encourage any and all institutional arrangements that help foster more of it. Nothing in this statement, however, should be understood to be saying that we believe that all decision makers, all individual citizens, all voters, should have making the objectively correct decision as their primary goal in life. The payoffs for any individual correct vote are far too minuscule for us to ever argue that. For many (and probably most) individuals, making oneself feel better, validating a world view, justifying a superficial consideration of the alternative candidates in an election so one can concentrate on other more pressing demands, or even deciding it just isn't worth the trouble to vote at all is a perfectly reasonable thing

Table 10.2. *Effect of Decision Strategies on Correct Voting,*
Primary Election Campaign

	Equation 1		Equation 2		Equation 3	
	B	S.E.	B	S.E.	B	S.E.
Age	−1.148*	(.525)	−1.212*	(.521)	−.975*	(.497)
Education	−.489	(.546)	−.432	(.545)	.149	(.520)
Income	−.134	(.360)	−.117	(.358)	−.038	(.345)
Female	−.060	(.240)	−.089	(.239)	−.251	(.342)
Strength of party ID	.052	(.354)	−.047	(.351)	.757*	(.342)
Conservative ID	−.508	(.529)	−.451	(.528)	.072	(.510)
Political sophistication	1.566*	(.825)	1.535*	(.820)	.339	(.783)
# of candidates manipulation	−1.534***	(.265)	−3.278***	(.264)	−1.385***	(.250)
Perceived difficulty of choice	−.777*	(.446)	−.742*	(.444)	−.562@	(.430)
Model 1	−.299	(.377)	−1.606*	(.590)	−.425	(.363)
Model 2	−.407	(.423)	−2.204***	(.591)	−.280	(.393)
Model 3	.435	(.450)	−.854	(.645)	−.449	(.427)
Model 4	.600*	(.340)	−.716	(.560)	−.033	(.327)
# of Candidates X Model 1			2.088*	(.891)		
# of Candidates X Model 2			2.470*	(1.119)		
# of Candidates X Model 3			2.454*	(1.256)		
# of Candidates X Model 4			1.916*	(.847)		
Constant	.866*	(.421)	2.090**	(.695)	1.172**	(.410)
Correctly classified	71.6%		71.9%		66.9%	
Nagelkerke Pseudo R^2	.26		.29		.17	
Model χ^2 (df)	88.52 (15)		97.28 (19)		56.29 (15)	
Significance	$p < .000$		$p < .000$		$p < .000$	

@$p < .10$, *$p < .05$, **$p < .01$, ***$p < .001$

Note: Table entries are logistic regression coefficients. Equation 3 employs the kitchen sink definition of correct voting. All models include dummy variables representing the different studies. Significance tests for directional hypotheses are one-tailed. $N = 402$.

to do. There is absolutely nothing wrong with Model 2 decision making, then, from any individual's standpoint. It is just less likely to result in something that we (as concerned citizens, etc.) care about.

To consider the effects of information processing on correct voting, we first added our continuous measures of depth of search, equality of search, and utilization of systematic search sequences (either within-candidate or within-attribute) to our baseline model. If cognitive limits were not a problem, we would expect all three of these variables to have positive effects. They do not. In fact, the only measure to achieve statistical significance is the depth-of-search measure in the primary election, and it had a negative effect on the probability of a correct vote: The deeper the information search is, the lower the probability of a correct vote will be. Using systematic search sequences approaches conventional levels of statistical significance in the general election model, but it too has a negative sign. If our readers have any doubts that cognitive limits are real, these results should put them to rest.

But adding these different measures of information search to our regression model is not the best way to examine the effects of information processing on the quality of the vote decision. Theoretically, it is different combinations of these variables that should matter, combinations that we have defined a priori as indicating different models of decision making. Hence, we replaced the continuous measures of information search with dummy variables presenting the different decision strategies and added them to our baseline model.

The results of the full logistic regression analyses for the primary and general election campaigns are reported in equation 1 of Tables 10.2 and 10.3. The data from the primary election conform very nicely with our theoretical expectations. The two types of decision strategies that rely on relatively deep information search are both negatively (albeit, non-significantly) related to correct voting. But the two categories of decision strategies that rely on relatively shallow search – both the compensatory Model 3 fast and frugal strategy and the noncompensatory Model 4 strategy are positively related to correct voting, with the latter achieving conventional levels of statistical significance ($p < .04$).

Figure 10.4 translates the logistic regression coefficients into probabilities of a correct vote for a female voter in the easier two-candidate condition with median values on all of the remaining control variables. Such a median voter employing some undifferentiated decision strategy[3] was correct 59% of the time. If instead this voter employed either Model 1

---

[3] That is, a voter with median levels of depth of search (between the 45th and 55th percentiles) who could not be classified into one of our four categories of decision strategies.

Table 10.3. *Effect of Decision Strategies and Memory on Correct Voting, General Election Campaign*

	Equation 1		Equation 2		Equation 3	
	B	S.E.	B	S.E.	B	S.E.
Age	.246	(.519)	.154	(.569)	−.031	(.547)
Education	−.001	(.534)	.082	(.548)	1.005*	(.526)
Income	.171	(.355)	.118	(.365)	−.278	(.352)
Female	.009	(.232).	.091	(.240)	.098	(.230)
Strength of party ID	.998**	(.343)	1.017**	(.354)	.173	(.340)
Conservative ID	.669	(.530)	.687	(.534)	.422	(.508)
Political sophistication	−.446	(.777)	−1.151	(1.221)	−.568	(.775)
Ideological dis-tinctiveness	.033	(.261)	.005	(.265)	−.274	(.260)
Perceived difficulty of choice	−.390	(.448)	−.475	(.459)	−.693@	(.442)
Model 1	.089	(.485)	−.404	(.558)	.800*	(.485)
Model 2	.866*	(.482)	.911@	(.569)	1.340**	(.478)
Model 3	.672@	(.505)	1.302@	(.689)	1.647***	(.518)
Model 4	.988*	(.482)	.606	(.578)	1.375**	(.481)
Political sophistication X Model 1			1.125*	(.547)		
Political sophistication X Model 2			−.166	(.561)		
Political sophistication X Model 3			−1.021	(.701)		
Political sophistication X Model 4			.711	(.566)		
Net accurate memories	1.326@	(.936)	1.359@	(.962)	.333	(.896)
Constant	.060	(.529)	.220	(.549)	−.581	(.533)
Correctly classified	70.4%		70.9%		68.2%	
Nagelkerke pseudo R^2	.10		.13		.08	
Model χ^2 (df)	29.01 (16)		39.79 (20)		22.19 (16)	
Significance	$p < .03$		$p < .01$		$p < .14$	

$@p < .08$, $*p < .05$, $**p < .01$

Note: Table entries are logistic regression coefficients. Equation 3 employs the kitchen sink measure of correct voting. All models include dummy variables representing the different studies. Significance tests for directional hypotheses are one-tailed. $N = 402$.

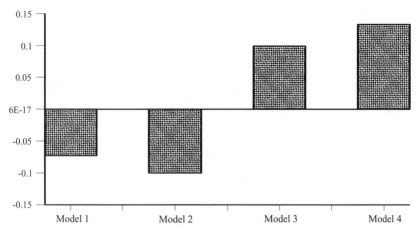

Note: Data reflect change from an overall base of a *.59* probability of being correct for a median voter in the two-candidate experiment condition.

Figure 10.4. Effect of decision strategies on change in probability of a correct vote, primary election.

or Model 2, the two strategies relying on relatively deep information search, his or her probability of a correct vote dropped to 52 and 49%, respectively – essentially chance levels in a two-candidate election. The lack of success of Model 2 in a primary election is not at all surprising because there is little advantage to Model 2 decision making when party provides no basis for making a choice. But the indifferent success of Model 1 *is* a little disappointing because we expected that if Model 1 were to prove efficacious anywhere in a primary election, it could only do so in a relatively easy decision context such as a two-candidate election.

As predicted, the two categories of decision strategies that increased the probability of correct voting the most were the two shallow search strategies. The median voter employing the fast and frugal Model 3 decision strategy voted correctly over 69% of the time. And voters employing more intuitive, noncompensatory Model 4 decision strategies did the best of all, voting correctly almost 73% of the time, all else being equal.

Our framework for studying the vote decision (Figure 2.1) led us to examine interactions between choice of decision strategy and several of the "prior" variables in our framework – political sophistication, variation in contextual factors which affect the objective difficulty of the choice, and the subjective perceived difficulty of that choice. As shown in equation 2 of Table 10.2, the interaction between decision strategy and the number-of-candidates manipulation provides interesting results. The main effect of each decision strategy is now interpreted as the effect of employing that strategy in the easier two-candidate condition, while the four interaction

Two-Candidate Condition (Base .88 probability of a correct vote)

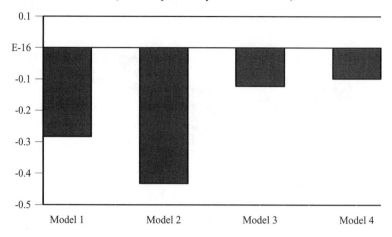

Four-Candidate Condition (Base .22 probability of a correct vote)

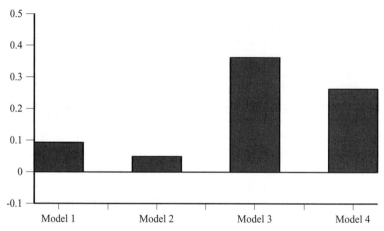

Note: Data reflect change in the probability of a correct vote for a median voter in the easier two-candidate condition (top half of the figure) or the more difficult four-candidate condition (bottom half of the figure).

Figure 10.5. Effect of decision strategies and objective difficulty of decision on change in probability of a correct vote, primary election campaign.

terms are the change in the probability of a correct vote associated with using each strategy in the more difficult four-candidate condition. Figure 10.5 translates the logistic coefficients into probabilities. In brief, the story is this: In the more difficult four-candidate condition, Models 1 and 2 are no better than chance; in the easier two-candidate condition, they

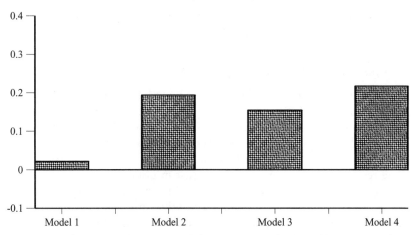

Note: Data reflect change from an overall base of a .55 probability of being correct for a median voter in the two-candidate experiment condition.

Figure 10.6. Effect of decision strategies on change in probability of a correct vote, general election campaign.

are noticeably worse than chance. In contrast, Models 3 and 4 are little different from chance in the easier two-candidate condition, but there is a big improvement over chance in the more difficult four-candidate condition.

The data from the general election campaign show a somewhat different pattern than that from the primary, but again they accord pretty closely to our theoretical predictions. Detailed statistics are presented in Table 10.3, but Figure 10.6 reports the change in the probability of a correct vote associated with each decision strategy for the median voter over a baseline of 55% correct. Rational Model 1 voters do no better than the baseline, but each of the other decision strategies prove to be significant improvements over baseline. Once again, our intuitive Model 4 voters perform the best, with fast and frugal Model 3 voters not too far behind. But this time the *American Voter's* Model 2 confirmatory decision makers do almost as well as Model 4 voters. In a general election campaign, when party differentiates the candidates, Model 2 proves to be a very efficacious decision strategy.

Is there no situation, or subset of voters, for whom Model 1 provides any improvement in the quality of decision making? Equation 2 of Table 10.3 presents an analysis where each of the decision strategies are interacted with political sophistication. The only significant interaction involves Model 1. Whereas political novices who try to employ a rational Model 1 decision strategy do about 10% worse than baseline, political experts who employ such a strategy do significantly better than novices, and about 4% over baseline.

This is the best picture we can paint for Model 1 voters, and it is not overly impressive. These results are very consistent with our theoretical expectation (based on a great deal of prior research in cognitive psychology), but they are extremely important because they so clearly run counter to the promises of classic economic rational choice theory. What these results are telling us is that, at least in politics, *more information does not always result in better decisions.* In fact, it often results in worse decisions. This finding sounds counterintuitive until we remember that all decision makers have cognitive limits. Evidently additional information beyond cognitive capacity often confuses voters (or tires them out?) and actually lowers the probability of a correct value-maximizing decision.

Or at least that is how we view our results. But we have been pressed by colleagues who have heard preliminary versions of this research to push a bit harder on this point. What if we have it absolutely wrong, and it is not that most people are overwhelmed by too much information, but that our criteria for calling someone a rational Model 1 voter are in fact too low? In other words, some people really can process a great deal of political information, and we are wrongly including too many people in the Model 1 category. Perhaps true rational choice voters should be in the 65th or even 75th percentiles of depth of search, rather than the upper 55th as we have employed here.

To explore this possibility, we defined the Model 1 category with these two higher limits and reran the basic (equation 1) analyses from Tables 10.2 and 10.3. These results are available from the authors for interested readers, but we can characterize them pretty easily here. In the primary, raising the depth of search criteria for Model 1 from the 55th to the 65th percentile has almost no effect whatsoever, apart from reducing the sample by fifteen cases. The coefficient associated with Model 1 changes from − .299 to − .162, a slight improvement. Raising the criterion on depth of search to the 75th percentile makes a somewhat bigger change, so that now the coefficient associated with Model 1 is zero (to three decimal places). The coefficients for the remaining three decision strategies remain virtually identical to those reported in Table 10.2. In the general election, the coefficient associated with Model 1 increases from .089 originally to .152 with the first raising of the bar, but then falls to .064 with the toughest criterion, even lower than it was originally. None of these changes lead us to change our interpretation of these results.

Another possible explanation for the relatively poor performance of Model 1 involves the definition of "correct voting" rather than the operationalization of the different decision strategies. Recall from Chapter 4 that our normatively naive definition of correct voting is based on each individual voter's judgment of what criteria are important to them in deciding how to vote. We get this information by observing each voter's behavior, by looking at what attributes they actually examine for two or more candidates, and then by making the normative judgment that they should have looked at that same information for every alternative in the choice set. This procedure gives each voter a pretty strong voice in determining what is "correct," which was our intent. But it also means that the standards for correctness differ across voters and differ in proportion to the amount of information that is actually considered. It is simply much easier for a voter who in practice only examines two or three different attributes for multiple candidates to be counted as voting correctly, compared to a voter who considers fifteen or twenty different attributes for multiple candidates. By this reasoning, our normative-naive measure of correct voting could have inadvertently "built in" a bias against decision strategies which rely on relatively deep information search.

To examine this possibility, we go to the other extreme in defining correct voting and say that, regardless of what our voters may have actually wanted to learn about these candidates, they nonetheless should have looked at every bit of available information about every candidate in the choice set, even though for all intents and purposes this was physically impossible to do in our experiments. We refer to this as our "kitchen sink" measure of correct voting. We find such a definition of correct voting harder to justify normatively, but it does fit with the assumptions of classic economic rational choice and should bias our results in favor of Model 1 and Model 2, the two types of decision strategies that employ the deepest search.

The results of these new analyses are reported in equation 3 of Tables 10.2 and 10.3. In the primary, the change in definition of correct voting had the effect of lowering the apparent effectiveness of every decision strategy except Model 2, and its coefficient is still clearly negative. Model 1 voters do not do any better with the kitchen sink definition of correct voting compared to our original normative-naive measure; in fact, they do somewhat worse. In the general election, the changes went in the opposite direction, as the apparent efficacy of all four decision strategies improves. Model 1 now has a significant positive coefficient – but it is still roughly half the size of the coefficients associated with the remaining three decision strategies. Again, we see no reason to change our interpretation of our basic findings.

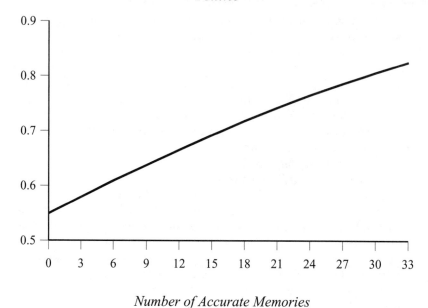

Number of Accurate Memories

Figure 10.7. Effect of accurate memory on the probability of a correct vote.

MEMORY

Finally we reach the last stage of our framework for studying voter decision making, where we examine the role of memory. Proposing a role for memory runs counter to the on-line model, yet the logic of why memory should matter to the quality of decision making (if not person impression) seems clear to us. A vote choice involves a comparison of two or more alternatives, and memory is almost always required to make such comparisons. We consider now not the affective nature of memory, which helped explain the direction of the vote, but the accuracy of memory. Inaccurate (affective) memories can help justify a decision, along with the accurate affective memories, but they should not improve its quality. If we are right, then net accurate memories (i.e., accurate memories minus inaccurate memories) should be positively related to correct voting. We will limit this analysis to the general election because of the availability of memory data there.

Although we have not discussed it yet, all of the equations in Table 10.3 include a measure of net accurate memories, and as predicted it has a (marginally) significant positive effect on correct voting. Figure 10.7 shows the predicted increase in the probability of a correct vote as a function of net accurate memories for a median voter. That probability increases from .58, for a voter with no accurate memories, to more than

.64 for a net of ten accurate memories. The inter-quartile range for this measure is 3 to 10, and thus it is a fair indication of the magnitude of the effect. If we consider the entire range of net memories, the probability of a correct vote would increase from .55 to more than .82 from this one variable alone (for a median voter, controlling, again, for everything else in the equation). The bottom line seems obvious here: Memory matters to the quality of the vote decision, and it matters a lot.

CONCLUSION

This chapter has presented a number of very important findings. We began with an analysis of a commonsense model predicting correct voting, one we would suspect most people would find quite reasonable. This base-line model, whether applied to the primary or general election campaigns of our experimental data, or to survey data from actual U.S. presidential elections, did an excellent job of explaining correct voting, accurately classifying over two thirds of the voters across the different studies. As expected, the most important explanatory variables were political sophistication and experimental manipulations (or pseudo manipulations in the survey data) of the objective difficulty of the decision. Strength of party identification was also an important predictor in the baseline model, but quite reasonably only in a general election campaign where the candidates differ by party affiliation.

Despite the strength of this baseline model, in both the primary and general election campaigns our information processing variables significantly improved the predictive ability of the equations. We focused our analysis on the different types of decision strategies that have been presented in this book. Let us consider now how they each performed in practice according to a criterion of correct voting – which, recall, is only one of the two major motivations (along with making an easy decision) guiding decision makers.

We begin with the most conventional model of voter decision making in political science, the confirmatory Model 2 strategy of *The American Voter*. This strategy performed the worst of all four decision-making strategies in the primary election campaign – but then, it was never designed to do well in such a situation. In politics, party identification is the driving force behind Model 2 decision making, and party identification has very little to do with choice among party candidates in a primary election.[4] But in the general election, when the choice was generally perceived by our voters to be easy, Model 2 was the second-best

---

[4] Party identification – at least strength of party identification – has a lot to do with who bothers to vote in primary elections, and hence has a very important indirect

performer. This is nonetheless a striking finding, if we can reiterate a point already made. Nothing about Model 2 would lead us to believe that it should be associated with unusually high-quality decisions even in a general election campaign, because accuracy is not the primary motivation of those voters. In that very common electoral situation, however, Model 2 voters do as well and often better than voters using any other decision strategy. Let us take this opportunity to offer four cheers to Campbell, Converse, Miller, and Stokes, who have advanced the study of voting behavior in so many ways for those of us who have come after them, even in ways (such as correct voting) that fall outside of their own wide-ranging concerns!

The other widely known decision strategy in political science is rational choice – our Model 1. Theoretically, Model 1 should guarantee the highest probability of a correct vote (or in rational choice language, a value-maximizing decision). In practice, however – at least in the context of our experiments – it does not. Model 1 voters did a bit better than voters following a confirmatory Model 2 strategy in the primary election, but noticeably worse than Model 3 and Model 4 in the primary, and worse than voters using any other decision strategy during the general election. This finding may surprise some political scientists, but it did not surprise us. The presumed superiority of Model 1 decision making is based on the assumption of an unlimited ability to process information more or less efficiently. Most people, most of the time, do not have that ability – nor do most people, most of the time, have sufficient motivation to even seriously try. What is important about our results is not that they show us that cognitive limits are real; no one who has studied or even seriously thought about the subject can doubt that. What our results suggest is that excess information – information beyond an individual's ability to process – does not randomly disappear like rain off a duck's back. It somehow interferes with the processing of information that, had it not been obtained, might have been more effectively utilized. It is as if more and more rain makes the poor duck waterlogged, and increasingly difficult to keep afloat.

Do these results prove, or even suggest, that voters are irrational? Absolutely not. "Rationality" is a very loaded term, and humans like to think of themselves as possessing a high degree of that characteristic. To quote a colleague and friend[5] who did not like or agree with the implications of these results for rational choice theory: "Rational decision processes

---

effect on the outcome of primary elections. But we did not give our subjects the option of not voting in either of our experimental campaigns, so we cannot say anything about the turnout decision.

[5] Who was admittedly somewhat inebriated when he made this argument, and will consequently remain anonymous.

are any processes that lead to a value maximizing decision." That is one definition of rationality, but to paraphrase James Buchanan, the Nobel prize–winning economist, it is a scientifically vacuous one. It removes the concept of rational choice from the realm of falsifiability.[6]

Our meaning of "rational choice" is much more restrictive in definition, based on the decision theory literature meaning of "rationality." Classic rational choice (and the recommendations of many psychologists as well – see Janis and Mann, 1977) holds that decision makers should gather as much information about every conceivable alternative course of action as they can before making a decision. Our results clearly contradict that recommendation.

Rationality is associated with any number of good, positive things, virtually all of which we agree with and strive for ourselves. But one of the most important good things typically associated with rational choice is the highest probability of reaching a value-maximizing decision. It is one of the most important normative justifications underlying social choice theory. That justification may have to be reconsidered.

In the primary election, our two low-information strategies – the fast and frugal Model 3 and the intuitive Model 4 – outperformed both the Model 1 rational choice and the confirmatory Model 2. We had hypothesized that these two strategies would be particularly effective in more difficult decision contexts, and the difference was particularly pronounced

---

[6] Many proponents of rational choice theory take rationality as a starting assumption rather than a testable proposition (Friedman, 1953). According to MacDonald (2003), this *instrumentalist–empiricism* epistemology views rationality as a useful fiction that allows for the generation of empirical predictions about some aspect of the social world. The rationality assumption facilitates the construction of general hypotheses about human behavior and thus is immune itself from empirical test (Lakatos, 1970). Whether people actually act in a manner prescribed by the theory is irrelevant, according to this view; what matters is the ease with which testable propositions can by generated, the generality of those propositions, and of course the accuracy of the predictions that are made from the theory (see Hempel, 1965; Popper, 1959).

In contrast, those adopting a *scientific realism* epistemology wish to develop theories about entities and phenomena that actually exist and operate in the real world. The emphasis is on accurate description of real processes. Conceptual clarification and description of causal mechanisms are at the heart of theory building and are at least as important as the empirical testing of theoretically derived propositions. Similarly, describing a (potentially limited) universe in which a theory is believed to operate is more important than striving for theories that are universally applicable (see Bhaskar, 1997; Putnam, 1982). Thus from the scientific realism perspective, rational choice involves a set of observable decision processes that may, or may not, describe actual behavior and that may, or may not, result in normatively preferred outcomes. Our research clearly adopts this latter perspective.

in the objectively more difficult four-candidate experimental condition. In the general election campaign, Model 4 was our best performer, and Model 3 did almost as well.

What we are calling Model 4 decision making, to the extent it encompasses Simon's (1955) satisficing (which more precisely is Model 4c to us), is familiar to many political scientists – and certainly all political psychologists. Herbert Simon was, after all, a political scientist by training, and his influence, although felt more strongly in psychology, economics, and organizational theory, also extended to his home discipline. A theory of human behavior based on limited cognitive abilities is beginning to be explicitly adopted by a growing number of political scientists as they explore public opinion, voting behavior, and elite decision making (e.g., Geva and Mintz, 1997; Lodge, McGraw, and Stroh, 1989; Lupia, 1992, 1994; Lupia and McCubbins, 1998; Mintz, 1997; Popkin, 1991; Sniderman, Brody, and Tetlock, 1991). The assumption is that people have no choice but to adopt some heuristic-based strategy for making judgments and reaching decisions, and the hope is that these strategies lead to good enough judgments and decisions, at least most of the time. Our results provide strong evidence that these hopes and assumptions are in fact true. Indeed, our results go a step further in suggesting that limited information decision strategies not only may perform as well as, but in many instances may perform better than, traditional rational Model 1 decision strategies. We will discuss some of the implications of this finding – which go well beyond assuming that low-information strategies can do almost as well as more in-depth decision making – in our final chapter.

We doubt that many political scientists have heard of fast and frugal decision making – our Model 3.[7] Like Model 4, it is based on relatively shallow information search; unlike Model 4, it also assumes a relatively comparable search across alternatives. The researchers of the ABC research group who coined the "fast and frugal" term have also provided evidence that, in some instances, it can prove superior to decisions based on more information (Goldstein and Gigerenzer, 1999). We have provided additional information on this point. Indeed, we suspected that the comparability of search across alternatives would prove beneficial often enough that, on average, Model 3 might actually outperform Model 4. We found no evidence that this was the case, however, at least in an electoral setting.

---

[7] We have all heard of single-issue voters, who in many ways seem to be fast and frugal at least to the extent that they might actually compare all of the candidates on the one issue they really care about.

We also found strong evidence that accurate memory contributes to correct voting, just as it contributed to our ability to predict the direction of the vote. This one variable alone added significantly to the predictive power of our general election equation for correct voting, after all the other variables in the model had been added to the equation. We have every reason to believe that memory would be just as important to correct voting in a primary election as it is in a general election campaign, although we do not have much evidence on that point.[8]

We see no contradiction between our finding and Lodge's on-line model (Lodge, McGraw, and Stroh, 1989), however. The on-line model argues that there is no necessary relationship between candidate evaluation – which is continually updated as new information about a candidate is encountered – and the affective content of memory (i.e., net positive memories), which is a function of the full range of factors that affect memory (saliency, recency, repetition) and may not fairly represent the range of information that went into the evaluation. But when two (or more) candidates are being compared, as they are in an election, memory plays a much bigger role. The voter – at least one motivated to make a good decision – wants to be able to compare apples to apples, and even though we doubt that the "information matrix" is ever very complete, as it would be in an ideal world (and on a static information board), accurate information leads both to more reliable judgments and to higher quality decisions.

We have now completed presenting the basic evidence for our information processing approach to studying the vote decision. We have been guided by the general framework of the vote choice presented in Figure 2.1 and the hypotheses presented at the end of Chapter 2. But in wanting to get the basic story "out there," we have skimmed over several politically

---

[8] In pretests for these experiments, we tried to gather memories at the end of the general election campaign for all six candidates from the primary. We quickly found, however, that subjects could remember next to nothing about any of the candidates save the two who ran in the general election. People certainly could have reported more memories for the candidates from the primary had we asked them after their initial vote choice but before the general election campaign began. But the very task of gathering that information could very easily change how people processed information during the general election campaign because many of them would be expecting to have to report memories again. We did not want to take that risk and, therefore, gave up trying to gather memories from the primary campaign. What little evidence we have on memory from the primary (presented in Chapters 8) comes from the one experiment that did not include a general election campaign (see Redlawsk, 2001a).

interesting topics that are only tangentially related to the underlying theory of this research, but that are nonetheless quite interesting. Some of those topics must be reserved for future research, presented in other venues. But one topic is so closely related to an information processing perspective that we want to devote an entire chapter to it here. In the penultimate chapter of the book, then, we explore cognitive heuristics, and more specifically how they relate to decision strategies.

II

Political Heuristics

We argued in Chapter 2 that one of the ways that decision makers overcome their cognitive limits is by employing cognitive shortcuts or heuristics that reduce processing demands. It has become conventional wisdom in political science to assume (1) that pretty much all voters employ such heuristics, and (2) that they help voters make reasonable judgments and decisions despite their lack of detailed knowledge about political candidates and issues. These are the two fundamental – but largely untested – assumptions about political heuristics. They are so widely assumed now that we think it is safe to refer to them as a new conventional wisdom in political science. In some real sense, "low information rationality" (Popkin, 1991) has become a catch-all term, a verbal solution to tricky analytic problems that is consistent with certain stylized facts about the electorate, a verbal solution that allows researchers to move on to other problems they find more tractable (see also Sniderman, 1993). The terms "cognitive shortcuts" or "heuristics" or "low information rationality" have become so pervasive in the field that it now seems they can mean almost anything – which is getting dangerously close to meaning nothing. As Bartels (1996) warns, however, it is far easier to assume that information shortcuts allow uninformed voters to act as if they were fully informed, than to demonstrate that in fact they do.[1] Indeed, it is far easier to assume that voters use cognitive heuristics in the first place than to carefully define and actually demonstrate their use. We as a field can do better than that, and we have to, if we are going to be anything more than bit players in the cognitive revolution.

Bartels's (1996) demonstration of very real and politically consequential effects of information per se on the political preferences of otherwise similar individuals illustrates the dangers of merely assuming that cognitive

---

[1] See Kuklinski and Quirk (2001) for a recent critique of this literature.

shortcuts somehow overcome most of the problems of cognitive limitations and political ignorance. Bartels's findings should also remind us of a possible liability of cognitive heuristics, one emphasized much more by psychologists than by political scientists: Heuristics can sometimes introduce serious bias, along with cognitive efficiency, into decision making.[2]

We will start by making an important distinction that seems to have gotten lost in the translation from cognitive psychology to political science. "Low information" is not the same thing as "heuristic-based." Low information by itself simply means relatively less information bearing on a decision than high information. Just because someone makes a choice based on relatively little information does not mean he or she employed heuristics to reach that decision. If decision makers are restricted to or decide to limit search to a relatively small amount of information, and if some subset of the total information available were particularly diagnostic, then decision makers might be wise to concentrate search on such highly diagnostic information. This is surely what Popkin (1991) means by "low information rationality." But there are a lot of hypotheticals in the preceding sentence, and it makes no more sense to equate low information with heuristic-based, than it does to assume that heuristics compensate for a dearth of real information, or that all voters can use them equally efficiently, or that heuristic-based decisions are as good as decisions reached on the basis of more detailed information.

We will try to avoid all such assumptions in this chapter. We will start by attempting to operationalize "heuristic use" in a manner that can be directly observed and is independent of total information search. We will then be able to see whether the assumption that "virtually all voters employ heuristics" is accurate. In trying to operationalize heuristic use, we know that we should be looking for particularly diagnostic information. We will next test whether heuristics (as we have operationalized them) actually serve the function they are purported to serve: to provide for cognitive efficiency, to reduce the need for more detailed information.

And most importantly, we will look to see whether heuristics are used effectively by voters of all stripes. In many ways, this is the crucial question because most political scientists who talk about cognitive shortcuts assume they are one mechanism by which those with little

---

[2] In one interesting study, Nicholson, Pantoja, and Segura (2002) find that foreign-born Latino voters are more likely to use relatively easy heuristics such as partisanship and whether a candidate speaks Spanish, compared to native-born Latinos. Moreover, they are also more likely to vote for a Spanish-speaking candidate who may fail to represent their policy interests than for a non-Spanish-speaking candidate who is in line with them. Thus, the use of cognitive heuristics in this group appears to result in a bias away from the closer candidate.

interest in and information about politics can nevertheless participate reasonably effectively in politics. This is certainly one possibility. But it is also possible that a certain level of political expertise is required before political heuristics can help voters fulfill their citizen duties. Delli Carpini and Keeter express this idea nicely: "Political information is to democratic politics what money is to economics: it is the currency of citizenship" (1996, p. 8). And to keep their simile going, it could be that political heuristics are yet one more way that the rich get richer, in that they are most useful to those who already have the most political information to begin with.

Finally, we will look to see whether and how our four types of decision strategies are related to heuristic use. We have defined the four categories of decision strategies in part by depth of information search. Heuristics should in part substitute for a more extended information search. But there is no restriction against decision makers employing one of our deeper search strategies (Models 1 and 2) from also utilizing heuristics, nor any requirement that voters utilizing one of the shallow search strategies (Models 3 and 4) must rely inordinately upon them. If political heuristics really do provide great cognitive savings, and their use is restricted largely to Model 3 and Model 4 voters, then we would have discovered a primary route by which voters employing a low information decision strategy can nonetheless vote correctly (as we saw, in Chapter 10, that they often do).

OPERATIONALIZING HEURISTIC USE

What, exactly, would "employing a cognitive heuristic" look like? Heuristics are usually employed automatically, without any conscious awareness on the decision maker's part that he or she is using such a device. As such, they are very well-learned – perhaps even genetic – cognitive predispositions. Yet no heuristic can be employed in any particular situation without at least some very basic information that a certain heuristic is applicable. We cannot use gender or racial or partisan stereotypes, for example, without knowing that we are looking at a female or male, black or white, Democrat or Republican candidate. Without this basic information, a heuristic cannot be applied. Thus, utilizing heuristics means noticing, or seeking out, the crucial information. We have just the data for observing such behavior.

In Chapter 2, we listed a number of common heuristics that could easily be employed by voters in an election. The design of our mock election, with totally new candidates voters had never seen before, precludes the use of three of these heuristics – affect referral, familiarity, and habit – all of which are based on some previous experience with and knowledge of one or more of the candidates. But four of those heuristics – endorsements, partisan and ideological schemata, person stereotypes, and viability – could be employed by voters in our elections. Let us consider each of them in turn.

- *Group endorsements* are one type of political information that has obvious heuristic value. In contrast to carefully considering each candidate's stands on all policies that affect women in a particular election, for example, a voter could instead simply learn a relevant interest group's endorsement (e.g., the National Organization of Women) as a summary of all the difficult candidate- and issue-specific information processing. In essence, voters who rely on endorsements defer the tough cognitive effort to trusted others. All that is necessary is to learn the candidate endorsed by a group, and one's own attitude toward the endorsing group, and an obvious and cognitively efficient inference can be made (see Brady and Sniderman, 1985; Sniderman, Brody, and Tetlock, 1991). We can only presume that voters can readily retrieve their evaluation of different well-known political interest groups (the voters had noted those evaluations on the initial political attitudes questionnaire).[3] But they must actively seek out the group's endorsement before we will say they are employing the heuristic.

- *Partisan and ideological schemata* or stereotypes are among the richest and most widely shared in American politics (Conover and Feldman, 1986, 1989; Hamill, Lodge, and Blake, 1985; Kuklinski and Hurley, 1994; Lodge and Hamill, 1986; Nicholson, 2005; Rahn, 1993 Sniderman et al., 1986). If the salient characteristics of a particular politician are consistent with or representative of the prototypic Republican, say, then voters may readily infer that she is for a strong defense, low taxes, against government intervention in the economy, against abortion, and so on, and will probably have a readily available affective response (what Fiske and Pavelchak, 1986, call a schema-based affective response) to the party label. Relying on stereotypes or schemata provide an obvious cognitive saving, to the extent that particular attributes (e.g., issue stands) are assumed "by default" rather than learned individually in each specific instance. Although these two heuristics are quite similar, party cues are somewhat simpler

---

[3] Or at least something very close. The questionnaire specifically mentioned some interest groups: The American Civil Liberties Union (ACLU), the American Medical Association (AMA), and the National Rifle Association (NRA). In other cases, we followed the ANES in gathering evaluations of "Business groups," "Labor Unions," "Groups that Work to Protect the Environment," the "Women's Movement," and so on, and associated those evaluations with endorsements provided by the "National Association of Manufacturers," the "AFL-CIO," the "Environmental Defense Fund," and the "National Organization of Women (NOW)," respectively.

to grasp and noticeably more prevalent on the American political scene (and thus in our experiment). For theoretical reasons, it will be convenient to treat them as distinct.[4] We consider seeking out candidate's party affiliation as an indication of using a partisan schema, and seeking out candidate's "Basic Political and Social Philosophy" and their "Basic Economic Philosophy" as indicators of employing an ideological schema.

- *Person stereotypes* are possibly the most important (or at least most frequently employed) heuristic in politics for the simple reason that they are not restricted to the political realm but are used by people in all aspects of their social lives. Visual images are so pervasive in the social world that researchers rarely consider their heuristic value. A single picture or image of a candidate may not be worth quite a thousand words, but pictures do provide a tremendous amount of information about that candidate, including gender, race, and age, and often general "likableness," which immediately brings many social stereotypes into play (Riggle et al., 1992).[5] Visual images can also trigger emotions, which can have a great impact on candidate evaluation (Marcus, 1988; Marcus and MacKuen, 1993). People who know absolutely nothing about politics nonetheless know a great deal about people and make social judgments of all types with great cognitive efficiency with these social stereotypes (Rosenberg, Kahn, and Tran, 1991). Voters had three ways of obtaining such information in our experiments: by actively seeking out a candidate's picture, by passively looking at that picture during a candidate's political advertisement, and by actively seeking out specific information about a candidate's age, education, family background, military experience, religion, and so on. Because the latter information seeking provides

---

[4] We may be bucking the current tide in political science by employing the "schema" term. We agree with critics who claim the term has been used far too energetically and uncritically by political scientists, and that the older terms of "attitudes" or "stereotypes" could be substituted into much of the published work on political schemata with little loss of meaning (Kuklinski, Luskin, and Bolland, 1991). If there are any areas in which this criticism does not hold true, however, it is in treating party and ideology as cognitive schemata. Researchers in these domains have carefully documented the memory, processing, and heuristic value of these two concepts (Conover and Feldman, 1984, 1986, 1989; Hamill and Lodge, 1986; Hamill, Lodge, and Blake, 1985; Lau, 1986, 1989; Lodge and Hamill, 1986), and we feel on safe ground by utilizing the schema concept here.

[5] The psychology literature often treats these individual characteristics as distinct heuristics or stereotypes influencing person judgments. Because in practice these are all based on a person's appearance, however, we will combine them into a single heuristic.

only very specific information about a single candidate, compared to the very rich information and broad-based inferences that can be drawn from a single image, we restrict our measure of employing person stereotypes as a political heuristic to seeking out candidates' images. Because all subjects were exposed to at least one advertisement from each candidate, the design of our experiments forced the availability of person stereotypes onto all voters. Still, voters did not know that they would eventually see at least one ad – and thus at least one image – of each candidate, and they could have chosen to seek out additional opportunities to look at a picture of a candidate – or to do so sooner – which builds important variance into this measure.

- *Candidate viability* is an important way to reduce cognitive overload during an election campaign. Although it is typical to derogate political polls as merely "horse race" information, poll results tell voters which candidates are ahead in a campaign and which are hopelessly behind and could never win. Particularly early in the primary season when there are often many candidates competing for a nomination, polls can help the voter eliminate several alternatives from consideration. Reducing the choice set from four candidates to two, say, immediately provides a 50% reduction in the amount of information that must be processed. Moreover, seeing a candidate leading in the polls provides a type of "consensus information" that could motivate a voter who had previously rejected or ignored a candidate to more closely consider that alternative (McKelvey and Ordeshook, 198b; Mutz, 1997). Seeking out poll results is the obvious indicator of employing this heuristic.

Figure 11.1 shows the amount of what we will call "heuristic search" during our election campaigns. The mean number of times information relevant to each of our five political heuristics, as defined earlier, were accessed in the primary and general election campaigns are shown in Figure 11.1. For perspective, we also show two types of nonheuristic search, candidate-specific issue stands and personal information. Two points are clear from the figure. First, there is a lot of heuristic search going on. Almost half of all information accessed during the primary election fell into this category (48.8%), while a third (33.7%) of all search during the general election, on average, was heuristic-based. Of course, we must put these numbers in perspective. Much of the information available would also be called heuristic: 46.3% in the primary, 43.5% in the general election. Thus, voters selected heuristic information slightly (and nonsignificantly) more than would be expected by chance in the primary election, and significantly less than would be expected by chance in the general election ($p < .001$).

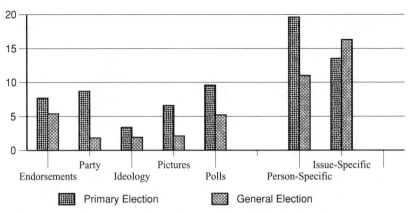

Figure 11.1. Heuristic (and nonheuristic) search during election campaigns.

And that is the second point we would like to make from this figure – there was much more heuristic search during the primary than during the general election, even controlling on the slightly lesser availability of that information during the general election. There are two likely explanations for this decline, both involving the need for using heuristics. First, there are six candidates running in the primary election, compared to only two in the general election campaign. At the very least, voters would have to learn candidate's party affiliations before they could figure out which ones were running in their party's primary. It is conceivable that people could keep a reasonable amount of specific information about two alternatives in mind while making a decision; beyond that, it is simply too difficult to imagine. And second, the two remaining candidates in the general election are already somewhat familiar to voters. Much of the heuristic information available during the general election was not new (candidate's pictures, ideology, and party affiliation) in that it could have been examined during the primary campaign. Only the polls and group endorsements were new to the general election campaign. So, there is less need for heuristic information during the general election, both because (a) there are fewer candidates running, and (b) much of if has already been learned.

DO ALL VOTERS UTILIZE POLITICAL HEURISTICS?

We are now prepared to address the first crucial assumption of cognitive heuristics, at least as they relate to voting. Do virtually all voters employ political heuristics? The answer is a clear and emphatic "Yes." Every one of our voters employed at least three of the different heuristics during the primary, and at least one during the general election. In both campaigns, the modal number was five – that is, employing every one of the political heuristics at least once. So the first fundamental assumption about political heuristics is absolutely true, at least as far as we can judge from our experiments: Political heuristic use is nigh onto universal.

Figures 11.1 only presents one way in which heuristic use can be measured, however. Given that information availability was the same for every voter, we could argue that if one voter examined five group endorsements during the primary election, say, and another voter examined ten, then the second voter is using the endorsement heuristic to a greater extent than the first. We cannot conclude that a voter is using a heuristic correctly or efficiently from these raw counts, however. Some of the heuristic use during the primary could be for the out-party, and it is not clear what purpose this is serving. Certainly it is not rational to learn anything about the out-party candidates during the primary, most of whom will not make it to the general election. Moreover, raw counts of information access like those reported in Figure 11.1 do not allow us to compare the relative use of the different heuristics because the availability of information across heuristic categories varied considerably, and we cannot discount the very strong possibility that some of this search was random.

Fortunately, there are two other measures of search available to us, measures that get at slightly different aspect of "use." One asks not how much information was gathered but what proportion of all of the relevant information available was examined. This measure differs in two ways from the raw counts reported in Figure 11.1, besides controlling on (dividing by) the total amount of information that could have been learned. First, relevant information is defined relative to the candidates in the voter's choice set. By this definition, information about out-party candidates during the primary is irrelevant, and is thus not counted. Second, every time a voter looks at a particular bit of heuristic information, it adds to the raw count total, but if something has already been examined, then looking at it again does not increase the proportion of relevant information examined. That is, if there are four candidates in an election, this measure records the proportion of those four for whom a picture, say, has been accessed. Accessing the same picture more than once would not increase this proportion.

A third measure of heuristic use is the relative priority with which information from a particular category is accessed. If a heuristic is useful to a voter, then the sooner it is examined the more useful it ought to be. The most straightforward measure of priority of access would be to simply record whether an item was examined first, second, or 123rd during a campaign. The lower the number is, the higher the priority of access will be. We could note the first time any information from a particular category was accessed, or perhaps average the priority of access for every item selected within a particular category. Such a procedure would work for a static information board, where all information is always available, and a decision maker can look at whatever he or she pleases, whenever he or she wants. But with a dynamic information board like ours, such information would be very misleading because all information is not always available, and some of it is not available until late in the campaign.

As an alternative, we kept track of when every bit of relevant information for a particular heuristic became available and simply noted whether a voter accessed the first available item from each category, the second available item, and so on. This gives us a different priority score for each category (i.e., each heuristic) but controls on the differential availability of relevant information across categories. With this measure, it is possible for a subject to receive a lower priority score for one heuristic compared to another, even though they could have looked at information relevant to the first heuristic sooner than information relevant to the second. What matters here is not how soon any item was accessed in any absolute sense but how soon it was accessed given how soon it became available.[6]

This gives us three somewhat different measures of using each heuristic: a raw count of the number of items examined that were relevant to a particular heuristic (or rather, to control for the total number of items a voter examined, the proportion of all items examined that fell into a particular category); the proportion of all relevant information from a category that was examined; and the priority with which the first item from any category was examined. We can calculate these measures separately for the primary and general election campaigns. But if we are correct in calling all three of these variables "measures of heuristic use," then they all ought to be positively correlated with each other, after we reverse the priority scores such that a high priority is associated with a high score.

---

[6] There is one somewhat awkward aspect to using priority scores: What happens when no item from a particular category is ever accessed? The measure is undefined in a strict sense, although treating these instances as missing data seems to be throwing away valuable information. If a heuristic is never examined, then it should have a very low priority score, it seems to us. In such instances, rather than counting the priority score as missing, we always assumed that a voter would have looked at the next available item from a category, if only one more had been available. As an example, consider group endorsements. There were fourteen of these in the general election campaign, each available only once. If a voter examined the first available endorsement, he or she received a priority score of 1. If a voter only looked at the last available endorsement, he or she received a priority score of 14. If a voter never examined an endorsement during the general election, he or she was assigned a priority score of 15 – one greater than the highest possible nonmissing value.

These correlations are available from the authors upon request. But the results can be summarized quite easily. As expected, all of these correlations are positive, significantly different from 0, and reasonably large by the standards of these type of data. We are therefore justified in making summary measures of heuristic use by combining the three different indicators of each heuristic. Summary scales created in this manner are typically more reliable in a statistical sense (i.e., they include less random error) than any of the individual items, and they also tend to be more valid in that they can represent a broader meaning of any conceptual variable. When throughout this chapter we examine heuristic use, we will be referring to these summary scales.[7]

Pressing a Little More: Is "Information Acquisition" the Same Thing as "Heuristic Use"?

We would hold that directly observing and measuring heuristic use is superior to indirectly inferring heuristic processing from some simple experimental manipulation or significant regression weight in an analysis.[8] Still, one could ask with our operationalizations of heuristic use, is gathering relevant information the same thing as using a certain heuristic? At one level the answer is obvious: Voters cannot use a heuristic if they do not know it is applicable (e.g., if they do not know the party affiliation of candidates). But we are not employing simple dichotomous operationalizations of heuristic use: Frequency and time of information acquisition are also part of our measures. And even with simple information acquisition, how do we know the information is actually being processed and used in a heuristic manner?

The political science literature provides no guidance on this issue, and the psychology literature is little better. But what heuristics should do, if they are to provide the cognitive saving they are alleged to provide, is to encourage more efficient information processing and/or to reduce

---

[7] Reliabilities (coefficient alpha) of the group endorsement scales were .79 and .85 from the primary and general elections, respectively. The candidate appearance scales had reliabilities of .73 in both campaigns. The ideology heuristic scales had reliabilities of .71 and .61 in the two campaigns, while the viability heuristic was measured with reliabilities of .77 and .83 in the primary and general election campaigns. Finally, the partisan schema had reliabilities of .52 and .67 in the two election campaigns. The somewhat lower reliability of the partisan schema in the primary campaign may reflect the fact that the context pretty much demanded that everyone access at least one candidate's party affiliation early in the campaign, irrespective of any greater desire to rely on partisan cues.

[8] The following three sections elaborates upon an analysis presented earlier in the *American Journal of Political Science* (Lau and Redlawsk, 2001b).

subsequent information processing needs. Learning a candidate's party affiliation, say, by itself does not have to do either of these things. Party could be just another bit of information, like a specific issue stand or personality judgment.

Our experiments gathered a great deal of subsidiary information that can be used to help determine if our heuristics are providing either of these crucial services. We focus the analysis on party, ideology, and endorsement heuristics because we have the most relevant evidence concerning these three.[9] The data are presented in Table 11.1. To begin with, heuristic use tends to be positively correlated with memory for relevant information. These positive correlations provide evidence that relevant information is at least processed, although we cannot say anything yet about efficiency.

After subjects had voted in the general election campaign of our last experiment, we asked them to place the candidates on five different issue scales. Controlling on general political sophistication, both the ideology and endorsement heuristics – but not party – are associated with more accurate placement of the two candidates on the issues. Here is direct evidence for what we might call "efficiency," for something that clearly ought to improve decision making. Even more telling (again controlling on political sophistication), all three of these heuristics are associated with more accurate placement of candidates on issues in the absence of actually learning the candidates' stand on the issues. This is direct evidence that heuristic use provides cognitive efficiency by allowing accurate inferences in the absence of more cognitively taxing procedures of information gathering and processing. Ideology and endorsements – but again, not

---

[9] Although we would argue that poll results generally have a great deal of heuristic value, particularly in campaigns with more than two candidates, the experiments required that it be possible for any of the candidates from the primaries to win their party's primary and advance to the general election campaign. To maintain plausibility across election campaigns, it was therefore necessary for all candidates to have roughly similar popular support during the primary campaign, as indicated in polls. In practice, then, there was little heuristic value to accessing poll results during our experiments, although of course no subjects knew this going into the experiment. But we cannot provide any validity evidence for the viability heuristic. Likewise, candidate appearance can very efficiently provide a great deal of information to voters, although there is much less variance in the "type" of people running for president than there is for lesser offices (a narrowness mirrored by our experiments), reducing in practice the heuristic value of the appearance heuristic for our experiments. Moreover, because all voters saw every candidate's picture at least once during each campaign (whenever the candidate's political ads aired), there is less meaningful variance in the use of the appearance heuristic compared to the others available in this study.

Table 11.1. *Further Validity Evidence for Measures of Heuristic Use*

	Party Schema	Ideology Schema	Endorsement Heuristic
Memory for relevant items	$r = .25^{***}$	$r = .02$	$r = .22^{***}$
Accuracy of perception of issue stands	NS	$r = .16^{**}$	$r = .17^*$
Accuracy of inference absent actual knowledge	$b = 11.44^{**}$	$b = 10.73^{**}$	$b = 4.62^*$
Substitutes for information search in four-candidate primary condition	NS	$b = -1.32^{**}$	$b = -2.82^{***}$

$^*p < .10$, $^{**}p < .05$, $^{***}p < .01$.

Note: Data in the first two rows of the table are partial correlations between the measure of heuristic use and the relevant criteria, controlling for Political Sophistication and Total Item Search. "Accuracy" in rows 2 and 3 is defined as agreement with experts' ratings of the candidates' actual issue stands. Data in the third row reports the regression weight for the interaction between the heuristic of interest and not actually accessing a candidate's issue stand, thus requiring inference. In the fourth row, we report the regression weight for the interaction between heuristic use and the two- or four-candidate manipulation, where the dependent variable is the average number of issue stands accessed for in-party candidates. All regressions also controlled for political sophistication. Because these various criteria were not available in every experiment, N is 285 in the first row, 110 in the second and third rows, and 364 in the last row.

party – also tend to substitute for accessing detailed issue information in the more taxing four-candidate primary condition, in that they were associated with less accessing of specific issue stands per candidate. Together, the data presented in Table 11.1 strongly validate our measures of political heuristic use by indicating they truly are associated with heuristic processing of information. We know of no similar evidence in the social science literature.

Is Political Sophistication Related to Heuristic Use?

Just because everyone uses political heuristics does not mean that everyone uses them equally early or equally often. Have political novices learned to employ heuristics disproportionately to compensate for their general lack of political knowledge? Or (which sounds more likely to us) have political experts learned how efficient acquiring particular types of political information (our five heuristics) can be? To answer this question, we regressed each of our five measures of heuristic use on our overall scale of political sophistication, along with controls for gender, race, education, family income, ideology, and strength of partisanship. These regressions are shown in Table 11.2. We are primarily concerned with

Table 11.2. *Effect of Political Sophistication on Use of Political Heuristics*

	Endorsements	Party	Ideology	Appearance	Polls
Sophistication	.29*** (.06)	−.06@ (.04)	.07 (.06)	−.12* (.06)	.02 (.06)
Age	−.19*** (.04)	.03 (.03)	−.18*** (.04)	−.03 (.04)	−.09* (.04)
Education	.06 (.04)	−.00 (.03)	.19* (.04)	−.09* (.04)	−.01 (.04)
Income	.06* (.03)	.00 (.02)	−.01 (.03)	.01 (.03)	.04 (.03)
Female	−.01 (.02)	.01 (.01)	.01 (.02)	.03 (.03)	−.05** (.02)
Strength of PID	.03 (.03)	−.01 (.02)	.06* (.03)	−.07@ (.04)	.04 (.03)
Conservatism	−.09* (.04)	−.03 (.03)	.03 (.04)	−.01 (.04)	.08* (.04)
Constant	.54*** (.03)	.66*** (.01)	.48*** (.02)	.59*** (.02)	.53*** (.02)
Adjusted R^2	.15	.04	.06	.12	.10
Standard error	.18	.11	.17	.17	.18

@ $p < .10$, * $p < .05$, ** $p < .01$, *** $p < .001$.
Note: All variables have a 1-point range. Regression also includes dummy variables representing the different studies. $N = 405$.

the relationship between political sophistication and heuristic use, and will focus our discussion upon it. There is a significant negative relationship between sophistication and use of both the candidate appearance and party heuristics ($p < .09$ in the latter case). These two heuristics apparently substitute for more detailed political knowledge. But group endorsements are employed much, much more by political experts, and even though the relationship between sophistication and use of the ideology heuristic is not statistically significant, it too is positive and larger than its standard error. Moreover the relationship between education and use of the ideology heuristic is positive and significant. These two heuristics, then, seem to complement rather than substitute for detailed political sophistication. To translate these regression coefficients into items accessed, experts accessed about seven more group endorsements, and about one more ideology item, than novices, but novices accessed about three more pictures, and checked a candidate's party affiliation about once more, compared to experts. Only the use of the viability heuristic (i.e., polls) is totally unrelated to political sophistication.[10]

[10] The negative relationship between expertise and utilizing the party heuristic – probably the most useful of all political cues – gives us the opportunity to address a tricky problem in the creation of our summary measures of heuristic use. Our measures of heuristic use combined tapping heuristic-relevant information early and often. Seeking party information early in the primary is a very efficient and sophisticated search strategy; seeking party information often, however, is not, in that once party information is learned about one candidate it is learned about all of them, given the color coding of the information available on the computer screen. Thus it is not clear just what seeking party information early and often really represents. Expertise

Thus, we find a mixed answer to the question of how heuristic use is related to political sophistication. If we were to rate how difficult each heuristic were to use, or rather how much prior political knowledge is required to make sense of the cues, then surely endorsements and ideology would seem to require the most political understanding, while party cues, candidate appearance, and poll results would seem to require little particularized (i.e., political) knowledge to provide valuable information. In retrospect, this seems like an obvious explanation for the pattern of results we observed.

But it also provides a very important caveat on how we think about heuristic use. Just as all voters are not the same, so all heuristics are not created equal. Some truly are simplifying strategies that can be employed by virtually anyone to make the task of deciding how to vote somewhat easier. But others require substantial domain-specific expertise before they are widely utilized. We will turn to the question of efficacy, of how useful in practice these heuristics prove to be, after considering several situational factors that should also influence heuristic use.

When Are Heuristics Employed? Situational Factors and Heuristic Use

If heuristics help voters stem the overwhelming information tide of a major election campaign, they ought to be utilized more often, and sooner, in more difficult decision contexts than in simpler ones. We have already seen one example of this – the heavier use of heuristics during the primary campaign (when all candidates were new, there were often four of them

is negatively related to using a party heuristic only if we relax our standards of statistical significance – but nothing else relates to it any more strongly.

We thus considered two alternative measures of using party cues efficiently. The first simply indicates the percentage of all information (from the primary election) that concerned in-party candidates accessed after the party affiliation of any candidate is first learned. The idea here is to use party to focus information seeking during the primary for in-party candidates. The second measure combines the first and our measure of the priority of seeking out-party information. So here the idea is not only focusing search during the primary to in-party candidates, but also doing it as soon as possible. Both education and strength of party identification – two variables strongly correlated with expertise – are significantly related to focusing search on in-party candidates. But controlling on these two variables, expertise per se adds no additional explanatory power. The same pattern of results holds for the variable that combines focusing search on in-party candidates with seeking party information early. The only thing we can conclude is that political experts do not utilize party information any more regularly or efficiently than nonexperts. We return to this point in the conclusion to this chapter.

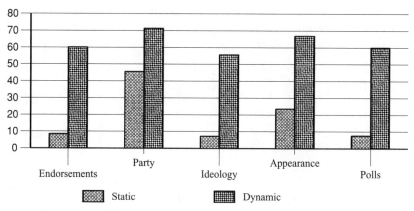

Figure 11.2. Effect of static–dynamic manipulation on heuristic use.

in the choice set, all sharing the same party affiliation) compared to the general election campaign (only two, more familiar candidates, differing in party affiliation). This difference was not a random manipulation, of course – it was more of a "naturally occurring" difference. But our experiments involved several manipulations of the difficulty of the decision task, none more dramatic than the difference between the ideal world of a static decision board and the more realistic, and much less controllable, dynamic decision board we created for these experiments. Our last experiment actually manipulated which format subjects were exposed to, and although we have restricted attention to the dynamic scrolling format so far in this book, we want to introduce the static data here because it is by far the strongest manipulation of task difficulty available. To test our hypothesis, we conducted a multivariate analysis of variance (MANOVA) with the five heuristic use variables (averaged across the primary and general election campaigns) as the dependent variables, the static-dynamic manipulation as the sole between-subjects factor, and age and political sophistication as covariates.

The data are shown in Figure 11.2, and as with the difference between the primary and general elections, every one of the heuristics is utilized much more in the more difficult dynamic condition than in the ideal world of a static information board. In the ideal world, when voters can learn anything they want to learn about the candidates, whenever they want to learn it, there is apparently little reason to utilize any of the heuristics, save perhaps party. These differences are so stark there is hardly any need for statistics. The effect of the static–dynamic manipulation is very significant ($p < .001$), as is the effect of political sophistication ($p < .003$). But there is also a significant interaction between sophistication and the

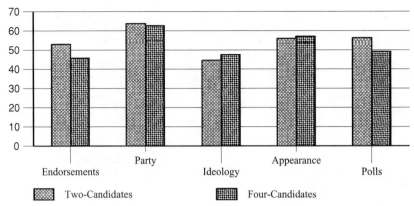

Figure 11.3. Effect of number of candidates running in the primary on heuristic use.

static–dynamic manipulation on heuristic use (multivariate $p < .05$). A closer examination of this interaction suggests that the greater use of heuristics in the more difficult dynamic condition is due primarily to experts, for every heuristic except candidate appearance, where there is no difference between relative novices and experts.

We did not find any consistent general relationship between political sophistication and heuristic use, but here for the first time we get reasonably consistent evidence that heuristics could be more beneficial for experts than novices. At least they are used more frequently by experts in more difficult choice contexts, when they ought to be the most beneficial.

The primary campaign in several of our experiments included another strong manipulation of choice difficulty, the number of candidates running in the primary. We look only at data from the more realistic dynamic format from here on. Again, we conducted a MANOVA with the five heuristic use variables from the primary campaign as the dependent variables, the number-of-candidates manipulation and dummy variables for experiment as between-subjects factors, and age and political sophistication as covariates. The effect of the number-of-candidates manipulation was highly significant ($p < .001$) on heuristic use during the primary, but as shown in Figure 11.3, this time its effect was not consistent across the five measures of heuristic use. As expected, voters were more likely to utilize the ideology heuristic in the more difficult four-candidate condition ($p < .05$). Although there were no differences across conditions on the use of candidate appearance or party heuristics, voters were significantly more likely to utilize the endorsement and viability heuristics in the easier

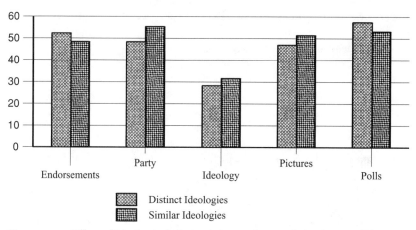

Figure 11.4. Effect of ideological distinctiveness of general election candidates on heuristic use.

two-candidate condition. These latter two results run counter to the second crucial assumption about political heuristic use, that all voters use information shortcuts in a manner that helps compensate for an overall dearth of political information resulting from lack of interest and cognitive limits. If all voters were uniformly following that dictum, then each of our political heuristics should have been employed more widely in the four-candidate condition, but that clearly was not the case. We also looked to see if there was an interaction between political sophistication and the number-of-candidates manipulation, but it was trivial.

A similar prediction would be made about the ideological distinctiveness manipulation in the general election campaign of our last study. It should be harder to choose between two ideologically similar candidates; consequently voters may need to rely more upon heuristics. Once again, we conducted a MANOVA with this manipulation as the between subjects factor, sophistication and age as covariates, and the five heuristic use measures from the general election as the dependent variables. As predicted, the manipulation was statistically significant ($p < .03$), but as seen in Figure 11.4, the only heuristic that seemed to be strongly affected by this manipulation was the party heuristic, which was utilized much more heavily in the more difficult ideologically similar condition. Ideology and candidate appearance were also relied upon somewhat more heavily in the more difficult similar ideologies condition, but group endorsements and polls were used a little more in the easier distinct-ideologies condition. So once again, although we have a multivariate significant effect of the experimental manipulation, the effect of the manipulation differs across heuristics.[11]

We are beginning to see a pattern in these data. Our strongest manipulations of task difficulty were the static versus dynamic decision board manipulation, and the difference between the primary and general election campaigns. Every one of the five heuristics were employed more frequently by voters in the more difficult situations. In most cases, the differences are attributable disproportionately to experts, who are apparently more aware than political novices of the benefits of utilizing heuristics when the going gets tough. But when the manipulated differences in choice difficulty are not quite so strong, as was the case with the number-of-candidates manipulation and the ideological distinctiveness manipulation, the pattern begins to break down. In these latter two situations, group endorsements and polls are both employed more frequently in the easier two-candidate and distinct-ideologies conditions. We have no ready explanation – and certainly no a priori hypothesis – for this interesting pattern of results. More heuristic use in more difficult contexts was our clearest theoretical prediction, but it was true for all five of the heuristics only for our strongest manipulations of choice difficulty. We were also led by theory to look for an interaction between political sophistication and the various manipulations of choice difficulty, but again it was only observed for really big differences in the difficulty of the decision context. All we can say for sure is that any assumption that cognitive shortcuts will be employed by all decision makers (or even by more sophisticated decision makers) when task demands get sufficiently high, is at best an oversimplification, and in some situations (and with many possible heuristics) out-and-out wrong.

Decision Strategies and Use of Political Heuristics

As we have discussed earlier, one of the best documented facts in all of political science is the low levels of interest, awareness, and knowledge of most political matters exhibited by common citizens (Converse, 1975; Delli Carpini and Keeter, 1996; Kinder, 1998). Nonetheless, there is considerable evidence that public opinion often tracks – and sometimes leads – changes in public policy, and that public opinion, at least in the aggregate, appears to be quite reasonable (see Page and Shapiro, 1992, for a very careful and comprehensive review). And of course there is our own evidence, presented in Chapter 10, that large majorities of American voters appear to vote correctly, at least in presidential elections.

---

[11] And once again, there is no hint of an interaction between the manipulation and political sophistication.

The typical explanation for this seeming paradox is cognitive heuristics, which allow citizens to act as if they are informed. Our answer, to this point, is somewhat different. We have shown that in many situations, Model 3 and Model 4 decision strategies, both of which rely on relatively little information, can provide at least as good decisions as strategies relying on much greater information gathering. The gist of our argument has been that a great deal of information about a choice at hand can in practice be as much a hindrance as a help to quality decision making. It is very possible, however, that we have mistakenly equated relatively shallow search with low-information search, and what Model 3 and Model 4 voters are doing is relying disproportionately on highly efficient heuristic-based search. If so, then the true information difference between Model 1 and Model 2 voters, on the one hand, and Model 3 and Model 4 voters, on the other, is not as great as we thought. We doubt that this argument is correct because it would be just as rational for Model 1 voters to rely on highly efficient heuristic-based information, and we know that Model 2 voters will, at the very least, rely heavily upon the party heuristic. But there is no need to speculate because we have the data and we can test the (null) hypothesis of no relationship between decision strategy and heuristic use.

We therefore specified separate MANOVAs for the primary and general election campaigns, where the dependent variables were four measures of heuristic use and the independent variables were a variable distinguishing the four decision strategies, the manipulation of choice difficulty, dummy variables representing the different studies, and measures of age, education, political sophistication, and total information search. We drop use of the viability heuristic (i.e., polls) because we are now preparing to look at correct voting, and in our studies the poll results never provided information that suggested that one or more candidates was hopelessly behind (see note 9 in this chapter). It is important to control for total information search in this analysis, however, because we know that Model 1 and Model 2 voters will have more information search than Model 3 and Model 4 voters; therefore, just by chance we would also expect them to have more heuristic-based search.

These analyses have a lot of power, and they each find that decision strategies are strongly related to political heuristic use ($p < .001$ in both the primary and general election campaigns). Even when we consider the dependent variables one at a time we find highly significant differences in every case except use of the candidate appearance heuristic in the primary election. Figure 11.5 shows the residualized mean differences, where the effects of all independent variables except decision strategies have been removed. The most obvious (and consistent across election campaigns) finding is that group endorsements are used much less by Model 4 voters

Primary Election Campaign

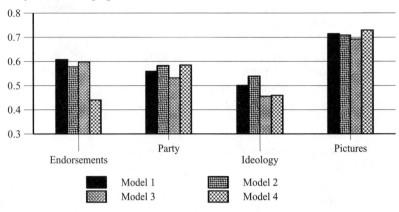

General Election Campaign

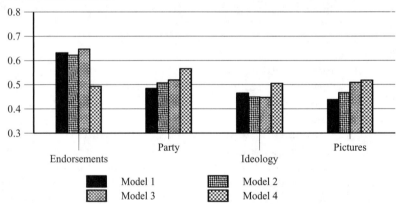

Note: Figures display the relative use of the different heuristics, controlling for the age, education, political sophistication, manipulations of the nature of the campaign, and total information search during the campaign.

Figure 11.5. Decision strategies and use of political heuristics.

than by any of the other three types of decision strategies. But in five of the six remaining cases Model 4 voters employ the other three heuristics as much as or more frequently than any of the other types of voters: They employ the party heuristic as much as (and actually slightly more than) Model 2 voters in the primary and more than anyone else in the general election; they use the ideology heuristic more than any other group in the general election; and they use the candidate appearance heuristic more than any other group in the primary election (although the means do not differ significantly here) and more than Model 1 and Model 2 voters in the general election.

We see no other clear pattern in the data. Unlike Model 4 voters, Model 3 voters are not particularly heavy users of political heuristics. But then neither do Model 1 and Model 2 voters shun their use. But now we have another possible explanation as to why Model 4 seemed to be a particularly effective strategy for voting correctly: Model 4 voters rely disproportionately on political heuristics, and those heuristics are particularly efficient means of gathering valuable information. To see whether decision strategies and political heuristics independently contribute to correct voting, however, we must include them both in an analysis.

Effect of Political Heuristics on Correct Voting

As we have seen, the argument for the efficacy of cognitive heuristics presumes two essential points, that virtually everyone utilizes heuristics, and that their utilization compensates for a more general lack of political information. We have already provided strong evidence for the first point, but we have also observed enough indirect evidence that heuristics are not always employed in those situations where they ought to be the most useful, nor are they disproportionately employed by voters for whom they ought to make the biggest difference, to be rather skeptical of the second point.

We nonetheless believe that the use of cognitive heuristics will generally be associated with higher quality decisions. Our reasoning is simple: If heuristics did not work, at least most of the time, they would not be developed and utilized. Heuristics should be particularly efficacious in the most difficult choice situations – the four-candidate condition of our primary election. Paradoxically, however, heuristic use may only be efficacious for political experts. This is paradoxical because if heuristics serve to compensate for a lack of knowledge, they should be less necessary for the politically sophisticated. But as Sniderman, Brody, and Tetlock have put it, the "comparative advantage [of experts] is not that they have a stupendous amount of knowledge, but that they know how to get the most out of the knowledge they do possess" (1991, p. 24). In other words, not only will experts be more likely to employ certain cognitive heuristics, as we have already seen, but they should also be more likely to employ them appropriately.

We therefore return to our final equations, which predict correct voting in the primary and general election campaigns from Chapter 10 (equation 2 of Tables 10.2 and 10.3), and initially add just our four measures of heuristic use (again, dropping the viability heuristic because, in our experiments, polls had no heuristic value). Only one of these new variables added significantly to the explanatory value of the equation, the endorse-ment heuristic in the primary election.[12] Controlling for all of the other variables in our equations, then, we find scant evidence that political heuristics play much of a role in helping people vote correctly.

But these initial equations do not test our more refined hypotheses about when or for whom political heuristics will be most efficacious. To test these hypotheses, we must add another set of interaction terms to our equa-tions, interactions between heuristic use and the number-of-candidates manipulation, in the primary, and interactions between heuristic use and political sophistication, in the general election.[13] Figure 11.6 illustrates the hypothesized effect of heuristic use on the probability of voting correctly. In the primary election, our hypothesis is rather strongly supported. All four of the interaction terms involving the political heuristics are positive, as expected, and three of the four are statistically significant (or nearly so). Political heuristics evidently do not contribute much beyond decision strategies themselves in the simpler two-candidate condition, but they are a big aid to voters in the more difficult four-candidate condition. The evidence is not quite as good in the general election. There, three of the four new interaction terms have the hypothesized positive signs, but only two of them have a net positive effect, and only one of those (involving the party heuristic) is statistically significant.

Two very important general points can be made from these more refined analyses. First, political heuristics do seem to contribute to the probabil-ity of a correct vote, but only in particularly difficult choice situations and/or only for political experts. Heuristic use by political novices slightly decreased the probability of a correct vote. These results provide strong support for the hypothesis that heuristic use will be particularly efficacious in more difficult choice situations, and somewhat weaker support for the hypothesis that political sophistication and heuristic use would interact in predicting correct voting. Second, heuristic use does not explain away

---

[12] To save space, we do not present the results of these equations, but they are available from the authors upon request.

[13] The results of these final logistic regression analyses are again available from the authors upon request. Our hypothesis on the interaction between heuristic use and political sophistication would apply equally well to the primary election, but we have our strongest manipulation of task difficulty in the primary and will limit our formal test of the interaction of sophistication and heuristic use to the general election campaign. If we ignore the hypothesized interaction between heuristic use and the number-of-candidates manipulation in the primary and instead examine the interaction of heuristic use and sophistication, the evidence is actually a lit-tle stronger than that which we found for the general election. The endorsement and ideology heuristics provide the strongest interactions, but only the former is statistically significant.

Primary Election

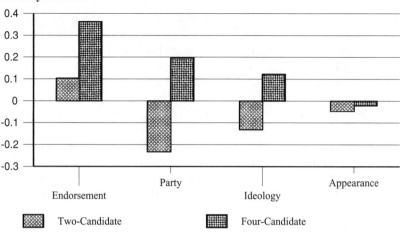

General Election

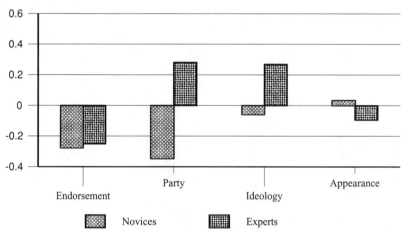

Note: All figures reflect the change in the probability of a correct vote from a median voter who does not use the heuristic at all, to a median voter who uses the heuristic a great deal in the specified situations.

Figure 11.6. Effect of heuristic use by novices and experts on probability of a correct vote.

the effect of decision strategies, which continue to have significant effects on correct voting. Thus both decision strategies and political heuristics combine to lead to more correct voting. The two sets of predictors are complementary, rather than competing, explanations for correct voting.

CONCLUSION

To summarize what we have learned about the efficacy of cognitive heuristics for the vote decision, heuristics are definitely not the saving grace for the apathetic American voter. They have no broad, across-the-board ameliorative effect on the quality of the vote decision. Heuristics often improve the decision quality of experts – who are otherwise interested and engaged in political affairs anyway – but do little to improve (and occasionally hurt) the decision making of novices. This is an extremely important point for those who study political behavior to remember. Heuristics are, however, apparently quite useful in the most difficult choice situations, where cognitively limited voters need all the help they can get. The bottom line is an ever-improving explanation for correct voting, but one that never eliminates the role of political interest, experience, and knowledge.

Part IV. Conclusion

12

A Look Back and a Look Forward

Political scientists have for some time had a pretty good sense of why people vote the way they do, based on such factors as socioeconomic status, group affiliations, partisanship, and issue agreement. There have been arguments over the relative importance of these different antecedents of the vote – and in fact, they have probably changed over time – but most models can readily predict the direction of the vote. In a general election in our current era of somewhat renewed partisanship, simply knowing the party identification of a voter gives us a pretty good idea of how he or she will vote. So there does not seem to us to be much more to mine within this particular genre of voting research.

While traditional models of the vote do a reasonably good job of predicting election outcomes, they do not do as good a job explaining why voters do what they do. Traditional voting models take as given that voters process information, but they do little to open the black box that surrounds how information is acquired and used. They typically view the information environment as fixed and exogenous and give voters little role in shaping their own personal information environments. Thus, one of the goals of this book has been to shed light on the process of voter decision making during political campaigns, to try to understand what people actually do as they try to shape the political information they encounter, and how they use it to make sense of the choices they face.

At the heart of our work is the assertion that information processing matters. For us, the black box of traditional voting models is actually the most interesting part, yet it is clearly the least well understood. In the real world of politics, campaigns know that information matters, and they work hard to provide it, often in overwhelming quantities. Even though the information may or may not be the detailed issue positions and hard facts that many argue should be the stuff of voter decision making, there is still a lot of it, especially in presidential campaigns. Voters may or may not pay much attention to politics, but in the heat of campaign season, they can hardly avoid at least some exposure. Once exposed, whether through active information search or passive reception of campaign ads that appear while watching *Desperate Housewives*, something happens; some impression is left on the voter.

Ultimately, casting a vote is a decision-making process and needs to be studied from a decision-theoretic perspective. Our approach has been guided by behavioral decision theory, a perspective that takes as given that how and what people learn about their alternatives has significant implications for the choice they will make. And the how and what is structured by both the nature of the decision environment – its complexity, the type of information available, and the like – and by the characteristics of the decision maker, in ways that are both systematic and predictable. Our experiments attempt to mimic a particular decision environment, presidential elections, allowing us to trace from beginning to end how information is acquired and used.

We have now concluded all the planned analyses of this book, and then some. We hope the end result has been well worth the price. For the first time, we have hard evidence on what people actually do during an election campaign as they make their vote decision. Our experimental methodology makes us extremely confident that the causal inferences we have been drawing are accurate ones. Of course, that confidence comes with a price – lower external validity due to the fact that those vote decisions occurred during a mock presidential election campaign run in our laboratory. Do voters in actual elections decide in the same manner, or rather, decide following the same contingencies, as voters in our experiments? We cannot say for sure, and certainly there would have to be some differences. But every time we could, we compared what our experimental voters did to survey data from actual presidential elections, and we never came across an instance in which our experimental subjects looked grossly different from these survey respondents. In fact, they usually looked amazingly similar.[1]

---

[1] Survey respondents are typically drawn from much more representative samples than our subject pool. But a survey, just like a laboratory experiment, is its own special social situation, which may well establish certain contingencies that simply do not exist for voters in real elections who are not actively being observed by social scientists. We compare our finding to survey data not because such data are real and unbiased while ours are not, but because surveys are the much more familiar standard for studying voting behavior. *All* research designs, experiments, and sample surveys alike, have their own shortcomings.

A Look Back and a Look Forward

Information processing matters. Our basic decision-making framework presented initially in Chapter 2 suggests that voter characteristics combine with the decision environment (i.e., the task demands) and the level of sophistication to generate a perceived sense of the ease or difficulty of the choice. This perceived nature of the decision task then influences the information processing strategies that voters use to make sense of a potentially chaotic information environment. In general, when the task is perceived to be especially difficult – with multiple candidates, little differentiation between choices, and/or disproportionate resource allocations – many voters employ simplifying strategies that result in unbalanced and/or shallow search. Thus, we see greater use of such intuitive noncompensatory Model 4 strategies as satisficing and Elimination-by-Aspects, where either some alternatives are given little consideration or some attributes are more or less ignored. We also find use of a fast and frugal Model 3 strategy where voters do in fact consider all candidates but only on a limited set of attributes. In any case, none of these strategies come close to meeting the classically rational Model 1 criteria of becoming informed about the full range of attributes for the complete set of alternatives.

Rather than representing a failure, however, Model 3 and Model 4 strategies actually represent an adaptive response to a complicated decision and, under many conditions, may actually result in a better decision than an attempt to learn everything about everyone. When the task at hand is simple, with only two candidates, for example, it becomes a more reasonable proposition for voters to study all the options in depth and to better approximate a rational Model 1 decision. And in fact, this is what we find happens. More voters choose the deeper, more comparable strategies in these cases. But this tack does not appear to pay off particularly well, at least in terms of the quality of the choices made.

Decision strategies not only include particular patterns of search – depth, comparability, and sequence – but also the type of information that is the focus of search. In particular, voters can choose to learn detailed information about the candidates, their issue positions, backgrounds, and the like, or they can look for shortcuts, the cognitive heuristics that potentially let them learn a lot from just a little information. Another advance of this book has been to clearly distinguish between overall strategies of information search and decision making – our Models 1 through 4 – and the more specific or particular attributes to be learned about the alternatives at hand, some of which, like party affiliation, ideology, candidate appearance, endorsements, and poll results, are particularly efficient or heuristic-based. Voters employing all four of our broad decision strategies utilize these cognitive heuristics more or less equally.

Political scientists have long considered partisanship to be a simplifying mechanism, a way for voters to summarize quickly a whole lot of affect toward a candidate. Within political science more recently there has been an ongoing argument that the use of such shortcuts may allow voters to act as if they were fully informed without needing to spend the cognitive effort necessary to actually become fully informed. Because we know exactly what information our voters examine as they learn about their choices, we know who uses heuristics and who doesn't, and the extent to which these cognitive shortcuts pay off. We know, for example, that the nature of the election itself has effects: We see greater heuristic use in the more difficult primary election, where the ultimate heuristic of partisanship is irrelevant. Thus once again, the perceived difficulty of the task has implications for information search. But unlike the intuitive Model 4 decision strategies, which appear to work reasonably well, these more specifically defined cognitive heuristics are not the saving grace for the apathetic American voter. In fact, if anyone benefits from using heuristics, it is political experts, who possess the store of knowledge needed to properly assess these shortcuts for what they mean about candidates.

In our approach, the information processing choices voters make – their search strategies and heuristic use – also have effects on memory. Voters who learn more about the candidates using deeper, more comparable search strategies, also remember more. These memories come into play when it comes time to vote. Here we find that, contrary to the on-line model of candidate evaluation, memory matters. Having more net affectively positive memories about a candidate predicts voting for that candidate, even in the face of the on-line evaluation counter, which also plays a role. And having more accurate memories of the candidates means a higher likelihood of voting correctly. Thus, we argue that voting in a competitive election – inherently a comparative *choice* rather than simply an evaluation – implicates both on-line processing and memory.

Finally, the particular decision strategy engaged in learning about choices in an election may well influence both the direction of the vote and its accuracy. Model 1 strategies that require relatively deep search across all the candidates in the choice set may result in a greater likelihood of voting for someone other than the perceived default candidate – the modal candidate in the primary or the in-party candidate in the general election – compared to strategies that result in never learning much about the full range of choices.

CORRECT VOTING

A second goal of this book, and one we believe marks an important and substantive change in direction for the field, is to understand what we call correct voting. We focus ultimately not on the outcome of an election but on whether democratic citizens are able to get it right when faced with a chaotic information environment with multiple candidates advancing competing claims for their vote. By redefining the dependent variable as decision quality rather than direction, we open up a new line of research into the important issue of whether election outcomes accurately reflect the needs and desires of voters. If voters can live through an election campaign and in the end choose the candidate or party who best reflects their interests, then at least one leg upon which democracy stands is firm. But if they cannot, if voters are easily bamboozled into voting for candidates they should not support by a flashy appeal, a pretty face, or a simple message repeated over and over again, then what happens to the basic link between the governors and the governed? Our work provides a framework for asking this question, by first establishing what it means to vote correctly and then identifying factors that lead to correct (or incorrect) votes.

Which search strategy is used has clear effects on voting correctly. Decision-simplifying Model 3 and Model 4 strategies improve decision making in primary elections (especially when the choice is particularly difficult, as when there are four candidates competing for the nomination), and in general election campaigns as well. Even what we have called confirmatory Model 2 strategies do a pretty good job in a general election campaign where the two competing alternatives differ by party. Rational choice Model 1 strategies, on the other hand, based on relatively deep search, typically do not improve decision making, and sometimes seem to hurt it.

The analyses presented in this book have largely supported our general theory of voter decision making. A wide range of factors – voter characteristics, the election environment, expertise – influence how a particular choice is perceived and the ways in which voters learn about their options. These then go on to affect both the direction and quality of the vote decision. Without taking the space here to review all the particular findings from earlier chapters, Figure 12.1 reprises our list of theoretical predictions from the end of Chapter 2. The research presented in this book has not tested all of them, nor has every hypothesis that could be tested been supported, but the vast majority of them have. No single study can provide the definitive test of any hypothesis (much less a broader theory), and how many of the findings reported in this book will stand the test

Basic Premises

Factors that should lead to a priority on one of the goals over the other include:

Making a Good Decision (NONE TESTED)	*Making an Easy Decision*
• Increasing perceived importance	• Competing obligations/interests
• Increasing stakes	• Familiarity/complacency (SUPPORTED)
• Increasing anxiety	• Increasing task difficulty (SUPPORTED)
• Novelty	• Time pressure

Factors That Affect Information Processing and Choice of Decision Strategy

Model 1 (Rational Choice): As the most cognitively difficult decision strategy, albeit one that promises a value-maximizing outcome, Model 1 is more likely to be chosen when there are only two alternatives in the choice set (SUPPORTED), by experts in any particular domain (SUPPORTED), and when decision makers are primarily motivated to make good decisions (NOT TESTED).

Model 2 (Confirmatory Decision Making): Model 2 is most likely to be chosen by strong political partisans (SUPPORTED), and in situations of high anxiety or otherwise high perceived "importance" of an election (NOT TESTED). Model 2 decision makers should be motivated to learn candidates' party affiliations as soon as possible (NOT TESTED – TRUE BY DEFINITION). And particularly when they are exposed to information that might lead them to question their standing decision, they should be motivated to seek disproportionate information about their in-party candidate which should serve to bolster or confirm their long-standing predispositions (SUPPORTED).

Model 3 (Fast and Frugal Decision Making): Model 3 is most likely when a decision is particularly difficult (SUPPORTED), or decision makers are working under severe time pressure (NOT TESTED)

Model 4 (Semiautomatic Intuitive Decision Making): Any factor that leads decision makers to be primarily motivated by desires to make an easy decision, particularly increasing task difficulty (SUPPORTED), should lead to great use of Model 4 decision strategies.

Expected Consequences of Decision Strategies

Model 1: More moderate, less polarized candidate evaluations (SUPPORTED); higher quality decisions when decision tasks are relatively easy (DISCONFIRMED), or when strategy employed by a relative expert (SUPPORTED).

Model 2: Polarized candidate evaluations (SUPPORTED);

Model 3: More moderate, less polarized candidate evaluations (SUPPORTED); better quality decisions when decisions are – or are perceived to be – very difficult (SUPPORTED).

Model 4: Polarized candidate evaluations (SUPPORTED); better quality decisions when decisions are (perceived to be) relatively difficult (SUPPORTED).

Figure 12.1. Scorecard on theoretical assumptions and predictions.

A Look Back and a Look Forward

Factors Affecting Memory

*   *Depth of search* should be positively related to amount of recall (SUPPORTED), although the effect should be curvilinear due to cognitive limitations (NO).

*   *Ordered search sequences* should be positively related to accuracy of recall (DISCONFIRMED).

  • Holistic (within-candidate) search should be related to both amount and accuracy of recall when candidate-oriented memories are requested (DISCONFIRMED);

  • Dimensional (within-candidate) search should be related to both amount and accuracy of recall when attribute-oriented memories are requested (DISCONFIRMED).

*   *Expertise* should be positively related to both amount and accuracy of recall (SUPPORTED).

Consequences of Memory

*   There is no necessary, deterministic relationship between the affective nature of memory and candidate evaluation (WE HAVE NOTHING TO SAY ABOUT NECESSITY, BUT IN OUR DATA THERE IS AN EMPIRICAL RELATIONSHIP BETWEEN AFFECTIVE MEMORY AND CANDIDATE EVALUATION).

*   But the affective nature of memory should be related to candidate choice (SUPPORTED).

*   And *accuracy* of memory should be related to quality of decision making (SUPPORTED).

Figure 12.1 *(continued)*.

of time is, of course, yet to be seen. But the record so far is pretty good. In presenting and developing this theory, we believe we have gone a long way toward opening up the black box of voter decision making.

DIRECTIONS FOR FUTURE WORK

When we started this project back in the dark ages before the World Wide Web and before ready access to personal computers, one of our major concerns was that the environment we were creating was highly artificial, relying as it does on the computer to present information about candidates to voters. In addition to problems with finding adequate desktop computing power to actually run the experiments, we routinely ran across subjects with little computer experience, and especially limited understanding of how to use a mouse to choose among options presented on a screen. In short, our experimental environment suffered substantially from a lack of mundane realism.

Fast forward ten years. Desktop computers are essentially ubiquitous. Campaigns now use the Web as a key part of their information strategy (Corrado and Firestone, 1996; Winneg and Jomini, 2004). A candidate without a web site – especially in a national campaign – is simply not a serious candidate. As a consequence, more and more voters are getting political information from exactly that unrealistic source we used in these experiments – a computer screen! We would not argue that our environment looks anything like a web site; nonetheless, there is no longer anything odd about learning about candidates and campaigns while sitting in front of a computer. And no doubt this trend is accelerating as candidates find more and better ways to communicate with potential supporters over the Internet.

This leads to interesting questions for anyone who believes information processing matters. Could it be that the way in which candidate Web sites (and also nonpartisan sites that provide information about multiple candidates) format their information might be another factor in the decision environment leading to variations in information processing by voters? Our research operates under the assumption that, even though voters play an active role in selecting the limited information they access from a much larger pool, they have very little control over what is available for access at any given time. In traditional political campaigns – the type that have existed over the past two centuries – most information that came to voters was ephemeral in nature, here today and gone tomorrow. Further, it was rare that a voter would be able to easily compare candidates side by side in some easy-to-process manner, though occasionally newspapers do run candidate comparison boxes on a select set of issues.

Now, however, the potential exists for voters to control their own destiny, to manage information the way they want it. Sites that first appeared during the 2000 presidential election, such as *presidentmatch.com* and *selectsmart.com*, allow voters to specify their own issue positions and interests and get back a ranked list of candidates based on where the candidates stand on the issues. Voters can then compare candidates side by side to see which one best represents their interests. This level of control over the flow of information in a campaign is unprecedented and has the potential to change the way voters learn about their choices.

But we know little about how voters interact with this kind of information. To the extent that such presentations simplify information processing, we would expect voters to become better informed about the full range of candidates. We have shown that task complexity has a significant impact on whether a decision maker will use a simplifying strategy or attempt to learn a lot about all the options, thus coming closer to the elusive rational ideal. On the other hand, the use of the Internet has the potential to increase information overload, to provide an environment so information-rich that it becomes impossible to wade through it all. And even if the Web has the potential to increase the ease with which information can be acquired, it is not at all certain that more information is always better, given our correct voting standard. During the 2004

U.S. presidential election campaign, we heard a lot of speculation about a great partisan divide in information sources, with liberals getting their political information from one set of media outlets and Web sites and conservatives getting their information from another set of media outlets and Web sites. Whatever the case, this would seem to be a fruitful area for future work.

We also believe more has to be learned about the role of correct voting in a democratic society. Democratic theory has long argued that an informed citizenry is a necessary condition to a working democracy. The logic seems impeccable; voters unaware of the issues and of what their representatives are doing seem unlikely to be able to hold those representatives to account. And there is plenty of evidence that most voters have a relatively limited store of knowledge about politics. Yet, when we investigate correct voting in American presidential elections, we find that over 70% of voters do, in fact, vote correctly. We have tried to show the myriad of ways citizens during an election campaign attempt to compensate for a rather shallow understanding of politics to still make reasonable – and in many cases, the best possible – decision.

But is 70% correct enough? Is it the best we can do? Without some sort of benchmark against which to compare our findings, we can only speculate. But there is no reason that the correct voting concept cannot be extended to democracies outside of the United States. It should be possible to assess the prevalence of correct voting as we define it – voting in accordance with one's fully informed preferences – in any kind of election, whether presidential or parliamentary, single or multi-member district, first-past-the-post or proportional representation. In theory, we merely need to know voter preferences and candidate positions to make the assessment.

Extending our work beyond the American context could provide just the benchmark needed to assess not only how well Americans are doing but how different democratic systems facilitate citizens' ability to learn about their choices and to translate that learning into a high-quality decision. This idea is not unique. Scholars have used voter turnout, for example, as a way to assess relative differences between democratic systems (Franklin, 1996). But turnout, while perhaps indicative of the viability of a democracy, does not tell us whether voters are capable of meeting the requirements of good democratic citizenship. It could easily turn out that a system with higher turnout actually has a lower incidence of correct voting. Given a choice, which would be preferred: a relatively low turnout of high-quality votes or a relatively high turnout of low-quality votes? What would be best for a vibrant democracy, of course, is a system that enhances both turnout and correct voting. Applying our correct voting standard cross-nationally should provide insight into what type of democratic system, if any, can do both.[2]

We began this work with a relatively narrow micro-level question about how voters use information, and we end it with a much broader question of how democracy works best and whether voters can and do make use of the information candidates provide in order to choose leaders who represent their interests. Although everybody does not do this effectively, our studies convince us that human beings have a great capacity for making sense of complicated information environments. At the same time, there is no question that information environments can be structured in ways that increase the chance that voters will sort through the noise and excitement to find the right choice. Our studies move us along the path to understanding how this can be accomplished, but much additional work is needed. We hope that we have set the groundwork to move voting research into a recognition that understanding what voters actually *do* is at least as important as being able to predict how they will vote.

Ultimately, of course, it does not matter if any of the findings reported in this book stand the test of time. What matters is that they are tested again, in many and varied different research settings. Eventually some reader of this book, smarter than its authors, will invent a new process-tracing technique that will allow the information processing of voters in actual elections to be studied. We cannot wait for that day to come. Until then, we hope that our general framework of voter decision making will prove as useful to others as it has to us. We have laid out a set of interesting questions to be addressed, and provided preliminary answers to many of them. More importantly, we have devised a number of conceptual measures – and provided at least one concrete operationalization of those concepts – that can be used to address those questions.

The great social psychologist Kurt Lewin taught his students that anything about human society could be operationalized and studied experimentally. As the students of Lewin's students, we strive to keep that Lewinian spirit alive. That, we hope, will be the greatest contribution of this work.

---

[2] Lau et al. (2005) provide preliminary answers to many of these questions.

Appendix A. Detailed Examples of Decision Strategies in Action

This appendix follows the efforts of a hypothetical voter Ralph as he negotiates a choice between three candidates in an election for governor of New Jersey. For convenience, we will set up a static information board that lists the three candidates across the top and eight attributes down the side. The structure of the board is shown in Figure A.1.[1] Ralph's job is to determine which candidate he supports based on the information he has at hand about the candidates.

COMPENSATORY STRATEGIES

Model 1: Rational Choice

Weighted Additive and Expected Utility Strategies. The *Weighted Additive Rule* (WAdd) and the *Expected Utility Rule* (EU) are both formal variants of rational choice, and are thus often considered normative standards in the behavioral decision theory literature. They suggest that decision makers evaluate each alternative according to the utilities of all relevant attributes or outcomes associated with it, form an overall evaluation of each alternative, and then choose the most highly evaluated one. The two approaches differ in that the Weighted Additive Rule assumes that decision makers further consider the relative importance of each attribute to the decision at hand, whereas the Expected Utility Rule assumes that decision makers consider the probability that each outcome will occur. Hence, they both involve great cognitive complexity. Of course, there is no reason a hybrid strategy could not consider both differential importance

---

[1] Information boards are one of the traditional ways of capturing process-tracing information useful to understanding decision making. Here we simply employ the information board as an easy way to visualize the task that our voter, Ralph, faces in making his choice.

	Candidate A	Candidate B	Candidate C	Voter's Import. Weights
Political Experience	4th term in House of Representatives [+.6]	Lieutenant governor [+.8]	Member of state assembly [0]	1
Education	BA political science from Princeton; Law degree from NYU [+.8]	Engineering degree from University of Iowa; MBA from Rutgers [+1.0]	Bachelor's and Master's degrees in biology from Monclair State Univ. [+.4]	.3
Family	Married; daughter in college, son in high school [+1.0]	Single; never married [+.5]	Divorced after 20 years of marriage; two grown daughters, three grandchildren [0]	.1
Party Affiliation	Democrat [−.5]	Republican [+1.0]	Independent Good Government Party [+.1]	.5
Policy on Abortion	Pro-Choice, but accepts parental notification laws "with appropriate safe-guards" for minors seeking abortions [+.8]	Pro-Life, except in cases of rape or incest, or when the mother's life is endangered [−.6]	Pro-Choice; believes government has no business regulating people's private lives [+1.0]	.8
Policy on Gun Control	Favors registration of all guns, a ban on cheap "Saturday night specials" and making possession of any semiautomatic weapon a felony [+1.0]	Opposes registration of guns, but would accept bans on privately owned machine guns and anti-tank weapons [−.2]	Opposes any limitation on private gun ownership; again, this is not the government's business [−.9]	.6
Policy on Homeland Defense	Would ask commander of state police to work with federal officials and coordinate anti-terror efforts with neighboring states [+.1]	Would appoint special commission to study problem and make recommendations [−.1]	Proposes special identification card which all immigrants and foreign visitors to the U.S. must carry at all times [+.5]	.4
Tax Policy	Proposes lowering taxes on the middle class and raising them on the rich, but keeping current tax revenues about the same [−.1]	Proposes an across-the-board 9% tax cut, spread equally over three years, to "spur the state's economy" [+1.0]	Proposes eliminating all taxes on businesses, and all tax deductions, and establishing a flat 2% income tax on all incomes above $40,000 [+.8]	.8

Figure A.1. Information board for three-candidate election with all cells exposed, showing utilities and importance weights for a hypothetical voter.

weights and differential probabilities, although this would involve yet another magnitude of complexity. Both of these rules assume that conflicts are explicitly confronted and resolved via the different weights or probabilities.

If our voter Ralph were to employ either WAdd or EU with the information board shown in Figure A.1, he would gather information by going down the columns, by selecting one candidate at random and learning everything there was about that candidate, associating a subjective utility and an importance weight (or a probability) to every attribute, and calculating an overall evaluation of the candidate once all the information is gathered. The process would be repeated for every candidate. Since everything must be learned about every candidate, there is no reason to select one attribute before any other, nor any reason to consider any particular candidate before any of the others.

To give substance to this decision rule (and the others we will consider), the utility Ralph associates with each particular cell is shown in Figure A.1 (in brackets). For simplicity, we have adopted the convention that a decision maker's most preferred outcome for each dimension of judgment is given a utility of $+1$, acceptable but not ideal positions or outcomes have utilities between 0 and 1, and unacceptable or disliked positions have a utility between 0 and -1. These particular numbers are arbitrary, of course, but we want to use positive numbers to represent preferred outcomes or attributes and negative numbers to represent disliked outcomes or attributes, to make more salient when and where value tradeoffs will be required.

The relative importance of each attribute or dimension of judgment to this same decision maker is displayed in the right-hand column.[2] The most important consideration for this decision is given a weight of 1.0, attributes that have absolutely no bearing of the decision would be given a weight of 0, with relative importance between these two extremes represented by appropriate values between 0 and 1. The range the weights take on is again arbitrary; we have used a 0 to 1 range to mirror what these "weights" would look like if they were probabilities.

Ralph is a pretty typical New Jersey Republican: conservative on economic issues, but liberal on many social issues. Ralph would probably be a "weak Republican" according to the well-known measure of party identification, judging by the greater utility he associates with the Republican candidate (Candidate B) over the Democrat (Candidate A) and the .5

---

[2] This example lends itself more to relative importance than to expected outcomes, so formally this example describes the use of the Weighted Additive model, but it would work exactly the same for the Expected Utility model if we replaced the importance weights with probabilities.

Weighted Additive Rule

	Candidate A	Candidate B	Candidate C
	1.0(.6)	1.0(.8)	1.0(0)
	.3(.8)	.3(1.0)	.3(.4)
	.1(1.0)	.1(.5)	.1(0)
	.5(−.5)	.5(1.0)	.5(.1)
	.8(.8)	.8(−.6)	.8(1.0)
	.6(1.0)	.6(−.2)	.6(−.9)
	.4(.1)	.4(−.1)	.4(.5)
	.8(−.1)	.8(1.0)	.8(.8)
$\sum w_i(U_{ij})$ =	1.89	1.80	1.27
	Choose A		

Additive Difference Rule

	A vs. B	A vs. C	B vs. C
	1.0(.6 − .8)	1.0(.6 − 0)	1.0(.8 − 0)
	.3(.8 −1.0)	.3(.8 − .4)	.3(1.0 − .4)
	.1(1.0 − .5)	.1(1.0 − 0)	.1(.5 − 0)
	.5(−.5 − 1.0)	.5(−.5 − .1)	.5(1.0 − .1)
	.8(.8 + .6)	.8(.8 − 1.0)	.8(−.6 − 1.0)
	.6(1.0 + .2)	.6(1.0 + .9)	.6(−.2 + .9)
	.4(.1 + .1)	.4(.1 + .5)	.4(−.1 − .5)
	.8(−.1 − 1.0)	.8(−.1 − .8)	.8(1.0 − .8)
$\sum w_i(U_{ij} - U_{ik})$	+.06	+.62	+.54

Candidate A is preferred to both B and C, so whatever order candidates are considered, the decision using this rule is **Choose A**.

Figure A.2. Examples of Model 1 rational choice compensatory decision rules.

importance he attributes to this attribute. Political experience is his most important consideration for governor, followed by the candidates' abortion and tax policies and then gun control. All of these policy considerations are more important to Ralph than a candidate's party affiliation.

The top part of Figure A.2 illustrates the calculations Ralph would need to make a decision by the Weighted Additive Rule. The figure reproduces the utilities and weights from Figure A.1. The Weighted Additive Rule says that you simply multiply the different utilities by the weights and then sum the resulting products. In this example, some of the products for each candidate are negative, but these negative values are compensated by a greater number of positive values. As it turns out, each of these three candidates is evaluated positively by Ralph, although candidate A is liked the most and is therefore the vote choice by this decision rule.

Additive Difference Rule. The *Additive Difference Rule* (AddDif) is logically equivalent to the Weighted Additive model, and therefore should result in the same decision. The major difference is that here decision makers are assumed to compare alternatives one attribute at a time and to calculate and retain the differences between alternatives. As with WAdd, all information is assumed to be considered, and the differences are weighed in terms of their relative importance to the decision maker. If more than two alternatives are available, this decision rule is exceedingly complex.

Unlike the Weighted Additive strategy, which focuses on a candidate-oriented search, the Additive Difference Rule dictates search "across the rows" of the information board, with the additional proviso that, given more than two alternatives, search is limited to two candidates at a time. So decision makers following this rule should pick two candidates arbitrarily, say A and B, then compare these two candidates on every attribute available. With each pair of attributes considered, the decision maker would decide which candidate has the better "position" on this attribute, and by how much, and then weight that difference by the importance of that attribute to the overall comparison. After all available information about these two candidates is considered, these weighted differences are combined to determine which candidate is preferred. This procedure is repeated, with the winning candidate compared to each remaining candidate in turn.

The bottom half of Figure A.2 shows the results of these calculations for our hypothetical voter Ralph, whose preferences have not changed since they were first introduced. And the results are exactly the same as those produced by the Weighted Additive Rule, as they should be: Candidate A comes out as the vote choice, no matter which pair of candidates is considered first.

No one thinks that people actually make decisions in this way, whether via an alternative-oriented WAdd strategy or an attribute-oriented AddDif approach, although social scientists employing rational choice models sometimes write as if they do.[3] Given what we know about cognitive limits, it is not really credible to assume that people actually make anything save the simplest decisions in such a manner. Neither relative utilities nor importance considerations are stored in the mind as numbers, and even if they were, the math alone would be pretty difficult for the unaided decision maker.[4] The real question for our purposes is whether this method is a

---

[3] Lau (2003) discusses several cognitively simpler variants of WAdd and AddDif. We will not be able to distinguish empirically between these closely related decision strategies, however, so we present only the purest variants of the strategies here.

[4] Go ahead and try to check the math in Figure 2.3 without paper and pencil or a calculator, in a situation where there are some distractions but basically where you can safely ignore what is going on around you and concentrate on this simple task. (Imagine, for example, the typical faculty meeting.) *Hint:* There is a small error in the calculations.

reasonable approximation – a mathematical formalization – of how decision makers actually reach a decision, without necessarily going through all the math. It does have some intuitive appeal. Certainly it is the case that some considerations matter more than others for most decisions. And the idea that we like certain outcomes or attributes more than others is true for everyone.

What is more difficult to accept are some of the implicit assumptions of this example: first, that any decision maker would actually have the same information about every alternative and, second, that the values or outcomes would all be commensurable. If these conditions are met, and if the decision maker has enough time to think about his or her decision, and if the amount of available information is not too overwhelming, the Weighted Additive model could be a reasonable approximation of actual decision making. If these conditions or assumptions do not hold, however, then for all practical purposes, it is simply impossible to use such a decision strategy. The remaining three strategies we review are much more likely to actually be used by cognitively limited decision makers.

Model 3: *Fast and Frugal Decision Making (Take the Few Best Rule)*

WAdd and AddDif are pretty unrealistic in most situations because of their exceedingly high cognitive demands, but a simpler compensatory strategy might well be employable. We propose a new strategy, based loosely on the fast and frugal heuristics of Gigerenzer, Todd, and their colleagues of the ABC research group (Gigerenzer and Todd, 1999). Decision makers employing this rule would *Take the Few Best* (FewBest) attributes – presumably the ones they care the most about, but only those few – under consideration in reaching a decision. A "few" could be as many as four or five, if there are only two alternatives under consideration, and is probably no more than two – and in the extreme, could be only one – if there are any more than two alternatives in the choice set.

Initially, every attribute is valued as simply good or bad. Decision makers are presumed to add up the good and bad features associated with each alternative from among the few attributes considered, subtract the number of bad from the number of good, and choose the alternative with the highest net positive score. If this initial, first-cut procedure does not result in a single alternative being selected, the decision maker must go back and make more fine-grained discriminations between the attributes associated with each alternative (i.e., give them values other than $+1$ or -1), and in all likelihood compensates for the greater cognitive effort by eliminating one or more attribute that was initially considered. This procedure continues until a single, most highly evaluated alternative results. This rule is agnostic about whether alternative-based or attribute-based

Take the Few Best Rule

Initial Search	Candidate A	Candidate B	Candidate C
Political Experience	+	+	−
Tax Policy	−	+	+
Policy on Abortion	+	−	+
$\Sigma + - \Sigma -$	1	1	1

No single best choice results, requiring more refined information processing (but on a smaller subset of available information) than initially assumed.

Refined Search	Candidate A	Candidate B	Candidate C
Political Experience	+.6	+.8	0
Tax Policy	−.1	+1.0	+.8
Σ	.5	1.8	.8
		Choose B	

Figure A.3. Example of Model 3 fast and frugal compensatory decision rule.

search is followed, as such decisions are probably in practice a function of the information environment (i.e., which type of search is easier to conduct).

As shown in Figure A.3, if Ralph were using this decision rule, with three alternatives, he would probably consider each candidate's political experience, tax policy, and stand on abortion – the three attributes he cares the most about. To make this example more interesting, let us also assume that experience in the state legislature is not considered sufficient experience to be governor, so this attribute for Candidate C is considered negative. If this were the case, Ralph's initial consideration of the candidates would result in a three-way tie, as each candidate would have a net positive score of +1. Ralph would then have to expend the additional cognitive effort to reconsider the attributes he has already examined about the three candidates and produce finer evaluations of each attribute. Assuming he compensates for the greater effort required in forming these evaluations by dropping the last attribute from consideration, a clear preference for Candidate B results.

Notice that if our decision maker were somewhat less interested in politics, or had fewer cognitive resources to spare, and only considered the first two attributes, a clear decision would result from the initial, fast and frugal examination of the alternatives: vote for Candidate B, with two positives. A decision maker with greater cognitive resources or more interest in politics might retain all three attributes in the second stage of decision making, in which case a choice for Candidate C would result.

Appendix A

We would like to add one subtle additional consideration to our Few Best strategy. As described earlier, this procedure, like all compensatory strategies, assumes that all attributes under consideration are *commensurable* – that is, their values can be compared on some utility scale. But what if this is not the case? What if the attributes under consideration are inherently incommensurable? In that case, this decision strategy reduces to *Take the Best* (One) because the decision maker has no choice but to consider only a single attribute and make a decision based on it (Gigerenzer and Todd, 1999).

NONCOMPENSATORY STRATEGIES

Compensatory strategies all assume that voters can compare apples to oranges by converting both to "utility." But a good argument can be made that such a process is very difficult to carry out. Just how does one convert real things – like feelings about abortion – to some generic comparative rubric, so that abortion can be compared, say, to preferences on Middle East policy? Cognitively such a task is extremely difficult, if not impossible. The answer for many decision makers may be to apply one of the *noncompensatory* rules, which by their very nature do not require difficult tradeoffs to be made. As such, noncompensatory strategies are all examples of Model 4 decision making. We consider two well-known approaches: a satisficing rule and an elimination-by-aspects rule.

Model 4: "Intuitive" Semiautomated Heuristic-Based Decision Making

Satisficing. Satisficing is one of the first and most famous decision rules identified in the behavioral decision theory literature (Simon, 1957). Satisficing assumes that decision makers set target or aspiration levels for every attribute they care about and then consider alternatives one at a time in random order. Information search continues until an alternative that meets or exceeds the target level for every criterion is discovered. Once such an alternative is found, search stops, and this alternative is chosen. If no such alternative is found, target levels must be lowered, and the process is repeated until an alternative that satisfies all criteria is found.

Satisficing involves relatively simple cognitive processes. Conflict and incommensurability are avoided by seeking an alternative that is satisfactory on every criterion of judgment and by not comparing the alternatives to each other. Indeed, some alternatives may be totally ignored, and there is no guarantee that anything approaching the "best" alternative will be selected. Obviously the order in which alternatives are considered

Decision Strategies in Action

<u>Satisficing</u>

Example: Consider only attributes 1, 5, and 8, the three most important to voter.

	Candidate A	Candidate B	Candidate C
	[+.6, +.8, −.1]	[+.8, −.6, +1.0]	[0, +1, +.8]
Target $U_{ij} > 0$	Reject	Reject	Reject
Lower Target: $U_{ij} \geq 0$	Reject	Reject	**Accept C**

<u>Elimination-by-Aspects</u>

Example: Eliminate any candidate with $U_{ij} < $ o.

Consider Most Important Attribute (1):	[+.6] Retain	[+.8] Retain	[0] Retain
Consider 2nd Most Important Attribute (5):	[+.8] Retain	[−.6] Eliminate	[+1] Retain
Consider 3rd Most Important Attribute (8):	[−.1] Eliminate		[+1] Choose C

Note, if the decision is to eliminate any $U_{ij} \leq $ o, Candidate C would be eliminated on the first attribute, and Candidate B would be eliminated on the second, leaving Candidate A as the choice.

Figure A.4. Examples of Model 4 intuitive *non*compensatory decision rules.

can completely determine which is selected, if more than one alternative would meet the target level for the attributes deemed important enough to consider.

If our hypothetical voter Ralph were satisficing, he would first determine which attributes were important to him, and what an acceptable position on each would be. This would normally be a subset of all the attributes available, such that satisficing typically includes a less than thorough information search even for the selected alternative. Suppose Ralph decided the only attributes he really cares about in a governor were that the candidate had some political experience, that the candidate was unlikely to raise taxes, and that the candidate was Pro-Choice on the abortion issue – the three attributes with the highest weights in Figure 2.3. Suppose his initial target level was that he simply like (i.e., have a positive utility for) the position of a candidate on these three attributes. Unfortunately for Ralph, each candidate would fail to satisfy one of these criteria, and he would be forced to lower his target level. Lowering it only slightly to aspire to not dislike a position (i.e., feeling neutral is okay) would now yield a satisfactory choice, Candidate C. These considerations – certainly far easier to compute than those involving addition and/or multiplication – are shown in the top half of Figure A.4.

Appendix A

To give another example of satisficing, suppose Ralph's sister (Ralphina) held the same values as Ralph (so her utilities would be the same as her brother's), but she only really cared that a governor had a good education and that the candidate was Pro-Choice. She would restrict search to attributes 2 and 5. Candidate B would prove to be unsatisfactory, but either Candidate A or Candidate C would be acceptable, and Ralphina would choose whichever candidate she happened to consider first. No attempt is made to trade off Candidate A's presumably better education against Candidate C's superior stand on the abortion issue. If Ralphina were satisficing, the choice between Candidate A and Candidate C would be completely determined by the order in which alternatives were considered.

Elimination-by-Aspects Rule. The *Elimination-by-Aspects Rule* (EBA) is another well-known noncompensatory decision strategy. It is similar to satisficing but focuses on an attribute-oriented search (Tversky, 1972). Decision makers are assumed to rank the attributes of judgment in terms of importance and then to consider the most important attribute first. Like satisficing, decision makers are assumed to have something like a target level of every attribute, and alternatives are eliminated if they do not meet or exceed this target. The procedure continues with additional attributes of judgment in decreasing order of importance until only one alternative remains. Like satisficing, EBA avoids conflicts by eliminating alternatives as soon as any conflict occurs.

If Ralph were utilizing EBA to make his vote decision, as detailed in the bottom half of Figure A.4, he would first set a target level and then consider all three candidates on the different attributes in their order of importance. Suppose Ralph, having learned from experience not to expect too much from politics, sets his target level at just wanting nonnegative utilities. He considers first the candidate's political experience and finds them all to have an acceptable political background. He then considers tax policy and eliminates Candidate A for fear that candidate might raise taxes. He then looks at Candidates B's and C's abortion stands, and finding C's position far preferable to B's, his decision process comes to an end and he selects Candidate C.

The Special Case of Model 2: Socialized Attitudes and Cognitive Consistency

Despite Model 2's prevalence in political science, the behavioral decision theory literature does not provide any prominent examples of individual decision strategies that fit clearly under this category.[5] When writers in the Michigan tradition come closest to describing a decision process (e.g., Converse and Markus, 1979; Kelley and Mirer, 1974; Miller and Shanks, 1996, chapter 8), it is clearly a compensatory one. It is presumably a comparison of the virtues and vices of the competing candidates which leads, ultimately, to the vote choice.

Just as surely, however, these processes are not identical to those of Model 1, nor are they entirely compensatory in their orientation. To a limited but very real extent, Model 2 voters use their information search not to decide how to vote, but to bolster or justify a standing decision provided by their long-term party identification. It will take a great deal of disconfirming information about one's own candidate before a partisan Model 2 voter would defect to the other side – much more than should be necessary given a "objective" reading of the evidence.

One of the methods available to Model 2 decision makers is to distort the perception of incoming information in a partisan manner; another method is to disproportionately seek out information the decision maker expects to bolster his or her standing decision; a third would be to increase the perceived importance of information that is consistent with one's predispositions and decrease the perceived importance of contradictory information. We believe many decision makers do all of these things. To the extent the decision comes first and the information search – the decision making strategy – follows from it, we can certainly understand why a literature focused on decision making would have little to say about such a strategy. Nonetheless we will try to detail such a strategy here.

Confirmatory Decision Making. We call this strategy *Confirmatory Decision Making* because its aim, at least in part, is ensuring that one's prior predispositions are confirmed. The first thing a decision maker following a confirmatory strategy has to learn is the party affiliation of the different candidates. Because the underlying motivational biases are coming from personal identifications, confirming that one's own candidate is "good" is probably more important than confirming that the opponent is "bad." Hence, we would expect disproportionate search directed toward in-party candidates. Fine-grained utility calculations are unnecessary as long as simpler positive or negative or neutral evaluations of particular attributes will work. Likewise importance weights are unnecessary (unless they are required to avoid dissonance and make the calculations come out right).

---

[5] Although one of the best-known labels for describing (bad) group-based decision processes, *groupthink* (Janis, 1972), is consistent with many aspects of this model.

Confirmatory Decision Rule

Initial Search	Candidate A	Candidate B	Candidate C
Party Affiliation	−	+	0
Policy on Abortion	+	−	+
Political Experience	+	+	−
$\sum + - \sum -$	1	1	0

The initial search yields no clear choice as the best alternative, and no confirmation of the voter's early-learned Republican partisan leaning. This should motivate additional information seeking, particularly about the in-party candidate.

Supplementary Search	Candidate A	Candidate B	Candidate C
Tax Policy		+	
$\sum + - \sum -$	1	2	0

Choose B

Figure A.5. Example of Model 2 confirmatory decision making.

We would expect decision makers following this strategy to seek out a little more information than may be the norm because the decision should be more important to them than it is to many other people, but there would be no requirement (even in theory) to engage in the comprehensive information search that a Model 1 decision maker would pursue in the ideal world. This would be particularly true if decision makers encountered some information that was inconsistent with their predispositions because they likely would be motivated to seek out additional, presumably consistent information about the alternatives.

If Ralph were utilizing the Confirmatory Decision Making strategy, he would first find the candidates' party affiliations and then try to learn some issue stands – say their stands on abortion – and something about their personal backgrounds or qualifications, such as their political experience. If Ralph were to consider only these three items, his initial evaluation of the candidates (as shown in Figure A.5) would result in a tie between the Republican and (egads!) the Democrat. Such a result would be inconsistent with Ralph's Republican Party identification, and he would certainly be motivated to learn more about his in-party candidate. Suppose Ralph then went out and learned the Republican's stand on tax policy. This is a solid Republican position, and Ralph is very pleased with it. At this point, search may well stop, and Ralph could be comfortable with his choice of Candidate B. (Why bother searching any more? Ralph knows all

Democrats want to tax and spend, and those Good Government party members are pretty crazy.)

SUMMARY

We have spent a good deal of ink detailing these various decision strategies – Weighted Additive, Additive Difference, Few-Best, satisficing, EBA, Confirmatory, and so on – because they are the key variables in our quest to understand how information processing affects evaluation and choice. We have focused our discussion on distinct decision strategies, but this should not be read to suggest that decision makers employ one and only one decision strategy, no matter what the task. There is little evidence for systematic individual differences in the use of the various strategies. People do not specialize; instead, all decision makers employ multiple decision strategies, sometimes even during the course of making a single decision (see Mintz et al., 1997). This is a complication for the latter half of the book. There we test the effects of using each of these different strategies, not only on the vote choice itself but also on the likelihood that voters choose the candidate who best represents their informed interests.

Appendix B. How the Dynamic Information Board Works

The dynamic information board is the most reasonable way to track information processing during a political campaign. The dynamic board allows the experimenter to establish any number of experimental conditions and randomly assign subjects to those conditions. The system used in these experiments can be employed to study both a primary and a general election campaign cycle. Further, the number of candidates can be varied, as can the amount of time available, along with other attributes of the campaign.[1]

Information was presented to the subject on a computer screen, and the subject used a mouse to make selections from whatever is currently available on the screen. The order in which information was presented varied randomly according to the relative likelihood of any particular piece of information becoming available at different points in the campaign. These probabilities were based on the data from the 1988 presidential election campaign summarized in Figure 3.1.

There are four distinct areas on the main screen. The central area (see Figure 3.2 for an example) contains the six information boxes, which continuously move down the screen, with the box at the bottom disappearing, and a new information box appearing at the top of the stack. This is the area that subjects click on in order to learn more details about issues, candidate personalities, polls, endorsements, candidate backgrounds, and any other information the experimenter makes available. Clicking on one of the boxes presents a new screen containing written information relating to the label in the box; for example, a detailed description of a candidate's position on welfare. Figure B.1 illustrates one such screen. When the subject finishes reading the information, another click of the mouse returns

---

[1] The dynamic information board was written in a computer language called *Toolbook* and run on Windows-based personal computers. For details on the technical aspects of the system design, see Redlawsk, 1992, 1995a.

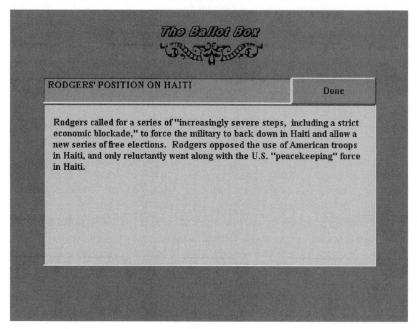

Figure B.1. Dynamic information board information card.

to the main screen, which is similar to Figure 3.2. The computer is continually recording the information boxes that are presented to the subject, the order and time in which they are presented, and which ones have been selected by the subject. As a subject makes a selection, the time is recorded when the selection is made, as is the time when the subject finishes reading the details and returns to the main screen – although inevitably one at least slightly different from the last one seen, as the scrolling has continued in the background while the specific information is considered (although this is hidden from subjects). Thus, the time spent examining each piece of information can be easily calculated.

At the top of the main screen is a box in which "newspaper headlines" appear and disappear from time to time. These headlines represent the type of information a voter might obtain by simply passing by a newsstand and scanning the newspaper headlines. Most of these headlines referred to the presidential campaign, but many did not (e.g., "BASEBALL STARTS TODAY: YANKS AT HOME, METS IN PITTSBURGH"). There is no additional information behind the headlines themselves, unlike the information boxes in the center of the screen. However, the experimenter can link specific headlines to specific pieces of information that will then appear on the screen in the information boxes after the headline disappears. Directly below the headlines and above the information boxes is a small area that informs the subject what the current "calendar month" is during the election cycle. For the primary election, the subject begins in February and ends in April, when the New Jersey primary election is held.[2] As the campaign continues, the month label changes appropriately. Information boxes are keyed to the month, so that the "Gallup Poll for early April" shows up when the month is April. This provides a significant amount of realism to the experiment.

Finally, the fourth area on the screen, to the left of the information boxes and the month, includes a timer and an indication of whether the subject is in the early, middle, or late part of the primary election. The timer counts down in real time the number of minutes remaining in the simulation. This was added in order to give subjects a sense of the pacing of the campaign and to help them realize when they must make a decision. While the time frame is dramatically shorter – twenty minutes in the present experiments – the effect is to remind subjects that they vote on a certain date, just as they do in a real primary election.

In addition to the main screen shown in Figure 3.2 and the detailed information screen that is reached by clicking on an information box, the system has several other screens. Most important is the campaign video screen (Figure B.2). At appropriate intervals during the campaign, the system can present recorded campaign commercials, with both video and audio. These are designed to take over the main screen so that when it is time for a campaign ad to air, the information boxes are completely covered over by the video, interrupting the scrolling and allowing a subject to do nothing else while the video is showing. Once the ad finishes running, the main screen reappears, and the subject can continue to examine additional text-based information until the next campaign commercial. If the subject was in the middle of reading some detailed information when an ad begins, they are returned to that screen. If they are at the main screen and hence between choices when an ad begins, they are returned there – but again, it will have almost completely new alternatives available, because the scrolling has continued while the ad was being played. Thus, the system is designed to mimic both of the major ways in which voters receive significant campaign information – through newspapers and through television.

---

[2] In the real world outside of the lab, the New Jersey primary is actually held in June and is one of the last primaries. The result is that New Jersey's presidential primary is usually meaningless, with the nomination having been determined earlier in the year. For the simulation, subjects were told that in 1996 the primary would be held earlier, as part of a "Super-Duper Tuesday" string of primaries that would undoubtedly determine the nominees of the two parties – a proposal that was actually considered by New Jersey politicians before the 1996 national election but not actually implemented.

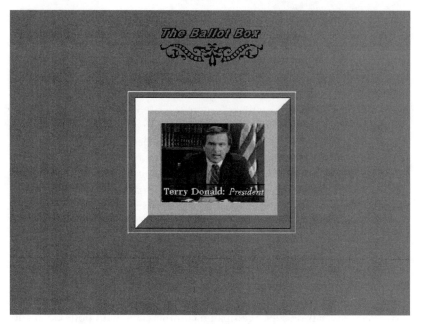

Figure B.2. Dynamic information board video screen.

The system contains a number of additional screens, including one on which subjects click on a thermometer scaled from 0 to 100 to record their global evaluation of each candidate. As the assessment is made, the computer records the rating and the amount of time required to make it. The voting screen presents the candidates from whom the subject may choose when the campaign is over. The subject simply clicks on a candidate name, and the vote is recorded, along with the amount of time required to make the choice. Finally, there are a number of introductory information screens that provide subjects with instructions and the election scenario. Figure B.3 illustrates one of these.

The dynamic information board resolves many of the problems associated with traditional information board approaches and allows us to go well beyond the data normally available through survey methods. It allows us to trace the decision-making process as it occurs, but it does so in an environment that more closely mimics that of a presidential election than does the classic static information board. Information comes and goes, its availability determined in accordance with real-world campaigns. In choosing to look at one piece of information, voters have to forgo learning something else. Time is limited, and information can be overwhelming. Subjects have to do the very tasks they must perform in real campaigns: learn about candidates, compare them to each other,

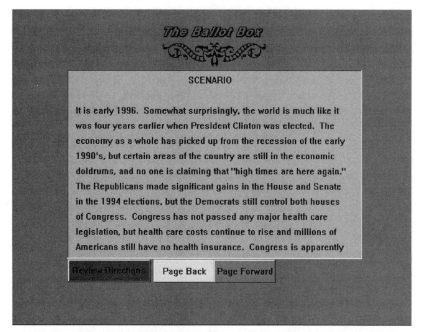

Figure B.3. Dynamic information board scenario page.

determine what issues and other information are most important, and ultimately make a choice. This new approach to process tracing, where information flow is important, allows us to collect a comprehensive set of data designed specifically to better understand what voters actually do when they encounter campaign information.

THE SPECIAL PROBLEM OF PARTY, POLLS, AND ENDORSEMENTS

Two points deserve special attention, for they are additional ways we have adapted standard information boards to better fit an election context. Primary elections in most states (and in our experiment) involve two simultaneous and semiindependent election campaigns, one in each party. As long as the party's choice has not been determined, both campaigns get considerable political attention, and the candidates involved in those campaigns spend most of their time addressing each other. Thus, during primary elections, most of the available information is (a) grouped by party and (b) available to anyone who is interested.

We wanted to incorporate both of those features into our campaign, and we ultimately decided that the best way to do it was to color-code the information from the different parties. So, during the primary campaign, all the labels scrolling down the screen were either red or blue, with all the information pertinent to the candidates in the Democratic primary in one of those colors, and all the information pertinent to the Republicans in the other. The computer randomly assigned colors to parties at the beginning of the primary campaign, and voters had to learn, by accessing the party affiliation of any candidate, which was which. Logically, because there are only two parities, and two colors in our campaign simulation, once subjects have learned the party affiliation of one candidate, they have learned it for all candidates.[3] This same color-coding was maintained for the general election, although by then the problem of separate campaigns (and therefore separate decisions) disappears. But during the primary election, voters were free to look at any information about any candidate from either party, although only information about candidates from their own party was relevant to the first decision they had to make.

The second somewhat unusual point about much information available during an election campaign is that, rather than being tied to any particular alternative, it inherently provides information about multiple candidates simultaneously. Poll results, a pervasive part of all presidential campaigns, always list the current support for all (viable) candidates. The absolute level of support does not usually matter in our winner-take-all elections, just the support of one candidate relative to all the others in the election. It is impossible to learn that one candidate is ahead in the polls without simultaneously learning that other candidates are behind.

Similarly, group endorsements are inherently comparative, and thus provide information about all candidates in an election. Learning that the AFL-CIO endorses Candidate A simultaneously tells you that the group chose not to endorse Candidates B, C, and D. Thus, even though our description of information boards has led the reader to believe that all information comes from one particular cell of an underlying attributes-by-alternatives matrix – and, indeed, that is the case in every information board study we have seen – these two types of information essentially represent receiving an entire row of that matrix simultaneously.

Thus, polls and endorsements provide two types of problems for us: the first practical, the second analytic. We discuss the analytic problems in Chapter 5, where we present most of our basic measures of information search. Here we address the practical problem of how to flag this special type of information for voters. The problem is multiplied during the primary season, where the multiple-candidate comparisons are limited to the candidates within each party. Our practical solution was to write the labels for these two types of information in all capital letters, so that they would stand out from the candidate-specific information, where at

---

[3] In practice, however, very few subjects accessed party affiliation only once.

most the first letter of a word (or candidate's name) would be capitalized. During the primary, the labels for endorsements and poll results for the different parties were in the same blue or red color as all of the candidate-specific information from that party. During the general election, when the specific information about one of the relevant candidates had red labels and the other blue labels, the labels for this multiple-candidate information were in a third color (a purplish mixture of red and blue).

Appendix C. Overview of Experimental Procedures

In this appendix we provide many of the nuts and bolts details of different experiments that we have conducted using our new dynamic process-tracing methodology and the presidential campaign simulation created to go with it. We begin with a description of the subjects who participated in the experiments and the methods by which they were recruited. We then discuss the general procedures that were followed in actually running the experiments. We conclude with a little more detail on the eight mock candidates who "ran" in our mock campaigns.

SUBJECTS

As mentioned briefly in Chapter 3, our requirements for participation in our experiments were only two: (1) Subjects had to be eligible to register and vote in U.S. elections (i.e., they had to be U.S. citizens at least 18 years of age), and (2) subjects could not be currently enrolled in a college or university. In practice, the studies also required subjects to be literate, as much of the experimental material was presented in written form. Our subject recruitment procedure differed between the first three experiments, when we had funding to pay subjects, and the last, when we did not. For the first three experiments, we could pay each subject $20 for participating – which, as will be detailed later, lasted about two hours – and some subjects were obtained by advertisements in local newspapers or community bulletin boards. As we suspected, however, it turns out that $20 is not a very strong incentive for most people for two hours of their free time; moreover, we feared that people who would volunteer to participate in a study of political decision making would be inordinately interested in politics – a bias we wanted to avoid.

In a wonderful example of framing effects, however, it turns out that relatively few people will work an extra two hours to put $20 in their own wallets, but they will gladly work that same amount of time to put the

$20 in the coffers of some voluntary organization to which they belong.[1] Thus we recruited most of our subjects by approaching voluntary associations in central New Jersey – churches, PTAs, and the full gamut of local community organizations – briefly describing the study, and telling them, in essence, that we would give them $20 for every member of their organization who would participate in our study. Such organizations are always fund-raising, and most were happy to approach some of their members with this idea.

The last study was run as a group project in several research methods classes at Rutgers University. The instructor (one of the authors) first ran each of the students in the class through the experiment, provided additional instruction on being an experimenter, and then gave the students (as a major class assignment) the task of recruiting and then running three or four non-college-student adult U.S. citizens through the experiment. The subjects in the last experiment participated mostly as a favor to the students in our classes, although they were each entered into a lottery (conducted on the last day of class) to win $100. Data resulting from those sessions where the Rutgers students themselves were subjects are not included in the data analyzed here.

Table C.1 describes the 664 subjects who participated in the four experiments we conducted for this project. A little more than half our subjects were female, most were white, married, currently employed, with a median family income of about $45,000 and a median age of 45.5. A little less than half had a college degree. Over a third of the subjects were Catholic, a quarter Protestant, and 17% were Jewish. Thirty-eight percent of our subjects identified themselves as Democrats, 27% were Republican, with the remainder, 35%, independent.[2] We make no claims that our subjects are representative of any larger population, although their background characteristics are broadly similar to the area of central New Jersey from which they were recruited. The important point is that most of these people had the opportunity for a lot more political involvement than is possible for your typical college sophomore.

---

[1] "Rationally," those people who wanted to help their organizations more then they already were should presumably have saved their time and simply donated another $20 to the organization, but we did not make this suggestion, nor, evidently, did many people come up with this idea themselves.

[2] We used the standard ANES branching question to gather party identification. Of these independents, 14% leaned toward the Democratic Party, 8% leaned toward the Republican Party, and 13% claimed to be pure independents with no leanings toward either party. We provide these details because we required all subjects in our experiments to register as Democrats or Republicans before the primary campaign began, so that they, and we, knew in which party's primary they would be voting.

Table C.1. *Characteristics of Experimental Subjects*

Gender		Race		Age	
Female	54%	African American	7%	Range	18–84
Male	46%	Asian American	3%	Mean	45.4
		Hispanic	3%	Median	45.5
		White	84%	Std. Dev.	19.0
		Other	2%		

Education		Family Income		Marital Status	
< High school	6%	Less than $15,000	11%	Married	55%
High school grad	17%	$15,000–$24,999	12%	Single, never married	30%
Some college	31%	$25,000–$34,999	15%	Separated	2%
College grad	26%	$35,000–$49,999	17%	Divorced	7%
Advanced degree	21%	$50,000–$74,999	19%	Widowed	6%
		Over $75,000	26%		

Employment		Religion		Church Attendance	
Working now	59%	Catholic	35%	Never	28%
Unemployed	3%	Jewish	17%	Few times a year	24%
Laid off	1%	Protestant	25%	Once/twice a month	10%
Retired/disabled	25%	Other	11%	Almost every week	10%
Homemaker	13%	None/no preference	13%	Every week	28%

Party Identification		Political Ideology	
Democrat	38%	Very liberal	4%
Independent	35%	Somewhat liberal	34%
Republican	27%	Moderate	28%
		Somewhat conservative	30%
		Very conservative	3%

We should make one more point while describing the subjects who participated in our experiments. The figures in Table C.1 summarize across the four different experiments, but it is also important that sufficient subject variation exist within each of the four experiments. Fortunately, this was the case. We might expect the largest differences between subjects in the first three experiments compared to the last, given the less formal recruitment procedure used in that last experiment, and this was indeed the case. The one noticeable difference across studies was age and variables related to it (being retired, widowed, etc.). For example, the mean age was 48 for the first three experiments, 39 for the last, with a slightly lower standard deviation as well (17 vs. 18). But again, the main point is a reasonable amount of variance in subject characteristics – and this we have, in all four experiments.

Appendix C

EXPERIMENTAL PROCEDURE

About half of our subjects were run in our laboratory at Rutgers University. The remaining subjects were run in reasonably quiet and private settings provided by the organizations whose members were volunteering their time. In this case, we lugged our own computer and monitor to the organization's headquarters. This latter procedure was generally more convenient for the subjects than coming to Rutgers. In virtually every case, subjects were run individually through the experiment, with an experimenter carefully explaining the study, making sure subjects understood how the computer, and the program, worked, and then staying nearby in case the subject had any questions.

Informed Consent. After introducing her- or himself, the experimenter gave a brief overview of the study, explaining that we were interested in how people make vote decisions (assuring subjects that we did not expect subjects to know much about politics), that eventually they would experience and vote in a mock presidential election campaign, that all their responses would be treated confidentially, and that the entire procedure would last about two hours.

Initial Political Attitudes Questionnaire. The first task for subjects was to complete a political attitudes questionnaire, most of which was done on the computer. The political attitudes questionnaire asked a fairly standard set of questions designed to measure subjects' political preferences, including their party identification, their general liberal or conservative ideology, their policy preferences in a wide variety of different domains (all crucial for determining candidate support), their liking for different groups involved in politics (important for determining how voters should react to learning about an endorsement from one of these groups), and their general level of political sophistication. This was also where we obtained the background information about our subjects, listed in Table C.1. All these questions were modeled after, and in most cases taken directly from, recent ANES surveys, except that our subjects read these questions themselves and responded directly on the computer.[3]

---

[3] The advantages of having subjects respond to this political attitudes questionnaire directly on the computer (rather than having the subject or an interviewer write the responses on a printed questionnaire) were fourfold. First, it is obviously very cost-efficient, as we ultimately need this data in the computer for analysis, and we do not have to take the time and expense to have a research assistant (or worse, ourselves) put this data into the computer. Less obviously, this also eliminates a level of data errors, where mistakes in data entry can add random noise to the data. Second, we can unobtrusively measure how long it takes subjects to answer each question, another

Instructions and Practice. Next, subjects were introduced to the dynamic information board and given practice learning how to use it. They were told that the scrolling represents the ongoing flow of information during a presidential election campaign, and that the experiment would expose them to a considerably compressed election campaign with both a primary and a general election. The practice session presented information about George H. Bush and Michael Dukakis from the 1988 U.S. presidential election in our dynamic scrolling format. The purpose of the practice session was (1) to give subjects experience using the mouse to access desired information – a skill that does not take too much practice to develop, but nonetheless a skill that many of our subjects, too old to have been raised on video games, did not yet have – and (2) to familiarize people with the type of information that was available so that people would know what to expect if they chose to look at a candidate's issue stand, family history, a group endorsement, and the like. The experimenter warned the subject not to get frustrated by the scrolling, which made it impossible to look at everything a voter might want to look at. The practice session lasted about seven minutes.

Then subjects read a set of instructions that repeated much of the information the experimenter had told them during the practice session. Figure C.1 presents a slightly condensed version of the instructions subjects read on the computer for our first experiment, run in the fall of 1994. Essentially the same instructions were used for subsequent experiments, although for experiments run after the actual 1996 presidential election, the instructions asked subjects to imagine they were voting in the 2000 presidential campaign.

Campaign Scenario. Before the campaigns began, subjects read a brief scenario "setting up" the mock 1996 (or later 2000) presidential election campaign. According to our scenario, President Clinton, deciding he had achieved everything he had set out to accomplish except health care reform, had stunned the political world by announcing that he would retire from politics to "do some fishing, play the saxophone, and get to

---

measure of how important different beliefs are to voters. Bassili (1995), for example, has shown that response latencies measured on telephone surveys are good measures of the certainty with which respondents hold different expressed attitudes. Third, information from subjects that we might want to use to design specific experimental stimuli or manipulations, is immediately available in a form the computer can utilize. And fourth, answering questions on the computer gave subjects a chance to practice using the computer before the mock campaigns began, practice that was important to many subjects at a time when personal computers were not nearly as pervasive at home or in the workplace as they are now.

Your task is to "experience" (in a very short period of time) the 1996 presidential election campaign, with a few changes. We have substituted a new set of candidates for those who are likely to run [who ran] in 1996. None of these candidates are ones you have heard of before. (You may or may not be upset to learn that Bill Clinton is not running for reelection in our mock campaign.) In fact, the candidates in this election don't actually exist; they have all been "made up" for the purposes of this experiment. However, they have been created to be as realistic as possible – to be the type of candidates who typically run for president in the United States.

As usual, the year begins with the primary season and the selection of each party's flag-bearer. The first primary in 1996 is New Hampshire's, on February 20th, although the Iowa "caucuses" are scheduled 10 days earlier. "Super Tuesday," when about a quarter of the delegates needed to win the nomination are selected, occurs on March 14. In our mock election, New Jersey, California, New York, Ohio, and Texas have all coordinated their primaries to occur on Tuesday, April 24. As these states combined have slightly more delegates than those selected on Super Tuesday, we have coined the term "Super Duper Tuesday" for April 24th. These states hope that the party's nominees will not be selected before then (and it is a good bet they will not), so that voters in these states will have the final say on which candidates get the nominations.

Information about the Democratic candidates will be in one color on the screen and information about the Republicans will be in another, but you will have to find out which party's candidates are in which color. This year there are six candidates from the two parties running for president. Most of the information will be specific to one of these candidates (e.g., Joe Politician's Stand on the Economy), but some of the information will apply to more than one of the candidates in a party (e.g., Gallup Poll as the Primaries Heat Up). Information of this latter type will be in the same color that the party it is about appears. For example, the Gallup Poll for the Republicans will be in the same color as the other information for Republicans. As in any campaign, there will be far more information available than you can possibly comprehend in so short a time, and you will have to be selective in what you pay attention to. Of course the longer you look at any given bit of information, the less time there is remaining to learn anything else.

At the end of the primary you will be asked to vote for one of the candidates in one of the party's primary. You can certainly look at any information about any of the candidate's during the campaign, irrespective of party, but you can only vote in one of the primaries. And you will have to choose ahead of time (i.e., "register" before the primary begins) which primary to vote in.

After the primaries are over, the general election campaign will begin. One of the Democratic candidates will run against one of the Republicans. (You will have to wait to see which candidates win their party's nomination.) After the general election campaign is over, you will be asked to "vote" for one of the two candidates. Of course, you can vote for either candidate, regardless of who you voted for in the primary.

In general, the same type of information is available about every candidate. However, the candidates can adopt different campaign strategies, which could result in different probabilities of your ever learning certain information about different candidates. Please note that the information associated with any label (e.g., Joe Politician's Stand on the Economy) will never change during the course of the campaign. That is, you will probably have more than one opportunity to "access" or learn certain information – and you should feel free to do so – but the hidden information associated with a label will always be the same.

Figure c.1. Instructions to subjects.

know my family again." [This line was not needed for experiments conducted after the 1996 elections, when subjects were asked to imagine the 2000 election was upon us, and President Clinton could not run again.] Although Clinton had initially endorsed Al Gore as his successor, the vice president was tragically crippled when he broke his back trying to dance the bugaloo at a fund-raising affair in a Los Angeles disco, and he had to withdraw from public life. The president then announced that he would support whichever candidate his party nominated but would make no further endorsement during the primary. Thus the primary season began with no incumbent seeking reelection and no overwhelming favorite for either party's nomination.

The Election Campaigns. After all this initial data gathering, instruction, and practice (which typically took between forty-five and sixty minutes), the mock campaigns began. Subjects were first required to register as a Democrat or Republican, which would determine which party's primary they could vote in. This emulates a closed primary (the most common practice across the United States, and the one actually used in New Jersey, where our experiments were run), where only party members (as determined by registrations a month before the election) can vote in that party's primary election.

The primary campaign then started, which lasted about twenty minutes. Depending upon experiment and condition, there were a total of either four or six candidates running in the primaries, two or four in each party. At the end of the campaign, the scrolling stopped, and a message came on the computer screen announcing that it was Election Day. A screen then came up listing, in random order, all the candidates running in the primary of the party in which the voter had registered. After voting for one of these candidates, subjects were asked to rate, on a 101-point feeling thermometers, all the candidates running in both party's primaries, and also to rate how difficult the choice was and how certain they were that they had made the right decision.[4]

After answering these questions, subjects were given a two-minute break between the primary and general election campaigns.[5] The newspaper "headlines" continued to appear on the computer screen, however, which was how subjects learned (if they were watching the headlines),

---

[4] It would certainly be possible to give subjects the option of not voting on Election Day with our procedure, but none of our experiments offered this possibility.

[5] Except for subjects in Study 2, which did not include a general election campaign. These subjects moved immediately to the postcampaign data-gathering phase of the study.

which candidate had won their party's primary and would be running in the fall campaign.[6] We also had a thirty-second clip of such typical party convention hoopla as delegates with signs, party leaders making endless speeches, and balloons and confetti falling from the ceiling.

The general election campaign followed, always with only two candidates, one Democrat and one Republican. This campaign, with fewer and now more familiar candidates, lasted only twelve minutes, after which subjects voted for one of the two remaining candidates, evaluated both of them on feeling thermometers, and again answered the two questions about how difficult the choice was and how certain they were that they had made the right choice.

Postcampaign Data Gathering. Although information gathering and the vote choice during the two election campaigns were the focal point of the study, several vital bits of information still remained to be gathered. First, subjects were told that we were interested in the sort of things people remember from political campaigns. They were given two sheets of paper, one for each candidate running in the general election, and asked to write down everything they could remember about these two candidates. The two candidates were presented in random order. It is important to note that this is the first time subjects had heard of trying to remember anything about the candidates in the campaigns. The memory task was a little different for subjects in Study 2, which only involved the primary election campaigns. In this study, subjects were asked to remember as much as they could about all six candidates in both parties' primaries.

At this point the procedure diverged between the first two and the last two experiments. In Studies 1 and 2 subjects went through an elaborate procedure designed to determine whether they had voted correctly – that is, voted for the candidate they would have chosen had they had more time and complete information. This is the focus of Chapter 4, and we describe this procedure in detail there. This proved to be a very time-consuming task, and because we were able to devise an alternative measure of correct voting from data gathered in other parts of our standard experimental procedure (again described more fully in Chapter 4), in our last two studies we replaced it with "answering a few more questions about the two general election candidates." Specifically, subjects were asked to attribute several issue stands to these two candidates (abortion policy, affirmative action, health care reform, size of defense budget),

---

[6] Subjects also learned during the break that Al Gore had been release from Bethesda Hospital with a steel rod in his back – to which one of our voters commented, "How could you tell?"

judge their general liberalism–conservatism, rate how "attractive" they were (the candidate's standard picture appeared on the screen along with this question), and how much they would like to have this person as a friend.

Debriefing. Finally the study was over, and debriefing began. The experimenter explained some of the manipulations in the study, particularly those conditions the subject had not actually experienced, to illustrate the type of things we were interested in learning. Subjects were explicitly asked how realistic they thought the candidates were in the elections (the mean rating was midway between "Realistic" and "Extremely Realistic"), and whether they had any remaining questions. We collected mailing addresses from subjects who desired a brief summary of the results after the experiment was completed, and paid those subjects who were working for themselves. Subjects were thanked profusely for their time (by now, approaching and often exceeding two hours) and effort, and sent on their way.

After the subject had left, the experimenter rated, on a 4-point scale, how seriously they believed the subject had taken the experiment. A handful of subjects (8, out of 664) were rated by our experimenter as not having taken the experiment seriously, and these people are eliminated from the analyses reported here.[7] Figure C.2 summarizes the entire typical experimental procedure.

THE COMPETING PRESIDENTIAL CANDIDATES

The eight mock candidates were all designed to be very realistic, in that they had the type of political experience typical of serious presidential candidates, they were at least 45-years-old, they were dispersed along the ideological spectrum appropriate for their party, and so on. We were careful, however, not to make any of the candidates appear too much like

---

[7] Whenever subjects are eliminated from analysis, it is important to assure readers that this exclusion did not in any way affect the results of the study. We hereby provide that assurance, at least for all of the hypothesis-driven results reported in this book (and elsewhere: Lau and Redlawsk, 1997, 2001a, 2001b; Redlawsk, 2001a, 2001b, 2002). Another (surprisingly small) handful of subjects had to be eliminated because of computer bugs. These bugs resulted in the complete loss of data, so we have no way of knowing whether or how the results would have changed had these bugs been caught ahead of time. We can only assume that they occurred randomly, and that nothing systematic in the subject's information processing caused the computer to crash.

1. Political Attitudes Questionnaire

- Questions to measure subjects' political preferences;
- Political interest, participation, knowledge, and media usage;
- Importance of different types of political information for 1992 vote choice;
- Background/demographic information (*30–40 minutes*)

2. Mock Election Campaign

a. Practice session accessing scrolling information about 1988 presidential election (*about 8 minutes*)
b. Explicit instructions and campaign scenario; random assignment to different experimental conditions (hidden from subjects) (*about 5 minutes*)
c. Primary election campaign involving six candidates (*about 22 minutes*)
d. Vote in party's primary election; evaluate all six candidates; manipulation check on difficulty of choice (*about 3 minutes*)*
e. Break for party conventions; general election candidates selected (*about 2 minutes*)
f. General election campaign involving two candidates (*about 12 minutes*)
g. Vote in general election; evaluate two remaining candidates; manipulation check on difficulty of choice (*about 3 minutes*)

3. Unexpected Memory Task

Subjects asked to remember as much as they can about two general election candidates (*about 10 minutes*)

4. Correct Voting Determination (Experiments 1 and 2 only)

Subjects presented with complete information about two candidates from primary (the one they voted for, and the candidate closest to the subject on the issues, of the remaining candidates in that same party) and asked to decide which they would have voted for if they had obtained all of this information when they actually had to make their choice during the primary election (*10–15 minutes*)

4. Attribution of Policy Stands to General Election Candidates (Experiments 3 and 4)

Subjects asked to place the two general election candidates on the standard liberalism-conservatism scale and four specific issue scales. Subjects also indicated how "attractive" each candidate was, and how much they would like that person as a friend (*2–4 minutes*).

5. Debriefing

Subjects' general impressions of experiment gathered; any remaining questions answered; etc. (*about 5 minutes*)

Figure C.2. Outline of experimental procedure.

---

* Study 2 subjects completed the unexpected memory task (step 3) at this point for candidates in their party's primary, and then a detailed guided protocol analysis where they explained why they had selected the items they chose to examine during the primary, before determining their correct vote choice (step 4).

some actual individual, so that attitudes toward that (real) person would not influence attitudes toward any candidate in the experiments.[8]

Figure 2.3 describes the eight candidates as they appeared in most of our studies. They are arranged ideologically from left to right.[9] The figure only highlights the total information available about each candidate. For example, the candidate's "Basic Social/Political Philosophy," reported in the second row of Figure 2.3, was an attribute that could actually be accessed during our campaigns. But each candidate also took stands on twelve specific social issues, five specific economic issues, and six specific foreign policy/defense issues, stands which were drawn from various articles in the *New York Times, Wall Street Journal,* or *Washington Post.* All these specific issue stands were potentially accessible about every candidate. We had a panel of six political experts (the two authors, three graduate students at Rutgers, and one local elected official) read each of these stands and rate them on a 7-point liberal–conservative dimension. The mean ratings of our panel of experts represent the "objective" or "true" candidate stands on these issues, but the table reports only the mean of those objective ratings across all issues for each candidate. There were also seven individual items available about each candidate's background, much of which is summarized in the first row of the table, and six brief personality descriptions, two of which are reported in the fourth row of Figure 2.3. Finally, there were six items about the candidate's political experience, job performance, and campaign strategy. We are particularly proud of the inspiring (and totally vacuous) campaign slogans we wrote for our candidates, which are reported in the last row of Figure 2.3.

We included multiple items about the candidates' personal history, family, personality, and so on to flesh out our candidates as people. Both the *New York Times* and the *Washington Post* regularly run very long background articles about all the major presidential candidates, and we drew on these articles in devising our material. Of course the major way candidates present their images to the public is through pictures in ads and billboards, and better yet (from the candidate's perspective) through coverage by television news of live campaign events. The latter were too difficult to simulate realistically for our mock candidates, but the candidates'

---

[8] Today, most politically interested people know who the governor of Texas was during the late 1990s, and who the governor of Florida is now. Two of our mock candidates supposedly held those positions. But at the time our experiments were run, the actual holders of these two offices were pretty obscure and largely unknown politicians from distant states.

[9] In experiment 3, we manipulated the issue stands and personality descriptions of the candidates on the fly according to the political attitudes of the subject, so the candidates in that one experiment were some combination of the ones described here.

pictures were readily available during our campaigns, both as a candidate-specific item that could be selected in the same manner as an issue stand or personality stand, and as "free" (i.e., unchosen) information associated with every campaign commercial, all of which ended with five seconds of the candidate's name (e.g., Pat Thomas for President) and picture.

Pictures, of course, almost immediately provide what are probably the three most useful and pervasive bits of social information about another person: their gender, race, and age. In these experiments, all our candidates were white, and they varied in age only from the late 40s to the mid 60s. But we did have both genders represented among our candidates; in fact, we purposely chose their names to be ambiguously gendered so that voters would not know a candidate's gender until they saw a picture. The standard pictures employed in our studies are shown in Figure 2.4.

We suspected that these images of the candidates could have strong influences on the impressions voters formed of the candidates, particularly since they would stand out against the written format in which most of the other information about the candidates was presented. Although we chose these pictures to all be equally attractive and plausible images one might see of political candidates, still we did not want them to influence decision making inordinately. Hence, we paired one Democrat with one Republican – D1 with R4, D2 with R3, D3 with R2, D4 with R1 – and randomly varied which of the two pictures was associated with which candidate. When two males are involved, this random variation of pictures is simply a control for any inadvertent influence these images might have on decision making and is not considered in the analysis. When one of the pictures is a male and the other a female, however, we have a manipulation of candidate gender – one that we can only examine superficially here, but which we anticipate will be the focus of future analyses. We also made sure that if one of the female pictures was assigned to a Democratic candidate, the other female picture was assigned to the Republican. Thus, there could never be two females running in either party's primary, although it did happen, on occasion, that both of the general election candidates were female.

A methodological point to note in passing is that creating mock candidates provides crucial control over inevitable differences between subjects in prior knowledge of actual politicians. No one had any prior knowledge of any candidate before the mock campaign began. Thus, any advantages accruing from greater political sophistication will be expressed in terms of superior information search or decision-making processes rather than greater factual knowledge per se (although the ability to make more accurate schema-based inferences could also come into play).

Appendix D. Detailed Decision Scripts

Our classification scheme for determining which decision strategy a voter is using may seem fairly abstract to many readers. Figures D.1 through D.4 provide another way to illustrate different decision strategies, by listing very concretely each item a voter chose to examine. This information is easy to extract from the "scripts" that are produced by our computer program – complete listings of everything on the computer screen and every action a voter takes. These particular voters were all from the static information board ideal-world condition of Experiment 4, which makes it much, much easier to see coherent patterns in the search strategies voters adopt. This is important to keep in mind as we look at these scripts.[1]

We struggled with different ways of presenting this information, and the matrix method we finally came up with does the job fairly well, although it needs some explication. Consider the voter whose decision making is illustrated in Figure D.1. This person registered as a Republican and was randomly assigned to the two-candidate condition in the primary. The first thing this voter does is check Singer's party affiliation, indicated by the number "1" in the Party row under the Singer column. Recall that the information (i.e., the boxes that had to be clicked to access the information) was in one color for all the Democrats and in another color for all of the Republicans. This entire row is shaded, because in learning Singer's

---

[1] One of the biggest differences between the dynamic scrolling condition under which most of our subjects were run, and the ideal world of a static information board, is that voters gather a lot more information from the dynamic, less controllable format. It was simply much easier for voters to find exactly what they wanted in the static format and to base their decisions on that information. We mention this here only to note that we have to take this big format difference into consideration when we determine what is a relatively deep search. The median level was much lower in the static information board format than in the dynamic scrolling format, which emulates an actual political campaign much better.

Attribute	Primary Election Campaign					
	Rodgers	Thomas	Singer	Fischer	Martin	Donald
Party			1			
Candidate's Plans for the Economy	2	3				
Candidate's Campaign Slogan	5	4				
Work Experience Prior to Politics	6, 7	8				
Anecdote from Cand's Childhood		9				
Candidate's Advertisement	22 (28a)	20, 21 (34a)	(19a)	(9a)	(24a)	(14a)
Stand on Size of Defense Budget	11	10				
Candidate's Health Policy	12	13				
Candidate's Stand on Welfare Reform	15	14				
Candidate's Policy for the Homeless	16	17				
Evaluations of Job Performance	18	19, 25, 33				
Candidate's Stand on Abortion	23	24				
Campaign Strategy for Primaries	27	26, 28				
Stand on (former) Soviet Union	30	29				
A Political Opponent Describes Cand	31	32				
Position on Education/College Aid	34	35				
Candidate's Position on Gun Control	36	37				
Vote Choice		X				
Feeling Thermometer Eval.	30	75	30	50	50	45

Figure D.1. Model 1d: deep intra-attribute search, ideal world.

party the voter simultaneously learned all the other candidates' party affiliations. This voter immediately focuses on the in-party candidates. She learns the two Republicans' plans for the economy, their campaign slogans, and their work experience prior to politics. This voter actually accessed Rodgers' work experience prior to politics twice in a row (the sixth and seventh items accessed), which may have been an accident. The voter then learns an anecdote from Thomas's childhood, and probably decided this information was too stupid to use in choosing a candidate, so she doesn't look at it for any other candidate. At this point, the advertisement from Fischer, unsolicited by the voter, took over the screen for a short time, indicated by the "9a" in parentheses.

Next the voter examined the two Republicans' stands on the size of the defense budget, considered their positions on health policy, welfare reform (interrupted by an ad from Donald), and the candidates' policies toward the homeless; read evaluations of how well they were performing their current jobs (saw an ad from Singer), chose to look at the ad from Thomas, twice (as indicated by the numbers "20" and "21" not in parentheses in the Candidate's Advertisement row under the Thomas column) and then chose to look at Rodgers's ad. After seeing an unsolicited ad from Rodgers (which the voter had already seen, voluntarily), she examined the candidates' stands on abortion (interrupted by the ad from Martin), checked out Thomas's job performance evaluation again, read Thomas's campaign strategy, then Rodgers's, then reviewed Thomas's again. Next the voter examined the two Republicans' policies toward Russia, read brief personality descriptions of the two candidates from political opponents, returned for a third time to examine the evaluation of Thomas's performance in his current job, learned the two candidates' positions on education (interrupted by the last unsolicited ad, this time from Thomas), and finally viewed the two Republicans' positions on gun control. This subject voted for Thomas on Election Day, evidently liking him much more than Rodgers, judging by the evaluations provided after the vote choice. Notice also that this voter was able to evaluate the four Democrats as well, presumable based solely upon their advertisements, all of which had been seen unsolicited.

This voter provides a wonderful illustration of a very rational Model 1d decision process. The first item the voter examined was party, to sort out the Democrats from the Republicans. Attention is focused exclusively thereafter on the two in-party candidates, and search proceeds methodically on a dimensional (intra-attribute) basis. This is a relatively deep search,[2] with very comparable information learned about the two candidates. This is a perfect example of a compensatory decision making strategy such as the Additive Difference Rule described in Chapter 2, and it evidently adds up to a big edge for Thomas over Rodgers, in this voter's mind.

Our second voter is a Democrat who, much like our first voter, engaged in something pretty close to Model 1 rational decision procedure during the primary. (See Figure D.2.) She was assigned to the two-candidate condition, accessed one of the candidate's party affiliation pretty early on to find the Democratic candidates and focused most of her primary information search on them, eventually voting for Gerry Singer. She evidently

---

[2] One of the major differences between the static and dynamic information boards was the total amount of information voters felt they needed to gather about the candidates, with much greater total search in the uncontrollable dynamic situation. So "deep" must be understood (and operationalized) in terms of the ideal world of the static information board.

Attribute	General Election Campaign	
	Martin	Thomas
Candidate's Advertisement	1, 2, (2a), 3, (17a) (23a)	(4a) (9a) (13a)
B'NAI B'RITH ENDORSEMENT	4	
Candidate's Campaign Slogan	6	5
Candidate's Policy for the Homeless	7	8
Candidate's Stand on Taxes/Tax Reform	10	9
Candidate's Stand on Israel, Middle East	11	12
Candidate's Campaign Strategy	14	13
Candidate's Stand on Abortion	15	16
Candidate's Party Affiliation	17	
Candidate's Views on Crime	18	
Candidate's Stand on Term Limits	19	
Candidate's Views on the Environment	20, 22	21
Candidate's Trade Policy	23	
Vote Choice	X	
Feeling Thermometer Eval.	80	40

Figure D.2. Model 2: moderately deep intra-candidate search, ideal world.

liked both Democrats, however, as she rated Singer at 90 and her second choice, Gale Martin, at 70. But let us consider what she does during the *general* election campaign.

The general election involved her second choice in-party candidate, Gale Martin, and Pat Thomas from the Republicans. This voter does not simply have to ratify her earlier decision from the primary, then. Moreover, Martin and Thomas are the moderate candidates from their respective parties, and there is little objective policy difference between them. Our voter first watches the Democrat's three different ads (and as luck will have it, sees one of them again during a randomly scheduled time). She then looks at the endorsement of the B'nai B'rith – which is relevant to both candidates – and then starts a series of intra-attribute comparisons, considering each candidate's campaign slogan, their policies toward the homeless, their stands on tax reform, their positions on Israel and the

Attribute	Primary Election Campaign					
	Donald	Fischer	Martin	Singer	Thomas	Rodgers
Party			1			8
Candidate's Position on Gulf War					2	3
Candidate's Advertisement	(2a)	(8a)	(12b)	(12a)	7 (12c)	6 (6a)
NRA Endorsement					4	
Hoopla and Horserace					5	
Stand on Capital Punishment					10	9
Candidate's Campaign Slogan					12	11
Vote Choice						X
Feeling Thermometer Eval.	DK	DK	DK	DK	35	95

Figure D.3. Model 3: shallow intra-attribute search, ideal world.

Middle East, their general election campaign strategies, and their stands on abortion. She checks Thomas's party affiliation (to assure herself, we suppose, that he is a Republican), and then focuses the remainder of her search almost exclusively on her in-party candidate. On Election Day, she confidently votes for the Democrat, having learned enough about him to raise her initial evaluation to an 80, rating Thomas only at 40.

This second voter clearly illustrates the type of confirmatory decision making we expect of Model 2 voters. Search is reasonably deep and, at least to begin with, clearly compensatory. Because these two candidate are both moderates, they should be difficult to distinguish on policy grounds – if, of course, this voter perceived those issue stands as objectively as our panel of experts did. Two thirds of the way through the general election, the voter seems to decide the Democrat is worthy of her support, and from then on she only risks one additional consideration of the Republican's policy views. Confirming that your own candidate has a reasonable stand on an issue you care about, and presuming (but not checking) that the other candidate does not, is one way to differentiate between two alternatives which, objectively, do not differ very much.

Our third voter, like our first, was a Republican randomly assigned to the two-candidate condition in the primary. As shown in Figure D.3, this voter first examined Martin's party affiliation, and distinguished the Democrats from the Republicans. The voter then looked at the two Republicans' positions on the Gulf War, checked out the endorsement of the National Rifle Association, looked at one poll from the Republican primaries, chose to watch Rodgers's campaign ad (and then, in a stroke of bad luck, was immediately shown that same ad again, unsolicited). The voter then chose to watch Thomas's campaign ad, and (perhaps finding

Attribute	Primary Election Campaign					
	Thomas	Green	Walker	Rodgers	Singer	Martin
Candidate's Campaign Strategy	1					
Party	2		15			
Candidate's Age	3	8				
Position on Education/College Aid	4					
Stand on (former) Soviet Union	5					
Candidate's Stand on the Environment	6	7				
Candidate's Advertisement	(16a)	(19a)	(6a)	(20b)	(20a)	(11a)
Position on Jobs/Unemployment		9				
Candidate's Health Policy		10				
Candidate's Stand on Abortion		11				
Candidate's Stand on Welfare Reform					12	
Candidate's Family					13	
Candidate's Race/Ethnicity		14				
Hoopla and Horse Race			16, 19		17	
Candidate's Campaign Slogan						18
Evaluations of Job Performance				20		
Vote Choice	X					
Feeling Thermometer Eval.	65	45	40	50	35	45

Figure D.4. Model 4: relatively shallow intra-candidate search, ideal world.

Thomas too liberal for his liking) examined Rodgers's party affiliation to make sure he got the parties correct. Then the voter examined the two Republicans' stands on capital punishment, considered their campaign slogans, and then relaxed for the remainder of the primary, having reached a clear decision. The voter selected Rodgers and evaluated his chosen candidate much more highly than the only alternative.

This third voter is the epitome of efficient decision making. He immediately distinguished the Republicans from the Democrats, and totally ignored the four out-party candidates for the remainder of the primary. The voter compared the two in-party candidates on two policies (three, if we include the NRA endorsement), considered their campaign ads and slogans, and made a very fast and frugal decision. This, clearly, is a Model 3 fast and frugal decision maker.

Figure D.4 illustrates the decision processes of yet another Republican voter, this one randomly assigned to the four-candidate condition in the primary. The first item examined was Thomas's campaign slogan, after which Thomas's party affiliation was learned (and thereby, the party affiliations of all the other candidates). The voter examined four more bits of information about Thomas – his age, position on education, policy toward Russia, and stand on the environment. After viewing an unsolicited ad for Walker, the voter turned to another Republican, Green, considering this candidate's stand on the environment, his age, his position on unemployment, his health policy, and his stand on abortion. Another unsolicited ad, this one from the Democrat Martin, turned the voter's attention briefly to the out-party, and Gerry Singer's position on welfare and her family are examined. The voter learned one more bit of information about Green, considered Walker's party affiliation (presumably making sure she has the parties correct), then looked at one of the polls from the Republican primary. This box is shaded under all four Republican candidates, as information relevant to all of them was provided in the poll.

After viewing an unsolicited ad from Pat Thomas, the voter looked at a poll from the Democratic primary, examined Martin's campaign slogan, looked at another poll from the Republican primary, saw an unsolicited ad from Green, and finally looked at evaluations of Rodgers's job performance. There were still several minutes left in the campaign,[3] but the voter chose to access no additional information. Only two additional unsolicited ads were viewed before the campaign ended and the voter selected Thomas.

This voter followed a much less "rational" decision process than those illustrated in figures D.1 and D.2. The search was relatively shallow; it was quite unequal between the four in-party candidates, and it was much more alternative-based than attribute-based. Sounds like a satisficer to us, and hence Model 4c. Notice also that six items were learned about both Thomas and Green, but there was actually very little comparable information learned about the two of them.

---

[3] You cannot tell this from the figure, but we can from the very detailed scripts that are produced by our program, which includes the time when everything happens during the campaigns.

Appendix E. Calculating the On-line
Evaluation Counter

To test the on-line model, we must first specify an on-line evaluation counter that incorporates the information voters encountered as they proceeded through the election. Three key questions have to be asked. First, what information should actually be counted in determining the evaluation counter? Second, should we weight some information more heavily than other information, since voters presumably do not consider everything to be of the same import? And third, how do we integrate this wide range of disparate information into a single running-tally evaluation of each candidate?

To begin with, we consider what information goes into a counter and how that information is evaluated. We incorporate four specific types of information in our counters: issues, group endorsements, candidate personality, and party identification.[1] Candidate–voter agreement on issue stands was calculated using the directional model (Rabinowitz and MacDonald, 1989), with the mean rating of seven experts providing an objective rating of where the candidates actually stood on the

---

[1] Thus, most information learned about a candidate figured into the evaluation. We have no way of knowing how subjects evaluated some of the available information about the candidates, however, particularly information about their personal backgrounds. Although we have no reason to believe there are systematic biases, it is quite possible that some individual subjects preferred senators over governors, people from Florida over people from California, lawyers over former reporters, men over women, 45-year-olds rather than 65-year-olds, and so on. Thus, it is important to note that our knowledge of subject's preferences, while very good, is incomplete. One way in which we will account for this is to include a measure of familiarity with the candidates, which is simply the total amount of information accessed for each candidate. This measure cannot account for any affective biases based on the information we do not incorporate in the counter, but it will give us an overall sense of how well known the candidates were.

issues.[2] Whenever a voter learned a candidate's stand on an issue, and that voter had expressed an opinion on that issue in our initial questionnaire, agreement or disagreement (rescaled to range from −1 to +1) was added into the candidate's summary evaluation. Group endorsements learned by a subject were scored +1 if a subject liked the group doing the endorsing (i.e., rated that group above the mean of all groups evaluated, and above the midpoint of the scale) and −1 if the subject disliked the group. The favorableness of personality descriptions and the attractiveness of candidate pictures were based on ratings by sixty-seven independent pretest subjects, again rescaled such that +1 was the highest possible evaluation and −1 was the lowest possible evaluation. Here we are assuming that these personality descriptions are universally appealing (or unappealing) within our subject pool. Finally, voters' party identifications were incorporated into the evaluation counters. Strong identification with a party counted as +1 for a candidate affiliated with that party, −1 for candidates affiliated with the other party. Similarly "weak" party identifiers and independent "leaners" counted ±.67 and ±.33, respectively, depending on whether the candidate in question affiliated with the voter's preferred party or the other party.

The second question is whether these pieces of information should be weighted as they are integrated into the evaluation counter. On the one hand, Dawes (1979) has shown that "improper" linear models, where coefficients are only valenced as positive or negative, work nearly as well as weighted models. However, this claim is based on analyses of relatively simple decision environments with only a few attributes for each alternative. Elections, as we have argued many times, are potentially overwhelming information environments. To suggest that voters would not view some types of information as more compelling than others seems counterintuitive. For example, we find it hard to accept that most voters would equate an anecdote from a candidate's childhood with evaluation of how well that candidate has performed in office, or the candidate's stand on an issue the voter holds dear. Thus, even though improper linear models may work well in some decision environments, the broad complexity of an election campaign combined with the widely varying types of information available clearly suggests the use of some kind of weighting scheme.

One indicator that our impressions about weighting information are reasonable ones comes from data collected in one of our studies. In this particular study, we have a treasure trove of information about what

---

[2] Recalculating issues-agreement with Euclidian distances does not make any significant change in any of our analyses. The experts were the two authors, a local elected official, and four Rutgers political science graduate students.

voters said they did, through a procedure where we reviewed each piece of information examined by those voters and asked them exactly what they were thinking as they accessed it. At the beginning of this process, we asked our subjects to explain why they had made the vote choice they had and what process they had tried to use to whittle down the candidates. Roughly half of all subjects volunteered that particular attributes of the candidates were specifically important to them, and thus figured prominently both in the information search and in their decision. Given that they were not prompted to say anything about what was important to them, this supports our contention that we need to consider some scheme for differentially weighting the importance of different candidate attributes.

We have two possible weights we can use: political chronicities (Lau, 1986, 1989) captured at the beginning of our preelection questionnaire, and a set of importance weights generated by asking subjects which particular attributes were important to them in casting a real-world vote in the 1992 (or 1996) presidential election. We chose the latter because it is a more straightforward measure and was collected with specific reference to an election campaign, where the chronicity scores came from questions focused on a range of political figures.

Finally, an important question in building the evaluation counter is how each piece of information is to be integrated into the overall evaluation. There are two obvious approaches – averaging or additive – both of which can be viewed as consistent with the general on-line processing model. A key difference between the two is how affectively neutral information has an impact on the evaluation. As should be obvious, a neutral item will neither increase nor decrease an additive counter, but it will cause a change in an averaging counter in the direction of the neutral point. Thus, new neutral information will have a greater impact on an averaging counter, while new affectively valenced information will have a greater impact on the additive counter.

For instance, if a voter considers five pieces of information and (using $+1$ for positive, -1 for negative, and 0 for neutral) and has evaluated them at 1, 1, 0, -1, and 1, an averaging evaluation counter would calculate to 0.4, while an *additive* counter would calculate to 2.0. Suppose a sixth item with an affective value of 0 is encountered. If averaging, this neutral item would lower the counter to $.333$, while having no effect on an additive counter. In this case the most recent information counts more in the averaging approach than the additive. Yet if the next item encountered carries an affective value of 1, both counters would increase: the averaging counter to $.43$ and the additive counter to 3.0. The last item has a stronger effect on the additive counter, increasing it by 50%, while it increases the averaging counter by only 30%. So now the most recent item has greater impact on the additive counter! Obviously, different scenarios would show different results, but the point is that they are, in fact, different.

The original on-line processing work by Lodge assumed averaging (Lodge, Steenbergen, and Brau, 1995), while Kelley and Mirer (1974), for example, adopt an additive approach. Existing research in social psychology on this question is not conclusive. Impression formation studies have often shown primacy effects (Anderson, 1965; Belmore, 1987), and some studies have found recency effects (Lichtenstein and Srull, 1987) especially when impression formation is interrupted. Thus, it is certainly possible that new information carries more weight than it is given in an averaging evaluation counter, much as Popkin (1991) has suggested that new bad information may drive out old good information.

We are left with unclear theory on the question of adding or averaging. And we have another twist. All previous work of which we are aware has either examined the evaluation of only a single individual or has assumed that evaluators have the same amount and type of information for each person to be evaluated. Neither situation is generally true in our studies. Subjects face multiple candidates in all our elections, and given the dynamic nature of the campaign, it is virtually certain that they learn a different set of information about each candidate. Thus, we think the only way to determine whether to use an averaging or additive evaluation counter is to see which does a better job of predicting global evaluations, that is, to use an empirical test.

We carried out a simple analysis comparing additive and averaging counters, using the information our subjects examined for each candidate adjusted by the importance weights for each information type. For analytic simplicity, we look only at in-party candidates, the candidates sharing the same party as the voter. We distinguish between the ideologically extreme, modal, moderate, and mixed in-party candidates, but collapse across the two parties.[3] In doing so, we are implicitly assuming that Democrats and Republicans evaluate candidates in a similar manner – an assumption we explicitly endorse here. In the general election, we also look at the candidates by their ideological types, though the extreme Democrat and Republican candidates were almost never in the general

---

[3] Recall that in Chapter 3 we listed our eight candidates as they were positioned on the ideological spectrum, from 1 to 4 for each party. Thus, the extreme (most liberal) Democrat is D1 while the extreme (most conservative) Republican is R4. In Table E.1, we combine parties so that D1 and R4, D2 (Modal Democrat) and R3 (Modal Republican), D3 (Moderate Democrat) and R2 (Moderate Republican), and D4 (Mixed Democrat) and R1 (Mixed Republican) are analyzed together.

Table E.1. *Comparison of Evaluation Integration Rules In-party Candidates Only*

	Primary Election Candidates				General Election Candidates		
	(D1/R4) Extreme	(D2/R3) Modal	(D3/R2) Moderate	(D4/R1) Mixed	(D2/R3) Modal	(D3/R2) Moderate	(D4/R1) Mixed
Mean (averaging)	−.130	.050	−.065	−.133*	.171**	−.052	−.087
Sum (additive)	.498***	.177**	.118*	.243***	.096	.244***	.164*
	$n = 232$	$n = 515$	$n = 368$	$n = 369$	$n = 199$	$n = 161$	$n = 122$

***$p < .01$, **$p < .05$, *$p < .1$

Note: Table entries are standardized OLS regression weights for models predicting the candidate feeling thermometer rating, simultaneously entering both measures of the evaluation counter and controlling for the mean feeling thermometer rating for all groups in the preexperiment questionnaire and for the different experiments. The evaluation counter measures incorporate only information actually examined about the candidate.

election and were dropped from analysis here.[4] This gives us seven different candidate evaluations to consider.

Table E.1 presents standardized regression weights for the importance-weighted averaging and additive evaluation counters as predictors of feeling thermometer rating for each candidate. Following their vote, subjects in our experiments were asked to evaluate each candidate in the primary election (whether in their party or not) and both candidates in the general election on this scale. The scale was anchored at 0 with the statement "very unfavorable," at 100 with the statement "very favorable," and at 50 with the statement "no feeling at all." The model we use here is very simple, the two predictors shown plus a control for a subject's tendency to evaluate everyone high or low, and dummy variables representing the different experiments.[5] Ultimately both additive and averaging measures are

---

[4] The extreme candidates were in the general election only 14 times out of 501 cases, less than 3% of the time.

[5] This approach for controlling for rating bias is used throughout this appendix and is the mean of all feeling thermometer evaluations made on the preexperiment questionnaire. Subjects rated twelve groups representing a range of positions from liberal to conservative. The subject means of these ratings gives us some sense of how each subject tends to use the thermometer scale and is an important control for those who tend to rate everyone high (or low) across the board. We might expect that in general individual people would be evaluated more highly than social groups – a "person positivity" effect (Lau, Sears, and Centers, 1979) – and thus the mean evaluation of

highly correlated. But when included together into a model, the stronger predictor should be clear (and positive), while the weaker one may well carry a negative sign.

The results of these analyses show that the additive evaluation counter is clearly the better predictor in six of the seven cases. Accordingly, we will use an additive evaluation counter throughout the book. There is an important consequence of this decision. An additive counter is on a scale that is necessarily different from an averaging counter. Again, looking at the example earlier, the averaging counter always remains within the bounds of -1 and 1 (assuming a -1, 1 scale for new information, as the example does). But an additive counter has no theoretical top (or bottom) end, limited only by the number of pieces of information that are incorporated within it. In our data, the additive evaluation counter for the modal candidates has a mean of .859, with a range from -1.93 to 7.71, while our averaging version of the counter has a mean of .361 and a range from $-.91$ to 1.0. In analyzing the results of our models, this simple difference must be kept in mind. One great advantage, though, is that our additive evaluation counter is directly comparable with our additive memory affect measure, which subtracts negative from positive memories, leaving a net positive memory score, which by necessity gives no weight to neutral information and is thus of a similar nature to our additive evaluation counter.

---

groups would tend to underestimate the evaluation of individual candidates. If so, this would only affect estimates of the constant in our regression models, a coefficient that does not concern us here. What we want is a measure of differential use of the feeling thermometer scale in general, and the mean rating of the social groups using that scale serves this purpose well.

References

Abelson, Robert P., and Ariel Levi. 1985. "Decision Making and Decision Theory." In Gardner Lindzey and Elliot Aronson (eds.), *Handbook of Social Psychology* (Volume I, 3rd edition, pp. 231–309). New York: Random House.

Abramowitz, Alan I. 1989. "Viability, Electability, and Candidate Choice in a Presidential Primary Election: A Test of Competing Models." *Journal of Politics* 51(November): 977–992.

Abramson, Paul R., John H. Aldrich, Phil Paolino, and David W. Rhode. 1992. "'Sophisticated' Voting in the 1988 Presidential Primaries." *American Political Science Review* 86(March): 55–69.

Achen, Christopher H. 1975. "Mass Political Attitudes and the Survey Response." *American Political Science Review* 69(December): 1218–1231.

Alba, Joseph W., and Howard Marmorstein. 1987. "The Effects of Frequency Knowledge on Consumer Decision Making." *Journal of Consumer Research* 14(June): 14–25.

Aldrich, John H. 1980. *Before the Convention: Strategies and Choices in Presidential Nomination Campaigns*. Chicago: University of Chicago Press.

Aldrich, John H. 1993. "Rational Choice and Turnout." *American Journal of Political Science* 37(February): 246–276.

Aldrich, John H., and R. Michael Alvarez. 1994. "Issues and the presidential primary voter." *Political Behavior* 16(September): 289–317.

Alexander, Herbert E. 1975. *Financing the 1972 Election*. Lexington, MA: Lexington Books.

Alexander, Herbert E. 1979. *Financing the 1976 Election*. Washington, DC: Congressional Quarterly.

Alexander, Herbert E. 1983. *Financing the 1980 Election*. Lexington, MA: Lexington Books.

Alexander, Herbert E., and Monica Bauer. 1991. *Financing the 1988 Election*. Boulder, CO: Westview Press.

Alexander, Herbert E., and Anthony Corrado. 1995. *Financing the 1992 Election*. Armonk, NY: M. E. Sharpe.

Alexander, Herbert E., and Brian A. Haggerty. 1987. *Financing the 1984 Election*. Lexington, MA: Lexington Books.

Allison, Graham T. 1971. *Essence of Decision: Explaining the Cuban Missile Crisis*. Boston: Little, Brown.

References

Allison, Graham T., and Philip D. Zelikow. 1999. *Essence of Decision: Explaining the Cuban Missile Crisis* (2nd edition). New York: Longman.

Anderson, John R. 1983. *The Architecture of Cognition*. Cambridge, MA: Harvard University Press.

Anderson, John R., and Gordon H. Bower. 1973. *Human Associative Memory*. New York: Wiley.

Anderson, John R., Michael D. Byrne, Scott Douglass, Christian Lebiere, and Yulin Qin. 2004. "An Integrated Theory of the Mind." *Psychological Review* 111(4): 1036–1060.

Anderson, Norman H. 1965. "Primacy Effects in Personality Impression Formation Using a Generalized Order Effect Paradigm." *Journal of Personality and Social Psychology* 2: 1–9.

Anderson, Norman H. 1981. *Foundations of Information Integration Theory*. New York: Academic Press.

Ansolabehere, Stephen, and Shanto Iyengar. 1995. *Going Negative: How Political Advertisements Shrink and Polarize the Electorate*. New York: Free Press.

Arrow, Kenneth J. 1951. *Social Choice and Individual Values*. New York: John Wiley and Sons.

Aschenbrenner, K. M., U. Bockenholt, D. Albert, and F. Schmalhofer. 1986. "The Selection of Dimensions When Choosing Between Multiattribute Alternatives." In R. W. Scholz (ed.), *Current Issues in West German Decision Research* (pp. 63–78). Frankfurt: Lang.

Bargh, John A. 1989. "Preconscious and Postconscious Automaticity in Social Perception." In J. S. Uleman and J. A. Bargh (eds.), *Unintended Thought* (pp. 3–51). New York: Guilford Press.

Bargh, John A., and R. R. Thein. 1985. "Individual Construct Accessibility, Person Memory, and the Recall-judgment Link: the Case of Information Overload." *Journal of Personality and Social Psychology* 49: 1129–1146.

Bartels, Larry M. 1988. *Presidential Primaries and the Dynamics of Public Choice*. Princeton, NJ: Princeton University Press.

Bartels, Larry M. 1996. "Uninformed Votes: Information Effects in Presidential Elections." *American Journal of Political Science* 40(February): 194–230.

Bassili, John N. 1995. "Response Latency and the Accessibility of Voting Intentions: What Contributes to Accessibility and How It Affects Vote Choice." *Personality and Social Psychology Bulletin* 21(July): 686–695.

Belmore, S. M. 1987. "Determinants of Attention during Impression Formation." *Journal of Experiment Psychology: Learning, Memory, and Cognition* 13: 480–489.

Ben Zur, Hasida, and Shlomo J. Breznitz. 1981. "The Effects of Time Pressure on Risky Choice Behavior." *Acta Psycologica* 47(February): 89–104.

Bennett, W. Lance. 1988. *News: The Politics of Illusion* (2nd ed.). New York: Longman.

Bennett, W. Lance. 1992. *The Governing Crisis: Media, Money, and Marketing in American Elections*. New York: St. Martin's Press.

Berleson, Bernard R., Paul F. Lazarsfeld, and William McPhee. 1954. *Voting: A Study of Opinion Formation in a Presidential Campaign*. Chicago: University of Chicago Press.

Berns, Walter. 1962. "Voting Studies." In Herbert Storing, *Essays on the Scientific Study of Politics* (pp. 1–62). New York: Holt, Rinehart and Winston.

References

Bettman, James R., Eric J. Johnson, M. F. Luce, and John W. Payne. 1993. "Correlation, Conflict, and Choice." *Journal of Experimental Psychology: Learning, Memory & Cognition* 19(July): 931–951.

Bhaskar, Roy. 1997. *A Realist Theory of Science*. New York: Verso.

Biggs, Stanley F., Jean C. Bedard, Brian G. Gaber, and Thomas J. Linsmeier. 1985. "The Effects of Task Size and Similarity on the Decision Behavior of Bank Loan Officers." *Management Science* 31(August): 970–987.

Billings, Robert S., and Stephen A. Marcus. 1983. "Measures of Compensatory and Noncompensatory Models of Decision Behavior: Process Tracing versus Policy Capturing." *Organizational Behavior and Human Performance* 31(June): 331–352.

Billings, Robert S., and Lisa L. Scherer. 1988. "The Effects of Response Mode and Importance on Decision-making Strategies: Judgment vs. Choice." *Organizational Behavior and Human Decision Processes* 41(1): 1–19.

Bockenholt, Ulf, Albert, Dietrich, Aschenbrenner, Michael, and Franz Schmalhofer. 1991. "The Effects of Attractiveness, Dominance and Attribute Differences on Information Acquisition in Multiattribute Binary Choice." *Organizational Behavior and Human Decision Processes* 49(August): 258–281.

Brady, Henry E. 1985. "The Perils of Survey Research: Inter-Personally Incomparable Responses." *Political Methodology* 11(3): 269–291.

Brady, Henry E., and Paul M. Sniderman. 1985. "Attitude Attribution: A Group Basis for Political Reasoning." *American Political Science Review* 79(December): 1061–1078.

Brunswik, E. 1957. "Scope and Aspects of the Cognitive Problem." In H. Gruber, K. R. Hammond, and R. Jessor (eds.), *Contemporary Approaches to Cognition* (pp. 5–31). Cambridge, MA: Harvard University Press.

Buchanan, Bruce. 1987. *The Citizen's Presidency: Standards of Choice and Judgment*. Washington, DC: Congressional Quarterly Press.

Buchanan, Bruce. 1988. "Sizing up Candidates in Private Lives and Public Careers." *PS: Political Science and Politics* 21(Spring): 250–256.

Burnham, Walter Dean. 1965. "The Changing Shape of the American Political Universe." *American Political Science Review* 59(March): 7–28.

Burnham, Walter Dean. 1974. "Theory and Voting Research: Some Reflections on Converse's 'Change in the American Electorate.'" *American Political Science Review* 68(December): 1002–1023.

Bystrom, Dianne G., Mary Christine Banwart, Lynda Lee Kaid, and Terry A. Robertson. 2004. *Gender and Candidate Communication: Videostyle, Webstyle, Newsstyle*. New York: Routledge.

Campbell, Angus, Gerald Gurin, and Warren E. Miller. 1954. *The Voter Decides*. Evanston, IL: Row, Peterson & Company.

Campbell, Angus, Philip E. Converse, Warren E. Miller, and Donald E. Stokes. 1960. *The American Voter*. Chicago: University of Chicago Press.

Campbell, Donald T., and Julian C. Stanley. 1963. *Experimental and Quasi-Experimental Designs for Research*. Chicago: Rand McNally.

Cantor, Nancy, and Walter Mischel. 1979. "Prototypes in Person Perception." In Leonard Berkowitz (ed.), *Advances in Experimental Social Psychology* (Volume 12, pp. 3–25). New York: Academic Press.

Carlston, Donal E. 1980. "The Recall and Use of Traits and Events in Social Inference Processes." *Journal of Experimental Social Psychology* 16(3): 303–328.

References

Carmines, Edward G., and James H. Kuklinski. 1990. "Incentives, Opportunities, and the Logic of Public Opinion in American Political Representation." In John A. Ferejohn and James H. Kuklinski (eds.), *Information and Democratic Processes* (pp. 240–268). Urbana: University of Illinois Press.

Carmines, Edward G., and James A. Stimson. 1980. "The Two Faces of Issue Voting." *American Political Science Review* 74, 78–91.

Carroll, John S., and Eric J. Johnson. 1990. *Decision Research: A Field Guide.* Beverly Hills, CA: Sage.

Chase, William G., and Herbert A. Simon. 1973. "Perception in Chess." *Cognitive Psychology* 4(January): 55–81.

Connolly, William E. 1972. "On 'Interests' in Politics." *Politics and Society* 2(Summer): 459–477.

Conover, Pamela J., and Stanley Feldman. 1984. "How People Organize Their Political World: A Schematic Model." *American Journal of Political Science* 28(February): 95–126.

Conover, Pamela J., and Stanley Feldman. 1986. "The Role of Inference in the Perception of Political Candidates." In Richard R. Lau and David O. Sears (eds.), *Political Cognition: The 19th Annual Carnegie Symposium on Cognition* (pp. 127–158). Hillsdale, NJ: Lawrence Erlbaum.

Conover, Pamela J., and Stanley Feldman. 1989. "Candidate Perception in an Ambiguous World: Campaigns, Cues, and Inference Processes." *American Journal of Political Science* 33 (November): 912–940.

Conover, Pamela Johnston, Virginia Gray, and Steven Coombs. 1982. "Single-Issue Voting: Elite-Mass Linkages." *Political Behavior* 4(December): 309–331.

Converse, Philip E. 1964. "Attitudes and Non-Attitudes: Continuation of a Dialogue." In Edward Tufte (ed.), *The Quantitative Analysis of Social Problems.* (pp. 206–261). Reading, MA: Addison-Wesley.

Converse, Philip E. 1975. "Public Opinion and Voting Behavior." In Fred Greenstein and Nelson Polsby (eds.), *Handbook of Political Science* (Volume 4, pp. 75–170). Reading, MA: Addison-Wesley.

Converse, Philip E., and Gregory B. Markus. 1979. "Plus ca Change: The New CPS Election Study." *American Political Science Review* 73(March): 32–49.

Corrado, Anthony. 1997. "Financing the 1996 Elections." In Gerald M. Pomper (ed.), *The Election of 1996* (pp. 135–172). Chatham, NJ: Chatham House Publishers.

Corrado, Anthony. 2001. "Financing the 2000 Elections." In Gerald M. Pomper (ed.), *The Election of 2000* (pp. 92–124). Chatham, NJ: Chatham House Publishers.

Corrado, Anthony, and Charles M. Firestone (eds.). 1996. *Elections in Cyberspace: Toward a New Era in American Politics.* Washington, DC: Aspen Institute.

Crawford, Mary E. 1995. *Talking Difference: On Gender ad Language.* Thousand Oaks, CA: Sage Publications.

Czerlinski, Jean, Gerd Gigerenzer, and Daniel G. Goldstein. 1999. "How Good Are Simple Heuristics?" In Gerd Gigerenzer, Peter M. Todd, and the ABC Research Group (eds.), *Simple Heuristics that Make Us Smart* (pp. 97–118). New York: Oxford University Press.

Dahl, Robert A. 1961. *Who Governs? Democracy and Power in an American City.* New Haven, CT: Yale University Press.

Dahl, Robert A. 1989. *Democracy and Its Critics.* New Haven, CT: Yale University Press.

References

Davis, Otto A., Melvin J. Hinich, and Peter C. Ordeshook. 1970. "An Expository Development of a Mathematical Model of the Electoral Process." *American Political Science Review* 64(June): 426–448.

Dawes, Robyn M. 1979. "The Robust Beauty of Improper Linear Models in Decision Making." *American Psychologist* 34(July): 571–582.

Dawes, Robyn M. 1988. *Rational Choice in an Uncertain World.* New York: Harcourt Brace Jovanovich.

Dawes, Robyn M. 1998. "Behavioral Decision Making and Judgment." In Daniel T. Gilbert, Susan T. Fiske, and Gardner Lindzey (eds.), *The Handbook of Social Psychology* (Volume I, 4th edition, pp. 497–548). Boston: McGraw-Hill.

DeClercq, Eugene, Thomas L. Hurley, and Norman Luttberg. 1976. "Voting in American Presidential Elections: 1956–1972." In Samuel A. Kirkpatrick (ed.), *American Electoral Behavior: Change and Stability.* Beverly Hills, CA: Sage.

Delli Carpini, Michael, and Scott Keeter. 1996. *What Americans Know About Politics and Why It Matters.* New Haven, CT: Yale University Press.

Downs, Anthony. 1957. *An Economic Theory of Democracy.* New York: Harper and Row.

Druckman, James N., and Arthus Lupia. 2000. "Preference Formation." *Annual Review of Political Science* 3: 1–24.

Easton, David. 1953. *The Political System: An Inquiry into the State of Political Science.* New York: Knopf.

Easton, David. 1965. *A Systems Analysis of Political Life.* New York: Wiley.

Einhorn, Hillel J. 1970. "The Use of Nonlinear, Noncompensatory Models in Decision Making." *Psychological Bulletin* 73: 211–230.

Einhorn, Hillel J., and Robin M. Hogarth. 1975. "Unit Weighting Schemes for Decision Making." *Organizational Behavior and Human Performance* 13(April): 171–192.

Einhorn, Hillel J., and Robin M. Hogarth. 1981. "Behavioral Decision Theory: Processes of Judgment and Choice." *Annual Review of Psychology* 32: 53–88.

Enelow, James M., and Melvin J. Hinich. 1984. *The Spatial Theory of Voting: An Introduction.* New York: Cambridge University Press.

Ericsson, K. Anders, and Herbert A. Simon. 1980. *Protocol Analysis: Verbal Reports as Data.* Cambridge, MA: MIT Press.

Ferejohn, John A., and Morris P. Fiorina. 1974. "The Paradox of Not Voting: A Decision Theoretic Analysis." *American Political Science Review* 68(June): 525–536.

Festinger, Leon. 1957. *A Theory of Cognitive Dissonance.* Stanford, CA: Stanford University Press.

Finnigan, Simon, Michael S. Humphreys., Dennis Simon, and Gina Geffen. 2002. "ERP 'Old/New' Effects: Memory Strength and Decisional Factors." *Neuropsychologia* 40: 2288–2304.

Fiorina, Morris P. 1976. "The Voting Decision: Instrumental and Expressive Aspects." *Journal of Politics* 38(May): 390–413.

Fiorina, Morris P. 1981. *Retrospective Voting in American National Elections.* New Haven, CT: Yale University Press.

Fischer, Gregory W., and Scott A. Hawkins. 1993. "Strategy Compatibility, Scale Compatibility, and the Prominence Effect." *Journal of Experimental Psychology: Human Perception and Performance* 19(June): 580–597.

Fischer, Gregory W., and Eric J. Johnson. 1986. "Behavioral Decision Theory." In Richard R. Lau and David O. Sears (eds.), *Political Cognition* (pp. 55–65). Hillsdale, NJ: Erlbaum.

References

Fischoff, Baruch, Paul Slovic, and Sarah Lichtenstein. 1978. "Fault Trees: Sensitivity of Estimated Failure Probabilities to Problem Representation." *Journal of Experimental Psychology: Human Perception and Performance* 4(May): 330–344.

Fishman, Mark. 1980. *Manufacturing the News*. Austin: University of Texas Press.

Fiske, Susan T., Donald R. Kinder, and W. Michael Larter. 1983. "The Novice and the Expert: Knowledge-Based Strategies in Political Cognition." *Journal of Experimental Social Psychology* 19(July): 381–400.

Fiske, Susan T., Richard R. Lau, and Richard A. Smith. 1990. "On the Variety and Utility of Political Knowledge Structures." *Social Cognition* 8(Spring): 31–48.

Fiske, Susan T., and Mark A. Pavelchak. 1986. "Category-Based versus Piecemeal-Based Affective Responses: Developments in Schema-Triggered Affect." In Richard M. Sorrentino and E. Tory Higgins (eds.), *The Handbook of Motivation and Cognition: Foundations of Social Behavior* (pp. 167–203). New York: Guilford.

Fiske, Susan T., and Shelley E. Taylor. 1991. *Social Cognition* (2nd edition). New York: McGraw-Hill.

Flanigan, William H., and Zingale, Nancy H. 1983. *Political Behavior of the American Electorate* (5th edition). Boston: Allyn and Bacon.

Ford, Gary T., and Ruth Ann Smith. 1987. "Inferential Beliefs in Consumer Evaluations: An Assessment of Alternative Processing Strategies." *Journal of Consumer Research* 14(December): 363–371.

Ford, Kevin J., Neal Schmitt, Susan L. Schechtman, Brian M. Hults, and Mary L. Doherty. 1989. "Process Tracing Methods: Contributions, Problems, and Neglected Research Questions." *Organizational Behavior and Human Decision Processes* 43(February): 75–117.

Frank, Thomas. 2004. *What's the Matter with Kansas? How Conservatives Won the Heart of America*. New York: Metropolitan Books.

Frankenberger, Kristina D., and Gerald S. Albaum. 1997. "Using Behavioral Decision Theory to Assess Advertisement Recognition Tasks by Level of Difficulty." *Psychology & Marketing* 14(March): 145–162.

Franklin, Mark N. 1996. "Electoral Participation." In Lawrence LeDuc, Richard G. Niemi, and Pippa Norris (eds.), *Comparing Democracies: Elections and Voting in Global Perspective* (pp. 216–235). Thousand Oaks, CA: Sage.

Friedman, Jeffrey (ed.). 1995. *The Rational Choice Controversy*. New Haven, CT: Yale University Press.

Friedman, Milton. (ed.). 1953. *Essays in Positive Economics*. Chicago: University of Chicago Press.

Gabrielcik, Adele, and Russel H. Fazio. 1984. "Priming and Frequency Estimation: A Strict Test of the Availability Heuristic." *Personality and Social Psychology Bulletin* 10(March): 85–89.

Gans, Herbert. 1979. *Deciding What's News*. New York: Vintage Books.

Gant, Michael M., and Dwight F. Davis. 1984. "Mental Economy and Voter Rationality: The Informed Citizen Problem in Voting Research." *Journal of Politics* 46(February): 132–153.

Gerber, Alan, and Donald Green. 1999. "Misperceptions about Perceptual Bias." *Annual Review of Political Science* 2: 189–210.

Gettys, Charles F., Rebecca M. Pliske, Carol Manning, and Jeff T. Casey. 1987. "An Evaluation of Human Act Generation Performance." *Organizational Behavior and Human Decision Processes* 39(February): 23–51.

References

Geva, Nehemia, and Alex Mintz (eds.). 1997. *Decisionmaking on War and Peace: The Cognitive-Rational Debate*. Boulder, CO: Lynne Rienner.

Gigerenzer, Gerd, and Daniel G. Goldstein. 1999. "Betting on One Good Reason: The Take the Best Heuristic." In Gerd Gigerenzer, Peter M. Todd, and the ABC Research Group (eds.), *Simple Heuristics that Make Us Smart* (pp. 75–95). New York: Oxford University Press.

Gigerenzer, Gerd, and Peter M. Todd. 1999. "Fast and Frugal Heuristics: The Adaptive Toolbox." In Gerd Gigerenzer, Peter M. Todd, and the ABC Research Group (eds.), *Simple Heuristics that Make Us Smart* (pp. 3–34). New York: Oxford University Press.

Gilbert, Daniel T. 1998. "Ordinary Personology." In Daniel Gilbert, Susan T. Fiske, and Gardner Lindzey (eds.), *The Handbook of Social Psychology* (Volume 2, 4th edition, pp. 89–150). Boston: McGraw Hill.

Gilliland, Stephen W., and Neal Schmitt. 1993. "Information Redundancy and Decision Behavior: a Process Tracing Investigation." *Organizational Behavior and Human Decision Processes* 54(2): 157–180.

Goldstein, Daniel G., and Gerd Gigerenzer. 1999. "The Recognition Heuristic: How Ignorance Makes Us Smart." In Gerd Gigerenzer, Peter M. Todd, and the ABC Research Group (eds.), *Simple Heuristics that Make Us Smart* (pp. 37–58). New York: Oxford University Press.

Graber, Doris A. 1984. *Processing the News: How People Tame the Information Tide*. New York: Longman.

Green, Donald P., and Ian Shapiro. 1994. *Pathologies of Rational Choice Theory: A Critique of Applications in Political Science*. New Haven, CT: Yale University Press.

Guterbock, Thomas M. 1980. "Social Class and Voting Choices in Middletown." *Social Forces* 58(June): 1044–1056.

Hamill, Ruth, and Milton Lodge. 1986. "Cognitive consequences of political sophistication." In Richard R. Lau and David O. Sears (eds.), *Political Cognition: The 19th Annual Carnegie Symposium on Congnition* (pp. 69–93) Hillsdale, NJ: Erlbaum.

Hamill, Ruth, Milton Lodge, and Fredrick Blake. 1985. "The Breadth, Depth, and Utility of Class, Partisan, and Ideological Schemata." *American Journal of Political Science* 29(August): 850–870.

Hastie, Reid. 1986. "A Primer of Information Processing Theory for the Political Scientist." In Richard R. Lau and David O. Sears (eds.), *Political Cognition: The 19th Annual Carnegie Symposium on Cognition* (pp. 11–39). Hillsdale, NJ: Erlbaum.

Hastie, Reid. 2001. "Problems for Judgment and Decision Making." *Annual Review of Psychology* (Volume 52, pp. 653–683). Stanford, CA: Annual Reviews.

Hastie, Reid, and Robyn M. Dawes. 2001. *Rational Choice in an Uncertain World*. Thousand Oaks, CA: Sage.

Hastie, Reid, and Purohit A. Kumar. 1979. "Person Memory: Personality Traits as Organizing Principles in Memory for Behavior." *Journal of Personality and Social Psychology* 37(January): 25–38.

Hastie, Reid, Thomas M. Ostrom, Ebbe B. Ebbesen, Robert S. Wyer, Jr., David L. Hamilton, and Donal E. Carlston (eds.). 1980. *Person Memory: The Cognitive Basis of Social Perception*. Hillsdale, NJ: Erlbaum.

Hastie, Reid, and Bernadette Park. 1986. "The Relationship Between Memory and Judgment Depends on Whether the Task Is Memory-based or On-line." *Psychological Review* 93(2): 258–268.

References

Hastie, Reid, and Nancy Pennington. 1988. "Notes on the Distinction Between Memory-based and On-line Judgments." In John N. Bassili (ed.), *On-line Cognition in Person Perception* (pp. 1–19). Hillsdale, NJ: Erlbaum.

Heider, Fritz. 1958. *The Psychology of Interpersonal Relations.* New York: Wiley.

Hempel, Carl G. 1965. *Aspects of Scientific Explanations.* New York: Free Press.

Henshel, Richard L. 1980. "The Purposes of Laboratory Experimentation and the Virtues of Deliberate Artificiality." *Journal of Experimental Social Psychology* 16(September): 466–478.

Herek, Gregory M., Irving L. Janis, and Paul Huth. 1987. "Decision Making During International Crises." *Journal of Conflict Resolution* 31(June): 203–226.

Herstein, John A. 1981. "Keeping the Voter's Limits in Mind: A Cognitive Process Analysis of Decision Making in Voting." *Journal of Personality and Social Psychology* 40(May): 843–861.

Higgins, E. Tory, and G. King. 1981. "Accessibility of Social Constructs: Information Processing Consequences of Individual and Contextual Variability." In Nancy Cantor and John F. Kihlstrom (eds.), *Personality, Cognition, and Social Interaction* (pp. 69–122). Hillsdale, NJ: Erlbaum.

Hinich, Melvin J., and Michael C. Munger. 1994. *Ideology and the Theory of Political Choice.* Ann Arbor: University of Michigan Press.

Hinich, Melvin J., and Michael C. Munger. 1997. *Analytical Politics.* New York: Cambridge University Press.

Hogarth, Robin M. 1975. "Cognitive Processes and the Assessment of Subjective Probability Distributions." *Journal of the American Statistical Association* 70(June): 271–289.

Hogarth, Robin M. 1987. *Judgment and Choice* (2nd edition). New York: Wiley.

Holbrook, Thomas M. 1996. "Reading the Political Tea Leaves: A Forecasting Model of Contemporary Presidential Elections." *American Politics Quarterly* 24(October): 506–519.

Huang, Li-Ning. 2000. "Examining Candidate Information Search Processes: The Impact of Processing Goals and Sophistication." *Journal of Communication* 50(Winter): 93–114.

Huang, Li-Ning, and Vincent Price. 2001. "Motivations, Goals, Information Search, and Memory about Political Candidates." *Political Psychology* 22: 665–692.

Huntington, Samuel P. 1968. *Political Order in Changing Societies.* New Haven, CT: Yale University Press.

Jacobson, Gary C. 1987. *The Politics of Congressional Elections* (2nd edition). Boston: Little, Brown.

Jacobson, Gary C., and Samuel Kernell. 1981. *Strategy and Choice in Congressional Elections.* New Haven, CT: Yale University Press.

Jacoby, Jacob, Carol Kohn, and Donald E. Speller. 1974. "Brand Choice Behavior as a Function of Information Load." *Journal of Marketing Research* 11(February): 63–69.

Jacoby, J., Donald E. Speller, and C. Kohn Berning. 1974. "Brand Choice Behavior as a Function of Information Load: Replication and Extension." *Journal of Consumer Research* 1(February): 33–40.

Jacoby, Jacob, R. W. Chestnut, K. C. Weigl, and W. Fischer. 1976. "Pre-Purchasing Information Acquisition: Description of a Process Methodology, Research Paradigm, and Pilot Investigation." *Advances in Consumer Research* 5(6): 546–554.

References

Jacoby, Jacob, James Jaccard, Alfred Kuss, Tracy Troutman, and David Mazursky. 1987. "New Directions in Behavioral Process Research: Implications for Social Psychology." *Journal of Experimental Social Psychology* 23(March): 146–175.

Janis, Irvine L. 1972. *Victims of Groupthink.* Boston: Houghton Mifflin.

Janis, Irvine L., and Mann, Leon. 1977. *Decision Making: A Psychological Analysis of Conflict, Choice, and Commitment.* New York: The Free Press.

Jervis, Robert. 1976. *Perception and Misperception in International Politics.* Princeton, NJ: Princeton University Press.

Johnson, Eric J., and J. E. Russo. 1984. "Product Familiarity and Learning New Information." *Journal of Consumer Research* 11(August): 542–550.

Johnson, Michael D. 1984. "Consumer Choice Strategies for Comparing Noncomparable Alternatives." *Journal of Consumer Research* 11(December): 741–753.

Johnson, Michael D. 1986. "Modeling Choice Strategies for Noncomparable Alternatives." *Marketing Sciences* 5(Winter): 37–54.

Johnson, Mitzi M. S. 1993. "Thinking about Strategies During, Before, and After Making a Decision." *Psychology and Aging* 8(3): 231–241.

Jones, Bryan D. 1994. *Reconceiving Decision-Making in Democratic Politics: Attention, Choice, and Public Policy.* Chicago: University of Chicago Press.

Jones, Bryan D. 1999. "Bounded Rationality." *Annual Review of Political Science* 2: 297–321.

Just, Marion R., Ann N. Crigler, Dean E. Alger, Timothy E. Cook, Montague Kern, and Darrell M. West. 1996. *Crosstalk: Citizens, Candidates, and the Media in a Presidential Campaign.* Chicago: University of Chicago Press.

Kahneman, Daniel. 1994. "New Challenges to the Rationality Assumption." *Journal of Institutional and Theoretical Economics* 15(1): 18–36.

Kahneman, Daniel, and Amos Tversky. 1972. "Subjective Probability: A Judgment of Representativeness." *Cognitive Psychology* 3(July): 430–454.

Kahneman, Daniel, and Amos Tversky. 1973. "On the Psychology of Prediction." *Psychological Review* 80(March): 237–251.

Kahneman, Daniel, and Amos Tversky. 1979. "Prospect Theory: An Analysis of Decision Under Risk." *Econometrica* 47(May): 263–291.

Kahneman, Daniel, and Amos Tversky. 1982. "The Psychology of Preferences." *Scientific American* 246(February): 160–173.

Kahneman, Daniel, and Amos Tversky. 1984. "Choices, Values, and Frames." *American Psychologist* 39(April): 341–350.

Kahneman, Daniel, Paul Slovic, and Amos Tversky. 1982. *Judgment Under Uncertainty: Heuristics and Biases.* New York: Cambridge University Press.

Keller, Kevin L., and Richard Staelin. 1987. "Effects of Quality and Quantity of Information on Decision Effectiveness." *Journal of Consumer Research* 14(September): 200–213.

Keller, L. R., and J. L. Ho. 1988. "Decision Problem Structuring: Generating Options." *IEEE Transactions on System, Man, and Cybernetics* 18: 715–728.

Kelley, Stanley, Jr. 1983. *Interpreting Elections.* Princeton, NJ: Princeton University Press.

Kelley, Stanley, Jr., and Thad W. Mirer. 1974. "The Simple Act of Voting." *American Political Science Review* 68(June): 572–591.

Kerstholt, Jose H. 1992. "Information Search and Choice Accuracy as a Function of Task Complexity and Task Structure." *Acta Psychologica* 80: 185–197.

References

Kessel, John H. 1972. "Comment: The Issues in Issue Voting." *American Political Science Review* 66(June): 459–465.

Key, V. O., Jr. 1966. *The Responsible Electorate.* Cambridge, MA: Belknap Press.

Kinder, Donald R. 1998. "Communication and Opinion." *Annual Review of Political Science* (Volume 1, pp. 167–197). Stanford, CA: Annual Reviews.

Kinder, Donald R., G. S. Adams, and Paul W. Gronke. 1989. "Economics and Politics in the 1984 American Presidential Election." *American Journal of Political Science* 33(May): 491–515.

Kinder, Donald R., and D. Roderick Kiewiet. 1979. "Economic Discontent and Political Behavior: The Role of Personal Grievances and Collective Economic Judgments in Congressional Voting." *American Journal of Political Science* 23(May): 495–527.

Kinder, Donald R., and Thomas Palfrey (eds.). 1993. *Experimental Foundations of Political Science.* Ann Arbor: University of Michigan Press.

Kinder, Donald R., and Lynn Sanders. 1990. "Mimicking Political Debate with Survey Questions: The Case of White Opinion on Affirmative Action for Blacks." *Social Cognition* 8(1): 73–103.

Kirkpatrick, Samuel A. (ed.). 1976. *American Electoral Behavior: Change and Stability.* Beverly Hills, CA: Sage.

Kirkpatrick Samuel A., William Lyons, and Michael R. Fitzgerald. 1976. "Candidates, Parties, and Issues in the American Electorate: Two Decades of Change." In Samuel A. Kirkpatrick (ed.), *American Electoral Behavior: Change and Stability.* Beverly Hills, CA: Sage.

Klayman, J. 1985. "Children's Decision Strategies and Their Adaptation to Task Characteristics." *Organizational Behavior and Human Decision Processes* 35(April): 179–201.

Kleinmuntz, Don N., and David A Schkade. 1993. "Information Displays and Decision Processes." *Psychological Science* 4(July): 221–227.

Krosnick, Jon. A. 1990. "Government Policy and Citizen Passion: A Study of Issue Publics in Contemporary America." *Political Behavior* 12(March): 59–92.

Kuklinski, James H., and Norman L. Hurley. 1994. "On Hearing and Interpreting Political Messages: A Cautionary Tale of Citizen Cue Taking." *Journal of Politics* 56(August): 729–751.

Kuklinski, James H., and Paul J. Quirk. 2001. "Conceptual Foundations of Citizen Competence." *Political Behavior* 23(September): 285–311.

Kuklinski, James H., Robert C. Luskin, and James Bolland. 1991. "Where is the Schema? Going Beyond the 'S' Word in Political Psychology." *American Political Science Review* 85(December): 1341–1356.

Kunda, Z. 1987. "Motivated Inference: Self-Serving Generation and Evaluation of Causal Theories." *Journal of Personality and Social Psychology* 53(4): 636–647.

Kunda, Z. 1990. "The Case for Motivated Reasoning." *Psychological Bulletin* 1083: 480–498.

Lakatos, Imre. 1970. "Falsification and the Methodology of Scientific Research Programmes." In Imre Lakatos and Alan Musgrave (eds.), *Criticism and the Growth of Knowledge* (pp. 91–196). New York: Cambridge University Press.

Lane, Robert E. 1962. *Political Ideology: Why the American Common Man Believes as He Does.* New York: The Free Press.

Langley, P., Herbert A. Simon, G. L. Bradshaw, and J. M. Zytkow. 1987. *Scientific Discovery* (Volume 1). Cambridge, MA: MIT Press.

Lau, Richard R. 1982. "Negativity in Political Perception." *Political Behavior* 4(December): 353–378.

References

Lau, Richard R. 1986. "Political Schemata, Candidate Evaluations, and Voting Behavior." In R. R. Lau and D. O. Sears (eds.), *Political Cognition* (pp. 95–126). Hillsdale, NJ: Erlbaum.

Lau, Richard R. 1989. "Construct Accessibility and Electoral Choice." *Political Behavior* 11(March): 5–32.

Lau, Richard R. 1992. *Searchable Information during an Election Campaign.* Unpublished manuscript, Rutgers University.

Lau, Richard R. 1995. "Information Search During an Election Campaign: Introducing a Process Tracing Methodology for Political Scientists." In M. Lodge and K. McGraw (eds.), *Political Judgment: Structure and Process* (pp. 179–205). Ann Arbor: University of Michigan Press.

Lau, Richard R. 2003. "Models of Decision Making." In David O. Sears, Leonie Huddy, and Robert Jervis (eds.), *Oxford Handbook of Political Psychology* (pp. 19–59). New York: Oxford University Press.

Lau, Richard R., and Ralph Erber. 1985. "An Information Processing Perspective on Political Sophistication." In Sidney Kraus and Richard Perloff (eds.), *Mass Media and Political Thought* (pp. 17–39). Beverly Hills, CA: Sage.

Lau, Richard R., Parina Patel, Dalia F. Fahmy, and Robert R. Kaufman. 2005. "Correct Voting Across 30 Democracies." Paper presented at the 2005 annual meeting of the Midwest Political Science Association, Chicago, IL, April 7–10.

Lau, Richard R., and David P. Redlawsk. 1992. "How Voters Decide: A Process Tracing Study of Decision Making During Political Campaigns." Paper presented at the annual meeting of the American Political Science Association, Chicago, IL.

Lau, Richard R., and David P. Redlawsk. 1997. "Voting Correctly." *American Political Science Review* 91(September): 585–599.

Lau, Richard R., and David P. Redlawsk. 2001a. "An Experimental Study of Information Search, Memory, and Decision Making During a Political Campaign." In J. Kuklinski (ed.), *Political Psychology and Public Opinion* (pp. 136–159). New York: Cambridge University Press.

Lau, Richard R., and David P. Redlawsk. 2001b. "Advantages and Disadvantages of Cognitive Heuristics in Political Decision Making." *American Journal of Political Science* 45(October): 951–971.

Lau, Richard R., and David O. Sears. 1986. "Social Cognition and Political Cognition." In Richard R. Lau and David O. Sears (eds.), *Political Cognition: The 19th Annual Carnegie Symposium on Cognition* (pp. 347–366). Hillsdale, NJ: Erlbaum.

Lau, Richard R., David O. Sears, and Richard Centers. 1979. "The 'Positivity Bias' in Evaluations of Public Figures: Evidence Against Instrument Artifacts." *Public Opinion Quarterly* 43(Fall): 347–358.

Lazarsfeld, Paul F., Bernard R. Berelson, and Hazel Gaudet. 1944. *The People's Choice.* New York: Columbia University Press.

Levy, Jack S. 2003. "Political Psychology and Foreign Policy." In David O. Sears, Leonie Huddy, and Robert Jervis (eds.), *Oxford Handbook of Political Psychology* (pp. 253–284). New York: Oxford University Press.

Lewin, Kurt. 1939. "Field Theory and Experiment in Social Psychology: Concepts and Methods." *American Journal of Sociology* 44(3): 868–896.

Lewin, Kurt. 1946. "Action Research and Minority Problems." *Journal of Social Issues* 2(1): 34–46.

Lewin, Kurt. 1951. *Field Theory in Social Science.* New York: Harper & Brothers.

References

Lewis-Beck, Michael S., and Tom W. Rice. 1992. *Forecasting Elections*. Washington, DC: Congressional Quarterly Press.

Lichtenstein, Sarah, and Paul Slovic. 1971. "Reversals of Preference between Bids and Choices in Gambling Decisions." *Journal of Experimental Psychology* 89(July): 46–55.

Lichtenstein, Meryl, and Thomas K. Srull. 1987. "Processing Objectives as a Determinant of the Relationship Between Recall and Judgment." *Journal of Experimental Social Psychology* 23(March): 93–118.

Lindberg, Eric, Tommy Garling, and Henry Montgomery. 1989. "Differential Predictability of Preferences and Choices." *Journal of Behavioral Decision Making* 2(October–December): 205–219.

Lindblom, Charles E. 1965. *The Intelligence of Democracy*. New York: Free Press.

Lippmann, Walter. 1955. *Essays in the Public Philosophy*. Boston: Little, Brown.

Lodge, Milton. 1995. "Toward a Procedural Model of Candidate Evaluation." In M. Lodge and K. McGraw (eds.), *Political Information Processing* (pp. 111–139). Ann Arbor: University of Michigan Press.

Lodge, Milton, and Ruth Hamill. 1986. "A Partisan Schema for Political Information Processing." *American Political Science Review* 80(June): 505–519.

Lodge, Milton, and Kathleen M. McGraw (eds.). 1995. *Political Judgment: Structure and Process*. Ann Arbor: University of Michigan Press.

Lodge, Milton, Kathleen M. McGraw, and Patrick Stroh. 1989. "An Impression Driven Model of Candidate Evaluation." *American Political Science Review* 83(June): 399–419.

Lodge, Milton, and Patrick Stroh. 1993. "Inside the Mental Voting Booth." In S. Iyenger and R. McGuire (eds.), *Political Psychology* (pp. 225–263). Durham, NC: Duke University Press.

Lodge, Milton, Patrick Stroh, and John Wahlke. 1990. "Black-box Models of Candidate Evaluation." *Political Behavior* 12(March): 5–18.

Lodge, Milton, Marco R. Steenbergen, and Shawn Brau. 1995. "The Responsive Voter: Campaign Information and the Dynamics of Candidate Evaluation." *American Political Science Review* 89(June): 309–326.

Lodge, Milton, and Charles Taber. 2000. "Three Steps Toward a Theory of Motivated Political Reasoning." In Arthur Lupia, Mathew D. McCubbins, and Samuel L. Popkin (eds.), *Elements of Reason* (pp. 183–213). Cambridge: Cambridge University Press.

Luce, R. Duncan, and Howard Raiffa. 1957. *Games and Decisions: Introduction and Critical Survey*. New York: Wiley.

Lodge, Milton, Charles Taber, and Christopher Weber. *Forthcoming*. "First Steps Towards a Dual-Process Accessibility Model of Political Beliefs, Attitudes, and Behavior." In David P. Redlawsk (ed.), *Feeling Politics: Emotion in Political Information Processing*. New York: Palgrave-Macmillan.

Lupia, Arthur. 1992. "Busy Voters, Agenda Control, and the Power of Information." *American Political Science Review* 86(June): 390–403.

Lupia, Arthur. 1994. "Shortcuts Versus Encyclopedias: Information and Voting Behavior in California Insurance Reform Elections." *American Political Science Review* 88(March): 63–76.

Lupia, Arthur, and Mathew D. McCubbins. 1998. *The Democratic Dilemma: Can Citizens Learn What They Really Need to Know?* New York: Cambridge University Press.

Lupia, Arthur, Mathew D. McCubbins, and Samuel L. Popkin. 2000. "Beyond Rationality: Reason and the Study of Politics." In Arthur Lupia, Mathew

References

D. McCubbins, and Samuel L. Popkin (eds.), *Elements of Reason: Cognition, Choice, and the Bounds of Rationality* (pp. 1–20). New York: Cambridge University Press.

Lynd, Robert S., and Helen Merrell Lynd. 1929. *Middletown*. New York: Harcourt, Brace & World.

Lynd, Robert S., and Helen Merrell Lynd. 1937. *Middletown in Transition*. New York: Harcourt, Brace & World.

Macaluso, Theodore F. 1975. "Candidate Image: Personal Attribute and Issue Content." Paper presented at the annual meeting of the Southern Political Science Association, Nashville, TN.

MacDonald, Paul K. 2003. "Useful Fiction or Miracle Maker: The Competing Epistemological Foundations of Rational Choice Theory." *American Political Science Review* 97 (November): 551–565.

Mackelprang, A. J., Bernard Grofman, and Thomas N. Keith. 1976. "Electoral Change and Stability: Some New Perspectives." In Samuel A. Kirkpatrick (ed.), *American Electoral Behavior: Change and Stability*. Beverly Hills, CA: Sage.

Malhotra, Naresh K. 1982. "Information Load and Consumer Decision Making." *Journal of Consumer Research* 8(March): 419–430.

Mansbridge, Jane J. 1983. *Beyond Adversary Democracy*. Chicago: University of Chicago Press.

March, James G. 1978. "Bounded Rationality, Ambiguity, and the Engineering of Choice." *Bell Journal of Economics* 9(Autumn): 578–608.

March, James G. 1988. *Decisions and Organizations*. Oxford: Blackwell.

March, James G. 1994. *A Primer on Decision Making*. New York: Free Press.

March, James G., and Johan P. Olson. 1989. *Rediscovering Institutions: The Organizational Basis of Politics*. New York: Free Press.

March, James G., and Herbert A. Simon. 1958. *Organizations*. New York: Wiley.

Marcus, George E. 1988. "The Structure of Emotional Response: 1984 Presidential Candidates." *American Political Science Review* 82(September): 737–761.

Marcus, George E., and Michael B. MacKuen. 1993. "Anxiety, Enthusiasm, and the Vote: The Emotional Underpinnings of Learning and Involvement During Presidential Campaigns." *American Political Science Review* 87(September): 672–685.

Marcus, George E., W. Russell Neuman, and Michael MacKuen. 2000. *Affective Intelligence and Political Judgment*. Chicago: University of Chicago Press.

Markus, Gregory B., and Philip E. Converse. 1979. "A Dynamic Simultaneous Equation Model of Electoral Choice." *American Political Science Review* 73(December): 1055–1070.

McClosky, Herbert. 1964. "Consensus and Ideology in American Politics." *American Political Science Review* 58(June): 361–382.

McDermott, Rose. 2002. "Experimental Methods in Political Science." *Annual Review of Political Science* 5(1): 31–61.

McGinniss, Joe. 1969. *The Selling of the President*. New York: Trident Press.

McGraw, Kathleen M. 2000. "Contributions of the Cognitive Approach to Political Psychology." *Political Psychology* 21(December): 805–832.

McGraw, Kathleen M., Mark Fischle, and Karen Stenner. 2000. "What Politicians 'Know' Depends on How They are Asked." Unpublished manuscript.

McGraw, Kathleen M., Milton Lodge, and Patrick Stroh. 1990. "On-line Processing in Candidate Evaluation: The Effects of Issue Order, Issue Salience, and Sophistication." *Political Behavior* 12(March): 41–58.

References

McGraw, Kathleen M., and Neil Pinney. 1990. "The Effects of General and Domain-specific Expertise on Political Memory and Judgment." *Social Cognition* 8(Spring): 9–30.

McKelvey, Richard D., and Peter C. Ordeshook. 1986. "Information, Electoral Equilibria, and the Democratic Ideal." *Journal of Politics* 48(November): 909–37.

McPhee, William. 1961. "Note on a Campaign Simulator." *Public Opinion Quarterly* 25(Summer): 184–193.

Meehl, Paul E. 1954. *Clinical versus Statistical Predictions: A Theoretical Analysis and Review of the Evidence*. Minneapolis: University of Minnesota Press.

Meehl, Paul E. 1977. "The Selfish Voter and the Thrown-Away Vote Argument." *American Political Science Review* 71(March): 11–30.

Mellers, Barbara A., Alan Schwartz, and Alan Cooke. 1998. "Judgment and Decision Making." *Annual Review of Psychology* 49: 447–477.

Milech, Dan, and Melissa Finucane. 1998. "Decision Support and Behavioral Decision Theory." In Kim Kirsner and Craig Speelman (eds.), *Implicit and Explicit Mental Processes* (pp. 291–307). Mahwah, NJ: Lawrence Erlbaum Associates.

Miller, Arthur H., Martin P. Wattenberg, and Oksana Malanchuk. 1986. "Schematic Assessments of Presidential Candidates." *American Political Science Review* 80(June): 521–540.

Miller, George A. 1956. "The Magical Number Seven, Plus or Minus Two: Some Limits on Our Capacity for Processing Information." *Psychological Review* 63(1): 81–97.

Miller, Warren E. 1976. "The Challenges of Electoral Research." In Samuel A. Kirkpatrick (ed.), *American Electoral Behavior: Change and Stability*. Beverly Hills, CA: Sage.

Miller, Warren E., and J. Merrill Shanks. 1996. *The New American Voter*. Cambridge, MA: Harvard University Press.

Mills, Charles W. 1971. *The Power Elite*. London: Oxford University Press.

Mintz, Alex. 1997. "The Decison to Attack Iraq: A Noncompensatory Theory of Decisionmaking." *Journal of Conflict Resolution* 37(December): 595–618.

Mintz, Alex, and Nehemia Geva. 1997. "The Poliheuristic Theory of Foreign Policy Decisionmaking." In Nehemia Geva and Alex Mintz (eds.), *Decisionmaking on War and Peace: The Cognitive-Rational Debate* (pp. 81–101). Boulder, CO: Lynne Rienner Publishers.

Mintz, Alex, Nehemia Geva, Steven B. Redd, and Amy Carnes. 1997. "The Effects of Dynamic and Static Choice Sets on Decision Strategy." *American Political Science Review* 91(September): 553–566.

Mondak, Jeffrey J. 1993. "Public Opinion and Heuristic Processing of Source Cues." *Political Behavior* 15(June): 167–192.

Morrell, Holly E. R., Santino Gaitan, and John T. Wixted. "On the Nature of the Decision Axis in Signal-Detection-Based Models of Recognition Memory." *Journal of Experimental Psychology: Learning, Memory, & Cognition.* 28(November): 1095–1110.

Mueller, John E. 1970. "Presidential Popularity from Truman to Johnson." *American Political Science Review* 64(March): 18–34.

Mueller, John. 1992. "Democracy and Ralph's Pretty Good Grocery: Elections, Equality, and Minimal Human Beings." *American Journal of Political Science* 36(November): 983–1003.

References

Mutz, Diana C. 1997. "Mechanisms of Momentum: Does Thinking Make it So?" *Journal of Politics* 59(February): 104–125.

Nicholson, Stephen P. 2005. *Voting the Agenda: Candidates, Elections and Ballot Propositions*. Princeton, NJ: Princeton University Press.

Nicholson, Stephen P., Adrian Pantoja, and Gary M. Segura. 2002. "Ich bin ein Latino: Sophistication, Symbolism, Heuristics and Latino Preferences in the 2000 Presidential Election." Paper presented at the annual meeting of the American Political Science Association, Boston, MA, August 29–September 1.

Nie, Norman H., and Kristi, Andersen. 1974. "Mass Belief Systems Revisited: Political Change and Attitude Structure." *Journal of Politics* 36(August): 541–591.

Nie, Norman H., Sidney Verba, and John R. Petrocik. 1976. *The Changing American Voter*. Cambridge, MA: Harvard University Press.

Niemi, Richard G., and Larry M. Bartels. 1985. "New Measures of Issue Salience: An Evaluation." *The Journal of Politics* 47(November): 1212–1220.

Nisbett, Richard E., and Lee Ross. 1980. *Human Inference: Strategies and Shortcomings of Social Judgment*. Englewood Cliffs, NJ: Prentice-Hall.

Nisbett, Richard E., and Timothy D. Wilson. 1977. "Telling More Than We Can Know: Verbal Reports on Mental Processes." *Psychological Review* 84(March): 231–259.

Norman, Donald A. 1976. *Memory and Attention: An Introduction to Human Information Processing*. New York: Wiley.

Norman, Donald A. 1982. *Learning and Memory*. San Francisco: Freeman.

Norusis, Marija J. 1994. *SPSS for Windows Advanced Statistics Release 6*. Chicago: SPSS.

Olshavsky, Richard W. 1979. "Task Complexity and Contingent Processing in Decision Making: A Replication and Extension." *Organization Behavior and Human Performance* 24(December): 300–316.

Page, Benjamin I., and Robert Y. Shapiro. 1992. *The Rational Public: Fifty Years of Trends in Americans' Policy Preferences*. Chicago: University of Chicago Press.

Patterson, Thomas E. 1980. *The Mass Media Election: How Americans Choose Their President*. New York: Praeger.

Payne, John W. 1976. "Task Complexity and Contingent Processing in Decision Making: An Information Search and Protocol Analysis." *Organizational Behavior and Human Performance* 16(August): 366–387.

Payne, John. W. 1980. "Information Processing Theory: Some Concepts and Methods Applied to Decision Research." In T. S. Wallsten (ed.), *Cognitive Processes in Choice and Decision Behavior*. Hillsdale, NJ: Erlbaum.

Payne, John W., James R. Bettman, and Eric J. Johnson. 1988. "Adaptive Strategy Selection in Decision Making." *Journal of Experimental Psychology: Learning, Memory, and Cognition* 14(July): 534–552.

Payne, John W., James R. Bettman, and Eric J. Johnson. 1992. "Behavioral Decision Research: A Constructive Processing Perspective." *Annual Review of Psychology* 43: 87–131.

Payne, John W., James R. Bettman, and Eric J. Johnson. 1993. *The Adaptive Decision Maker*. New York: Cambridge University Press.

Payne, John W., and Myron L. Braunstein. 1978. "Risky Choice: An Examination of Information Acquisition Behavior." *Memory & Cognition* 6(September): 554–561.

References

Payne, John W., Myron L. Braunstein, and John S. Carroll. 1978. "Exploring Pre-decisional Behavior: An Alternative Approach to Decision Research." *Organizational Behavior and Human Performance* 22(August): 17–44.

Perlmutter, Marvon. 1983. "Learning and Memory Through Adulthood." In Matilda White Riley, Beth B. Hess, and Kathleen Bond (eds.), *Aging in Society: Selected Reviews of Recent Research* (pp. 219–241). Hillsdale, NJ: Lawrence Erlbaum.

Pitz, Gordon, and Natalie Sachs. 1984. "Judgment and Decision: Theory and Application." *Annual Review of Psychology* 35: 139–163.

Plutzer, Eric, and John F. Zipp. 1996. "Identity Politics, Partisanship, and Voting for Women Candidates." *Public Opinion Quarterly* 60(Spring): 30–57.

Pomper, Gerald M. 1972. "From Confusion to Clarity: Issues and American Voters, 1956–1968." *American Political Science Review* 66(June): 415–428.

Pomper, Gerald M. 1976. "Impacts on the Political System." In Kirkpatrick, Samuel A. (ed.), *American Electoral Behavior: Change and Stability.* Beverly Hills, CA: Sage.

Pomper, Gerald M. 2001. *The Election of 2000.* New York: Chatham House.

Pool, Ithiel de Sola, and Robert Abelson. 1961. "The Simulmatics Project." *The Public Opinion Quarterly* 25(Summer):167–183.

Popkin, Samuel L. 1991. *The Reasoning Voter: Communication and Persuasion in Presidential Campaigns.* Chicago: University of Chicago Press.

Popper, Karl. 1959. *The Logic of Scientific Discovery.* New York: Basic Books.

Prothro, James W., and Charles W. Grigg. 1960. "Fundamental Principles of Democracy: Bases of Agreement and Disagreement." *Journal of Politics* 22(May): 276–294.

Purkitt, Helen E., and James W. Dyson. 1988. "An Experimental Study of Cognitive Processes and Information in Political Problem Solving." *Acta Psychologica* 68(September): 329–342.

Putnam, Hillary. 1982. "Three Kinds of Scientific Realism." *Philosophical Quarterly* 32(April): 195–200.

Quadrel, Marilyn J., Baruch Fischfoff, and William David. 1993. "Adolescent (In)vulnerability." *American Psychologist* 48(February): 102–116.

Rabinowitz, George, and Stuart Elaine MacDonald. 1989. "A Directional Theory of Issue Voting." *American Political Science Review* 83(March): 93–121.

Rahn, Wendy M. 1993. "The Role of Partisan Stereotypes in Information Processing about Political Candidates." *American Journal of Political Science* 37(May): 472–496.

Rahn, Wendy M., John H. Aldrich, and Eugene Borgida. 1994. "Individual and Contextual Variations in Political Candidate Appraisal." *American Political Science Review* 88(March): 193–199.

Rahn, Wendy M., John H. Aldrich, Eugene Borgida, and John L. Sullivan. 1990. "A Social-Cognitive Model of Candidate Appraisal." In John A. Ferejohn and James H. Kuklinski (eds.), *Information and Democratic Processes.* Chicago: University of Illinois Press.

Rahn, Wendy M., Jon A. Krosnick, and Marijke Breuning. 1994. "Rationalization and Derivation Processes in Survey Studies of Political Candidate Evaluation." *American Journal of Political Science* 38(August): 582–600.

Raiffa, Howard. 1968. *Decision Analysis: Introductory Lectures on Choices Under Uncertainty.* Reading, MA: Addison-Wesley.

References

Reder, Lynn M., and John R. Anderson. 1980. "A Partial Resolution of the Paradox of Interference: The Role of Integrating Knowledge." *Cognitive Psychology* 12(October): 447–472.

Redlawsk, David P. 1992. "Using Hypermedia to Develop a Political Science Simulation." Paper presented at the 25th annual meeting of the Association of Small Computer Users in Education (ASCUE), Myrtle Beach, SC.

Redlawsk, David P. 1995a. "Conducting Political Science Research Using Multimedia." Paper prepared for the 28th annual meeting of the Association of Small Computer Users in Education (ASCUE), Myrtle Beach, SC.

Redlawsk, David P. 1995b. "How voters use campaign information." Paper presented at the annual meeting of the American Political Science Association, Chicago.

Redlawsk, David P. 2001a. "You Must Remember This: A Test of the On-line Voting Model." *Journal of Politics* 63(February): 29–58.

Redlawsk, David P. 2001b. "Implications of Motivated Reasoning for Voter Information Processing." Paper presented at the annual meeting of the Midwest Political Science Association, Chicago, and at the annual meeting of the International Society for Political Psychology, Cuernavaca, Mexico.

Redlawsk, David P. 2002. "Hot Cognition or Cool Consideration? Testing the Effects of Motivated Reasoning on Political Decision Making." *Journal of Politics* 64(November): 1021–1044.

Redlawsk, David P. 2004. "What Voters Do: Information Search During Election Campaigns." *Political Psychology* 25(4): 595–610.

Redlawsk, David P., and Richard R. Lau. 1995. "The Miserly Voter: Heuristics and Rational Voting Behavior." Paper presented at the annual meeting of the Midwest Political Science Association, Chicago.

Redlawsk, David P., and Richard R. Lau. 2003. "Do Voters Want Candidates They Like of Candidates They Agree With? Affect vs. Cognition in Voter Decision Making." Paper presented at the Shambaugh Conference on Affect and Cognition in Political Action, University of Iowa, March 6–9, and the annual meeting of the Midwest Political Science Association, Chicago, April 3–6.

Reyes, R. M., W. C. Thompson, and Gordon H. Bower. 1980. "Judgmental Biases Resulting from Differing Availabilities of Arguments." *Journal of Personality and Social Psychology* 39(July): 2–12.

Riggle, Ellen D. B., Mitzi M. S. Johnson, and Scot Hickey. 1996. "Information Monitoring of Strategic Decision Making: a Process Tracing Demonstration." Paper presented at the annual meeting of the Midwest Political Science Association, Chicago.

Riggle, Ellen D., Victor Ottati, Robert S. Wyer, James Kuklinski, and Norbert Schwartz. 1992. "Bases of Political Judgments: The Role of Stereotypic and Nonstereotypic Information." *Political Behavior* 14(March): 67–87.

Riker, William H., and Peter C. Ordeshook. 1968. "A Theory of the Calculus of Voting." *American Political Science Review* 62(March): 25–42.

Riker, William H., and Peter Ordeshook. 1973. *An Introduction to Positive Political Theory.* Englewood Cliffs, NJ: Prentice-Hall.

Rosch, Ellen. 1978. "Principles of Categorization." In Ellen Rosch and B. B. Lloyd (eds.), *Cognition and Categorization* (pp. 28–50). Hillsdale, NJ: Lawrence Erlbaum.

Rosenberg, Shawn W., Shulamit Kahn, and Thuy Tran. 1991. "Creating a Political Image: Shaping Appearance and Manipulating the Vote." *Political Behavior* 13(December): 345–367.

References

Rosenstone, Steven J. 1983. *Forecasting Presidential Elections*. New Haven, CT: Yale University Press.

Rossi, Peter H. 1959. "Four Landmarks in Voting Research." In Eugene Burdick and Arthur J Brodbeck (eds.), *American Voting Behavior*. New York: Free Press.

Rothkopf, Ernst Z., Monica Dashen, and Kim Teft. "Aggregation in Memory of Episodic Influences on Rule-Guided Decisions." *Journal of Experimental Psychology: Learning, Memory, & Cognition* 28(September): 983–998.

Rubenstein, Albert H. 1998. *Modeling Bounded Rationality*. Cambridge, MA: MIT Press.

Russo, J. Edward. 1977. "The Value of Unit Price Information." *Journal of Marketing Research* 14(May): 193–201.

Russo, J. Edward, and Barbara A. Dosher. 1983. "Strategies for Multiattribute Binary Choice." *Journal of Experimental Psychology: Learning, Memory and Cognition* 17(September): 676–696.

Sargent, T. J. 1993. *Bounded Rationality in Macroeconomics*. Oxford: Clarendon Press.

Savage, Leonard J. 1954. *The Foundations of Statistics*. New York: Wiley.

Schattschneider, Elmer E. 1960. *The Semi-Sovereign People: A Realist's View of Democracy in America*. New York: Holt.

Sears, David O. 1975. "Political Socialization." In Fred I. Greenstein and Nelson W. Polsby (eds.), *Handbook of Political Science* (Vol. 2, pp. 93–127). Menlo Park, CA: Addison-Wesley.

Sears, David O. 1986. "College Sophomores in the Laboratory: Influences of a Narrow Database on Social Psychology's View of Human Nature." *Journal of Personality and Social Psychology* 51: 515–530.

Sears, David O., and Carolyn Funk. 1991. "The Role of Self-Interest in Social and Political Attitudes." In L. Berkowitz (ed.) *Advances in Experimental Social Psychology* (Vol. 24, pp. 1–91). New York: Academic Press.

Sears, David O., Richard R. Lau, Tom R. Tyler, and Harris M. Allen, Jr. 1980. "Self-Interest versus Symbolic Politics in Policy Attitudes and Presidential Voting." *American Political Science Review* 74(September): 670–684.

Shaffer, William R. 1972. *Computer Simulations of Voting Behavior*. New York: Oxford University Press.

Shanteau, J. 1988. "Psychological Characteristics and Strategies of Expert Decision Makers." *Acta Psychological* 68(2): 203–215.

Shanteau, J. 1992. "How Much Information Does an Expert Use? Is It Relevant?" *Acta Psychologica* 81(1): 75–86.

Shugan, Steven M. 1980. "The Cost of Thinking." *Journal of Consumer Research* 7(September): 99–111.

Simon, Herbert A. 1947. *Administrative Behavior*. New York: Macmillan.

Simon, Herbert. 1955. "A Behavioral Model of Rational Choice." *Quarterly Journal of Economics* 69(February): 99–108.

Simon, Herbert. 1956. "Rational Choice and the Structure of the Environment." *American Psychologist* 63(February): 129–138.

Simon, Herbert A. 1957. *Models of Man: Social and Rational*. New York: Wiley.

Simon, Herbert A. 1979. "Information Processing Models of Cognition." *Annual Review of Psychology* 30: 363–396.

Simon, Herbert A. 1985. "Human Nature in Politics: The Dialogue of Psychology with Political Science." *American Political Science Review* 79(June): 293–304.

Simon, Herbert A. 1995. "Rationality in Political Behavior." *Political Psychology* 16(March): 45–61.

References

Slovic, Paul, Baruch Fischhoff, and Sara Lichtenstein. 1977. "Behavioral Decision Theory." *Annual Review of Psychology* 28: 1–39.

Slovic, Paul, Baruch Fischhoff, and Sara Lichtenstein. 1982. "Response Mode, Framing, and Information Processing Effects in Risk Assessment." In Robin Hogarth (ed.), *New Directions for Methodology of Social and Behavioral Science: The Framing of Questions and the Consistency of Response* (pp. 21–36). San Francisco: Jossey-Bass.

Slovic, Paul, and Sara Lichtenstein. 1971. "Comparison of Bayesian and Regression Approaches to the Study of Information Processing in Judgment." *Organizational Behavior and Human Performance* 6(4): 649–744.

Smith, Elliot. 1989. *The Unchanging American Voter*. Berkeley: University of California Press.

Smith, Elliott R. 1998. "Mental Representation and Memory." In Daniel T. Gilbert, Susan T. Fiske, and Gardner Lindzey (eds.), *The Handbook of Social Psychology* (Volume I, 4th edition, pp. 391–445). Boston: McGraw-Hill.

Sniderman, Paul M. 1993. "The New Look in Public Opinion Research." In Ada W. Finifter (ed.), *Political Science: The State of the Discipline II* (pp. 219–245). Washington, DC: American Political Science Association.

Sniderman, Paul M., Richard A. Brody, and Philip E. Tetlock. 1991. *Reasoning and Choice: Explorations in Political Psychology*. New York: Cambridge University Press.

Sniderman, Paul M., Michael G. Hagen, Philip E. Tetlock, and Henry E. Brady. 1986. "Reasoning Chains: Causal Models of Policy Reasoning in Mass Publics." *British Journal of Political Science* 16(July): 405–430.

Squire, Pevrill. 1992. "Challenger Quality and Voting Behavior in U.S. Senate Elections." *Legislative Studies Quarterly* 17(May): 247–263.

Srull, Thomas K. 1981. "Person Memory: Some Tests of Associative Storage and Retrieval Models." *Journal of Experimental Psychology: Human Learning and Memory* 7(November): 440–463.

Staelin, Richard, and John W. Payne. 1976. "Studies of the Information-Seeking Behavior of Consumers." In J. S. Carroll and J. W. Payne (eds.), *Cognition and Social Behavior*. Hillsdale, NJ: Erlbaum.

Steenbergen, Marco. 2001. "The Reverend Bayes Meets John Q. Public: Patterns of Political Belief Updating in Citizens." Paper presented at the annual meeting of the International Society of Political Psychology, Cuernavaca, Mexico.

Steenbergen, Marco, and Milton Lodge. 1998. "Process Matters: Cognitive Models of Candidate Evaluations." Paper presented a the annual meeting of the American Political Science Association, Boston, MA.

Stigler, George J. 1961. "The Economics of Information" *Journal of Political Economy* 69(2): 213–225.

Stokes, Donald E., Angus Campbell, and Warren E. Miller. 1958. "Components of Electoral Decision." *American Political Science Review* 52(June): 367–387.

Svenson, Ola. 1979. "Process Descriptions of Decision Making." *Organizational Behavior and Human Performance* 23(February): 86–112.

Taber, Charles S., and Marco R. Steenbergen. 1995. "Computational Experiments in Electoral Behavior." In Milton Lodge and Kathleen M. McGraw (eds.), *Political Judgment: Structure and Process* (pp. 141–178). Ann Arbor: University of Michigan Press.

Tannen, Deborah. 1990. *You Just Don't Understand: Women and Men in Conversation*. New York: Morrow.

References

Taylor, Shelley E. 1981. "The Interface of Cognitive and Social Psychology." In John Harvey (ed.), *Cognition, Social Behavior, and the Environment* (pp. 189–211). Hillsdale, NJ: Erlbaum.

Tetlock, Philip E. 1993. "Cognitive Structural Analysis of Political Rhetoric: Methodological and Theoretical Issues." In Shanto Iyengar and William J. McGuire (eds.), *Explorations in Political Psychology* (pp. 380–405). Durham, NC: Duke University Press.

Trilling, Richard J. 1976. "Party Image and Electoral Behavior." In Samuel A. Kirkpatrick (ed.), *American Electoral Behavior: Change and Stability*. Beverly Hills, CA: Sage.

Tversky, Amos. 1969. "Intransitivity of Preferences." *Psychological Review* 76(January): 31–48.

Tversky, Amos. 1972. "Elimination by Aspects: A Theory of Choice." *Psychological Review* 79(May): 281–299.

Tversky, Amos, and Daniel Kahneman. 1973. "Availability: A Heuristic for Judging Frequency and Probability." *Cognitive Psychology* 5(April): 207–232.

Tversky, Amos, and Daniel Kahneman. 1974. "Judgment Under Uncertainty: Heuristics and Biases." *Science* 185(4157): 1124–1131.

Tversky, Amos, and Daniel Kahneman. 1981. "The Framing of Decisions and the Psychology of Choice." *Science* 211(4481): 453–463.

Tversky, Amos, and Daniel Kahneman. 1986. "Rational Choice and the Framing of Decisions." *Journal of Business* 59(October): S251–S278.

Tversky, Amos, and Daniel Kahneman. 1992. "Advances in Prospect Theory: Cumulative Representation of Uncertainty." *Journal of Risk and Uncertainty* 5(October): 297–323.

Tversky, Amos, and Shmuel Sattath. 1979. "Preference Trees." *Psychological Review* 86(September): 542–573.

Tversky, Amos, Shmuel Sattath, and Paul Slovic. 1988. "Contingent Weighting in Judgment and Choice." *Psychological Review* 95(July): 371–384.

von Neuman, John, and Oscar Morgenstern. 1947. *Theory of Games and Economic Behavior*. Princeton, NJ: Princeton University Press.

Vriend, Nicolaas J. 1996. "Rational Behavior and Economic Theory." *Journal of Economic Behavior & Organization* 29(March): 263–285.

Wahlke, John C. 1979. "Pre-Behavioralism in Political Science." *American Political Science Review* 73(March): 9–31.

Wattenberg, Martin P. 1981. "The Decline of Political Partisanship in the United States: Negativity or Neutrality?" *American Political Science Review* 75(December): 941–950.

Weir, Blair T. 1975. "The Distortion of Voter Recall." *American Journal of Political Science* 19(February): 53–62.

Williams, Daniel C., Stephen J. Weber, Gordon A. Haaland, Ronald H. Mueller, and Robert E. Craig. 1976. "Voter Decisionmaking in a Primary Election: An Evaluation of Three Models of Choice." *American Journal of Political Science* 20(February): 37–49.

Winneg, Kenneth, and Talia Jomini. 2004. "The Internet as a Source of Campaign Information: An Analysis of its use in the 2004 Democratic Presidential Primary Campaign." Paper presented at the annual conference of the American Association for Public Opinion Research, Phoenix, AZ.

Winter, S. G. 1975. "Optimization and Evolution in the Theory of the Firm." In R. H. Day and T. Groves (eds.), *Adaptive Economic Models* (pp. 73–118). New York: Academic Press.

References

Wright, P. 1975. "Consumer Choice Strategies: Simplifying vs. Optimizing." *Journal of Marketing Research* 12(February): 60–67.

Wyer, Robert S., and Thomas K. Srull. 1980. "The Processing of Social Stimulus Information: A Conceptual Integration." In Reid Hastie, Thomas M. Ostrom, Ebbe E. Ebbesen, Robert S. Wyer, Jr., David L. Hamilton, and Donal E. Carlston (eds.), *Person Memory: The Cognitive Basis of Social Perception*. Hillsdale, NJ: Erlbaum.

Wyer, Robert S., and Thomas K. Srull. 1986. "Human Cognition in its Social Context." *Psychological Review* 93(July): 322–359.

Wyer, Robert S., and Thomas K. Srull. 1988. "Understanding Social Knowledge: If Only the Data Could Speak for Themselves." In Daniel Bar-Tal and Arie W. Kruglanski (eds.), *The Social Psychology of Knowledge*. Cambridge: Cambridge University Press.

Zajonc, Robert B. 1968. "Attitudinal Effects of Mere Exposure." *Journal of Personality and Social Psychology* 9(January): 1–27.

Zaller, John R. 1992. *The Nature and Origin of Mass Opinion*. New York: Cambridge University Press.

Zimmermann, Manfred. 1989. "The Nervous System in the Context of Information Theory." In R. F. Schmidt and G. Thews (eds.), *Human Physiology* (2nd edition, pp. 166–173). Berlin: Springler-Verlag.

Index

Books in the series